# South Carolinians
## *in the*
# Revolution

## With Service Records *and* Miscellaneous Data

*Also*

### Abstracts *of* Laurens County, SC Wills, 1775-1855

By:
Sara Sullivan Ervin

Southern Historical Press, Inc.
Greenville, South Carolina

This volume was reproduced
from a personal copy located in
the Publishers private library

Please direct all correspondence and book orders to:
**SOUTHERN HISTORICAL PRESS, Inc.**
**PO Box 1267**
**Greenville, SC    29602-1267**

Originally printed: 1949
New Material Copyright 2023 by:
    Southern Historical Press, Inc.
ISBN #978-1-63914-018-3
*Printed in the United States of America*

# DEDICATION

THIS VOLUME IS RESPECTFULLY AND GRATEFULLY DEDICATED TO THE INTREPID PIONEERS OF LAURENS COUNTY, SOUTH CAROLINE, (PART OF OLD NINETY-SIX DISTRICT) WHO "SACRIFICED THEIR LIVES AND THEIR FORTUNES" IN THE GREAT STRUGGLE FOR INDEPEND- ENCE, AND WHO SERVED THEIR COUNTRY IN THE FOUNDING AND BUILDING OF OUR AMERICAN NATION, THE MILITARY RECORDS AND WILLS OF MANY OF WHOM WILL BE FOUND WITHIN THESE PAGES.

LAURENS COUNTY COURT HOUSE, LAURENS, S. C.

# Carolina

## The State Song

Call on thy children of the hill,
Wake swamp and rive, coast and rill,
Rouse all thy strength and all thy skill,
              Carolina!

Cite wealth and science, trade and art,
Touch with thy fire the cautious mart,
And pour thee through the people's heart,
              Carolina!

Hold up the glories of thy dead,
Say how thy elder children bled,
And point to Eutaw's battle-bed,
              Carolina!

Tell how the patriot's soul was tried,
And what his dauntless breast defied,
How Rutledge ruled and Laurens died,
              Carolina!

Cry! till thy summons, heard at last,
Shall fall like Marion's bugle-blast,
Re-echoed from the haunted past,
              Carolina!

Thy skirts indeed the foe may part,
Thy robe be pierced with sword and dart,
They shall not touch thy noble heart,
              Carolina!

Throw thy bold banner to the breeze,
Front with thy ranks the threatening seas,
Like thine own proud armorial trees,
              Carolina!

Girt with such wills to do and bear,
Assured in right, and mailed in prayer,
Thou wilt not bow thee to despair,
              Carolina!
              —Henry Timrod.

# State Flag

## State Flower of South Carolina

### The Yellow Jessamine

"As fair as Southern chivalry
  As pure as truth, and shaped like stars."

## State Tree
PALMETTO

# FOREWORD

Students of the Revolutionary Period, historical and genealogical researchers and all patriotic souls, have for years suffered because of the meager records of South Carolina for this momentous era. Buried in books and places inaccessible to the public generally and in local and private sources, are names and evidence of service of thousands of soldiers of the American Revolution. To run down a Revolutionary ancestor in South Carolina, may mean a long trek beginning in our capital city and visiting there the State Historical Commission, Secretary of State's Office and the State Library, then journey on to the city of Charleston to read the early wills and finally to Washington, D.C. to search at The Library of Congress and the National Archives . Many have followed this procedure but not being entirely successful, they realize that after all the missing link must be back home. In many old South Carolina communities, there has been little migration and it is not unusual to find the present generation attending the same church in which nearby cemetery their Revolutionary ancestors are buried. So the searcher now visits local cemeteries, examines church and Bible records, visits the county Court House and County Library. If he is diligent and persevering, he may find here that vital "missing link." Probably the richest field of undiscovered records today lies in these old communities where the pioneers settled. The National Society, Daughters Of The American Revolution, is doing a great work in unearthing much of this unpublished data and filing all of it in one place, their library in Washington. To help fill that urgent need for more accessible information about the soldiers and patriots of South Carolina who rendered service in the American Revolution, and for the convenience of those persons whose county and state libraries do-not contain the necessary records, the compiler has collected from various sources much data on this subject and brought it all together into one volume. You will find in this book the names with proof of service of many persons who rendered Revolutionary service, both men and women.

Referring to the Table of Contents: "South Carolina Pension Roll" - These records were found in the office of the Clerk of Court in the Laurens County Court House. The original document is fifty-three, finely-printed, loose-leaf pages, size about 8 x 4 inches, yellowed and spotted by time. It was rolled and wrapped in a paper addressed "To the Clerk of The Court Laurens, South Carolina." A round hole in the wrapper suggests that the package was fastened with a seal. The compiler of this volume, contacted the State Historian, the National Archives and The Library of Congress in an effort to learn more about this Pension Roll. The information I get is that it was part of a report published by the United States Government, probably in 1835. The present incumbent of the office of Clerk of Court, Mr. V. R. Fleming, kindly gave exclusive permission to the compiler (as representative of the Sullivan-Dunklin chapter, South Carolina, State Society, Daughters of the American Revolution, it being the only group in the county composed of descendants of Revolutionary soldiers) to reproduce this document. The South Carolina Society, D.A.R., held their State Conference at Greenwood, on March 24-27, 1942. The above described, "S.C. Pension Roll," was awarded at that time, the state history prize.

Contents "Names of Officers of S.C. Regiments, Continental Establishment," was "published by order of the General Assembly 1886." It appeared in the Year Book of the City of Charleston, S.C. in 1893. Contents "Medical Men of S.C. Who Served in the Revolution" was ab - stracted from the "Army Medical Bulletin no. 25" and other sources. Contents "The Roll of General Sumter's Brigade" was published by the "57th Congress, 1st Session---Senate---Document 447. Date 1902." The compiler was able to get this paper (and other data) through the courtesy of Miss Helen M. McMackin, Librarian General, N.S. D.A.R. It was contributed by J. T. Gantt and was published in the 4th volume D.A.R. Report to the Smithsonian Institution. This roll has been checked by other records in South Carolina, corrections made in spelling of names and some data added in lists of regimental officers.

Contents "Some Revolutionary War Prisoners of S.C." was obtained by permission, of Mr. J. H. Easterby, V-Pres., S.C. Historical Society, and is taken from the S.C. Historical and Genealogical Magazine, published at Charleston, Vols: 33, 34, 10.

Contents "South Carolina Women of the Revolution" was compiled from many sources: Mr. A. S. Salley, State Historian, kindly gave permission for me to abstract names of women who received Revolutionary Indents, from the twelve books edited by him, which were issued by the South Carolina Historical Commission; other records are from the S.C. Historical and Genealogical Magazine; South Carolina D.A.R. chapters; Lineage Books of N.S. D.A.R.; Sequi-Centennial and Anniversary Editions of S.C. Newspapers; County Histories; Family Genealogies and private papers.

Contents "Ancestral Roll of South Carolina D.A.R.," was used by permission of the State Regent of the S.C. Daughters of the American Revolution, Mrs. Henry J. Munnerlyn, and also by permission of the State Registrar, Mrs. James R. Carson, who in addition, kindly checked the list for misspelled names. Contents 15----- "Some Revolutionary Soldiers Claimed by Missouri, Texas, Iowa, etc:" The list of Missouri soldiers was sent to the compiler by Mrs. John F. McKinney. The compiler also obtained written permission from Mr. Floyd C. Shoemaker, Secretary of the State Historical Society of Missouri, to use these names, which appeared in Vol. 2, no. 1, pp. 55-60, Oct. 1907, and p. 128, Oct. 1940 of the Missouri Historical Review. Some of this information previously appeared as a report of the State Historian, Missouri D.A.R. in 1903, and other data appeared in the Sedalia Democrat of July 1, 1940 and the Huntsville Randolph County Times-Herald of May 16, 1940. For other data I am indebted to Mrs. Brenda R. Gieseker, Librarian of the Missouri Historical Society, who kindly gave permission to copy

"Death Notices of Some Soldiers of the American Revolution Published in Missouri Newspapers," which appeared in the "Missouri Historical Society Collections, Vol. 7, no. 2, in Feb. 1928. Mrs. Harriet Smither, State Archivist of Texas State Library, obligingly sent the list of Revolutionary Soldiers buried in Texas, the information being taken from newspaper clippings giving an account of a contest conducted among Texas school children by W. P. Webb, Prof. of History at the University of Texas. The Revolutionary Soldiers of Iowa was received in exchange for a similiar list of S.C. soldiers, from the Librarian of the Historical Library, Iowa State Department of History and Archives.

Contents "Miscellaneous Notes and Data," in addition to the sources named: By permission, from the D.A.R. Magazine, issues of March and August 1945, published at 1720 D. St. N. W., Washington, D. C., which can also be checked by: Memoirs of the Revolution by Drayton, Vol. 1, p. 226; S.C. Under The Royal Government 1719-1776 by Edw. McCrady, pp. 743-744; History of the Old Cheraws by Gregg, p. 221; Anecdotes Of The Revolutionary War in America by Alex. Garden, p. 165; Diary of Josiah Smith & S.C. Histl. & Geneal. Magazine.

Contents 17------ Abstracts of the wills 1775-1855, of my home county, Laurens: Many of these were collected over a period of years as needed in my work as a genealogist. Some two years ago, on discovering that I already had so many, the decision was taken to try to get the rest of the old wills and so have a more complete record. If written out in full, these wills would fill several large volumes. Therefore abstractions were made, they were arranged alphabetically, and eliminations used in order to prepare them in such a manner that they could easily be incorporated in one book. By using these devices, it is believed that the wills will be more accessible for quick reference and much less expensive to purchase. Proper or surnames are not repeated in listing children if the name is the same as that of the person who made the will, but if different, the name is written out in full. The first date used is when the will was made or written, and the second date, when proved. If dates and other data are not shown, it is because they were not available.

Advice and help in compiling this volume has been received from many persons and many sources. Among these were: Mr. A. S. Salley, State Historian; The South Carolina Historical Society; Miss Ellen Perry, Greenville, S.C. Public Library; Mrs. Phil Huff, Laurens County Library. The pictures in this book were used by permission of Everett Waddy Company of Richmond, Va., except that of Rebecca Moote which was obtained through the courtesy of Mrs. Mary Simms Oliphant, author of "The New Simms History of South Carolina, pub. 1940. by The State Co., Columbia, S.C.

Service records are available for the men and women of the Revolution, named in this book, but lack of space prevents including much of such data in this volume.

The matter of copyrighted material has been thoroughly examined. The Institute of American Genealogy searched some of the data used. The Hon. Jos. R. Bryson, Congress of U.S., advised us that "Title 17 of the U.S. Code states that government publications are not subject to copyright. It is my understanding that ... if you wish to copyright your work, your copyright would cover only the portions that were your own, and not the quotations." Miss Estellene P. Walker, Executive Secretary of the S.C. Library Board and Miss Lois Barbare, rendered valuable help and put us in touch with Miss Sarah Leverette, Librarian, University of S.C. School of Law. Finally a search was made at the Copyright Office, The Library of Congress, Washington, D.C. Letters and reports were received from Mr. Sam B. Warner, Register of Copyrights, Mr. Arthur Fisher, Associate Register of Copyrights, and Mr. Richard S. MacCarteney, Chief, Reference Division. The latter advised, "...no copyright can subsist in any publication of the U.S. Government. Such publications are deemed to be public property and free for... use and reproduction by anyone..." (a report on various items to be searched was included) In another letter the Copyright Office advised that "the first term of copyright is 28 years with a possibility of renewal for an additional 28 years if an application is properly made during the final year of the original term."

It is hoped that this book will make revolutionary service records more accessible to the descendants of South Carolina soldiers who are now scattered over the whole United States. Also that it will furnish information to patriotic persons who are interested in these Heroes who lived in the most crucial period of our country's history and who won the independence of our nation. Finally perhaps this volume will help perpetuate the cherished memories and the spirit of patriotism of that period so that descendants may find in these records the stimulus helpful in acquiring the faith, the courage, and the strength of their forbears and realize that they have an obligation to play well their part on the stage of life and so dedicate themselves to the betterment of mankind and the freedom of the world.

"ERVIN-DALE"                                  (Mrs.) Sara Sullivan Ervin
Ware Shoals, Route 1
Laurens County
South Carolina

HAND SPINNING WHEEL

# KEY TO ABBREVIATIONS

A-acre
acct-account
adm-administration
aft-after
AMER-American
amt-amount
b-born
beq-bequest
bk-book
bwt-between
Bro-brother
bptz-baptized
bur-buried
bx-box
Bh-bachelor
b.l.-bro-in-law
c-circa (about)
cem-cemetery
ch-church
CHN-children
ck-creek
Cpt-captain
Col-colonel
cos-cousins
CO-company
Com-committee
Daus-daughters
dec'd-deceased
div-divided
Dist-district
?-doubtful
dur-during
d-died

dept-department
est-estate
EXR-executors
et al(& elsewhere)
educ-educate
fam-family
fem-female
fks-forks
f.l.-father-in-law
Gr.chn-grand chn.
GRD-guardian
grt-great
Hist'l-historical
hus-husband
ibid-ibidem(in same place)
IS-issue
Invt-inventory
M-mother
m.l.-mother-in-law
Md-married
min-minor
Maj-Major
mgr-manager
ment-mentioned
memb-member
No.-number
O.B.-order book
Ods-oldest
p-page
Par-parish
pkg-package
Pres-president
prop-property

pvd-proved
pt-part
pesn-pension
plant-plantation
Qt-quarterly
Rec-recorded
recv'd-received
Regt-regiment
rem-remainder
rept-report
rd--road
Rev-Reverend
Revo.S--RevolutionaryS
riv-river
sect'y-secretary
sm-small
sps-springs
Sgt-sergeant
sub-submit
s.l.-son-in-law
Treas-treasurer
unmd-unmarried
Viz-namely
wid-widow
Wit-witnesses
w-wife
yrs-years
yg-youngest
Surg-surgeon
phy-physician
Chap-chaplain

A FLINT-LOCK GUN.

MATCHLOCK-GUN.

*George Washington*

*Commander-in-Chief of the Armies of the United States
of America in the War of the Revolution*

# TABLE OF CONTENTS

# SOUTH CAROLINA PENSION ROLL.

# SOUTH CAROLINA PENSION ROLL

*A statement showing the names, rank, &c., of Invalid Pensioners residing in the district of Abbeville, in the State of South Carolina.*

| NAMES. | Rank. | Annual allowance. | Sums received. | Description of service. | When placed on the pension roll. | Commencement of pension. | Ages. | Laws under which inscribed; and remarks. |
|---|---|---|---|---|---|---|---|---|
| James Armstrong | Private | 60 00 | 266 64 | - | - | Nov. 15, 1911 | - | Act July 5, 1812. |
| Do | Do | 96 00 | 946 89 | - | - | April 24, 1916 | - | Act April 24, 1816. |
| Lewis Howland | Do | 96 00 | 1,660 75 | U. S. rifle reg't | Sept. 5, 1816 | Nov. 11, 1814 | - | Act military establishment. Died February 26, 1882. |
| John Martin | Do | 30 00 | 153 32 | - | - | Nov. 15, 1811 | - | Act July 5, 1812. Died February 5, 1822. |
| Do | Do | 48 00 | 277 57 | - | - | April 24, 1816 | - | Act April 24, 1816. |
| | | | 3,285 17 | | | | | |

*A statement showing the names, rank, &c., of Invalid Pensioners residing in the district of Anderson, in the State of South Carolina.*

| NAMES. | Rank. | Annual allowance. | Sums received. | Description of service. | When placed on the pension roll. | Commencement of pension. | Ages. | Laws under which inscribed; and remarks |
|---|---|---|---|---|---|---|---|---|
| Sion Holly | Private | 63 96 | 1,152 15 | N. C. militia under General Martin | Mar. 27, 1818 | Feb. 28, 1816 | - | Act March 3, 1817. |
| John Looney | Do | 21 42 | 173 78 | - | - | March 1, 1808 | - | Act April 25, 1808. |
| Do | Do | 34 12 | 592 52 | - | - | April 24, 1816 | - | Act April 24, 1816. |
| | | | 1,918 45 | | | | | |

*A statement showing the names, rank, &c., of Invalid Pensioners residing in the district of Barnwell, in the State of South Carolina.*

| NAMES. | Rank. | Annual allowance. | Sums received. | Description of service. | When placed on the pension roll. | Commencement of pension. | Ages. | Laws under which inscribed; and remarks. |
|---|---|---|---|---|---|---|---|---|
| Daniel Odom* | Captain | 55 78 | 1,422 39 | Mil. regt. commanded by Col. Hardin | - | Sept. 4, 1789 | - | Transferred from Georgia from March 4, 1815. |
| Do | Do | 55 78 | 63 62 | - | - | March 4, 1815 | - | |
| Do | Do | 89 12 | 1,591 98 | - | - | April 24, 1816 | - | |
| | | | 3,077 99 | | | | | |

*A statement showing the names, rank, &c., of Invalid Pensioners residing in the district of Chester, in the State of South Carolina.*

| NAMES. | Rank. | Annual allowance. | Sums received. | Description of service. | When placed on the pension roll. | Commencement of pension. | Ages. | Laws under which inscribed; and remarks. |
|---|---|---|---|---|---|---|---|---|
| Joseph Gaston | Private | 95 00 | 113 03 | U. S. rifle regt. | Oct. 1, 1833 | Jan. 1, 1833 | - | Act March 2, 1833. |
| John Halcomb | Do | 72 00 | 1,051 97 | | Jan. 11, 1821 | July 26, 1819 | - | Act military establishment. |
| | | | 1,165 00 | | | | | |

* The books do not show when this pensioner was placed on the invalid pension list: and the papers upon which his claim was established were burnt in 1814, when the War Office was destroyed by the British troops. Hence no information on this point can be furnished.

For the same reason, information required in other cases, marked thus, (*) cannot be given.

N. B. In all cases where the ages are not indicated in the appropriate column, they could not be ascertained.

3

*A statement showing the names, rank, &c., of Invalid Pensioners residing in the district of Charleston, in the State of South Carolina.*

| NAMES. | Rank. | Annual allowance. | Sums received. | Description of service. | When placed on the pension roll. | Commencement of pension. | Ages. | Laws under which inscribed; and remarks. |
|---|---|---|---|---|---|---|---|---|
| Joseph Clark* | Private | 48 00 | 340 26 | 1st regt. U. S. rifle | Feb. 24, 1817 | Aug. 3, 1815 | - | Acts ex. military establishment. |
| William Laval | Captain | 240 00 | 369 80 | 3d U. S. regt. | March 3, 1830 | Feb. 19, 1830 | - | Act April 10, 1806. Dropped under act May 1, 1820. |
| George Petrie | 2d lieut. | 240 00 | 428 38 | S. C. cont'l line | May 29, 1818 | May 22, 1818 | - | |
| Do | Do | 180 00 | 1,144 93 | Col. Pinkney's reg. | July 30, 1823 | July 3, 1823 | - | Act February 4, 1822. Died July 12, 1831. |
| | | | 2,283 37 | | | | | |

*A statement showing the names, rank, &c., of Invalid Pensioners residing in the district of Edgefield, in the State of South Carolina.*

| NAMES. | Rank. | Annual allowance. | Sums received. | Description of service. | When placed on the pension roll. | Commencement of pension. | Ages. | Laws under which inscribed; and remarks. |
|---|---|---|---|---|---|---|---|---|
| Turner Crooker | Captain | 240 00 | 1,496 69 | 9th regt. U. S. inf. | Dec. 11, 1819 | Dec. 10, 1819 | - | Act mil'y establish't. Transferred from Georgia March 24, 1826. |
| Do | Do | 240 00 | 1,738 06 | Do | Do | Do | - | Died May 31, 1833. |
| | | | 3,234 75 | | | | | |

4

*A statement showing the names, rank, &c., of Invalid Pensioners residing in the district of Fairfield, in the State of South Carolina.*

| NAMES. | Rank. | Annual allowance. | Sums received. | Description of service. | When placed on the pension roll. | Commencement of pension. | Ages. | Laws under which inscribed; and remarks. |
|---|---|---|---|---|---|---|---|---|
| Joseph Kerr | Private | 60 00 | 1,470 00 | - | - | March 4, 1789 | - | Act Sept. 29, 1789. Transfer from North Carolina from Sept. 4, 1813. Dead. |
| Do | Do | 60 00 | 158 45 | | | Do | | Do |
| Do | Do | 96 00 | 370 89 | | | April 24, 1816 | | Act April 24, 1816. |
| Joseph King | Do | 30 00 | 75 49 | | | Oct. 19, 1813 | | Act April 18, 1814. |
| Do | Do | 48 00 | 113 44 | | | April 24, 1816 | | Act April 24, 1816. |
| | | | 2,188 27 | | | | | |

*A statement showing the names, rank, &c. of Invalid Pensioners residing in the district of Greenville, in the State of South Carolina.*

| NAMES. | Rank. | Annual allowance. | Sums received. | Description of service. | When placed on the pension roll. | Commencement of pension. | Ages. | Laws under which inscribed; and remarks. |
|---|---|---|---|---|---|---|---|---|
| Thomas Smith, 1st | Private | 60 00 | 1,568 45 | Army of the rev. | Oct. 19, 1821 | March 4, 1790 | - | Act Sept. 29, 1789. Transferred from North Carolina from 4th March, 1826. |
| Do | Do | 96 00 | 946 89 | Do | Do | April 24, 1816 | - | Act April 24, 1816. |
| Do | Do | 96 00 | 768 00 | Do | Do | March 4, 1826 | - | Do. |
| | | | 3,283 34 | | | | | |

*A statement of the names, &c., of the Heirs of non-commissioned Officers, Privates, &c., who died in the United States' service; who obtained five years' half pay in lieu of bounty land, under the second section of the act of April 16, 1816, and who resided in Greenville district, in the State of South Carolina.*

| Names of the original claimants. | Rank. | Description of service. | Time of decease. | Names of the heirs. | Annual allowance. | Sums received. | When placed on the roll. | Commencement of pension. | Ending of pension. |
|---|---|---|---|---|---|---|---|---|---|
| Noah Coleman - | Private | 3d regt. inf. | Aug. 27, 1813 | Eliza and Mahala Coleman - | 48 00 | 240 00 | Aug. 20, 1817 | Feb. 17, 1815 | Feb. 17, 1820 |
| John Duncan - | Do | Do | Nov. 13, 1813 | James and Rebecca Duncan - | 48 00 | 240 00 | Mar. 23, 1818 | Do | Do |
| Atha Saxton - | Do | Do | Mar. or April, 1815 | Luraney, Noah, Polly, John, and Atha Saxton - - - | 48 00 | 240 00 | Mar. 5, 1818 | Do | Do |

*A statement of the names, &c., of the Heirs of non-commissioned Officers, Privates, &c., who died in the United States' service; who obtained five years' half pay in lieu of bounty land under the second section of the act of April 16, 1816, and who resided in Marlborough district, in the State of South Carolina.*

| Names of the original claimants. | Rank. | Description of service. | Time of decease. | Names of the heirs. | Annual allowance. | Sums received. | When placed on the roll. | Commencement of pension. | Ending of pension. |
|---|---|---|---|---|---|---|---|---|---|
| Joseph Clark | Private | 18th regt. inf. | Mar. 21, 1814 | Obedience, Henrietta, and Jesse Clark - - - - | 48 00 | 240 00 | May 10, 1820 | Feb. 10, 1820 | Feb. 10, 1825 |

6

*A statement of the names, &c., of the Heirs of non-commissioned Officers, Privates, &c., who died in the United States' service; who obtained five years' half-pay in lieu of bounty land, under the second section of the act of April 16, 1816, and who resided in Pendleton district, in the State of South Carolina.*

| Names of the original claimants. | Rank. | Description of service. | Time of decease. | Names of the heirs. | Annual allowance. | Sums received. | When placed on the roll. | Commencement of pension. | Ending of pension. |
|---|---|---|---|---|---|---|---|---|---|
| Jno. Cunningham | Private | 3d regt. inf. | March, 1815 | Catharine, Elizabeth, Elias, Jno. B., and Sarah Cunningham - | 48 00 | 240 00 | Dec. 17, 1817 | Feb. 17, 1815 | Feb. 17, 1820 |
| Thomas Pointer - | Do | Do | Feb. 20, 1815 | Katy, Leanna, Polly, Melinda Fleming, Elizabeth, Lucinda John, and Jackson Pointer - | 48 00 | 240 00 | Do | Do | Do |

*A statement of the names, &c., of the Heirs of non-commissioned Officers, Privates, &c., who died in the United States' service; who obtained five years' half-pay in lieu of bounty land, under the second section of the act of April 16, 1816, and who resided in Richland district, in the State of South Carolina.*

| Names of the original claimants. | Rank. | Description of service. | Time of decease. | Names of the heirs. | Annual allowance. | Sums received. | When placed on the roll. | Commencement of pension. | Ending of pension. |
|---|---|---|---|---|---|---|---|---|---|
| Henry Williams - | Corporal | 18th regt. inf. | Sept. 18, 1812 | Mary, George, and Henry Williams - - - - | 48 00 | 240 00 | June 6, 1818 | Feb. 17, 1815 | Feb. 17, 1820 |
| Jesse Holder - | Private | Do | Jan. 21, 1814 | Jesse Holder - - - - - | 48 00 | 240 00 | Sept. 23, 1819 | Do | Do. |

A statement of the names, &c., of the Heirs of *non-commissioned Officers, Privates, &c., who died in the United States' service; who obtained five years' half-pay in lieu of bounty land, under the second section of the act of April 16, 1816, and who resided in Spartanburgh district, in the State of South Carolina.*

| Names of the original claimants. | Rank. | Description of service. | Time of decease. | Names of the heirs. | Annual allowance. | Sums received. | When placed on the roll. | Commencement of pension. | Ending of pension. |
|---|---|---|---|---|---|---|---|---|---|
| Benjamin Wells | Private | 8th regt. inf. | Nov. 9, 1814 | Priscilla, Nancy, and Alexander Wells - - - - | 48 00 | 240 00 | Sept. 23, 1819 | Feb. 17, 1815 | Feb. 17, 1820 |

*A statement showing the names, rank, &c., of Invalid Pensioners residing in the district of Pickens, in the State of South Carolina.*

| NAMES. | Rank. | Annual allowance. | Sums received. | Description of service. | When placed on the pension roll. | Commencement of pension. | Ages. | Laws under which inscribed; and remarks. |
|---|---|---|---|---|---|---|---|---|
| Andrew McAllister* | Private | 21 42 | 121 88 | - - | - - | Sept. 4, 1810 | | Act April 24, 1816 |
| Do | Do | 34 12 | 508 47 | - - | - - | April 24, 1816 | | |
| | | | 630 35 | | | | | |

*A statement showing the names, rank, &c., of Invalid Pensioners residing in the district of Spartansburgh, in the State of South Carolina.*

| NAMES. | Rank. | Annual allowance. | Sums received. | Description of service. | When placed on the pension roll. | Commencement of pension. | Age. | Laws under which inscribed; and remarks. |
|---|---|---|---|---|---|---|---|---|
| Jesse Vincent - - | Private | 48 00 | 89 18 | 7th regt. U. S. inf. | Nov. 1, 1831 | Oct. 27, 1831 | - | Acts ex. military establishment. |
| | | | 89 18 | | | | | |

2

*A statement showing the names, rank, &c., of Invalid Pensioners residing in the district of Union, in the State of South Carolina.*

| NAMES. | Rank. | Annual allowance. | Sums received | Description of service. | When placed on the pension roll. | Commencement of pension. | Ages. | Laws under which inscribed; and remarks. |
|---|---|---|---|---|---|---|---|---|
| Joseph Davidson - | Private | 30 00 | 127 58 | | | Jan. 23, 1812 | - | Act Aug. 2, 1813. Died October 12, 1832. |
| Do - - | Do | 48 00 | 769 44 | | | April 24, 1816 | - | Act April 24, 1816. |
| Joseph McJunkin - | Major | 144 00 | 2,792 20 | U. States army | Dec. 23, 1811 | Oct. 18, 1808 | - | Act March 3, 1809. |
| Do - - | Do | 200 00 | 786 07 | Do | Do | March 7, 1828 | - | Act April 24, 1816. |
| Do - - | Do | 225 00 | 503 58 | Do | Do | Feb 11, 1832 | - | Do do. |
| Jasper Tomiton - | Private | 30 00 | 131 23 | | | Dec. 10, 1811 | - | Act July 5, 1812. Died December 31, 1828. |
| Do - - | Do | 48 00 | 417 00 | | | April 24, 1816 | - | Act April 24, 1816. |
| Thomas Young - - | Do | 72 00 | 430 23 | Army of revolution | April 18, 1828 | March 12, 1828 | - | Act February 4, 1822. |
| | | | 5,957 33 | | | | | |

9

A statement showing the names, rank, &c. of Invalid Pensioners residing in the district of York, in the State of South Carolina.

| NAMES. | Rank. | Annual allowance. | Sums received. | Description of service. | When placed on the pension roll. | Commencement of pension. | Ages. | Laws under which inscribed; and remarks. |
|---|---|---|---|---|---|---|---|---|
| Alexander Haynes* | Private | 42 00 | 351 26 | U. States army | Jan. 28, 1822 | Sept. 4, 1808 | - | Transferred from North Carolina, from Sept. 4, 1826. Died Feb. 2, 1828. |
| Do | Do | 67 20 | 427 62 | Do | Do | April 24, 1816 | - | Act April 24, 1816. |
| Do | Do | 48 00 | 192 00 | Do | Do | Sept. 4, 1822 | - | Act March 3, 1819. |
| Do | Do | 48 00 | 67 74 | Do | Do | Sept. 4, 1826 | - | |
| James McClain | Do | 96 00 | 155 61 | Ballarde's co. 3d rifl. | Jan. 19.1828 | Jan. 19, 1828 | - | Acts military establishment. Died August 31, 1829. |
| Samuel Rose | Do | 20 00 | 14 04 | 3d regt. U. S. rifle | - | Aug. 6, 1815 | - | Acts military establishment. |
| Do | Do | 32 00 | 251 62 | Do | - | April 24, 1816 | - | Act April 24, 1816. |
| Isaiah Twitchall | Do | 60 00 | 57 66 | Howards' co. 25 inf. | - | May 14, 1815 | - | Acts ex. military establishment. Transferred from Connecticut, from March 4, 1824. |
| Do | Do | 96 00 | 754 92 | Do | - | April 24, 1816 | - | Acts April 24, 1826. |
| Do | Do | 96 00 | 960 00 | Do | | | | |
| | | | 3,232 47 | | | | | |

A list of Invalid Pensioners who have been in the receipt of pensions at the agency of Charleston, in the State of South Carolina, and whose residence cannot be ascertained in consequence of the destruction of the papers in the War Office in 1801 and 1814,

| NAMES. | Rank. | Annual allowance. | Sums received. | Description of service. | When placed on the pension roll. | Commencement of pension. | Ages. | Laws under which inscribed; and remarks. |
|---|---|---|---|---|---|---|---|---|
| John Calhoun - | Private | 21 42 | - | - | - | - | - | Act April 25, 1808. |
| Do - | Do | 34 12 | - | - | - | April 24, 1816 | - | Act April 24, 1816. |
| William Dunlap* - | Do | 21 42 | - | - | - | | - | Do do. |
| Do - | Do | 34 12 | - | - | - | Do | - | Act July 5, 1812  Died May 26, 1820. |
| Malcom Keys - | Do | 48 00 | 213 31 | - | - | Nov. 15, 1811 | - | |
| Do - | Do | 76 80 | 314 23 | - | - | April 24, 1816 | - | Act April 24, 1816. |
| George Mason* - | Do | 55 12 | - | - | - | March 4, 1809 | - | Dead. |
| David Witherspoon* - | Do | 21 42 | 76 04 | - | - | - | - | Dead. |
| Henry Weems* - | Do | 60 00 | 108 28 | - | - | Nov. 15, 1811 | - | Act July 5, 1812.  Dead. |
| | | | 711 86 | | | | | |

11

*A statement showing the names, rank, &c., of persons residing in the district of Abbeville, in the State of South Carolina, who have been inscribed on the pension list under the act of Congress passed the 18th March, 1818.*

| NAMES. | Rank. | Annual allowance. | Sums received. | Description of service. | When placed on the pension roll. | Commencement of pension. | Ages. | Laws under which they were formerly inscribed on the pension roll; and remarks. |
|---|---|---|---|---|---|---|---|---|
| William Ashley - | Corporal - | 96 00 | 360 56 | Pulaski's legion | Sept. 24, 1818 | Aug. 11, 1818 | 77 | Dropped under act May 1, 1820. Restored, commencing Dec. 27, 1831. |
| James Devlin - - | Private | 96 00 | 674 60 | S. C. cont'l line | March 5, 1819 | Aug. 26, 1818 | 75 | Died November 26, 1825. |
| Hugh Houston - - | Do | 96 00 | 1,149 82 | N. C. do | Nov. 25, 1819 | June 8, 1818 | 79 | Dropped under act May 1, 1820. Restored, commencing June 10, 1823. |
| Benjamin Kennard - | Do | 96 00 | 949 56 | Penn. do | July 31, 1819 | June 14, 1819 | 83 | Dropped under act May 1, 1820. Restored, commencing September 4, 1821. |
| Edward Lyon - - | Do | 96 00 | 425 02 | Virginia do | March 5, 1819 | Aug. 9, 1818 | 71 | Died January 12, 1823. |
| Andrew Mellog - - | Do | 96 00 | - | S. C. do | March 5, 1821 | Nov. 13, 1818 | - | Dropped under act May 1, 1818. |
| Henry Magner - - | Do | 96 00 | 1,415 43 | N. C. do | Aug. 19, 1819 | June 7, 1819 | 68 | |
| Joshua Pruett - - | Do | 96 00 | 1,511 16 | N. C. do | Sept. 6, 1819 | June 8, 1818 | 80 | |
| James Russell - - | Do | 96 00 | 438 20 | S. C. do | March 5, 1819 | Aug. 12, 1818 | 90 | Died December 4, 1823. |
| | | | 6 924 35 | | | | | |

*A statement showing the names, rank, &c., of persons residing in the district of Anderson, in the State of South Carolina, who have been inscribed on the pension list under the act of Congress passed the 18th March, 1818.*

| NAMES. | Rank. | Annual allowance. | Sums received. | Description of service. | When placed on the pension roll | Commencement of pension. | Ages. | Laws under which they were formerly inscribed on the pension roll; and remarks. |
|---|---|---|---|---|---|---|---|---|
| William Day - | Private - | 96 00 | 1,490 57 | Virginia cont'l line | Jan. 18, 1819 | Aug. 26, 1818 | 78 | |
| Coodman Harris - | Do | 96 00 | 1,506 06 | N. C. do | March 5, 1819 | July 1, 1818 | 76 | |

| | | | | | | | | |
|---|---|---|---|---|---|---|---|---|
| John Lewis | Do | 96 00 | 340 57 | Virginia do | Feb. 5, 1829 | Feb. 3, 1829 | 78 | Act March 18, 1818. Transferred from Rutherford co., N. Carolina, from September 4, 1833. |
| Do | Do | 96 00 | 48 00 | Do Do | Feb. 5, 1829 | Feb. 3, 1829 | 78 | |
| William Noble | Do | 96 00 | 1,489 56 | N. C. do | March 5, 1819 | Sept. 2, 1818 | 90 | |
| James Young | Do | 96 00 | 1,509 83 | Virginia do | March 5, 1819 | June 13, 1818 | 80 | |
| | | | 6,384 59 | | | | | |

*A statement showing the names, rank, &c., of persons residing in the Beaufort district, in the State of South Carolina, who have been inscribed on the pension list under the act of Congress passed the 18th March, 1818.*

| NAMES. | Rank. | Annual allowance. | Sums received. | Description of service. | When placed on the pension roll. | Commencement of pension. | Ages. | Laws under which they were formerly inscribed on the pension roll; and remarks. |
|---|---|---|---|---|---|---|---|---|
| Isam Carter | Private | 96 00 | 1,511 96 | S. C. cont'l line | Aug. 2, 1819 | June 5, 1818 | - | |
| John Cook, 2d | Do | 96 00 | 323 92 | Do | Sept. 10, 1819 | Sept. 16, 1818 | 80 | Dropped under act May 1, 1820. Restored, commencing April 9, 1824. |
| George Gosling | Do | 96 00 | 123 96 | Do | Sept. 7, 1819 | Nov. 20, 1818 | - | |
| John Wickly | Captain | 240 00 | 422 58 | Do | Aug. 2, 1819 | June 1, 1818 | 78 | Dropped under act May 1, 1820. |
| Levi Weeks | Private | 96 00 | 1,169 06 | Maryland do | April 22, 1820 | July 1, 1818 | 78 | Dropped under act May 1, 1820. |
| | | | 3,551 48 | | | | | |

A statement showing the names, rank, &c., of persons residing in the district of Barnwell, in the State of South Carolina, who have been inscribed on the pension list under the act of Congress passed the 18th March, 1818.

| NAMES. | Rank. | Annual allowance. | Sums received. | Description of service. | When placed on the pension roll. | Commencement of pension. | Ages. | Laws under which they were formerly inscribed on the pension roll; and remarks. |
|---|---|---|---|---|---|---|---|---|
| Jesse Griffin - | Private | 96 00 | 1,377 56 | Pulaski's corps | Jan. 22, 1819 | Nov. 3, 1818 | 78 | |
| Dennis Scott - | Do | 96 00 | 777 03 | N. C. cont'l line | Feb. 23, 1826 | Feb. 1, 1826 | 74 | |
| | | | 2,154 59 | | | | | |

A statement showing the names, rank, &c., of persons residing in the district of Chester, in the State of South Carolina, who have been inscribed on the pension list under the act of Congress passed the 18th March, 1818.

| NAMES. | Rank. | Annual allowance. | Sums received. | Description of service. | When placed on the pension roll. | Commencement of pension. | Ages. | Laws under which they were formerly inscribed on the pension roll; and remarks. |
|---|---|---|---|---|---|---|---|---|
| James Alverson - | Private | 96 00 | 695 73 | Virginia cont'l line | Dec. 30, 1826 | Dec. 5, 1826 | 75 | |
| Joseph Brown - | Do | 96 00 | 1,357 18 | do | March 5, 1819 | July 16, 1818 | 75 | Died April 16, 1833. |
| Archibald Brown - | Do | 96 00 | 673 03 | do | Oct. 11, 1823 | March 1, 1823 | 74 | Died July 21, 1831. |
| James Black - | Do | 96 00 | 607 69 | Do | Nov. 19, 1827 | Nov. 6, 1827 | 77 | |
| William Cockrell - | Do | 96 00 | 1,501 15 | Do | March 5, 1819 | July 16, 1818 | 77 | |
| Robert Conley - | Do | 96 00 | 128 00 | Do | Sept. 23, 1819 | Nov. 4, 1818 | 66 | Dropped under act May 1, 1820. |
| Robert Cowley - | Do | 96 00 | 695 73 | Do | Dec. 30, 1826 | Dec. 6, 1826 | 81 | |
| John Dougherty - | Do | 96 00 | 686 47 | Penn. | April 19, 1819 | July 11, 1818 | 91 | |
| Lewis Hardin - | Do | 96 00 | 1,500 12 | do | Feb. 16, 1820 | July 20, 1818 | 63 | |
| William Knox - | Do | 96 00 | 1,164 15 | N. C. | March 5, 1819 | Do | 82 | |
| Charles Kea - | Do | 96 00 | 253 15 | S. C. | March 5, 1819 | July 16, 1818 | 85 | |
| James Kirkpatrick - | Do | 96 00 | 115 35 | Virginia | May 17, 1819 | Dec. 23, 1818 | - | Dropped under act May 1, 1820. |

14

| Names | Rank | Annual allowance | Sums received | Description of service | When placed on the pension roll | Commencement of pension | Ages | Laws under which they were formerly inscribed on the pension roll; and remarks |
|---|---|---|---|---|---|---|---|---|
| Hugh Knox - | Do | 96 00 | 128 77 | Do | Sept. 23, 1819 | Nov. 2, 1818 | - | Dropped under act May 1, 1820. |
| Spencer Kirkpatrick - | Do | 96 00 | 845 86 | Do | Sept. 23, 1819 | Nov. 13, 1818 | 72 | Dead. Reported December, 1828. |
| John Miller - | Do | 96 00 | 147 69 | Virginia do | March 5, 1819 | July 20, 1818 | - | Dropped under act May 1, 1820. |
| Benjamin Rowan | Do | 96 00 | 1,165 18 | S. C. do | March 5, 1819 | July 16, 1818 | 78 | Died December 3, 1830. |
|  |  |  | 11,665 25 |  |  |  |  |  |

*A statement showing the names, rank, &c., of persons residing in the district of Charleston, in the State of South Carolina, who have been inscribed on the pension list under the act of Congress passed the 18th March, 1818.*

| Names. | Rank. | Annual allowance. | Sums received. | Description of service. | When placed on the pension roll. | Commencement of pension. | Ages. | Laws under which they were formerly inscribed on the pension roll; and remarks |
|---|---|---|---|---|---|---|---|---|
| John Betsell or Bedsell | Private | 96 00 | 201 06 | Virginia cont'l line | Sept. 18, 1820 | Aug. 1, 1820 | 73 |  |
| Nathaniel Cudworth - | Major | 240 00 | 1,868 38 | do | May 4, 1818 | April 9, 1818 | 79 | Died January 21, 1826. |
| Francis Francum - | Private | 96 00 | 420 26 | Mass. do | May 17, 1825 | May 9, 1825 | 70 | Died September 23, 1829. |
| Henry Gray - | Lieutenant | 240 00 | 85 80 | S. C. Do | June 12, 1824 | March 10, 1824 | 75 | Died July 20, 1824. |
| John McCune - | Private | 96 00 | 243 91 | Do | March 19, 1827 | Feb. 19, 1827 | 76 |  |
| David Sardezas - | Lieutenant | 240 00 | 3,590 96 | Georgia do | Jan. 12, 1819 | May 19, 1818 | 73 | Dropped under act May 1, 1820. |
| James Stewart - | Private | 96 00 | 122 09 | Do | April 8, 1819 | Nov. 27, 1818 | - | Dead. Reported June 1, 1823. |
| James Waddell - | Sergeant | 96 00 | 381 15 | S. C. do | Aug. 3, 1820 | March 16, 1820 | 62 |  |
|  |  |  | 6,913 61 |  |  |  |  |  |

*A statement showing the names, rank, &c., of persons residing in the district of Chesterfield, in the State of South Carolina, who have been inscribed on the pension list under the act of Congress passed the 18th March, 1818.*

| NAMES. | Rank. | Annual allowance. | Sums received. | Description of service. | When placed on the pension roll. | Commencement of pension. | Ages. | Laws under which they were formerly inscribed on the pension roll, and remarks. |
|---|---|---|---|---|---|---|---|---|
| John Brown | Private | 96 00 | 1,368 54 | S. C. cont'l line | March 5, 1819 | Dec. 3, 1818 | 73 | |
| | | | 1,368 54 | | | | | |

*A statement showing the names, rank, &c., of persons residing in the district of Darlington, in the State South Carolina, who have been inscribed on the pension list under the act of Congress passed the 18th March, 1818.*

| NAMES. | Rank. | Annual allowance. | Sums received. | Description of service. | When placed on the pension roll. | Commencement of pension. | Ages. | Laws under which they were formerly inscribed on the pension roll, and remarks. |
|---|---|---|---|---|---|---|---|---|
| James Neal | Private | 96 00 | 485 88 | S. C. cont'l line | Feb. 12, 1829 | Feb. 12, 1829 | 79 | |
| | | | 485 88 | | | | | |

16

*A statement showing the names, rank, &c., of persons residing in the district of Edgefield, in the State of South Carolina, who have been inscribed on the pension list under the act of Congress passed the 18th March, 1818.*

| NAMES. | Rank. | Annual allowance. | Sums received. | Description of service. | When placed on the pension roll. | Commencement of pension | Ages. | Laws under which they were formerly inscribed on the pension roll; and remarks. |
|---|---|---|---|---|---|---|---|---|
| Richard Burton | Private | 96 00 | 1,513 83 | Georgia cont'l line | Sept. 18, 1818 | June 2, 1818 | 75 | |
| William Blaikley | Do | 96 00 | - | S. C. do | Dec. 14, 1818 | June 3, 1818 | - | Dropped under act May 1, 1818. |
| William Bryant | Do | 96 00 | 347 61 | N. C. do | March 24, 1819 | July 22, 1818 | 83 | |
| Joseph Croes | Do | 96 00 | 580 93 | Virginia cavalry | Jan. 4, 1819 | Aug. 17, 1818 | 76 | |
| Thomas Dean | Do | 96 00 | 840 76 | 3d reg't rangers | Sept. 18, 1818 | June 2, 1818 | 73 | |
| Julius Dean | Do | 96 00 | 359 16 | Georgia cont'l line | July 7, 1819 | June 8, 1819 | 80 | |
| Batte Evans | Do | 96 00 | 776 54 | Virginia do | March 5, 1819 | Ag. 3, 1818 | 74 | Dead. Reported June, 1832. |
| Samuel Garner | Do | 96 00 | 134 19 | S. C. do | March 24, 1819 | Oct. 16, 1818 | 73 | |
| John Glover | Ensign | 240 00 | 587 08 | Do | Feb. 3, 1820 | Oct. 17, 1818 | 70 | Died March 27, 1821. |
| Robert Hastings | Private | 96 00 | 1,513 83 | Delaware do | Sept. 18, 1818 | June 2, 1818 | 90 | Dropped under act May 1, 1830. Restored, commencing Nov. 14, 1825. Died July 25, 1827. |
| John Huffman | Do | 96 00 | 314 71 | Virginia do | Jan. 4, 1819 | Aug. 4, 1818 | 71 | |
| Stephen Hutchinson | Do | 96 00 | 1,499 35 | Do | April 15, 1819 | July 23, 1818 | 79 | |
| Joshua J. Jackson | Do | 96 00 | 504 79 | N. York do | Sept. 18, 1818 | June 2, 1818 | 89 | |
| Thomas Inlo | Do | 96 00 | 84 46 | Virginia do | Jan. 4, 1819 | Sept. 7, 1818 | 78 | Dropped under act May 1, 1820. |
| James King | Do | 96 00 | 159 73 | Do | March 24, 1819 | July 6, 1818 | 59 | do. |
| Basil Lowe | Do | 96 00 | 168 23 | Armand's legion | Sept. 18, 1819 | June 4, 1818 | 61 | do. |
| Dennis Lowe | Do | 96 00 | 1,240 28 | Do | Jan. 18, 1821 | Oct. 4, 1820 | 70 | |
| Isham Melton | Do | 96 00 | 1,223 96 | Virginia cont'l line | March 24, 1819 | June 5, 1818 | 74 | |
| William Martin | Do | 96 00 | 809 56 | S. C. do | Nov. 10, 1819 | Sept. 29, 1819 | 74 | Dead. Reported Dec., 1828. |
| Joshua Reams | Do | 96 00 | 793 80 | N. C. do | Sept 18, 1818 | June 2, 1818 | 74 | |
| Simeon Smith | Do | 96 00 | 1,368 79 | Do | Do | Do | 83 | |
| Charles Simpkins | Do | 96 00 | 1,509 83 | Mil. cont'l line | Dec. 14, 1818 | June 13, 1818 | 84 | Dropped under act May 1, 1820. Restored, commencing Feb. 14, 1827. Died June 2, 1829. |
| Moses Spivey | Do | 96 00 | 357 06 | S. C. do | Jan. 4, 1819 | Oct. 4, 1818 | 73 | |
| George Turner | Do | 96 00 | 168 76 | Geo gia do | Sept. 18, 1818 | June 2, 1818 | 75 | |
| Jonathan Taylor | Do | 96 00 | 136 77 | Virginia do | March 24, 1819 | Oct. 2, 1818 | 60 | Dropped under act May 1, 1820. Do |

*Statement of Edgefield district—Continued.*

| NAMES. | Rank. | Annual allowance. | Sums received. | Description of service. | When placed on the pension roll. | Commencement of pension. | Ages. | Laws under which they were formerly inscribed on the pension roll; and remarks. |
|---|---|---|---|---|---|---|---|---|
| Thomas Wiseman - | Private | 96 00 | 696 79 | Md. cont'l line | Jan. 4, 1819 | June 2, 1818 | 84 | |
| Henry Weaver - | Do | 96 00 | 168 76 | S. C. do | March 24, 1819 | Do | 83 | Dropped under act May 1, 1820. Restored, commencing Aug. 7, 1838. |
| | | | 17,859 56 | | | | | |

*A statement showing the names, rank, &c., of persons residing in the district of Fairfield, in the State of South Carolina, who have been inscribed on the pension list under the act of Congress passed March 18, 1818.*

| NAMES. | Rank. | Annual allowance. | Sums received. | Description of service. | When placed on the pension roll. | Commencement of pension. | Ages. | Laws under which they were formerly inscribed on the pension roll; and remarks. |
|---|---|---|---|---|---|---|---|---|
| John Smith - | Private | 96 00 | 1,081 01 | S. C. cont'l line | March 5, 1819 | July 16, 1818 | - | Dropped under act May 1, 1820. Restored, commencing July 21, 1824. |
| | | | 1,081 01 | | | | | |

A statement showing the names, rank, &c., of persons residing in the district of Georgetown, in the State of South Carolina, who have been inscribed on the pension list under the act of Congress passed March 18, 1818.

| NAMES. | Rank. | Description of service. | When placed on the pension roll. | Commencement of pension. | Ages. | Sums received. | Annual allowance. | Laws under which they were formerly inscribed on the pension roll; and remarks. |
|---|---|---|---|---|---|---|---|---|
| Peter Bacot - - | Captain | N. C. cont'l line | Sept. 28, 1818 | June 2, 1818 | 67 | 767 71 | 240 00 | Died August 13, 1821. |
| | | | | | | 767 71 | | |

A statement showing the names, rank, &c., of persons residing in the district of Greenville, in the State of South Carolina, who have been inscribed on the pension list under the act of Congress passed March 18, 1818.

| NAMES. | Rank. | Descript'on of service. | When placed on the pension roll. | Commencement of pension. | Ages. | Sums received. | Annual allowance. | Laws under which they were formerly inscribed on the pension roll; and remarks. |
|---|---|---|---|---|---|---|---|---|
| Charles Bryant - - | Private | Virginia cont'l line | Jan. 14, 1824 | Nov. 5, 1823 | 73 | 655 99 | 96 00 | Died January 10, 1831. |
| William Berry - - | Do | Do | May 10, 1826 | Nov. 2, 1825 | 79 | 752 79 | 96 00 | |
| William Duncan - | Do | N. C. do | July 30, 1824 | June 26, 1824 | 85 | 930 36 | 96 00 | |
| Isaac Gregory - - | Do | Do | April 3, 1819 | June 8, 1818 | 76 | 1,471 16 | 96 00 | |
| Blackman Ligan - | Do | Virginia do | March 5, 1819 | June 14, 1818 | 63 | 125 56 | 96 00 | Dropped under act May 1, 1820. |
| Nicholas Latner - | Do | S. C. do | Jan. 10, 1829 | Dec. 15, 1828 | 72 | 501 41 | 96 00 | |
| Thomas Masters - | Do | Virginia do | March 5, 1819 | Nov. 3, 1818 | 79 | 1,473 56 | 96 00 | |
| Gipson Southern - | Do | Georgia do | Feb. 9, 1819 | May 18, 1818 | 81 | 1,324 64 | 96 00 | |
| | | | | | | 7,235 47 | | |

19

*A statement showing the names, rank, &c., of persons residing in the district of Horry, in the State of South Carolina, who have been inscribed on the pension list under the act of Congress passed March 18, 1818.*

| NAMES. | Rank. | Annual allowance. | Sums received. | Description of service. | When placed on the pension roll. | Commencement of pension. | Ages. | Laws under which they were formerly inscribed on the pension roll; and remarks. |
|---|---|---|---|---|---|---|---|---|
| Henry Gunter - | Private | 96 00 | 609 28 | S. C. cont'l line | Dec. 13, 1821 | Oct. 31, 1820 | 83 | |
| William Hardee - | Do | 96 00 | 611 84 | N. C. do | Oct. 3, 1822 | April 4, 1821 | 71 | Died August 18, 1827. |
| Moses Milligan - | Do | 96 00 | 787 73 | S. C. do | Dec. 13, 1821 | Do | 73 | Died June 17, 1829. |
| Thomas Wallace - | Do | 96 00 | 808 26 | N. C. do | May 18, 1822 | Do | 80 | |
| | | | 2,817 11 | | | | | |

*A statement showing the names, rank, &c., of persons residing in the district of Kershaw, in the State of South Carolina, who have been inscribed on the pension list under the act of Congress passed March 18, 1818.*

| NAMES. | Rank. | Annual allowance. | Sums received. | Description of service. | When placed on the pension roll. | Commencement of pension. | Ages. | Laws under which they were formerly inscribed on the pension roll; and remarks. |
|---|---|---|---|---|---|---|---|---|
| John Artiss - | Private | 96 00 | 82 09 | S. C. cont'l line | Dec. 3, 1819 | April 27, 1819 | 79 | Dropped under act May 1, 1320. |
| Do | Do | 96 00 | 1,296 00 | Do | | Nov. 16, 18:9 | 91 | |
| Richard Britt - | Do | 96 00 | 1,085 03 | Do | Dec. 4, 1819 | June 20, 1818 | 78 | |
| Lewis Cook - | Do | 96 00 | 1,507 86 | Virginia do | March 5, 1819 | June 17, 1818 | 78 | |
| John Cook - | Do | 96 00 | 548 76 | S. C. do | Do | June 20, 1818 | - | Do |
| Johnson Elkins - | Sergeant | 96 00 | 163 96 | Do | July 27, 1819 | | | do. |

| NAMES. | Rank. | Annual allowance. | Sums received. | Description of service. | When placed on the pension roll. | Commencement of pension. | Ages. | Laws under which they were formerly inscribed on the pension roll; and remarks. |
|---|---|---|---|---|---|---|---|---|
| Abraham Kelly - - | Private | 96 00 | 875 58 | Do | Nov. 10, 1819 | Aug. 20, 1819 | 87 | Dropped under act May 1, 1820. Restored, commencing Nov. 21, 1823. Died June 18, 1832. |
| Oliver McHaffey - | Do | 96 00 | 755 49 | Do | May 11, 1826 | April 18, 1826 | 72 | Do |
| | | | 6,314 77 | | | | | |

*A statement showing the names, rank, &c., of persons residing in the district of Lancaster, in the State of South Carolina, who have been inscribed on the pension list under the act of Congress passed March 18, 1818.*

| NAMES. | Rank. | Annual allowance. | Sums received. | Description of service. | When placed on the pension roll. | Commencement of pension. | Ages. | Laws under which they were formerly inscribed on the pension roll; and remarks. |
|---|---|---|---|---|---|---|---|---|
| Joseph Haile - - | Private | 96 00 | 109 93 | N. C. cont'l line | Jun. 14, 1831 | Jan. 13, 1831 | 77 | Died July 13, 1832. |
| | | | 109 93 | | | | | |

*A statement showing the names, rank, &c., of persons residing in the district of Lexington, in the State of South Carolina, who have been inscribed on the pension list under the act of Congress passed March 18, 1818.*

| NAMES. | Rank. | Annual allowance. | Sums received. | Description of service. | When placed on the pension roll. | Commencement of pension. | Ages. | Laws under which they were formerly inscribed on the pension roll; and remarks. |
|---|---|---|---|---|---|---|---|---|
| John Reizer - - | Private | 96 00 | 593 03 | N. C. cont'l line | July 14, 1830. | Jan. 1, 1828 | 83 | Special act, passed May 20, 1830. |
| | | | 593 03 | | | | | |

A statement showing the names, rank, &c., of persons residing in the district of Laurens, in the State of South Carolina, who have been inscribed on the pension list under the act of Congress passed the 18th March, 1818.

| NAMES. | Rank. | Annual allowance. | Sums received. | Description of service. | When placed on the pension roll. | Commencement of pension. | Ages. | Laws under which they were formerly inscribed on the pension roll; and remarks. |
|---|---|---|---|---|---|---|---|---|
| John Alverson* | Private | 40 00 | 480 00 | Virginia cont'l line | - - | Sept. 4, 1802 | 70 | Transferred from North Carolina from September 4, 1814. |
| Do | Do | 40 00 | 65 63 | Do | - - | Do | 70 | |
| Do | Do | 64 00 | 278 26 | Do | - - | April 24, 1816 | 70 | Act April 24, 1816. Increased to $64 per annum per act April 24, 1816. |
| Do | Do | 96 00 | 814 00 | Do | April 7, 1820 | Sept. 4, 1820 | 70 | Act March 18, 1818. Relinquished his invalid pension for the benefit of the act of March 18, 1818. Died February 25, 1829. |
| John Butler | Do | 96 00 | 96 00 | Do | Jan. 19, 1819 | Sept. 25, 1818 | 58 | Dropped under act May 1, 1820. |
| Richard Butler | Do | 96 00 | 236 72 | Do | April 21, 1830 | April 21, 1830 | 82 | Died October 8, 1832. |
| William Canady | Do | 96 00 | 1,465 83 | Maryland do | May 9, 1820 | Nov. 28, 1818 | 83 | |
| Thomas Gains | Do | 96 00 | 762 86 | Virginia do | March 28, 1820 | Do | 80 | Dropped under act May 1, 1820. Restored, commencing July 4, 1827. |
| James Howerton | Do | 96 00 | 204 93 | S. C. Do | April 24, 1820 | June 21, 1819 | 67 | Died August 9, 1821. |
| James Saxon | Do | 96 00 | 1,429 83 | do | Feb. 16, 1830 | April 13, 1819 | 80 | |
| Flanders Thompson | Do | 96 00 | 848 50 | Virginia do | June 19, 1820 | March 30, 1819 | 73 | Dropped under act May 1, 1820. Restored, commencing March 1, 1823. Died January 27, 1831. |
| Thomas Turner | Do | 96 00 | 484 26 | Do | Sept. 5, 1820 | June 15, 1818 | 66 | Died September 19, 1823. |
| Thomas Word | Do | 96 00 | 382 70 | Do | March 10, 1830 | March 10, 1830 | 78 | |
| | | | 7,549 57 | | | | | |

*A statement showing the names, rank, &c., of persons residing in the district of Marion, in the State of South Carolina, who have been inscribed on the pension list under the act of Congress passed the 18th March, 1818.*

| NAMES. | Rank. | Annual allowance. | Sums received. | Description of service. | When placed on the pension roll. | Commencement of pension. | Ages. | Laws under which they were formerly inscribed on the pension roll; and remarks. |
|---|---|---|---|---|---|---|---|---|
| James Gassaway | Private | 96 00 | 588 37 | Virginia cont'l line | May 17, 1819 | March 16, 1819 | 74 | Dropped under act May 1, 1820. Restored, commencing January 8, 1829. |
| William Rozier | Do | 96 00 | 282 06 | S. C. do | July 14, 1819 | Oct. 27, 1818 | 72 | Died October 3, 1821. |
|  |  |  | 870 43 |  |  |  |  |  |

*A statement showing the names, rank, &c., of persons residing in the district of Newberry, in the State of South Carolina, who have been inscribed on the pension list under the act of Congress passed the 18th March, 1818.*

| NAMES. | Rank. | Annual allowance. | Sums received. | Description of service. | When placed on the pension roll. | Commencement of pension. | Ages. | Laws under which they were formerly inscribed on the pension roll; and remarks. |
|---|---|---|---|---|---|---|---|---|
| Charles Charity | Private | 96 00 | 641 80 | Virginia cont'l line | Aug. 9, 1827 | July 2, 1827 | 77 |  |
| John Ellis | Do | 96 00 | 379 86 | N. C. do | May 29, 1826 | March 21, 1826 | 76 | Died. Reported June, 1830. |
| John Inlow | Do | 96 00 | 1,063 76 | S. C. do | Jan. 30, 1819 | Aug. 6, 1818 | - |  |
| William Plantt, sen. | Do | 96 00 | 22 96 | Virginia do | May 25, 1820 | Dec. 9, 1819 | 62 | Dropped under act May 1, 1820. |
| John Smith, 2d | Do | 96 00 | 66 89 | S. C. do | April 27, 1820 | June 24, 1819 | 73 | Do do. |
| James Motes | Do | 96 00 | 982 70 | Do | March 28, 1820 | Dec. 14, 1819 | 82 | Do do. Restored, commencing September 1, 1823. |
|  |  |  | 3,157 97 |  |  |  |  |  |

*A statement showing the names, rank, &c. of persons residing in the district of Pickens, in the State of South Carolina, who have been inscribed on the pension list under the act of Congress passed the 19th March, 1818.*

| NAMES. | Rank. | Annual allowance. | Sums received. | Description of service. | When placed on the pension roll. | Commencement of pension. | Ages. | Laws under which they were formerly inscribed on the pension roll; and remarks. |
|---|---|---|---|---|---|---|---|---|
| Robert Farr | Private | 96 00 | 588 90 | Penn. cont'l line | Jan. 17, 1828 | Jan. 17, 1828 | 82 | |
| Stephen Fuller | Sergeant | 96 00 | 545 06 | Georgia do | Aug. 27, 1830 | Jan. 1, 1828 | 81 | Special act, passed May 20, 1830. |
| Levi Philips | Private | 96 00 | 768 76 | Virginia do | Nov. 26, 1819 | May 15, 1818 | 84 | |
| Edmund Singleton | Do | 96 00 | 1,378 06 | Do | June 2, 1820 | Oct. 18, 1819 | 80 | |
| John Wilson | Do | 96 00 | 1,282 83 | Do | Nov. 19, 1821 | Oct. 25, 1820 | 79 | |
| | | | 4,563 61 | | | | | |

*A statement showing the names, rank, &c. of persons residing in the district of Pendleton, in the State of South Carolina, who have been inscribed on the pension list under the act of Congress passed the 18th March, 1818.*

| NAMES. | Rank. | Annual allowance. | Sums received. | Description of service. | When placed on the pension roll. | Commencement of pension. | Ages. | Laws under which they were formerly inscribed on the pension roll; and remarks. |
|---|---|---|---|---|---|---|---|---|
| Robert Clannahan | Private | 96 00 | 1,115 61 | Maryland cont'l line | March 5, 1819 | May 17, 1818 | 74 | Died December 2, 1829. |
| Thomas Cooper | Do | 96 00 | 32 05 | Virginia do | Nov. 25, 1819 | Oct 28, 1819 | | Dropped under act May 1, 1830. |
| Pendleton Isbell | Do | 96 00 | 172 12 | Do | April 6, 1820 | May 20, 1818 | | Do do. |
| Robert Miller | Do | 96 00 | 274 35 | Do | July 16, 1821 | Oct. 27, 1818 | 77 | |
| John Powell | Do | 96 00 | 537 31 | Do | May 7, 1821 | Jan. 31, 1820 | 85 | |
| Peter Rowland | Do | 96 00 | 332 15 | S. C. do | April 6, 1820 | March 20, 1819 | 80 | |
| John Swords | Do | 96 00 | 87 43 | Do | June 2, 1820 | April 7, 1819 | | Do do. |
| John Winn | Do | 96 00 | 886 18 | Virginia do | Oct. 16, 1822 | May 16, 1818 | 84 | Died August 8, 1827 |
| | | | 3,437 21 | | | | | |

*A statement showing the names, rank, &c. of persons residing in the district of Richland, in the State of South Carolina, who have been inscribed on the pension list under the act of Congress passed the 18th March, 1818.*

| Names. | Rank. | Annual allowance. | Sums received. | Description of service. | When placed on the pension roll. | Commencement of pension | Ages. | Laws under which they were formerly inscribed on the pension roll; and remarks. |
|---|---|---|---|---|---|---|---|---|
| James Brown - | Private | 96 00 | 1,465 03 | S. C. cont'l line | March 5, 1819 | Dec. 1, 1818 | 77 | |
| John Barry, or Berry | Do | 96 00 | 81 83 | Georgia do | June 17, 1820 | April 28, 1819 | 81 | Transferred from Georgia from March 4, 1820. |
| Do | Do | | 816 00 | Do | Do | Do | 91 | |
| Thomas Cole - | Do | 96 00 | 1,182 22 | N. C. do | Oct. 5, 1819 | May 12, 1819 | – | |
| Deason Enlow - | Do | 96 00 | 162 89 | S. C. do | March 5, 1819 | June 24, 1818 | 66 | |
| Philip Martin Frey | Drummer | 96 00 | 115 61 | Do | Do | Dec. 22, 1818 | 79 | Dropped under act May 1, 1820. |
| Meshac Fuller | Private | 96 00 | 1,034 57 | Georgia do | Feb. 17, 1821 | May 26, 1818 | 80 | Do do. |
| James Strange | Matross | 96 00 | 1,522 36 | S. C. artillery | Oct. 14, 1818 | April 26, 1818 | 61 | |
| Edward Sims | Private | 96 00 | 125 56 | Virginia cont'l line | Sept. 7, 1820 | Nov. 14, 1818 | – | |
| Stephen Truhitt | Do | 96 00 | 130 35 | N. C. do | Nov. 29, 1819 | Oct. 26, 1818 | 71 | Do do. |
| William Taylor | Sergeant | 96 00 | 666 57 | S C. do | May 18, 1822 | March 26, 1821 | 71 | Do do. |
| William Ware | Private | 96 00 | 954 32 | Virginia do | May 12, 1823 | March 27, 1823 | 74 | Died June 10, 1828. |

*A statement showing the names, rank, &c. of persons residing in the district of Spartanburgh, in the State of South Carolina, who have been inscribed on the pension list under the act of Congress passed the 18th March, 1818.*

| NAMES. | Rank. | Annual allowance. | Sums received. | Description of service. | When placed on the pension roll. | Commencement of pension. | Ages. | Laws under which they were formerly inscribed on the pension roll; and remarks. |
|---|---|---|---|---|---|---|---|---|
| Robert Belcher - | Private | 96 00 | 1,279 69 | Virginia cont'l line | Dec. 28, 1821 | Nov. 6, 1820 | | Dropped under act May 1, 1820. Restored, commencing December 4, 1828. |
| Henry Cole - | Do | 96 00 | 508 74 | N.C. do | June 4, 1819 | Feb. 15, 1819 | 81 | |
| Martin Cole - | Do | 96 00 | 1,349 03 | Do | Do | Do | 76 | Died March 20, 1833. |
| Ellis Cannon - | Do | 96 00 | 251 89 | Virginia do | Feb. 18, 1830 | Jan. 21, 1830 | 86 | Died June 12, 1830. |
| James Flemming - | Do | 96 00 | 759 16 | N.C. do | Feb. 3, 1823 | April 8, 1822 | 76 | Died March 4, 1832. |
| James Fisher - | Do | 96 00 | 425 11 | Maryland do | Oct. 15, 1827 | Sept. 28, 1827 | 81 | Died April 13, 1828. |
| John Gunter - | Do | 96 00 | 303 74 | Virginia do | Feb. 25, 1825 | Feb. 7, 1825 | 87 | |
| Joshua Hawkins* - | Do | 36 00 | 185 07 | Do | - | March 4, 1811 | 80 | Act March 3, 1809. } Increased to $57 60 per annum, per act April 24, 1816. |
| Do - | Do | 57 60 | 251 33 | Do | - | April 24, 1816 | 80 | Act April 24, 1816 } |
| Do - | Do | 96 00 | 1,299 09 | Do | Feb. 9, 1819 | Aug. 24, 1818 | 80 | Relinquished his invalid pension for the benefit of the act of March 18, 1818. |
| James Halks - | Do | 96 00 | - | S. C. do | Sept. 23, 1819 | Dec. 28, 1818 | - | Dropped under act May 1, 1818. |
| Clairbourn Holt - | Do | 96 00 | 563 43 | Virginia do | May 17, 1828 | April 22, 1828 | 83 | |
| Robert Kimble - | Do | 96 00 | 854 36 | Do | Sept. 30, 1822 | April 11, 1822 | 77 | |
| John Low - | Lieutenant | 240 00 | 1,722 66 | N. C. | June 21, 1820 | April 5, 1819 | 80 | Died June 8, 1826. |
| James Lett - | Private | 96 00 | 1,143 16 | Do | Feb. 12, 1823 | April 8, 1822 | 85 | |
| Martin Martin - | Do | 96 00 | 1,441 03 | S. C. do | June 9, 1820 | March 1, 1819 | 78 | |
| Archibald McCrery - | Do | 96 00 | 534 19 | N. C. do | Aug. 27, 1828 | Aug. 12, 1828 | 89 | |
| John Peace - | Serg't maj. | 96 00 | 566 36 | Maryland do | Jan. 5, 1821 | April 11, 1820 | 79 | |
| Thomas Pope - | Private | 96 00 | 415 43 | Virginia do | April 10, 1822 | Nov. 7, 1820 | 66 | Dead. Reported June 30, 1825. |
| William West - | Do | 96 00 | 1,339 87 | S. C. do | April 13, 1821 | March 17, 1820 | 71 | |
| George Walker - | Do | 96 00 | 842 83 | Virginia do | June 17, 1825 | May 25, 1825 | 73 | |

*A statement showing the names, rank, &c., of persons residing in the district of Sumpter, in the State of South Carolina, who have been inscribed on the pension list under the act of Congress passed the 18th March, 1818.*

| NAMES. | Rank. | Annual allowance. | Sums received. | Description of service. | When placed on the pension roll. | Commencement of pension. | Ages. | Laws under which they were formerly inscribed on the pension roll; and remarks. |
|---|---|---|---|---|---|---|---|---|
| William Brown | Private | 96 00 | 1,510 09 | S. C. cont'l line | May 17, 1819 | June 12, 1818 | 83 | |
| Peter David | Do | 96 00 | 1,445 88 | Do | Do | Feb. 12, 1819 | 80 | |
| Samuel Francis | Do | 96 00 | 821 63 | Do | Nov. 20, 1819 | Feb. 13, 1819 | 99 | |
| Adam Gibhart | Do | 96 00 | 1,301 63 | Maryland do | Do | Do | 81 | |
| Thomas Garrett | Do | 96 00 | 804 38 | S. C. do | Dec. 13, 1825 | Oct. 19, 1825 | 83 | |
| David Garrett | Do | 96 00 | 321 32 | Do | April 30, 1830 | April 30, 1830 | 78 | |
| Thomas Kolb | Sergeant | 96 00 | - | Do | May 17, 1819 | Feb. 13, 1819 | - | Dropped under act May 1, 1820. |
| George St. George | Private | 96 00 | 166 09 | Conn. do | Do | June 12, 1818 | 82 | Do do |
| James Scott | Do | 96 00 | 790 12 | S. C. do | Do | Do | 81 | |
| John Thompson | Do | 96 00 | 419 35 | Do | Nov. 10, 1819 | Oct. 22, 1819 | 79 | |

*A statement showing the names, rank, &c., of persons residing in the district of Union, in the State of South Carolina, who have been inscribed on the pension list under the act of Congress passed the 18th March, 1818.*

| NAMES. | Rank. | Annual allowance. | Sums received. | Description of service. | When placed on the pension roll. | Commencement of pension. | Ages. | Laws under which they were formerly inscribed on the pension roll; and remarks. |
|---|---|---|---|---|---|---|---|---|
| John Bird | Lieut. | 240 00 | 3,758 70 | S. C. cont'l line | Jan. 8, 1819 | July 7, 1818 | 77 | |
| John Crawford | Private | 96 00 | 584 57 | Do | Sept. 23, 1819 | Feb. 3, 1819 | 82 | |

## Statement of the district of Union—Continued.

| NAMES. | Rank. | Annual allowance. | Sums received. | Description of service. | When placed on the pension roll. | Commencement of pension | Ages. | Laws under which they were formerly inscribed on the pension roll; and remarks. |
|---|---|---|---|---|---|---|---|---|
| Charles Dick - - | Private | 96 00 | 283 39 | S. C. cont'l line | March 5, 1819 | Oct. 15, 1818 | 88 | Dropped under act May 1, 1820. Restored, commencing October 15, 1825. Died June 7, 1827. |
| Perry Evans - - | Do | 96 00 | 152 21 | Maryland do | July 20, 1819 | Aug. 3, 1818 | 60 | Dropped under act May 1, 1820. |
| Joshua Foster - | Do | 96 00 | 148 64 | Virginia do | April 6, 1820 | Aug. 18, 1818 | 67 | Do |
| Thomas Owens - | Do | 96 00 | - | Penn. do | March 5, 1819 | Sept. 16, 1818 | - | Do |
| Nicholas Rochester - | Do | 96 00 | 148 64 | N. C. do | Do | Aug. 18, 1818 | 68 | Do |
| William Townsend - | Do | 96 00 | 92 90 | Virginia do | May 17, 1819 | March 16, 1819 | - | Do |

*A statement showing the names, rank, &c., of persons residing in the district of Williamsburgh, in the State of South Carolina, who have been inscribed on the pension list under the act of Congress passed March 18, 1818.*

| NAMES. | Rank. | Annual allowance. | Sums received. | Description of service. | When placed on the pension roll. | Commencement of pension. | Ages. | Laws under which they were formerly inscribed on the pension roll; and remarks. |
|---|---|---|---|---|---|---|---|---|
| Ludford Berry - | Private | 96 00 | 372 15 | Virginia cont'l line | March 5, 1819 | Oct. 20, 1818 | 79 | Dropped under act May 1, 1820. |
| Samuel Bratcher - | Do | 96 00 | - | N. C. do | Do | Do | 85 | Do |
| Grant Knowlton - | Do | 96 00 | 131 61 | S. C. do | Do | Oct. 22, 1818 | 66 | Do |
| Aaron Odam - | Do | 96 00 | 131 61 | N. C. do | Do | Oct. 20, 1818 | - | Do |
| Needham Perrit - | Do | 96 00 | 83 89 | Do | Do | Do | 72 | Do |
| William Smith - | Do | 96 00 | 110 18 | S. C. do | Sept. 22, 1819 | Do | - | Died December 12, 1819. |

A statement showing the names, rank, &c., of persons residing in the district of York, in the State of South Carolina, who have been inscribed on the pension list under the act of Congress passed March 18, 1818.

| NAMES. | | Rank. | Annual allow-ance. | Sums re-ceived. | Description of ser-vice. | When placed on the pen-sion roll. | Commencement of pension. | Ages. | Laws under which they were for-merly inscribed on the pension roll; and remarks. |
|---|---|---|---|---|---|---|---|---|---|
| Jesse Boswell | - | Private | 96 00 | 967 42 | Md. cont'l line | March 18, 1819 | Oct. 27, 1818 | 73 | Died November 23, 1828. |
| Peter Cherry | - | Sergeant | 96 00 | 1,098 51 | Penn, do | Jan. 31, 1820 | March 23, 1819 | 81 | Dropped under act May 1, 1820. Restored, com'g Sept. 8, 1823. |
| Daniel Gilmore | - | Private | 96 00 | 1,474 32 | Virginia do | March 5, 1819 | Oct. 27, 1818 | 79 | |
| Richard M. Head | - | Cornet | 240 00 | 2,174 33 | A'mand's legion | April 24, 1818 | April 24, 1818 | 82 | Died May 15, 1827. |
| Robert Marsh | o | Private | 96 00 | 1,430 07 | Virginia cont'l line | March 5, 1819 | April 17, 1818 | 76 | |

A statement showing the names, rank, &c., of persons residing in the State of South Carolina,* who have been inscribed on the pension list under the act of Congress passed March 18, 1818.

| NAMES. | | Rank. | Annual allow-ance. | Sums re-ceived. | Description of ser-vice. | When placed on the pen-sion roll. | Commencement of pension. | Ages. | Laws under which they were for-merly inscribed on the pension roll; and remarks. |
|---|---|---|---|---|---|---|---|---|---|
| Isaac Smith | - | Sergeant | 96 00 | - | Virginia cont'l line | March 10, 1820 | Feb. 8, 1820 | - | Dropped under act May 1, 1820. |

* District unknown.

A statement showing the names, rank, &c., of persons residing in the district of Anderson, in the State of South Carolina, who have been inscribed on the pension list under the act of Congress passed June 7, 1832.

| NAMES. | Rank. | Annual allowance. | Sums received. | Description of service. | When placed on the pension roll. | Commencement of pension. | Ages. | Laws under which they were formerly inscribed on the pension roll; and remarks. |
|---|---|---|---|---|---|---|---|---|
| Jelu Atkinson - | Private | 20 00 | 50 00 | Virginia line | July 19, 1833 | March 4, 1831 | 74 | |
| William Armstrong - | Do | 80 00 | 240 00 | do | April 30, 1834 | Do | 69 | |
| Reuben Broch - | Pri. of cav. | 25 00 | 75 00 | S. C. militia | Feb. 14, 1833 | Do | 80 | |
| William Brewster - | Private | 33 33 | 99 99 | Do | Do | Do | 77 | |
| Thomas Banister - | Do | 30 00 | 90 00 | Do | May 16, 1833 | Do | 71 | |
| Charles Bennett | Pri. & ser. | 30 00 | 90 00 | N. C. do | Aug. 17, 1833 | Do | 71 | |
| Benjam'n Bowen | Private | 46 66 | 139 98 | N. C. troops | Dec. 7, 1833 | Do | 78 | |
| James Brown - | Do | 75 10 | 225 30 | S. C. do | April 19, 1834 | Do | 75 | |
| Joshua Betterton - | Do | 50 00 | 150 00 | Do | | Do | - | |
| John Bagwell - | Do | 26 66 | - | N. C. line | May 14, 1834 | Do | 72 | |
| Abraham Campbell - | Do | 45 00 | - | S. C. do | May 16, 1833 | Do | 72 | |
| Harmen Comins - | Do | 96 00 | 138 86 | Virginia cont'l line | Nov. 26, 1819 | March 25, 1819 | - | Act March 18, 1818. Dropped under act May 1, 1820. |
| Do | Do | 80 00 | 240 00 | ‒ | Nov. 5, 1833 | March 4, 1831 | 75 | |
| William Dodd - | Do | 22 31 | 66 93 | S. C. troops | April 19, 1834 | Do | 70 | |
| David Galry - | Do | 20 00 | 60 00 | Virginia line | May 17, 1833 | Do | 70 | |
| Aaron Guyton - | Do | 31 66 | 94 98 | S. C. do | Oct. 24, 1833 | Do | 71 | |
| John Harris - | Do | 54 43 | 163 29 | Do | Dec. 9, 1833 | Do | 90 | |
| Andrew Hood - | Do | 20 00 | - | N. C. cont'l line | June 5, 1834 | Do | 80 | |
| John Looney - | Do | 80 00 | 240 00 | S. C. troops | April 8, 1834 | Do | | |
| William McIntosh | Do | 80 00 | 240 00 | Virginia cont'l line | Feb. 14, 1833 | Do | | |
| William Moore - | Do | 20 00 | 60 00 | S. C. line | May 16, 1833 | Do | 71 | |
| James Merret - | Pri. of inf. & cav'y. | 36 97 | 92 42 | | | Do | 79 | |
| William Milwee - | Pri. & cap. | 373 38 | 1,119 96 | N. C. do | Aug. 27, 1833 | Do | 80 | |
| John Milford - | Private | 40 00 | 120 00 | S. C. do | Oct. 21, 1833 | Do | 74 | |
| Peter McMahon - | Do | 80 00 | 200 00 | N. C. do | Nov. 21, 1833 | Do | 78 | |
| George Oldham - | Ensign & captain. | 120 00 | 360 00 | Do | Aug. 7, 1833 | Do | 84 | |

| Names | Rank | Annual allowance | Sums received | Description of service | When placed on the pension roll | Commencement of pension | Ages |
|---|---|---|---|---|---|---|---|
| Frederick Owen | Private | 80 00 | 240 00 | S. C. do | Oct. 21, 1833 | Do | 81 |
| David Pressley | Do | 48 33 | 144 99 | Do | May 29, 1833 | Do | 70 |
| Richard Reid | Do | 33 33 | 99 99 | Do | May 16, 1833 | Do | 71 |
| George Reese | Do | 27 54 | 68 85 | N. C. do | Aug. 27, 1833 | Do | 81 |
| John Scott | Do | 23 33 | 69 99 | S. C. do | May 17, 1833 | Do | 92 |
| David Sadler | Do | 76 66 | 229 98 | Do | April 8, 1834 | Do | 72 |
| John Wilson | Pri. of inf. & cav'y | 58 33 | 174 99 | N. C. do | May 17, 1833 | Do | 78 |
| William Williamson | Private | 21 55 | 64 65 | Virginia cont'l line | Aug. 7, 1833 | Do | 69 |
| John Wornoch | Do | 80 00 | - | S. C. do | June 16, 1834 | Do | 76 |

*A statement showing the names, rank, &c., of persons residing in the district of Abberville, in the State of South Carolina, who have been inscribed on the pension list under the act of Congress passed June 7, 1832.*

| NAMES. | Rank. | Annual allowance. | Sums received. | Description of service. | When placed on the pension roll. | Commencement of pension. | Ages. | Laws under which they were formerly inscribed on the pension roll; and remarks. |
|---|---|---|---|---|---|---|---|---|
| Thomas Anderson | Private | 20 00 | 60 00 | Virginia troops | Dec. 7, 1833 | March 4, 1831 | 72 | |
| John Black, 1st | Pri. of art. | 50 88 | 152 64 | S. Carolina militia | Feb. 16, 1833 | Do | 71 | |
| Pollard Brown | Private | 20 00 | 50 00 | Virginia line | June 28, 1833 | Do | 71 | |
| William Buckhanan | Do | 52 11 | 130 27 | S. C. do | Do | Do | 72 | |
| Joseph Black | Do | 55 33 | 165 99 | N. C. do | Jan. 9, 1834 | Do | 71 | |
| Zachariah Carvil | Do | 80 00 | 240 00 | Virginia cont'l line | Dec. 28, 1832 | Do | 84 | |
| James Conner | Do | 30 00 | 75 00 | N. C. do | Aug. 7, 1833 | Do | 72 | |
| James Frazier | Do | 43 33 | 107 32 | S. C. do | May 29, 1833 | Do | 67 | |
| John Finley | Do | 60 00 | 180 00 | Do | July 8, 1833 | Do | 74 | |
| Frederick Gray | Pri, lieut, & captain | 260 01 | 780 03 | S. Carolina troops | Dec. 7, 1833 | Do | 76 | |
| George Green | Private | 53 33 | 159 99 | S. Carolina line | April 19, 1834 | Do | 71 | |

*Statement of the district of Abberville, South Carolina—Continued.*

| NAMES. | Rank, | Annual allowance. | Sums received. | Description of service. | When placed on the pension roll. | Commencement of pension. | Ages. | Laws under which they were formerly inscribed on the pension roll; and remarks. |
|---|---|---|---|---|---|---|---|---|
| John Hodges - | Private | 70 00 | 210 00 | S. Carolina line | April 20, 1833 | March 4, 1831 | 79 | |
| Solomon Hall, sen. - | Do | 52 78 | 158 34 | N. C. cont'l line | Aug. 7, 1833 | Do | 77 | |
| Andrew Logan - | Do | 27 21 | 68 02 | S. Carolina line | April 20, 1833 | Do | 69 | |
| Henry Livingston - | Do | 24 66 | 73 98 | S. Carolina troops | Dec. 7, 1833 | Do | 73 | |
| Thomas Moore - | Pri. of inf. & cavalry | 55 00 | 165 00 | S. Carolina line | May 29, 1833 | Do | 70 | |
| Joseph Moseley, sen. - | Private | 20 00 | 50 00 | Virginia do | July 19, 1833 | Do | 70 | |
| John McAdam - | Do | 80 00 | 240 00 | S. Carolina do | Aug. 7, 1833 | Do | 75 | |
| George McFarlin - | Do | 26 66 | 79 98 | Do | Feb. 5, 1834 | Do | 70 | |
| Thomas Norwood - | Do | 30 00 | 75 00 | Do | May 29, 1833 | Do | 73 | |
| Samuel Pruett - | Do | 33 44 | 100 32 | N. Carolina do | July 8, 1833 | Do | 84 | |
| Samuel Porter - | Do | 23 33 | 69 99 | Do | Aug. 7, 1833 | Do | 71 | |
| Alex. Patterson, sen. - | Do | 71 88 | - | S. Carolina do | April 8, 1834 | Do | 83 | |
| William Reeve - | Do | 23 22 | 58 05 | Virginia militia | May 29, 1833 | Do | 78 | |
| Willis Scoggins - | Do | 41 10 | 123 30 | N. C. cont'l line | April 20, 1833 | Do | 73 | |
| Austin Smith - | Do | 28 88 | 86 64 | S. Carolina line | Aug. 7, 1833 | Do | 71 | |
| Newell Walton - | Do | 25 99 | 64 97 | Virginia do | July 20, 1833 | Do | 71 | |
| Simpson Warren - | Do | 20 00 | 60 00 | S. Carolina do | Feb. 5, 1834 | Do | 72 | |

*A statement showing the names, rank, &c., of persons residing in the district of Barnwell, in the State of South Carolina, who have been inscribed on the pension list under the act of Congress passed June 7, 1832.*

| NAMES. | Rank. | Annual allowance. | Sums received. | Description of service. | When placed on the pension roll. | Commencement of pension. | Ages. | Laws under which they were formerly inscribed on the pension roll; and remarks. |
|---|---|---|---|---|---|---|---|---|
| Tarlton Brown | Lt. & cap. of inf. | 356 00 | 1,068 00 | S. C. cont'l line | June 10, 1833 | March 4, 1831 | 77 | |

*A statement showing the names, rank, &c., of persons residing in the district of Chesterfield, in the State of South Carolina, who have been inscribed on the pension list under the act of Congress passed June 7, 1832.*

| NAMES. | Rank. | Annual allowance. | Sums received. | Description of service. | When placed on the pension roll. | Commencement of pension. | Ages. | Laws under which they were formerly inscribed on the pension roll; and remarks. |
|---|---|---|---|---|---|---|---|---|
| Abraham Blackwell - | Private | 80 00 | 240 00 | S. Carolina militia | Feb. 17, 1834 | March 4, 1831 | 81 | |
| James James - | Do | 80 00 | - | N. Carolina do | April 17, 1834 | Do | 86 | |
| James McMillan - | Pri. of cav. | 100 00 | - | S. C. cont'l line | May 8, 1834 | Do | 81 | |
| William Roberts - | Private | 20 00 | 60 00 | S. C. militia | Oct. 21, 1833 | Do | 72 | |

*A statement showing the names, rank, &c., of persons residing in the district of Colleton, in the State of South Carolina, who have been inscribed on the pension list under the act of Congress passed June 7, 1832.*

| NAMES. | Rank. | Annual allowance. | Sums received. | Description of service. | When placed on the pension roll. | Commencement of pension. | Ages. | Laws under which they were formerly inscribed on the pension roll; and remarks. |
|---|---|---|---|---|---|---|---|---|
| John Hiott, sen. | Musician | 38 00 | 264 00 | S. C. cont'l line | Dec. 30, 1833 | March 4, 1831 | 78 | |
| Albert Strobel | Private | 46 66 | 139 98 | S. Carolina militia | Dec. 18, 1833 | Do | 74 | |

*A statement showing the names, rank, &c., of persons residing in the district of Chester, in the State of South Carolina, who have been inscribed on the pension list under the act of Congress passed June 7, 1832.*

| NAMES. | Rank. | Annual allowance. | Sums received. | Description of service. | When placed on the pension roll. | Commencement of pension. | Ages. | Laws under which they were formerly inscribed on the pension roll; and remarks. |
|---|---|---|---|---|---|---|---|---|
| James Adair | Private | 26 66 | 79 98 | S. Carolina militia | April 20, 1833 | March 4, 1831 | 82 | |
| John Allen | Pri. & ens. | 40 00 | 120 00 | N. Carolina do | April 8, 1834 | Do | 82 | |
| James Anderson | Pri. & lt. | 190 00 | 570 00 | S. Carolina do | Do | Do | 76 | |
| William Bobbit | Pri. inf. and cav. | 34 99 | 104 97 | N. Carolina do | May 16, 1833 | Do | 73 | |
| William Boyd | Private | 23 33 | 69 99 | S. Carolina do | July 19, 1833 | Do | 68 | |
| John Bishop | Do | 56 66 | 169 98 | S. C. cont'l line | April 8, 1834 | Do | 69 | |
| Stephen Crain | Do | 40 00 | 100 00 | N. Carolina militia | Sept. 3, 1833 | Do | 74 | |
| John Conn | Do | 66 66 | 199 98 | N. C. cont'l line | March 8, 1834 | Do | 79 | |
| Moses Grisham | Do | 50 00 | 150 00 | S. Carolina militia | April 8, 1834 | Do | 72 | |
| George Gill | Pri. cav. and inf. | 80 00 | 240 00 | Do | May 29, 1833 | Do | 75 | |
| | | 90 35 | 271 05 | Do | June 28, 1833 | Do | 73 | |

| NAMES. | Rank. | Annual allowance. | Sums received. | Description of service. | When placed on the pension roll. | Commencement of pension. | Ages. | Laws under which they were formerly inscribed on the pension roll; and remarks. |
|---|---|---|---|---|---|---|---|---|
| James Graham - | Private | 55 88 | 167 64 | Do | Aug. 7, 1833 | Do | 73 | |
| Joseph Gaston - | Do | 39 66 | 118 98 | Do | April 4, 1834 | Do | 71 | |
| James Harbison - | Do | 52 78 | 188 34 | S. C. cont'l line | Aug. 31, 1833 | Do | 72 | |
| Benjamin Jackson - | Do | 52 92 | 105 84 | N. Carolina militia | May 16, 1833 | Do | 76 | |
| James Jamieson - | Pri., lt., & capt. | 383 31 | 1,149 93 | N. Carolina do | June 12, 1833 | Do | 71 | |
| Joseph Morrow - | Private | 39 00 | 117 00 | S. Carolina do | July 19, 1833 | Do | 74 | |
| Thomas McClurken - | Do | 55 00 | 137 50 | Do | Aug. 7, 1833 | Do | 78 | |
| John McDill - | Do | 29 00 | 72 50 | Do | Do | Do | 72 | |
| Daniel McMillan - | Do | 41 55 | 124 65 | Do | Oct. 18, 1833 | Do | 82 | |
| James McCaw - | Do | 80 00 | 240 00 | Do | April 8, 1834 | Do | 72 | |
| Micajah Proctor - | Do | 32 33 | 80 82 | Virginia do | May 16, 1833 | Do | 74 | |
| Edward Steedman - | Do | 80 00 | 240 00 | S. Carolina do | April 8, 1834 | Do | 74 | |
| William White - | Do | 80 00 | 216 39 | Do | Do | Do | 80 | |
| George Wier - | Do | 60 00 | 180 00 | Do | Do | Do | 82 | Died November 18, 1833. |

*A statement showing the names, rank, &c., of persons residing in the district of Charleston, in the State of South Carolina, who have been inscribed on the pension list under the act of Congress passed June 7, 1832.*

| NAMES. | Rank. | Annual allowance. | Sums received. | Description of service. | When placed on the pension roll. | Commencement of pension. | Ages. | Laws under which they were formerly inscribed on the pension roll; and remarks. |
|---|---|---|---|---|---|---|---|---|
| Jeremiah Bunch | Private | 53 33 | 159 99 | S. Carolina militia | March 22, 1834 | March 4, 1831 | 72 | |
| Thomas Burbage | Do | 80 00 | 240 00 | Do cont'l | April 4, 1834 | Do | 74 | |
| David N. Cardozo | Sergeant | 60 00 | 180 00 | Do militia | Aug. 3, 1833 | Do | 80 | |
| John Cart | Pri. inf. & cav. | 29 66 | 88 98 | do | Oct. 16, 1833 | Do | 73 | |
| William Hasell Gibbes | Lt. art. | 400 00 | 1,176 52 | do | Dec. 26, 1832 | Do | 80 | |
| John Girardeau | Private | 80 00 | 240 00 | Georgia do | March 25, 1834 | Do | 78 | Died February 13, 1834. |
| Marks Lazarus | Pri. & ser. | 28 33 | 84 99 | S. Carolina do | Oct. 16, 1833 | Do | 77 | |
| Solomon Legare | Private | 68 00 | 204 00 | Do cont'l | Do | Do | 80 | |
| Job Palmer | Do | 22 33 | 66 99 | Do militia | Do | Do | 87 | |
| Do | Do | 50 00 | 150 00 | do | Do | Do | 73 | |

Statement of the district of Charleston, South Carolina—Continued.

| NAMES. | Rank. | Annual allowance. | Sums received. | Description of service. | When placed on the pension roll. | Commencement of pension. | Ages. | Laws under which they were formerly inscribed on the pension roll; and remarks. |
|---|---|---|---|---|---|---|---|---|
| Samuel Rivers | Private | 80 00 | 240 00 | S. Carolina militia | Jan. 6, 1834 | March 4, 1831 | 83 | |
| Joseph Righton | Sergeant | 120 00 | 360 00 | Do | June 20, 1834 | Do | | |
| Daniel Stevens | Ser. & lt. art. | 376 66 | 1,129 98 | Do | March 31, 1834 | Do | 88 | |
| Jacob Sass | Lieut. | 198 25 | 594 75 | N. Carolina do | Oct 16, 1833 | Do | 84 | |
| James Wallace | Private | 80 00 | 240 00 | Virginia do | June 28, 1833 | Do | 82 | |
| Richard Wall | Midship'n | 144 00 | 432 00 | Frigate Rd. P. Jones | Oct. 26, 1833 | Do | 80 | |

A statement showing the names, rank, &c., of persons residing in the district of Darlington, in the State of South Carolina, who have been inscribed on the pension list under the act of Congress passed June 7, 1832.

| NAMES. | Rank. | Annual allowance. | Sums received. | Description of service. | When placed on the pension roll. | Commencement of pension | Ages. | Laws under which they were formerly inscribed on the pension roll; and remarks. |
|---|---|---|---|---|---|---|---|---|
| Thomas Goodson | Private | 80 00 | 240 00 | S. C. cont'l line | March 22, 1833 | March 4, 1831 | 72 | |
| Ephraim Gaudy | Do | 60 00 | — | S. Carolina militia | March 6, 1834 | Do | 82 | |
| Jesse Hicks | Do | 20 00 | — | N. Carolina do | April 19, 1834 | Do | 72 | |
| Jehu Kolb | Do | 47 88 | — | S. Carolina do | March 14, 1833 | Do | 76 | |
| Nicholas Powers | Pri. & ser. | 103 04 | 309 12 | S. C. cont'l line | Feb. 5, 1834 | Do | 78 | |
| John Stewart | Private | 46 66 | — | S. Carolina militia | May 15, 1834 | Do | 72 | |
| Zachariah Winn | Do | 40 00 | — | N. C. cont'l line | March 31, 1834 | Do | 73 | |
| Henry Wilson | Do | 20 00 | 60 00 | S. Carolina militia | April 10, 1834 | Do | 73 | |
| Albert Fort | Do | 26 66 | — | Do | April 28, 1834 | Do | 76 | |

*A statement showing the names, rank, &c., of persons residing in the district of Edgefield, in the State of South Carolina, who have been inscribed on the pension list under the act of Congress passed June 7, 1832.*

| NAMES. | Rank. | Annual allowance. | Sums received. | Description of service. | When placed on the pension roll. | Commencement of pension. | Ages. | Laws under which they were formerly inscribed on the pension roll; and remarks. |
|---|---|---|---|---|---|---|---|---|
| Zachariah S. Brooks - | Private | 40 00 | 120 00 | S. Carolina militia | Feb. 14, 1833 | March 4, 1831 | 69 | |
| William Cooke - | Pri. cav. | 100 00 | 300 00 | Virginia cont'l line | July 8, 1833 | Do | 80 | |
| Richard Christmas - | Private | 20 00 | - | N. Carolina militia | Dec. 14, 1833 | Do | 70 | |
| Abner Corley - | Pri. inf. & cav. | 55 00 | 165 00 | S. Carolina do | Do | Do | 76 | |
| Robert Cochran - | Pri. & lt. | 93 33 | 279 99 | Do | March 8, 1834 | Do | 79 | |
| William Flinn - | Private | 47 00 | 141 00 | Virginia do | Jan. 6, 1834 | Do | 74 | |
| Drury Hearn - | Do | 80 00 | 240 00 | N. C. cont'l line | Jan. 24, 1833 | Do | 79 | |
| William Howl, sen. - | Do | 80 00 | 240 00 | Georgia militia | July 8, 1833 | Do | 80 | |
| Samuel Hammond - | Maj. & col. | 600 00 | 1,800 00 | Virginia do | July 11, 1833 | Do | 77 | |
| Peter Hilyard - | Private | 50 44 | 151 32 | S. C. do | Jan. 20, 1834 | Do | 78 | |
| Samuel Price - | Do | 80 00 | 200 00 | S. C. cont'l line | July 8, 1833 | Do | 82 | |
| Daniel Rogers - | Do | 73 33 | 219 99 | S. Carolina militia | March 8, 1834 | Do | 73 | |
| William S. Stubblefield - | Pri. & ser. | 67 66 | 169 15 | Virginia do | Sept. 20, 1833 | Do | 70 | |
| William Wash - | Sergeant | 120 00 | 360 00 | Geo. & Va. do | Jan. 24, 1833 | Do | 81 | |

*A statement showing the names, rank, &c., of persons residing in Fairfield district, in the State of South Carolina, who have been inscribed on the pension list under the act of Congress passed June 7, 1832.*

| NAMES. | Rank. | Annual allowance. | Sums received. | Description of service. | When placed on the pension roll. | Commencement of pension. | Ages. | Laws under which they were formerly inscribed on the pension roll; and remarks. |
|---|---|---|---|---|---|---|---|---|
| William Aiken - | Private | 20 00 | 40 00 | S. Carolina militia | May 21, 1833 | March 4, 1833 | 74 | |
| John Broom - | Do | 27 77 | 83 31 | Do | Sept. 18, 1833 | Do | 71 | |

Statement of the district of Fairfield, South Carolina—Continued.

| NAMES. | Rank. | Annual allowance. | Sums received. | Description of service. | When placed on the pension roll. | Commencement of pension. | Ages. | Laws under which they were formerly inscribed on the pension roll; and remarks. |
|---|---|---|---|---|---|---|---|---|
| Cannon Cason - | Private | 40 00 | 120 00 | S. Carolina militia | May 21, 1833 | March 4, 1833 | 80 | |
| Charnel Durham | Pri. & cap. | 263 33 | 789 99 | Do do | May 21, 1833 | Do | 81 | |
| William Hogan | Private | 35 33 | - | Do do | Do | Do | 74 | |
| David Hamilton | Pri. & q. m. | 144 16 | 432 48 | Do do | July 20, 1833 | Do | 75 | |
| John Hollis - | Private | 110 00 | 330 00 | Do do | Sept. 20, 1833 | Do | 77 | |
| Robert Kilpatrick | Pri. & Lt. | 102 50 | 307 50 | Do do | April 8, 1834 | Do | 95 | |
| John Lee - | Private | 80 00 | 200 00 | Do cont'l | April 18, 1833 | Do | 75 | |
| Robert McCreight | Pri. & Lt. | 151 88 | 455 64 | Do militia | July 20, 1833 | Do | 73 | |
| James Nelson, sen. | Private | 29 66 | 88 98 | Do do | Nov. 29, 1833 | Do | 86 | |
| William Robertson | Do | 30 00 | 75 00 | Do do | July 20, 1833 | Do | 74 | |
| John Sullivan - | Pri. & scr. | 94 83 | 284 49 | Do do | Sept, 17, 1833 | Do | 74 | |
| John Sloan - | Private | 80 00 | 240 00 | Do do | April 8, 1834 | Do | 73 | |
| Jacob Stone - | Do | 33 33 | 99 99 | Do do | April 17, 1834 | Do | 76 | |
| Meredith Taylor | Do | 46 66 | 116 65 | Do do | May 21, 1833 | Do | 70 | |
| Jeremiah Taylor | Do | 43 33 | 108 32 | Do do | Do | Do | 72 | |
| Dixsey Ward - | Do | 80 00 | 240 00 | Do do | July 20, 1833 | Do | 74 | |
| Bolling Wright | Do | 36 66 | - | Virginia do | May 31, 1834 | Do | 75 | |

38

## A statement showing the names, rank, &c., of persons residing in Greenville district, in the State of South Carolina, who have been inscribed on the pension list under the act of Congress passed June 7, 1832.

| NAMES. | Rank. | Annual allowance. | Sums received. | Description of service. | When placed on the pension roll. | Commencement of pension. | Ages. | Laws under which they were formerly inscribed on the pension roll; and remarks. |
|---|---|---|---|---|---|---|---|---|
| James Altorn | Private | 40 00 | 84 53 | N. Carolina militia | April 18, 1833 | March 4, 1831 | 81 | Died April 15, 1833. |
| David Burn | Do | 80 00 | 240 00 | Do | Dec. 3, 1832 | Do | 77 | |
| John Brookshire | Do | 55 00 | 165 00 | Do | April 17, 1834 | Do | 75 | |
| Joel Callahan | Do | 40 22 | 120 66 | S. Carolina do | June 28, 1833 | Do | 80 | |
| William Crane | Do | 20 00 | 60 00 | Do | Nov. 21, 1833 | Do | 68 | |
| Henry Cannon | Do | 33 33 | 99 99 | Virginia do | April 17, 1834 | Do | 83 | |
| Benjamin Dispair | Do | 26 66 | 79 98 | N. Carolina do | April 20, 1833 | Do | 77 | |
| Nathaniel Dacus | Do | 20 00 | 50 00 | S. Carolina do | May 17, 1833 | Do | 85 | |
| Jonathan Davis | Do | 32 44 | - | N. Carolina do | April 8, 1834 | Do | 75 | |
| David Dickey | Pri. & ser. | 37 50 | 112 50 | Do | April 20, 1834 | Do | 87 | |
| Philip Evans | Private | 50 00 | 150 00 | N. Carolina do | March 6, 1834 | Do | 75 | |
| Shadrach Farmer | Do | 33 33 | 99 99 | S. Carolina do | July 8, 1833 | Do | 79 | |
| John Farmer | Do | 40 00 | 120 00 | Do | Do | Do | 78 | |
| John Goodlett | Do | 24 88 | 74 64 | do | April 17, 1834 | Do | 78 | |
| Abraham Hester | Do | 22 88 | 68 64 | N. Carolina do | Nov. 21, 1833 | Do | 84 | |
| Stephen Huff | Do | 46 66 | 139 98 | S. Carolina do | Feb. 5, 1834 | Do | 78 | |
| Esle Hunt | Do | 38 66 | 115 98 | N. Carolina do | April 17, 1834 | Do | 76 | |
| Ezekiel Henderson | Do | 57 50 | 172 50 | Do | Do | Do | 71 | |
| Jacob Kytle | Pri. cor. & sergeant | 90 66 | 271 98 | Do cont'l | May 24, 1833 | Do | 74 | |
| Lewis Land | Private | 80 00 | 240 00 | Virginia do | April 18, 1833 | Do | 72 | |
| George Mitchell | Do | 36 66 | 109 98 | S. Carolina militia | Sept. 18, 1833 | Do | 82 | |
| Samuel Melson | Do | 80 00 | 240 00 | N. Carolina do | March 6, 1834 | Do | 98 | |
| Thomas Pander | Do | 60 00 | 180 00 | Do cont'l | July 8, 1833 | Do | 69 | |
| Henry Prince | Do | 40 00 | 120 00 | S. Carolina line | April 8, 1834 | Do | 86 | |
| John Waldrop | Do | 33 33 | 66 66 | N. Carolina do | April 20, 1833 | Do | 81 | |
| Asa Wright | Do | 80 00 | - | Do cont'l | April 8, 1834 | Do | 75 | |
| William Ward | Do | 30 00 | 90 00 | Do line | Do | Do | 82 | |
| John Young | Do | 80 00 | 240 00 | S. Carolina do | Sept. 18, 1833 | Do | 72 | |

A statement showing the names, rank, &c., of persons residing in the district of Horry, in the State of South Carolina, who have been inscribed on the pension list under the act of Congress passed the 7th June, 1832.

| NAMES. | Rank. | Annual allowance. | Sums received. | Description of service. | When placed on the pension roll. | Commencement of pension. | Ages. | Laws under which they were formerly inscribed on the pension roll; and remarks. |
|---|---|---|---|---|---|---|---|---|
| Nicholas Prince - | Pri. & gun'r | 102 00 | 306 00 | S. Carolina militia | Nov. 25, 1833 | March 4, 1831 | 76 | |

A statement showing the names, rank, &c., of persons residing in the district of Kershaw, in the State of South Carolina, who have been inscribed on the pension list under the act of Congress passed June 7, 1832.

| NAMES. | Rank. | Annual allowance. | Sums received. | Description of service. | When placed on the pension roll. | Commencement of pension. | Ages. | Laws under which they were formerly inscribed on the pension roll; and remarks. |
|---|---|---|---|---|---|---|---|---|
| John Brockington - | Pri. cav. | 46 80 | 140 40 | S. C. militia | Feb. 9, 1833 | March 4, 1831 | 70 | |
| Nathaniel Jones - | Pri.inf.cav. | 56 83 | 142 07 | Do | Feb. 5, 1834 | Do | 81 | |
| Samuel Jones - | Private | 80 00 | 240 00 | Virginia cont'l line | Jan. 10, 1834. | Do | 71 | |
| Kenneth McKaskell - | Do | 20 00 | - | N. C. troops | March 12, 1834 | Do | 74 | |
| William Nettles - | Captain | 480 00 | 1,200 00 | S. C. militia | Aug. 29, 1832 | Do | 92 | |
| David Scott - | Private | 96 00 | 166 09 | N. C. cont'l line | May 17, 1819 | June 12, 1818 | - | Dropped under act May 1, 1820. |
| Do - | Do | 80 00 | 240 00 | Do | July 14, 1832 | March 4, 1831 | | |

A statement showing the names, rank, &c., of persons residing in the district of Lancaster, in the State of South Carolina, who have been inscribed on the pension list under the act of Congress passed June 7, 1832.

| NAMES. | Rank. | Annual allowance. | Sums received. | Description of service. | When placed on the pension roll. | Commencement of pension. | Ages. | Laws under which they were formerly inscribed on the pension roll; and remarks. |
|---|---|---|---|---|---|---|---|---|
| James Cunningham | Private | 21 33 | — | S. Carolina militia | Dec. 18, 1833 | March 4, 1831 | 72 | |
| Do | Do | 30 00 | — | S. C. cont'l line | May 20, 1834 | Do | 72 | |
| Robert Gault | Do | 40 00 | 100 00 | S. Carolina militia | Aug. 27, 1833 | Do | 69 | |
| Philip Gruber | Do | 80 00 | 240 00 | Do | Nov. 21, 1833 | Do | 77 | |
| James Holliman | Do | 20 00 | 50 00 | N. Carolina do | Nov. 18, 1833 | Do | 84 | |
| Samuel Love | Do | 80 00 | 240 00 | S. Carolina do | Jan. 31, 1833 | Do | — | |
| Thomas McDow | Do | 20 00 | 60 00 | Do | Do | Do | 90 | |
| Thomas Mackey | Do | 33 33 | 99 99 | Do | May 29, 1833 | Do | 72 | |
| John McMurry | Do | 43 33 | 129 99 | Do | Aug. 7, 1833 | Do | 83 | |
| Henry Massey | Pri. inf. & cavalry | 63 33 | 189 99 | Do | Feb. 5, 1834 | Do | 72 | |
| William Owens | Private | 30 00 | 90 00 | Do | Jan. 31, 1833 | Do | — | |
| Wm. Valandingham | Do | 30 00 | 90 00 | N. Carolina do | Jan. 30, 1833 | Do | 81 | |

*A statement showing the names, rank, &c., of persons residing in the district of Laurens, in the State of South Carolina, who have been inscribed on the pension list under the act of Congress passed June 7, 1832.*

| NAMES. | Rank. | Annual allowance. | Sums received. | Description of service. | When placed on the pension roll. | Commencement of pension. | Ages. | Laws under which they were formerly inscribed on the pension roll; and remarks. |
|---|---|---|---|---|---|---|---|---|
| George Adams | Pri. inf. & cavalry | 67 50 | 202 50 | N. Carolina militia | Feb. 20, 1833 | March 4, 1831 | 92 | |
| David Anderson | Private | 80 00 | - | S. Carolina do | April 17, 1834 | Do | 69 | |
| Abraham Bolt, sen. | Do | 30 00 | 90 00 | Do | Feb. 20, 1833 | Do | 71 | |
| Andrew Burnsides | Do | 23 33 | 69 99 | Do | Do | Do | 71 | |
| Leonard Beasley | Pri. inf. & cavalry | 22 50 | 45 00 | Virginia militia | Do | Do | 67 | |
| William Blakely | Private | 21 10 | 52 75 | S. Carolina do | Sept. 17, 1833 | Do | 74 | |
| Thomas Blakely | Do | 30 00 | 75 00 | Do | Do | Do | 79 | |
| John Burns | Do | 43 33 | - | S. Carolina do | July 24, 1834 | Do | 74 | |
| Robert Culbertson | Do | 30 00 | 75 00 | N. Carolina do | Nov. 9, 1833 | Do | 83 | |
| John Colhoun | Do | 40 00 | 120 00 | N. C. cont'l line | Dec. 14, 1833 | Do | 77 | |
| Ellis Cheek | Do | 53 33 | 159 99 | S. Carolina militia | April 17, 1834 | Do | 74 | |
| William Dunlap | Do | 80 00 | 240 00 | S. Carolina do | Feb. 20, 1833 | Do | 79 | |
| James Dillard | Pri. lieut. & capt. | 160 00 | 480 00 | S. Carolina do | June 12, 1834 | Do | - | |
| Samuel Freeman | Private | 20 00 | 50 00 | S. Carolina do | Feb. 20, 1833 | Do | 69 | |
| Paul Finley | Do | 80 00 | 240 00 | S. Carolina do | Dec. 2, 1833 | Do | 72 | |
| Samuel Franks | Do | 40 00 | 120 00 | S. Carolina do | April 19, 1834 | Do | 70 | |
| Arthur Fuller | Do | 20 00 | 40 00 | N. C. cont'l line | Dec. 16, 1832 | Do | 78 | |
| Reuben Golding | Pri. & lt. | 51 79 | 155 37 | S. Carolina militia | Dec. 14, 1833 | Do | 91 | |
| Robert Long | Private | 40 00 | - | S. Carolina do | July 24, 1834 | Do | 71 | |
| Henry Meredith | Pri. inf. & cavalry | 47 50 | 118 75 | N. C. cont'l line | Dec. 28, 1832 | Do | 77 | Transf. from Granville co. N. C. |
| John McMahan | Private | 80 00 | 240 00 | Virginia cont'l line | March 25, 1834 | Do | 79 | |
| John Osborn | Do | 26 66 | 79 98 | Virginia militia | Feb. 20, 1833 | Do | 72 | |
| Richard Owings | Do | 40 00 | 100 00 | S. Carolina militia | Do | Do | 87 | |
| James Pool, sen. | Do | 40 00 | 120 00 | Virginia militia | Do | Do | 87 | |
| Henry Pitts | Do | 33 33 | - | S. Carolina do | June 26, 1834 | Do | 75 | |

| Names. | Rank. | Annual allowance. | Sums received. | Description of service. | When placed on the pension roll. | Commencement of pension. | Ages. |
|---|---|---|---|---|---|---|---|
| John Ridgeway | Do | 60 00 | 180 60 | S. Carolina militia | Nov. 29, 1833 | Do | 74 |
| Amos Strange | Pri. inf. & cavalry | 27 27 | 68 17 | N. Carolina do | Feb. 20, 1833 | Do | 75 |
| George F. Sloane | Ser. & mar. | 56 66 | 169 98 | Navy | March 15, 1834 | Do | 77 |
| Thomas Wilkes, sen. | Private | 30 00 | 90 00 | Virginia militia | Feb. 20, 1833 | Do | 75 |
| John Wait | Do | 80 00 | 240 00 | Virginia cont'l line | April 17, 1834 | Do | 77 |
| Calvin Williamson | Do | 31 10 | 93 30 | S. Carolina militia | April 19, 1834 | Do | 76 |

*A statement showing the names, rank, &c., of persons residing in Lexington district in the State of South Carolina, who have been inscribed on the pension list under the act of Congress, passed the 7th June, 1832.*

| NAMES. | Rank. | Annual allowance. | Sums received. | Description of service. | When placed on the pension roll. | Commencement of pension. | Ages. | Laws under which they were formerly inscribed on the pension roll; and remarks. |
|---|---|---|---|---|---|---|---|---|
| Nedom Busby | Private | 43 33 | 129 99 | S. Carolina militia | April 19, 1834 | March 4, 1831 | 82 | |
| Jacob Fulmer | Do | 40 00 | 120 00 | Do | Do | Do | 72 | |
| John Lohner | Do | 20 00 | 60 00 | Do | Oct. 16, 1833 | Do | 70 | |
| George Summer | Do | 51 66 | 154 98 | Do | Do | Do | 75 | |

*A statement showing the names, rank, &c., of persons residing in the district of Marlborough, in the State of South Carolina, who have been inscribed on the pension list under the act of Congress passed the 7th June 1832.*

| NAMES. | Rank. | Annual allowance. | Sums received. | Description of service. | When placed on the pension roll. | Commencement of pension. | Ages. | Laws under which they were formerly inscribed on the pension roll; and remarks. |
|---|---|---|---|---|---|---|---|---|
| Joshua Ammons | Private | 80 00 | 168 19 | S. C. cont'l line | May 16, 1833 | March 4, 1831 | 77 | Died April 11, 1833. |
| William Cox | Do | 56 66 | 169 98 | Do militia | Oct. 26, 1833 | Do | 71 | |
| Samuel Cox | Do | 50 00 | 150 00 | Do do | Dec. 7, 1833 | Do | 75 | |

Statement of the district of Marlborough, South Carolina—Continued.

| NAMES. | Rank. | Annual allowance. | Sums received. | Description of service. | When placed on the pension roll. | Commencement of pension. | Ages. | Laws under which they were formerly inscribed on the pension roll; and remarks. |
|---|---|---|---|---|---|---|---|---|
| John Haskew | Private | 26 66 | 79 98 | S. Carolina militia | March 11,1833 | March 4, 1831 | 81 | |
| William Hodges | Do | 26 66 | 79 98 | Do do | July 20, 1833 | Do | 72 | |
| William Johnson | Do | 29 00 | 87 00 | N. Carolina do | May 8, 1834 | Do | 75 | |
| William Lister | Do | 20 00 | 50 00 | S. Carolina do | Aug. 7, 1833 | Do | 74 | |
| John Morris | Pri. cav. | 100 00 | 300 00 | Virginia cont'l line | April 17, 1833 | Do | 75 | |
| Jesse Miles | Private | 50 00 | 124 52 | S. Carolina do | Oct. 16, 1833 | Do | 72 | |
| Sion Odom | Do | 80 00 | 240 00 | Do cont'l line | May 16, 1833 | Do | 79 | |
| Lewis Stubbs | Do | 40 00 | 100 00 | Do militia | Aug. 27, 1833 | Do | | Died August 31, 1833. |
| William Stubbs | Do | 56 66 | 169 98 | Do | April 9, 1834 | Do | 86 | |

A statement showing the names, rank, &c., of persons residing in the district of Marion, in the State of South Carolina, who have been inscribed on the pension list under the act of Congress passed the 7th June, 1832.

| NAMES. | Rank. | Annual allowance. | Sums received. | Description of service. | When placed on the pension roll. | Commencement of pension | Ages. | Laws under which they were formerly inscribed on the pension roll; and remarks. |
|---|---|---|---|---|---|---|---|---|
| John Booth | Private | 80 00 | 240 00 | S. Caroline militia | May 17, 1933 | March 4, 1831 | 74 | |
| Henry Braswell | Do | 26 66 | 79 98 | Do | Feb. 5, 1834 | Do | 68 | |
| Ezekiel Daniel | Do | 20 00 | 60 00 | Do | Aug. 7, 1833 | Do | 69 | |
| Archibald Kirby | Do | 22 22 | 66 66 | Do | Nov. 9, 1833 | Do | 70 | |
| Levi Odom | Do | 36 66 | 103 32 | N. Caroline militia | April 17, 1833 | Do | 75 | |
| Drura Pilkington | Do | 80 00 | 200 00 | Virginia do | May 2, 1833 | Do | 72 | |
| Nathan Wittington | Do | 21 10 | 63 30 | S. Carolina do | April 3, 1833 | Do | 72 | |

A statement showing the names, rank, &c., of persons residing in the district of Newberry, in the State of South Carolina, who have been inscribed on the pension list under the act of Congress passed the 7th June, 1832.

| NAMES. | Rank. | Annual allowance. | Sums received | Description of service. | When placed on the pension roll. | Commencement of pension. | Ages. | Laws under which they were formerly inscribed on the pension roll; and remarks. |
|---|---|---|---|---|---|---|---|---|
| William Calmes | Pri. & lt. | 130 00 | 390 00 | Virginia militia | Feb. 20, 1833 | March 4, 1831 | 72 | |
| James Caldwell | Private | 26 66 | - | S. Carolina do | May 12, 1834 | Do | 76 | |
| Henry Dominick | Do | 26 66 | 53 32 | Do do | Feb. 20, 1853 | Do | 77 | Died June 26, 1833. |
| John Davis | Do | 20 00 | - | Do do | Jan. 9, 1834 | Do | 78 | |
| John Floyd | Do | 22 22 | - | N. Carolina do | May 20, 1834 | Do | 75 | |
| Donald McDonald | Do | 33 33 | 99 99 | Pennsylvania do | Feb. 20, 1833 | Do | 77 | |
| William Morrow | Do | 21 55 | - | S. Carolina do | Feb. 5, 1834 | Do | 67 | |
| Thomas Perkins | Do | 40 00 | 120 00 | N. Carolina do | Feb. 20, 1833 | Do | 77 | |
| John Ritchie | Do | 80 00 | 240 00 | S. C. cont'l line | Do | Do | 76 | |
| Christopher Stockman | Do | 20 00 | - | S. Carolina militia | May 20, 1834 | Do | 79 | |
| Edward Thiveatt | Do | 20 00 | 60 00 | N. Carolina do | Feb. 20, 1833 | Do | 70 | |
| Peter Weedman | Do | 37 21 | 111 63 | S. Carolina do | Do | Do | 78 | |
| Peter Wilhelm | Do | 20 22 | 40 44 | Do do | May 16, 1833 | Do | 80 | |
| David Watts | Do | 80 00 | 240 00 | Do do | March 12,1834 | Do | 78 | |

A statement showing the names, rank, &c., of persons residing in the district of Orangeburgh, in the State of South Carolina, who have been inscribed on the pension list under the act of Congress passed the 7th June, 1832.

| NAMES. | Rank. | Annual allowance. | Sums received. | Description of service. | When placed on the pension roll. | Commencement of pension. | Ages. | Laws under which they were formerly inscribed on the pension roll; and remarks. |
|---|---|---|---|---|---|---|---|---|
| John Amaker | Private | 26 66 | 53 32 | S. Carolina militia | Feb. 12, 1833 | March 4, 1831 | 77 | |
| Leven Argor | Do | 53 33 | 159 99 | N. C. cont'l do | Feb. 5, 1834 | Do | 80 | |

Statement of the district of Orangeburgh, South Carolina—Continued.

| NAMES. | Rank. | Annual allowance. | Sums received. | Description of service. | When placed on the pension roll. | Commencement of pension. | Ages. | Laws under which they were formerly inscribed on the pension roll; and remarks. |
|---|---|---|---|---|---|---|---|---|
| Lazarus Chaves | Private | 46 66 | 139 98 | S. Carolina militia | Feb. 6, 1833 | March 4, 1831 | 77 | |
| Daniel Carn | Pri. art'y | 70 83 | 177 07 | N. Carolina do | Sept. 5, 1833 | Do | 71 | |
| Lewis Carn | Pri. cav. | 70 83 | 177 07 | Do | Dec. 14, 1833 | Do | 73 | |
| George Fisher | Steward | 120 00 | 360 00 | S. Carolina do | Do | Do | 76 | |
| Erasmus Gibson | Private | 30 00 | 90 00 | Virginia do | Do | Do | 74 | |
| Jacob Haigler | Do | 43 33 | 129 99 | S. Carolina do | Do | Do | 76 | |
| Andrew Houser | Do | 80 00 | 240 00 | Do | Do | Do | 79 | |
| Jeremiah Jones | Do | 35 83 | 107 49 | N. Carolina do | March 8, 1834 | Do | 75 | |
| Peter Oliver, sen. | Do | 80 00 | - | S. Carolina do | Dec. 24, 1833 | Do | 82 | Died October 27, 1832. |
| William Paulling | Pri. cav. | 41 66 | - | Do | May 16, 1833 | Do | 67 | |
| Hugh Philip | Private | 60 00 | 180 00 | New Jersey do | Dec. 14, 1833 | Do | 74 | |
| Joseph Winningham | Do | 33 33 | 99 99 | S. Carolina do | Feb. 8, 1833 | Do | 71 | |

A statement showing the names, rank, &c., of persons residing in Pickens district, in the State of South Carolina, who have been inscribed on the pension list under the act of Congress, passed June 7, 1832.

| NAMES. | Rank. | Annual allowance. | Sums received. | Description of service. | When placed on the pension roll. | Commencement of pension. | Ages. | Laws under which they were formerly inscribed on the pension roll; and remarks. |
|---|---|---|---|---|---|---|---|---|
| Jeoffrey Beck | Pri. inf. & cav. | 42 50 | 127 50 | N. Carolina militia | May 16, 1833 | March 4, 1831 | 82 | |
| Francis Bradley | Private | 80 00 | 240 00 | N. C. cont'l line | April 19, 1834 | Do | 82 | |
| Richard Carver | Do | 20 00 | 60 00 | Virginia militia | May 16, 1833 | Do | 70 | |
| James Carter | Do | 30 00 | 90 00 | S. Carolina do | May 18, 1833 | Do | 75 | |

| Name | Rank | Amount | Amount | Service / line | Date | Date | Age | Remarks |
|---|---|---|---|---|---|---|---|---|
| Joseph Chapman | Pri. inf. & cav. | 42 28 | 243 75 | Do militia | Oct. 26, 1833 | Do | 88 | |
| William Copeland | Pri. & cap. | 81 25 | 125 00 | . Do | March 6, 1834 | Do | 81 | |
| Stafford Graham | Private | 50 00 | 240 00 | N. Carolina do | Feb. 14, 1833 | Do | 77 | |
| John Gray | Do | 80 00 | 80 31 | Georgia do | June 28, 1833 | Do | 76 | |
| John Gresham | Do | 26 77 | 240 00 | Virginia do | July 20, 1833 | Do | 75 | |
| Benjamin Grist | Do | 80 00 | 240 00 | S. Carolina do | Sept. 18, 1833 | Do | 75 | |
| William Guest | Do | 80 00 | 240 00 | N. Carolina do | April 19, 1834 | Do | 71 | |
| David Humphreys, sr. | Captain | 240 00 | 720 00 | Do | Feb. 14, 1833 | Do | 81 | |
| William Hubbard | Private | 41 55 | 124 65 | S. Carolina do | May 17, 1833 | Do | 78 | |
| Jesse Hall | Corporal | 44 00 | - | N. C, cont'l line | June 24, 1833 | Do | 74 | Died April 25, 1833. |
| Ezekiel Howard | Private | 20 00 | 60 00 | Do militia | Oct. 23, 1833 | Do | 84 | |
| David Hamilton | Do | 80 00 | 240 00 | Do cont'l line | April 8, 1834 | Do | 72 | |
| Thomas Henderson | Lieuten't | 320 00 | 960 00 | S. Carolina militia | April 17, 1834 | May 15, 1818 | 81 | Act March 18, 1818. Dropped under act May 1, 1820. |
| Jacob Jones | Private | 96 00 | 173 41 | N. C. cont'l line | April 3, 1819 | | | |
| Do | Do | 80 00 | 240 00 | Do | May 16, 1833 | March 4, 1831 | 77 | |
| Elisha Jarvis | Do | 20 00 | 60 00 | Maryland militia | Oct. 23, 1833 | Do | 77 | |
| John Mason | Do | 80 00 | 240 00 | Virginia cont'l line | April 20, 1833 | Do | 71 | |
| Archibald McMahan | Do | 50 00 | 150 00 | N. Carolina militia | May 17, 1833 | Do | 75 | |
| Jesse Nevelle | Do | 80 00 | 240 00 | Do | July 20, 1833 | Do | 79 | |
| Tilson Oliver | Do | 30 00 | 90 00 | S. Carolina do | May 18, 1833 | Do | 75 | |
| John Peterson | Do | 24 16 | 60 40 | N. Carolina do | Feb. 14, 1836 | Do | 75 | |
| John Richey | Do | 56 66 | 169 98 | Do do | April 19, 1834 | Do | 70 | |
| James Southerland | Do | 20 00 | 60 00 | Do do | May 16, 1833 | Do | 75 | |
| Buckner Smith | Do | 80 00 | 240 00 | Do cont'l line | July 20, 1833 | Do | 79 | |
| James Standridge | Do | 20 00 | 60 00 | Do militia | Oct. 24, 1833 | Do | 75 | |
| John Thrift | Do | 20 00 | 60 00 | Do | July 20, 1833 | Do | 70 | |
| Charles Taylor | Do | 20 00 | 60 00 | S. Carolina militia | Sept. 20, 1833 | Do | 70 | |
| George Vandever | Do | 36 66 | 109 98 | Virginia do | Feb. 14, 1834 | Do | 71 | |
| John Verner | Do | 48 32 | - | S. C. do | July 24, 1834 | Do | 75 | |
| Levi Young | Do | 31 55 | 94 65 | Do | Oct. 26, 1833 | Do | 75 | |

*A statement showing the names, rank, &c., of persons residing in the district of Richland, in the State of South Caro- lina, who have been inscribed on the pension list under the act of Congress passed June 7, 1832.*

| NAMES. | Rank. | Annual allow- ance. | Sums re- ceived. | Description of ser- vice. | When placed on the pen- sion roll. | Commencement of pension. | Ages. | Laws under which they were for- merly inscribed on the pension roll; and remarks. |
|---|---|---|---|---|---|---|---|---|
| Hicks Chappell - | Lt. & cap. | 400 00 | 1,200 00 | S. C. cont'l line | Jan. 9, 1834 | March 4, 1831 | 77 | |
| Benjamin Hodge - | Private | 70 00 | 210 00 | Do | May 4, 1833 | Do | 82 | |
| Andrew Hamilton, sen. | Captain | 404 66 | - | S. Carolina militia | March 31, 1834 | Do | 80 | |
| Allen Jeffers - | Private | 80 00 | 240 00 | N. C. cont'l line | May 21, 1833 | Do | 74 | |
| Thomas Parrott - | Do | 80 00 | 240 00 | S. Carolina militia | Oct. 16, 1833 | Do | 74 | |
| Adam Team - | Do | 53 33 | 159 99 | Do | May 16, 1833 | Do | | |

*A statement showing the names, rank, &c., of persons residing in the district of Sumpter, in the State of South Caro- lina, who have been inscribed on the pension list under the act of Congress passed June 7, 1832.*

| NAMES. | Rank. | Annual allow- ance. | Sums re- ceived. | Description of ser- vice. | When placed on the pen- sion roll. | Commencement of pension. | Ages. | Laws under which they were for- merly inscribed on the pension roll; and remarks. |
|---|---|---|---|---|---|---|---|---|
| Ripley Copeland - | Private | 96 00 | 48 00 | N. C. cont'l line | Nov. 26, 1819 | Oct. 10, 1819 | 73 | Act March 18, 1818. Dropped under act May 1, 1820. |
| Do | Do | 80 00 | 240 00 | Do | Dec. 28, 1832 | March 4, 1831 | 73 | |
| John China, sen. | Do | 53 33 | 159 99 | S. Carolina militia | Sept. 17, 1833 | Do | 69 | |
| Staughan Conyers | Do | 30 00 | 90 00 | Do | April 8, 1834 | Do | 70 | |
| Peter Dubose - | Ens., lie't. & cap. | 410 00 | 1,230 00 | Do | June 21, 1833 | Do | 75 | |
| Elijah Johnson, sen. - | Private | 20 00 | 60 00 | N. C. cont'l line | March 6, 1834 | Do | 80 | |
| James Jenkins - | Do | 40 00 | 120 00 | S. Carolina militia | Mar. 12, 1834 | Do | 69 | |

| Names | Rank | Annual allowance | Sums received | Description of service | When placed on the pension roll | Commencement of pension | Ages | Remarks |
|---|---|---|---|---|---|---|---|---|
| John Mayrant, sen. | Lt. navy | 360 00 | 1,080 00 | S. Carolina navy | April 17, 1833 | Do | 72 | |
| William McIntosh | Pri. inf. & cav. | 83 33 | 208 32 | S. Carolina militia | May 4, 1833 | Do | 77 | |
| William McElveen, sr. | Private | 48 00 | 120 00 | Do | August 7, 1833 | Do | 75 | |
| John McDonald | Do | 80 00 | 240 00 | Do | Mar. 12, 1834 | Do | | |
| Redden McCoy | Ser. cav. | 180 00 | 540 00 | Do | June 7, 1834 | Do | 71 | Died January 2, 1833. |
| Robert Roberts | Private | 63 33 | 110 70 | S. Carolina do | Feb. 9, 1833 | Do | 85 | |
| Richard Rawlins | Do | 51 11 | 127 77 | S. Carolina do | Oct. 21, 1833 | Do | 75 | Died January 29, 1833. |
| James Spann | Do | 80 00 | 222 14 | N. Carolina do | March 1, 1833 | Do | 81 | |
| Charles Spann | Do | 33 33 | 99 99 | N. Carolina do | May 16, 1833 | Do | 79 | |
| Obadiah Spears | Do | 55 11 | 195 33 | S. Carolina do | April 19, 1834 | Do | 80 | |
| William Vaughan | Pri. cav. | 83 33 | 249 99 | N. Carolina do | Jan. 24, 1834 | Do | 78 | |
| Richard Williford | Pri. & ser. | 40 00 | - | S. Carolina do | Sept. 25, 1833 | Do | 79 | |
| Joseph West | Private | 80 00 | 240 00 | S. Carolina do | Feb. 5, 1834 | Do | | Died January 18, 1834. |
| Thomas Wilson | Do | 43 33 | 124 42 | S. Carolina do | Mar. 12, 1834 | Do | 70 | |

A statement showing the names, rank, &c., of persons residing in the district of Spartansburgh, State of South Carolina, who have been inscribed on the pension list under the act of Congress, passed June 7, 1832.

| Names | Rank | Annual allowance | Sums received | Description of service | When placed on the pension roll | Commencement of pension | Ages | Laws under which they were formerly inscribed on the pension roll; and remarks |
|---|---|---|---|---|---|---|---|---|
| James Byers | Private | 23 33 | 69 99 | S. Carolina militia | Sep. 25, 1833 | March 4, 1831 | 73 | |
| William Bishop | Do | 33 33 | 99 99 | Do | Oct. 18, 1833 | Do | 74 | |
| Abraham Crow | Do | 26 66 | 52 00 | North Carolina do | April 17, 1833 | Do | 71 | |
| Solomon Crocker | Do. | 26 66 | 79 98 | South Carolina do | May 4, 1833 | Do | 77 | |
| Anthony Crocker | Do | 26 66 | 79 98 | Do | Do | Do | 76 | |
| Paul Castlebury | Do | 63 33 | 189 99 | Georgia do | June 27, 1833 | Do | 73 | |
| Edmund Clement | Do | 80 00 | 240 00 | Virginia do | Aug. 27, 1833 | Do | 75 | |
| John Collins | Captain | 480 00 | 1,440 00 | South Carolina do | May 10, 1834 | Do | 80 | |
| William Caldwell | Private | 26 65 | 79 98 | Georgia do | June 10, 1834 | Do | 70 | |
| Henry Emerson | Do | 30 00 | 75 00 | N. C. cont'l line | Aug. 27, 1833 | Do | 71 | |

Statement of the district of Spartansburgh, South Carolina—Continued.

| NAMES. | Rank. | Annual allowance. | Sums received. | Description of service. | When placed on the pension roll. | Commencement of pension. | Ages. | Laws under which they were formerly inscribed on the pension roll; and remarks. |
|---|---|---|---|---|---|---|---|---|
| Thomas Farrow - | Pri. & lt. | 293 99 | 881 97 | N. Carolina militia | Jan. 24, 1834 | March 4, 1831 | 79 | |
| Isaac Gordin - | Private | 31 11 | 93 33 | Virginia cont'l line | April 17, 1833 | Do | 80 | |
| William Goode - | Do | 80 00 | 240 00 | Maryland  do | April 17, 1834 | Do | 72 | |
| Absalom Hastin - | Do | 43 00 | 107 50 | Virginia militia | Aug. 27, 1833 | Do | 73 | |
| Drury Hutchinson - | Do | 40 00 | 120 00 | Do | May 8, 1834 | Do | 89 | |
| Thomas Hanna - | Lt. & cap. | 320 00 | 960 00 | S. C.  do | July 8, 1834 | Do | 75 | |
| Howell Johnson - | Private | 20 00 | 60 00 | Virginia  do | Aug. 27, 1833 | Do | 72 | |
| Rowland Johnson - | Do | 21 66 | 64 98 | Do | Sept. 25, 1833 | Do | 76 | |
| Ellis Johnson - | Do | 50 22 | 150 66 | S. C.  do | April 28, 1834 | Do | 74 | |
| John King - | Do | 96 00 | 96 51 | Virginia cont'l line | May 17, 1819 | March 3, 1819 | 76 | Act March 18, 1818.  Dropped der act May 1, 1820. |
| Do | Do | 80 00 | 240 00 | Do | Nov. 2, 1832 | March 4, 1831 | | |
| James Lawrence - | Do | 53 33 | 159 99 | Virginia militia | Oct. 18, 1833 | Do | 74 | |
| Samuel Morrow - | Pri. & cor. | 81 32 | 243 96 | S. C.  do | Mar. 28, 1834 | Do | 75 | |
| John Meadows - | Private | 43 33 | - | Do | April 28, 1834 | Do | 72 | |
| Reuben Newman - | Do | 80 00 | 240 00 | N. C. cont'l line | June 6, 1833 | Do | 77 | |
| Samuel Noblit - | Do | 30 00 | 90 00 | Pennsylv'a militia | April 17, 1833 | Do | 90 | |
| John Osheals - | Do | 80 00 | 240 00 | S. Carolina  do | Mar. 12, 1834 | Do | 73 | |
| Drury Parham - | Do | 63 33 | 189 99 | S. Carolina  do | Mar. 2, 1833 | Do | 77 | |
| William Pollard - | Do | 34 66 | 103 98 | Virginia  do | April 17, 1834 | Do | 75 | |
| George Roebuck - | Do | 95 00 | 101 03 | N. C. cont'l line | June 4, 1819 | Feb. 15, 1819 | 77 | Act March 18, 1818.  Dropped under act May 1, 1820. |
| Do | Do | 80 00 | 240 00 | Do | Mar. 27, 1833 | March 4, 1831 | | |
| Joshua Richards - | Pri. inf. & cav. | 42 50 | 127 50 | N. Carolina militia | Oct. 22, 1833 | Do | 74 | |
| William Smith - | Captain | 480 00 | 1,200 00 | N. Carolina  do | March 2, 1833 | Do | 83 | |
| James Seay - | Private | 96 00 | 126 09 | Virginia cont'l line | Feb. 9, 1819 | Nov. 13, 1818 | 79 | Act March 18, 1818.  Dropped under act May 1, 1820. |
| Do | Do | 80 00 | 240 00 | Do | April 18, 1833 | March 4, 1831 | | |
| Ephraim Sizemore | Private | 30 00 | 90 00 | Virginia militia | Aug. 27, 1833 | March 4, 1831 | 86 | |

| Names | Rank | Annual allowance | Sums received | Description of service | When placed on the pension roll | Commencement of pension | Age |
|---|---|---|---|---|---|---|---|
| James Tinsley | Do | 80 00 | 200 00 | S. Carolina militia | Feb. 28, 1833 | March 4, 1831 | 74 |
| John Thomas | Do | 40 00 | 120 00 | Virginia cont'l line | July 8, 1833 | Do | 81 |
| Golding Tinsley | Do | 68 33 | - | N. Carolina do | March 6, 1834 | Do | 76 |
| Thomas Vaughan | Do | 80 00 | 240 00 | Virginia militia | Oct. 26, 1833 | Do | 73 |
| John Vaughan | Do | 21 10 | 63 30 | Virginia do | April 17, 1834 | Do | 74 |
| John Wood | Do | 20 00 | 60 00 | Virginia do | Aug. 27, 1833 | Do | 76 |
| Daniel White | Do | 34 88 | 87 20 | N.C. do | Do | Do | 73 |
| Newman Wilson | Do | 40 00 | 100 00 | Do | Aug. 31, 1833 | Do | 78 |
| William Wingo | Do | 80 00 | - | Virginia do | June 5, 1834 | Do | 74 |

*A statement showing the names, rank, &c., of persons residing in the district of Union, in the State of South Carolina, who have been inscribed on the pension list, under the act of Congress passed June 7, 1832.*

| Names. | Rank. | Annual allowance. | Sums received. | Description of service. | When placed on the pension roll. | Commencement of pension. | Age. | Laws under which they were formerly inscribed on the pension roll; and remarks. |
|---|---|---|---|---|---|---|---|---|
| Richard Addis | Private | $60 00 | 180 00 | S. Carolina militia | July 19, 1833 | March 4, 1831 | 86 | |
| Christopher Brandon | Do | 80 00 | 240 00 | Do | March 2, 1833 | Do | 70 | |
| William Bailey | Do | 80 00 | 240 00 | Virginia do | April 17, 1833 | Do | 74 | |
| Henry Cogburn | Do | 33 77 | 84 42 | N. Carolina do | July 19, 1833 | Do | 85 | |
| Mordecai Chandler | Do | 80 00 | 240 00 | Do do | Jan. 20, 1834 | Do | 72 | |
| Daniel Crownover | Do | 20 00 | - | S. Carolina do | Do | Do | 71 | |
| John Gibson | Do | 20 00 | 50 00 | Virginia do | April 20, 1833 | Do | 86 | |
| James Guthery | Do | 40 44 | 121 32 | N. C. cont'l line | Sept. 25, 1833 | Do | 78 | |
| Daniel Holder | Do | 46 66 | 139 98 | S. Carolina militia | March 2, 1833 | Do | 76 | |
| James Hollis | Musician | 66 00 | 198 00 | N. C. cont'l line | June 6, 1833 | Do | 77 | |
| John Hodge | Private | 23 33 | 57 32 | N. Carolina militia | Aug. 31, 1833 | Do | 72 | |
| Drury Harrington | Pri. & Lt. | 116 66 | 349 98 | Do do | April 17, 1833 | Do | 81 | |
| James Jeter | Private | 43 66 | 109 15 | S. Carolina do | Sept. 20, 1833 | Do | 75 | |
| William McBride | Sergeant | 35 00 | 105 00 | N. Jersey do | April 20, 1833 | Do | 78 | |
| William Mitchell | Private | 20 00 | 60 00 | Virginia cont'l line | July 8, 1833 | Do | 75 | |
| James Mosely, sen. | Do | 27 44 | 68 60 | S. Carolina militia | Aug. 7, 1833 | Do | 77 | |
| James McDonald | Do | 43 53 | 129 99 | Do | Jan. 20, 1834 | Do | 77 | |

## Statement of Union district, South Carolina—Continued.

| NAMES. | Rank. | Annual allowance. | Sums received. | Description of service. | When placed on the pension roll. | Commencement of pension. | Ages. | Laws under which they were formerly inscribed on the pension roll; and remarks. |
|---|---|---|---|---|---|---|---|---|
| James McWhiter | Private | 32 33 | - | S. Carolina militia | July 1, 1834 | March 4, 1831 | 74 | |
| Sherwood Nance | Do | 33 33 | 99 99 | N. C. cont'l line | July 8, 1833 | Do | 80 | |
| Stephen Neal | Do | 40 00 | 120 00 | N. Carolina militia | Jan. 20, 1834 | Do | 72 | |
| Hancock Porter | Do | 43 33 | 129 99 | S. Carolina de | July 8, 1833 | Do | 79 | |
| Joshua Palmer | Pri. & cap. | 280 00 | 700 00 | Do do | Aug. 7, 1833 | Do | 84 | |
| Matthew Patton | Captain | 260 00 | 780 00 | Do do | Mar. 14, 1834 | Do | 77 | |
| Daniel Palmer | Private | 44 66 | 133 98 | Virginia do | May 8, 1834 | Do | 78 | |
| Nathaniel Rogers | Do | 46 66 | 139 98 | S. Carolina do | Sept. 17, 1833 | Do | 73 | |
| James Smith | Do | 30 00 | 90 00 | Do do | July 8, 1833 | Do | 83 | |
| Thomas Sanders | Do | 37 21 | 111 63 | Do do | Da | Do | 76 | |
| Edmond Simpson | Do | 43 33 | 86 66 | N. Carolina do | July 19, 1833 | Do | 69 | |
| Samuel Smith | Do | 30 00 | 90 00 | S. Carolina do | Sept. 31, 1833 | Do | 79 | |
| James Tracy, sen. | Do | 53 33 | 159 99 | Do do | July 19, 1833 | Do | 74 | |
| John Van Lew | Do | 36 66 | 109 98 | N. Jersey do | April 20, 1833 | Do | 79 | |

*A statement showing the names, rank, &c. of persons residing in the district of York, in the State of South Carolina, who have been inscribed on the pension list under the act of Congress passed the 7th June, 1832.*

| NAMES. | Rank. | Annual allowance. | Sums received. | Description of service. | When placed on the pension roll. | Commencement of pension. | Ages. | Laws under which they were formerly inscribed on the pension roll; and remarks. |
|---|---|---|---|---|---|---|---|---|
| Jeremiah Blalock | Private | $20 00 | $50 00 | S. Carolina militia | Feb. 10, 1833 | March 4, 1831 | 80 | |
| Jacob Black | Do | 72 33 | 216 99 | Do | Feb. 16, 1833 | Do | 76 | |
| John Black, 2d | Do | 35 67 | 107 01 | Do | Do | Do | 80 | |

| Name | Rank | | | State/Line | Date | | Age |
|---|---|---|---|---|---|---|---|
| Joseph Bingham | Do | 35 55 | 106 65 | Do | Do | Do | 74 |
| Thomas Baily | Artificer | 144 00 | 432 00 | Do | May 17, 1833 | Do | 78 |
| Samuel Burns | Private | 30 00 | 75 00 | Do | July 8, 1833 | Do | 78 |
| James Campbell | Do | 28 21 | 70 52 | Pennsylvania militia | April 22, 1833 | Do | 79 |
| John Clark | Pri. & adj. | 169 99 | 424 97 | N. Carolina do | June 27, 1833 | Do | 87 |
| William Clark | Private | 26 99 | 80 97 | S. Carolina do | Dec. 24, 1833 | Do | 74 |
| George Davis | Do | 26 66 | 79 98 | N. Carolina do | July 8, 1833 | Do | 70 |
| Andrew Floyd | Pri. & adj. | 120 22 | 360 66 | S. Carolina do | Jan. 9, 1834 | Do | 85 |
| James B. Fulton | Private | 22 00 | 66 00 | Maryland cont'l line | March 14, 1834 | Do | 69 |
| James Glenn | Do | 50 00 | 150 00 | N. Carolina militia | Sept. 24, 1833 | Do | 75 |
| Samuel Henderson | Do | 43 33 | 108 32 | S. Carolina do | Feb. 2, 1833 | Do | 79 |
| Richard Horseley | Do | 33 33 | 99 99 | N. Carolina do | April 3, 1833 | Do | 79 |
| Robert Hanna | Pri. & lt. | 186 66 | 559 98 | S. Carolina do | June 12, 1833 | Do | 73 |
| Samuel Hutchison | Private | 94 66 | 236 65 | .S. C. cont'l line | Oct. 16, 1833 | Do | 80 |
| Joseph Jamieson | Do | 24 10 | 72 30 | S. Carolina militia | Feb. 4, 1833 | Do | 70 |
| Andrew Kerr | Do | 28 21 | 70 52 | Do | May 17, 1833 | Do | 78 |
| John Kenmoure | Do | 50 00 | 125 00 | Do | July 19, 1833 | Do | 74 |
| Joseph Moss | Do | 80 00 | 240 00 | N. C. cont'l line | Feb. 23, 1835 | Do | 83 |
| Thomas Martin | Pri. cav. | 25 00 | 62 50 | S. Carolina militia | April 22, 1833 | Do | 78 |
| James Martin | Captain | 480 00 | 1,440 00 | Do | May 4, 1833 | Do | 79 |
| John Moore | Private | 20 00 | 60 00 | N. Carolina do | Feb. 5, 1834 | Do | 79 |
| Daniel Quinn | Do | 76 66 | 229 98 | S. Carolina do | June 28, 1833 | Do | 74 |
| John Rooker | Do | 43 33 | 108 32 | S. Carolina do | Feb. 2, 1833 | Do | 79 |
| Henry Rea | Do | 80 00 | 240 00 | Do | June 12, 1833 | Do | 75 |
| William Summerford | Do | 40 00 | 120 00 | Do | May 29, 1833 | Do | 72 |
| Robert Wilson | Do | 80 00 | 240 00 | S. C. cont'l line | Jan. 16, 1833 | Do | 76 |
| Aaron Wood | Do | 63 33 | 158 32 | S. Carolina militia | Feb. 2, 1835 | Do | 77 |

The "Best Friend of Charleston" was the first locomotive entirely built in this    country.

# THE NAMES,

AS FAR AS CAN BE ASCERTAINED OF THE

# OFFICERS

WHO SERVED IN THE

# SOUTH CAROLINA REGIMENTS

ON THE CÓNTINENTAL ESTABLISHMENT

PREPARED BY

WILMOT G. DeSAUSSURE.

PUBLISHED BY ORDER OF THE GENERAL ASSEMBLY, 1886.

This list is made from the Journals of the Provincial Congress, so far as the same have been accessible; from the Journals of the Council of Safety, so far as the same have been accessible; from Moultrie Revolution, from Ramsay Revolution, from such orderly books of General William Moultrie and General Francis Marion as are accessible, from various books relating to the Revolution, from extracts from the revolutionary muster-rolls, &c., on file in the Department of State at Washington, and from whatever other sources information on this subject could be gathered.

The list is doubtless imperfect, but so many names as are here gathered, are by this list preserved from oblivion.

|  |  |  |
|---|---|---|
| Adair, William | Lieutenant 6th Regiment | |
| Alexander Charles | " " " | |
| Alexander, Nathaniel | Surgeon's mate | |
| Anderson, David | Captain 5th Regiment | |
| Armstrong, John | " " " | Died 3d October, 1778. |
| Armstrong, Robert | Lieutenant 1st Regiment | |
| Armstrong, William | Major " " | |
| Ashby, Anthony | Lieutenant 2d Regiment | Resigned Feb. 16, 1778. |
| Axson, Samuel J | Surgeon's mate | |
| Airs, —— | Surgeon | Died ——, 1777. |
| Bailey, —— | Lieutenant 3rd Regiment | Killed Savannah, 9th October. 1779. |
| Baker, Jesse | Captain " " | |
| Baker, Richard Bohun | " 2nd " | |
| Barnwell, John | " 1st " | Resigned, Dec. 11, 1775. |
| Beekman, Barnard | Colonel 4th Regiment Art'y | |
| Beekman, Samuel | Lieutenant — Regiment | |
| Belin, Allard | " 1st " | " 1777. |

GATEWAY TO FORTUNE WOODS PARK. CAPTAIN JOHN BUCHANAN, A SOLDIER OF THE REVOLUTION, GAVE THIS TRACT OF LAND TO HIS SLAVE, FORTUNE, WHEN HE GAVE HIM HIS FREEDOM. FORTUNE ACTED AS BODY-SERVANT TO LAFAYETTE WHEN THE LATTER WAS IN CAMP WITH CAPTAIN BUCHANAN AT GEORGE-TOWN DURING THE REVOLUTION.

OLD HIBBEN HOUSE, MT. PLEASANT, S. C., NEAR CHARLESTON. HERE STAYED GEN. WILLIAM MOULTRIE, GENERAL PINCKNEY AND OTHER CONTINENTAL OFFICERS ON PAROLE WHEN THE BRITISH OCCUPIED CHARLESTON IN 1781. WASHINGTON VISITED HERE IN 1791.

| | | |
|---|---|---|
| Blake, John | Lieutenant 2d Regiment | Resigned April 25, 1778. |
| Blameyer, William | Captain 5th " | " Nov. 1778. |
| Bowie, John | " " " | [tober 1779. |
| Boyce, Alexander | " 6th " | Killed Savannah, 9th Oc- |
| Boykin, Francis | Lieutenant 3d Regiment | |
| Bradwell, Nathaniel | " 1st " | |
| Bremar, Francis | Dep. Must. Mast. | |
| Brown, Charles | Lieutenant 1st Regiment | |
| Brown, John | Captain 5th " | |
| Brown, Richard | " 3d " | |
| Brown, William | " 6th " | Resigned Dec, 1778 |
| Brownfield. Robert | Surgeon's mate | |
| Brownson,[Nathaniel | Dep. Sun. Med. Dep't | |
| Buchanan, John | Captain 3d Regiment | |
| Budd, John Shivers | Surgeon 4th Reg't Artillery | |
| Burke, Ædanus | Lieutenant 2d Regiment | Resigned 22d Feb., 1778. |
| Bush, John | " " " | Killed Savannah, 9th Oc- |
| Buchanan, —— | | [tober, 1779. |
| Brown, Benjamin | " 6th ". | |
| Baker, S | " " " | |
| | | |
| Caddett, —— | Lieutenant — Regiment | |
| Caldwell, John | Captain 3d " | |
| Caldwell, William | " " " | |
| Cameron, Allan | Lieutenant " " | |
| Capers, William | " 2d " | |
| Carne, John | Ass't Dep't Apothecary | |
| *Caltell, Benjamin | Captain 1st Regiment | |
| *Caltell, William | " " " | |
| Charnock, William | " 2d " | Resigned Nov. 25, 1778. |
| Chesnut.;John | Paymaster 3d Regiment | |
| Cleiland. John | Surgeon's mate 3d Reg't | |
| Cogdell, George | Captain 5th Reg't | Resigned Sept. 3, 1778. |
| Coit, —— | " 6th " | |
| Conyers, Clement | " 5th " | |
| Cooper, Leonard | | |
| Crowther, Isaac | Lieutenant 3d Regiment | |
| Cor'terier, John | Capt. — Reg't Lt, Drag. | |
| Cole, —— | Ensign 2d " | |
| | | |
| Daniel, John | Lieutenant — Regiment | |
| Dark, John Sandford | Paymaster 1st " | |
| Davis, Harman | Captain — " | |
| Davis, John | Lieutenant 3d " | |
| Davis, William Ransom | Captain 5th " | |
| DeBraham, —— | Major Engineers | |
| D'Ellient, Andrew | Brigade Major | [tober, 1779. |
| DeSaussure, Louis | Lieutenant 3d Regiment | Killed Savannah, 9th Oc- |
| DeTreville, John LaB | Captain 4th Reg't Art'y | |
| Deveaux, —— | | [1779. |
| Dickenson, Benjamin | Lieutenant 1st Regiment | [tober, 1779. |
| Dixon, Henry | Brigade Inspector | Killed, Stono, June 20, |
| Doggatt. —— | Captain 6th Regiment | [tober, 1779. |
| Donaldson, James | Captain 3rd Regiment | Killed, Savannah, 9th Oc- |
| Donnom, William | " 4th Reg't Art'y | Resigned 6th October, |
| Downes, William | Adjutant 2nd Regiment | [1878. |
| D'Oyley, Daniel | Captain 1st Regiment | |
| Drayton, Charles | " 4th Reg't Ar'y | Resigned August, 1779. |
| Drayton, Glen | Lieutenant 2nd Regiment | |
| Drayton, Stephen | Dep. Quartermaster Gen'l | [tober, 1779. |
| Dubose, Isaac | Lieutenant 2nd Regiment | Killed,Savannah, 9th Oc- |
| Dubois, David | Captain — Reg't Drag. | |
| Duff, James | " 6th Regiment | |
| Dunbar, Thomas | Lieutenant 2d Regiment | |
| Dunham, —— | Captain 4th Reg't Art'y | |
| Dutarque, Louis | Lieutenant 3d Regiment | Resigned Jan. 30, 1776. |
| Doggatt, Joel | " 6th " | |
| | | |
| Earle, Samuel | Captain 5th Regiment | |
| Edmunds, David | Lieutenant — Regiment | |
| Elliott, Barnard | Lieut. Col. 4th " | Died 5th October, 1778. |
| Elliott, Joseph | Lieutenant 1st " | Died. |
| Elliot, Thomas | " 2d " | |
| Esom, John | Adjutant 3d " | |
| Evance, Thomas | Paymaster 2d " | Died 18th Dec., 1777. |
| Evans, George | Lieutenant " " | |
| Eveleigh, George | " " " | Died ——, 1777. |
| Eveleigh, Michael | Captain — " | Probably a mistake for |
| Eveleigh, Nicolas | Dep. Adjutant General | [Nicholas Eveleigh. |

* So in printed pamphlet, but believed to be misprint for *Cattell.*

|  |  |  |
|---|---|---|
| Edmunds. David | Lieutenant — Regiment | Died ——, 1778. |
| | | |
| Farr, John | Lieutenant 2d Regiment | |
| Farrar, Field | Captain 3d " | |
| Farrar, Thomas | Lieutenant — " | |
| Fayssoux, Peter | Paymaster and Surgeon | |
| Ferguson, —— | Major 3d Regiment | |
| Field, James | Lieut. 4th Reg't Art'y | |
| Fildloath, —— | " " " " " | |
| Fisby, —— | Lieut 2d Bat. Lt. Inf'y | |
| Fishburne, William | Lieutenant 1st Regiment | |
| Fitzpatrick, William | " 3d " | Resigned Aug. 24, 1778. |
| Flagg, Henry C. | Surgeon — | |
| Foissin, Peter | Lieutenant 2d Regiment | [15th March, 1781. |
| Forbes, John | Captain — ": | Killed, Guilford C. H., |
| Ford, Tobias | Lieutenant — Regiment | |
| Fraser, Alexander | " 1st " | |
| Frierson, John | " 2d " | |
| Fuller, Richard | " 1st " | Died. |
| | | |
| Gadsden, Christopher | Brigadier General | Resigned ——. 1777. |
| Gadsden, Thomas | Captain 1st Regiment | |
| Galvan, William | Lieutenant 2d Regiment | Resigned 5th July, 1778. |
| Garden, Alexander | Cornet Lee's Legion | [tober, 1779. |
| Gaston, Robert | Lieutenant 3d Regiment | Killed, Savannah, 9th Oc- |
| Gervais, John Lewis | Dep. Paym'r Gen., S. Dep. | |
| Giles, Thomas | Capt. — Reg't Lt. Drag. | |
| Glover, Wilson | Lieutenant 1st Regiment | |
| Goodwyn, John | Captain " " | |
| Goodwyn, John | " 4th Reg't Art'y | |
| Goodwyn, Richard | Capt. — Reg't Lt. Drag. | |
| Goodwyn, Robert | Captain 3d Regiment | Resigned May 30, 1778. |
| Goodwyn, Uriah | " 2d " | |
| Goodwyn, William | Lieutenant 3d Regiment | Resigned May 30, 1778. |
| Gray, George | " 1st " | Lost on schr Randolph. |
| Gray, Henry | " 2d " | Resigned Dec. 15, 1777. |
| Gray, James | " " " | Killed, Savannah, 9th Oc- |
| Gray, Peter | Captain 2d " | [tober, 1779. |
| Grayson, John | Lieut. 4th Reg't Art'y | |
| Grimke, John F | Lieut. Col. Dep. Adj. Gen. | |
| Guerry, Samuel | Lieutenant 2d Regiment | Died 12th July, 1779. |
| Guerry, Stephen | Captain 5th " | Resigned August, 1779, |
| Gould, —— | Surgeon 1st Regiment | |
| Gordon, —— | Lieutenant 5th Regiment | |
| | | |
| Hall, John | Quartermaster 2d Reg't | |
| Hall, Thomas | Captain " " | |
| Hambleton, —— | Lieutenant — " | |
| Hamilton, John | " 1st " | |
| Hampton, John | Capt. — Reg't Lt. Drag. | |
| Hampton, Richard | Lt. Col. — Reg't Lt. Drag. | |
| Hampton Wade | " " " " " | |
| Hardaway, Joel | Lieutenant 1st Regiment | |
| Harleston, Isaac | Major 6th " | |
| Harthorn, Joseph | Captain 6th " | Resigned Aug. 9, 1778. |
| Hart, John | " 2d " | |
| Hart, Oliver | Surgeon | |
| Hazzard, William | Lieutenant 1st Regiment | |
| Healtey, Charles | " 3d " | Resigned Jan. 30, 1776. |
| Heard, John | Lt. Fireworker 4th Reg't | |
| Henderson, William | Lieut Col. 6th Regiment | |
| Hennenton, John | Lieutenant " " | |
| Hext, William | Captain 1st " | |
| Hodges, Benjamin | Lieutenant 3d " | |
| Hogan, —— | Captain 5th " | |
| Hopkins, David | " 1st " | |
| Horry, Daniel, | " " " | |
| Horry, Peter | Lieut. Col. 2d " | |
| Hourston, James | Surgeon | [May, 1779. |
| Huger, Benjamin | Major 5th Regiment | Killed, Charlestown, 11th |
| Huger, Francis | Captain 1st Regiment | |
| Huger, Isaac | Brigadier General | |
| Hughes, Henry | Lieutenant 1st Regiment | [tober, 1779. |
| Hume, Alexander | " 2d " | Killed, Savannah, 9th Oc- |
| Hyrne, Edmund | Lieut. Col. Dep. Adj. Gen. | |
| Heyward, William | Lieutenant 1st Regiment | Resigned 22d Oct., 1777. |

| Name | Rank / Regiment | Notes |
|---|---|---|
| Hampton, Henry | Captain 6th Regiment | |
| Imhoff, John L. S. | Lieutenant 3d Regiment | |
| Joor, Joseph | Lieutenant 2d Regiment. | Lost on schr. Randolph |
| Jackson, Bazil | " — " | |
| Jackson, William | Captain 1st " | |
| Jenkins, Joseph | Lieutenant 1st " | |
| Jewey, Thomas | Capt. Dep. Must. Mast. | Resigned Nov. 1778. |
| Johnson, Robert | Hospital Physician | |
| Jones, John | Lieutenant 3d Regiment | |
| Jones Richard | " " " | |
| Jervey, —— | Captain 5th " | |
| Jones, —— | Lieutenant 5th " | |
| *Kaltiesen, Michel | Capt. Wagonmaster Gen'l | |
| Knap, John | Lieutenant 1st Regiment | |
| Keith, Alexander | Capt. 3d " | |
| Kennedy, James | Lieutenant 1st " | |
| Kershaw, Ely | Captain 3d " | Resigned October, 1777. |
| Kirkland, Moses | " " " | |
| Kobb, Josiah | Lieutenant 2d " | |
| Lacy, James | Lieutenant 6th Regiment | Died December 20, 1778. |
| Ladson, James | " 2d " | |
| Langford, Daniel | | |
| Laurens, John | Lieut. Col. of D. C | Killed, Combahee, Aug. [27, 1781. |
| Legare, James | Lieutenant 2d Regiment | |
| Lesesne, Thomas | Captain " " | Resigned 6th Aug. 1779. |
| Levacher, St. Marie | " 1st " | |
| Liddell, George | Lieutenant 3d " | |
| Lining, Charles | Captain 1st " | |
| Leston, Thomas | Lieutenant — Regiment | |
| Lisle, John | " 3d " | Resigned August, 1779. |
| Lloyd, Benjamin | " — " | |
| Lloyd Edward | " " " | |
| Lochman, John | Surgeon | |
| Lyell, Robert | Captain 3d Regiment | |
| Lynch, Thomas, Jr | " 1st " | |
| La Marzell, —— | Lieutenant 4th Regiment | Resigned ——, 1777. |
| Love, William | " 3d " | |
| Maham, Hezekiah | Capt. 5th Reg't Lt. Col. Reg- iment Light Drag. | |
| Marion, Francis | Lieut. Col. 2d Regiment | |
| Marion, Gabriel, Jr | Lieutenant " " | Killed ——, 1781. |
| Martin, James | Surgeon | |
| Martin, John | Captain 2d Regiment | |
| Mason, Luke | Lieutenant 3d Regiment | |
| Mason, Richard | Captain 2d " | |
| Mason, William | " 1st " | |
| Massey, William | Adjutant 1st " | |
| Mayson, James | Lieut. Col. 3d " | |
| Mazyck, Daniel | Captain 2d " | |
| Mazyck, Stephen | Lieutenant 2d " | |
| McDonald, Adam | Captain 1st " | Died ——, 1778. |
| McDonald, James | " " " | |
| McGinnis, Charles | Lieutenant — Regiment | |
| McGuire, Merry | " 2d " | |
| McIntosh, Alexander | Major " | |
| McQueen, Alexander | Lieutenant 1st " | |
| Middleton, Hugh | " 3d " | |
| Middleton, John | Cornet Lee's Legion | |
| Milling, Hugh | Capt. Lieut. 6th Regiment | |
| Mitchell, Ephraim | Major — Regiment | |
| Mitchell, James | Captain 4th Reg't Art'y | |
| Mitchell, William | Lt. Fireworker 4th Reg't | |
| Monaghan, David | Lieutenant 3d Regiment | Resigned 24th, ——, 1775. |
| Moore, Francis | Major | [October, 1779. |
| Moore, Henry | Lieut. 4th Reg't Art'y | Killed, Savannah, 9th |
| Motte, Charles | Captain 2d Regiment | Resigned Sept. 23, 1778. |
| Motte, Isaac | Lieut. Col. 2d Regiment | Resigned ——, 1777. |
| Moualt, William | Captain 1st " | Killed, Charlestown, [May, 1780. |
| Moultrie, Thomas | " 2d " | |
| Moultrie, William | Major General | |
| Moultrie, William | Lieutenant 2d Regiment | |

*So in printed pamphlet, but should be " Michael Kalteissen."

| Name | Rank / Regiment | Remarks |
|---|---|---|
| Mowatt, John | Lieutenant 1st " | |
| Marshall, —— | Captain 2d " | |
| Monterip, Richard | Lieutenant 5th " | |
| McNeill, Daniel | Surg. mate 2d " | |
| Marshall, Thomas | Captain 3d Regiment | |
| McKinney, James | Lieutenant 5th " | |
| | | |
| Nelson, John | Major | |
| Neufville, William | Regimental Surgeon | |
| Newson, Benjamin | Lieutenant 2d Regiment | [May, 1780. |
| Neyle, Philip | " 1st " | Killed, Charlestown, |
| Nixon, George | Adjutant 4th Reg't Art'y | |
| | | |
| Ogier, George | Lieutenant 2d Regiment | |
| Oliphant, David | Medical Director | |
| Oliphant, William | Lieutenant 2d Regiment | Resigned Oct. 20, 1777. |
| Ousby, Thomas | " — " | |
| | | |
| Paggett, —— | Captain — Regiment | |
| Parham, —— | Lieutenant 1st Regiment | |
| Parsons, —— | " 5th " | |
| Partridge, William | " 1st " | |
| Peronneau, Henry | " 2d " | Resigned July 15, 1778. |
| Peronneau, James | " 1st " | |
| Petrie, Alexander | Captain 5th " | Resigned 8th Oct. 1778. |
| Petrie, George [worth | Lieutenant 2d " | |
| Pinckney, Chas. Cotes- | Colonel 1st " | |
| Pinckney, Thomas | Major " | |
| Platen, Frederick Von | Lieut. 4th Reg't Ar'ty | |
| Pledger, Joseph | Lieutenant 3d Regiment | Resigned Jan. 30, 1776. |
| Polk, Ezekiel | Captain " " | |
| Pollard, Richard | " " " | |
| Postell, Benjamin | Lieutenant 1st " | |
| Potts, Thomas | Captain 5th " | |
| Poyas, John E | Hospital mate | |
| Prescott, Joseph | Surgeon | |
| Prince, Francis | Captain 5th Regiment | |
| Provaux, Adrian | " 2d " | |
| Purcell, Henry, Rev | Brigade Chaplain | |
| Purvis, John | Captain 3d Regiment | |
| Peronneau, John | Lieutenant 2d Regiment | Resigned Dec. 12, 1777, |
| | | |
| Ramsay, Henry | Lieutenant —— Regiment | |
| Ramsay, Joseph H | Surgeon | |
| Rasche, John Henry | Surgeon's mate 2d Reg't | |
| Rayford, —— | Captain —— Regiment | |
| Read, William | Physician and Surgeon | |
| Redmond, —— | Lieutenant 6th Regiment | |
| Richardson, Edward | Captain 3d " | Resigned Jan 30, 1776, |
| Richardson, Richard, Jr | " 6th " | |
| Richardson, William | " 5th " | [1779. |
| Roberts, Owen | Colonel 4th Reg't Artillery | Killed, Stono, 20th June, |
| Roberts, Richard Brooks | Captain " " " | |
| Roberson, James | Lieutenant 3d Regiment | |
| Rodgers, Alexander | Surgeon 3d " | |
| Rogers, Christopher, Jr | Lieutenant 2d " | |
| Rose, Hugh | Surgeon " " | |
| Rothmaler, Erasmus | Lieutenant — " | |
| Roux, Albert | Captain 2d " | |
| Russell, Thos. Com'ndr | Lieutenant 1st " | |
| Raphel, —— | Lieut 4th Reg't Art'y | Died October, 1777. |
| Rolando, —— | " 5th " | Resigned ——. 1777. |
| Rutledge, Andrew | Dep. Wagonmaster Gen'l | |
| | | |
| Sanders, Roger Parker | Captain 1st Regiment | Resigned 8th Oct. 1778. |
| Schreiber, Jacob | " Engineers | |
| Scott, William | Lieut Col — Regiment | |
| Screven, Benjamin | Capt — Reg't Lt Drag | |
| Senf, Christian | Captain Engineers | |
| Shubrick, Jacob | Lieutenant 2d Regiment | Died 27th April, 1778. |
| Shubrick, Richard | " " " | Died 8th Nov, 1777, |
| Shubrick, Thomas | Captain " " | |
| Simons, James | Cornet Lee's Legion | |
| Singleton, Richard | Lieutenant 1st Regiment | |

GENERAL CHRISTOPHER GADSDEN

1724-1805

AMERICAN PATRIOT AND REVOLUTIONARY
GENERAL. HE RECEIVED HIS EDUCATION IN
ENGLAND. HE WAS A DELEGATE TO THE
FIRST COLONIAL CONGRESS IN 1765, AND
MEMBER OF THE FIRST CONTINENTAL CON-
GRESS 1774-1776; AN OFFICER IN THE CON-
TINENTAL ARMY IN THE DEFENSE OF
CHARLESTON 1776-1780. AT THE BEGINNING
OF THE REVOLUTION HE ENTERED THE
ARMY AS A COLONEL. IN 1776 HE WAS PRO-
MOTED TO THE RANK OF BRIGADIER-GEN-
ERAL. HE WAS LIEUTENANT-GOVERNOR OF
SOUTH CAROLINA 1778-1780. IN 1782 HE WAS
ELECTED GOVERNOR.

FLAG BORNE BY AMERICAN
TROOPS AT THE SOUTH
AT THE BEGINNING OF THE
REVOLUTION.

The battle of King's Moun-
tain was the beginning of that great return wave which broke the
British power, and swept it, not only from South Carolina, but from all
the States which had declared for independence.

|  |  |  |
|---|---|---|
| Skirving, Charles | Lieutenant 1st " | |
| Smith, Aaron | " 2d " | |
| Smith, Daniel | Dep Med Surveyor | |
| Smith, John Caraway | Captain 2d Regiment | |
| Smith, Press | Lieutenant 1st Regiment | |
| Smith, Robert, Rt Rev | Hospital Chaplain | |
| Smith, Samuel | Lieutenant 1st Regiment | Resigned August 1779. |
| Springer, Sylvester | Surgeon's mate, 2d Regiment | |
| Stevens, Wm S | Junior Surgeon | |
| Sumter, Thomas | Lieut Col 6th Regiment | Resigned Sept. 23, 1778. |
| Sunn, Frederick | Reg't Surgeon. —— Reg't | |
| Shackelford, —— | Captain 5th " | Resigned 7th Dec. 1777. |
| Spencer, —— | " " " | |
| Simons, —— | Lieutenant —— Regiment | Lost on schr. Randolph. |
| Simpson, Robert | Adjutant 5th " | Resigned Nov. 1778. |
| | | |
| Taggart, William | Lieutenant 3d Regiment | |
| Tate, Wm | Capt Lieut 5th " | Resigned 22d Dec. 1777 |
| Taylor, Samuel | Major 6th " | |
| Theus, Jeremiah | Surgeon 2d " | |
| Theus, Simeon | Captain 1st " | |
| Thompson, William | Colonel 3d " | |
| Thompson, —— | Lieutenant 3d " | |
| Towles, Oliver | Captain " " | |
| Townsend, Paul | Paymaster 4th Reg't Artil'ry | |
| Tucker. Thomas Tudor | Physician and Surgeon | |
| Turner, George | Captain 1st Regiment | |
| Tutt. Benjamin | " 5th " | |
| Tutt, Richard | " " " | |
| Taylor, Thomas | " 3d " | Resigned October, 1777. |
| | | |
| Valentine, Wm | Lieutenant 1st Regiment | |
| Vanderhorst, James | " —— " | |
| Vanderhorst, John | Major 2d " | |
| Vaughan, —— | Surgeon | [October, 1779. |
| Vlieland, Cornelius Van | Lieutenant 2d " | Killed, Savannah, 9th |
| Vickars, Samuel | Hospital Physician | |
| | | |
| Wage, George | Captain 6th Regiment | |
| Wallace, John | Surgeon | |
| Walter, John Allen | Lieutenant 2d " | |
| Ward, John Peter | " 1st " | |
| Ward, Wm | " " " | |
| Warley, Felix | Captain " " | |
| Warley, George | " 2d " | |
| Warley Joseph | " " " | |
| Warley, Paul | Lieutenant " " | Resigned —— 1777. |
| Warren, Samuel | Captain 5th " | |
| Watson, Samuel | Lieutenant 3d " | |
| West, Cato | " " " | Resigned Sept. 14, 1778. |
| White, Sims | Captain 4th Reg't Art'ly | Resigned ——, 1777. |
| Wickley, John | " —— Regiment | [October, 1779. |
| Wickom, John | Ensign 2d " | Killed, Savannah, 9th |
| Williamson. John | Captain 1st " | |
| Wilson, —— | Capt. Lt 4th Reg't Art'ly | |
| Wilson, —— | Lieutenant " " | |
| Winn, Richard | Lieutenant 3d Regiment | [October, 1779. |
| Wise, Samuel | Major " " | Killed, Savannah, 9th |
| Withers, William R | Ensign —— " " | |
| Woodward, Thomas | Captain 3d " | Resigned Jan. 30, 1779. |

AMERICAN ARTILLERY DRAWN BY OXEN.

MORGAN.

Soldier of the Continental Army.

General Lincoln.

The following are the names of various different Military militia organizations which existed at and during the Revlutionary War. These names are taken from the various authorities cited, as the authorities from whom the names of the Militia officers hereinafter given are taken, to wit:

Charles Town Battalion of Artillery. Charles Town. 2 companies.

Charles Town Volunteers. Charles Town.
Charles Town Light Infantry. " "
Charles Town Fusileers, German. " "
True Blue Company. " "
Grenadier Company. " "
Cannon's Company of Volunteers. " "
Charles Town Rangers. " "
Beaufort Light Infantry. Beaufort.
Beaufort Artillery. "
Beaufort Company of Volunteers. Beaufort.
St. Helena Volunteers.
Euhaw Volunteers.
Huspa Volunteers.
Foot Rangers or Rovers, Raccoon Company.
James Island Company.
Salt Catcher Company.
Horry's Light Dragoons, — Regiment. State troops enlisted.

William Moultrie, commander of the
little fort on Sullivan's Island,
afterwards named in his honor.

MORGAN'S ESCAPE FROM THE INDIANS

Maham's Light Dragoons,—Regiment. State troops, enlisted.
Wade Hampton's Light Dragoons,—Reg't. " "          "
Richard Hampton's "          "     "   "   "   "          "
Boykin's Company of Catawba Indians.
Round O Volunteers.
Pon Pon Company.
Dozier's Company of Volunteers.
Indian Field Company.
Postell's Company of Volunteers.
Edisto Island Volunteers,
John's Island Company.
Kingstree Company.
Stono Company.
Militia Rangers Volunteers.
Wando Company, Christ Church.
Port's Company of Volunteers.
St. George's Company.
Georgetown Artillery.   Georgetown.
Light Horse, or Pocotaligo Hunters.
Oakely Creek Company.
St. Peter's Company.
Black Swamp Company.
Pipe Creek Company.
Boggy Gut Company.
New Windsor Company.
Upper Three Runs Company.

Brig. Gen. Francis Marion's Brigade consisted of—
Lieut. Col. McDonald's Regiment.
Col. Richardson's          "
Col. Irwin's          "
Col. Benbow's          "
Col. Maybank's          "

In Gen. Marion's Brigade, Jacob Brawler, who lived in
the present Marion County, and his 23 sons served ; he and
22 of his sons were killed or died in service, and the one
son who survived came out of the war a cripple, and imbe-
cile from exposure and hardships.

16

# LIST OF OFFICERS.

## OF THE MILITIA OF SOUTH CAROLINA WHO TOOK PART IN THE WAR OF THE REVOLUTION 1775–1783.

The sources from whence these names are obtained are set opposite to their respective names. Very often several of these authorities mention the same officer, and in this list where double authorities are cited, it is because the rank of the officer or the term of service has been of a different grade or different period.

In the citation of the Journal of the Council of Safety as authority, these citations should very frequently have been Journal of the Provincial Congress. When the Congress was in session, the officers were appointed by it; when it was not in session, the Council of Safety appointed; and hence the Journal of the Council is cited merely for uniformity of citation.

This list is doubtless very imperfect, but so many names as are here gathered are by this list preserved from oblivion.

LA FAYETTE.

Governor Rutledge.

Charles Pinckney,

Count Pulaski.

Henry Laurens

| Name | Rank | Service | Command | Reference |
|---|---|---|---|---|
| Abney, Nathaniel | Captain. | | | Gibbes's Documentary History, 19 Nov., 1775. |
| Alexander, James | Lieutenant. | | | Johnson's Traditions of Revolution, 1781. |
| Allen Jeremiah | Captain. | | | Gregg's History of Old Cheraws, 1782. |
| Allison, Robert | " | | | Gibbes's Documentary History, 1781. |
| Allston, John | " | Expedition under Major Williamson. | Marion Brigade, | Jour. Coun. Safety, 20 Dec., 1775 Moul. Rev. 1778. |
| Allston, William | | | " | Gibbes's Documentary History, 1781. |
| Ancrum, — | Major. | | | Moultrie's Revolution 1778. |
| Anderson, John | Captain. | | Marion Brigade | Gibbes's Documentary History, 19 Nov., 1775. |
| Anderson, Robert | " | Col. Peter Horry's Reg't Dragoons. Wounded. | | " |
| Andrews, John | Adjutant, Lieut. Colonel. | Expedition under Major Williamson. | | Ramsay's Revolution, 1780. |
| Adams, — | Captain. | " | | Gregg's History of Old Cheraws, 1780. |
| All, Jacob | | | Col. George Hick's Regiment. | |
| Bacot. Peter | Lieutenant. | Light Infantry Company. | South Carolina State Troops. | Johnson's Traditions of Revolution, 1781. |
| Bacot. Samuel | Captain. | | Marion Brigade. | Gregg's History of Old Cheraws, 1782. |
| Baddeley, John | Colonel. | | Charles Town Militia. | Jour. of Coun. of Safety, 22 Dec., 1775. Moultrie's [Rev., 1778. |
| Baker, John | Brig. General. | | | Gibbes's Doc. His., 1780. |
| Barnwell, John | Captain. | Beaufort Company. | | Garden's Anecdotes, 1781. |
| Barnwell, Robert | " | | | Moultrie's Revolution, 1779. |
| Barry, John | " | | | Johnson's Traditions of Revolution, 1780. |
| Barton, — | Major. | Wounded Quinby Bridge, 1782. | Col. William Harden's Command. | Gibbes's Documentary History, 1781. |
| Baxter, — | Lieutenant. | | | Moultrie's Revolution. 1781. |
| Beal, — | Captain. | | | Gibbes's Documentary History, 1781. |
| Beaty, — | " | | | Lossing's Field Book of Revolution, 1780. |
| Bennett, — | Lieutenant. | Wounded near Nelson's Ferry. | Marion Brigade. | Gibbes's Doc. His., 1781. [His., 1780. |
| Benson, — | Colonel. | | Charles Town Militia. | Lossing's Field Book of Rev., 1781. Gibbes's Doc. |
| Bentham, James | Captain. | | Marion Brigade. | Journal of Council of Safety. 22 Dec., 1775. |
| Benton, Sam | " | Expedition under Major Williamson. Prisoner at St. Augustine. | | Gibbes's Documentary History, 1781. |
| Berand, Matthew | " | | | 19 Nov., 1775. |
| Beresford. — | " | | Aide to Gen. William Moultrie. | Johnson's Traditions of Revolution, 1780. |
| Black, — | Major. | St. David's Parish. | Marion Brigade. | Gibbes's Documentary History, 1781. |
| Bleakney, John | Captain. | | | Journal of Council of Safety, 30 November, 1775. |
| Bleauford, — | " | | | Gibbes's Documentary History, 1781. |
| Bocquet, — | | | | " |
| Boroneau, — | Lieutenant. | Wounded Savannah, 9 October, 1779. | Marion Brigade. | Ramsay's Revolution, 1779. |
| Boroneau, — | | " Eutaw, 8 September, 1781. | | 1781. |
| Boon, — | Captain. | | | Gibbes's Documentary History, 1780. |
| Bossard, — | | Battalion of Artillery. | Charles Town Militia. | Garden's Anecdotes, 1780. |
| Bonnetheau, Peter | Lieutenant. | | | Ramsay's Revolution, 1780. |
| Bowman, — | Lieutenant. | Company of Catawba Indians Dragoons. | | Journal of Council of Safety, 14 Jan., 1776. |
| Boykin, Samuel | " | | | Johnson's Tradition of Revolution, 1780. |
| Boykin, T | Colonel. | | | Lossing's Field Book of Revolution, 1781. |
| Brandon, — | | Capt. Port's Co. Vols. St. David's Parish. | | Journal of Council of Safety, 30 Nov., 1775. |
| Bratton, William | Lieutenant. | Company of Volunteers. | | " 21 Feb., 1776. |
| Britton, Daniel | " | Light Infantry Company. | Charles Town Militia. | Johnson's Traditions of Revolution, 1781. |
| Britton, Henry | Captain. | | | Gibbes's Documentary History, 1781. |
| Brown, Archibald | " | | | Moultrie's Revolution, 1779. Ramsay's Revolution. |
| Brown, — | Lieutenant. | Wounded Stono, 1779. | Col. William Harden's Command. | Johnson's Traditions Revolution, 1781. |
| Brown, — | Captain. | | | |
| Brown, Tarleton | | | | |

| Name | Rank | Company / Notes | Regiment / Brigade | Reference |
|---|---|---|---|---|
| Buckholdt, Abraham | Major. | | Craven County Regiment. | Col. Isaac Hayne's Register, 1779. |
| Buckholdt, Peter | Captain. | | Granville County Regiment. | Gregg's History of Old Cheraws, 1775. |
| Bull, Stephen | Colonel. | | | Capt. Lining's Order Book, 1776. |
| Bull, — | Captain. | | | Journal of Council of Safety, 6 Dec. 1775. |
| Burton, Sam | Lieutenant. | Capt. Port's Co. Vols. St. David's Parish. | | 25 Jan., 1776. |
| Butler, James | Captain. | | | 30 Nov., 1775. |
| Butler, John | " | | | Johnson's Traditions of Revolution, 1776. |
| Butler, Pierce | Major. | | Col. Benton's Reg't, Marion Brigade. | Gregg's History of Old Cheraws, 1781. |
| Butler, William | Captain, Colonel. | | | Johnson's Traditions of Revolution, 1780. |
| Butler, William | Lieutenant. | | | Gibbes's Documentary history, 1781. |
| Butler, — | Major. | | | Johnson's Traditions of Revolution, 1780. |
| Burnett, Jacob | Lieutenant. | | | Moultrie's Revolution, 1778. |
| Basquin, William | | Col. Maham's Reg't Light Dragoons. | | 1782. |
| Bryan, John | Cornet. | " | | " |
| Barnett, William | Adjutant. | " | | " |
| Bachelor, Garner | Captain. | | | " |
| Benton, — | Lieutenant. | | | 1781. |
| Baxter, — | | | | |
| Cannon, Daniel | Captain. | Wounded Quinby Bridge. Cannon's Volunteers. | Charles Town Militia. | Journal of Council of Safety, 1 Dec., 1775. |
| Cantey, — | Lieutenant. | | | 9 " |
| Capers, William | Captain. | Volunteer Company, Beaufort. [Rovers. | Marion Brigade. | Johnson's Traditions of Revolution, 1783. |
| Cater, Thomas | Lieutenant. | | | Journal of Council of Safety, 26 Feb. 1776. |
| Clark, — | Captain. | Capt. John Allen's Foot Rangers, or Pon Pon Company. | | Gibbes's Documentary History, 1781. |
| Clegg, — | Lieutenant. | Capt. John Allen's Foot Rangers, or [Rovers. | | Journal of Council of Safety, 11 Feb., 1776. |
| Clefford, Charles | " | | | 30 Jan., " |
| Coachman, James | Captain. | Ordnance Storekeeper. | Colleton County Regiment. | 16 Dec., 1775. |
| Coachman, — | " | | | 15 " " |
| Cochran, Robert | " | Expedition under Major Williamson. | | 2 " " |
| Colson, Jacob | Adjutant. | | Col. Benton's Reg't, Marion Brigade. | Gibbes's Documentary History, 19 Nov. 1775. |
| Conn, Thomas | Captain. | | | Gregg's History of Old Cheraws, 1781. |
| Conyers, Daniel | Lieutenant. | Round O Volunteers. | Colleton County Regiment. | Gibbes's Documentary History, 1781. |
| Conyers, Daniel | Major. | | Marion Brigade. | Wallace's History of Williamsburg Church, 1780. |
| Cook, Wilson (with- [drawn]) | Lieutenant. | Capt. William Butler's Company. | | Journal of Council of Safety, 11 Jan., 1776. |
| Cooper, S [drawn] | Captain. | | | Gibbes's Documentary History, 1781. |
| Corley, John | " | | | Johnson's Traditions of Revolution, 1780. |
| Couturier, John | " | Wounded Eutaw, 8 September, 1781. | South Carolina State Troops. | Gregg's History of Old Cheraws. |
| Cowan, — | Major. | | | Gibbes's Documentary History, 1781. |
| Cranghead, — | Lieutenant. | Killed Fort Motte, 1781. | | Journal of Council of Safety, 28 Dec., 1775. |
| Crawford, Robert | | | | Lossing's Field Book of Revolution, 1780. |
| Crawford, — | | | | Johnson's Traditions of Revolution, 1780. |
| Cruger, — | | | | Lossing's Field Book of Revolution, 1780. |
| Culpeper, — | | Wounded at Eutaw, 8 September, 1781 | South Carolina State troops. | 1781. |
| Cunningham, Arthur | | Capt Edward Plowden's Company. | | Gibbes's Documentary History, 1781. |
| Campbell, Robert (mis) | | Col. Maham's Reg't Light Dragoons, | Col. Richardson's Regiment. | Journal of Council of Safety, 18 Jan., 1776. 1782. |
| Capers, William | Captain. | | | 1778. |
| Dabbs, Joseph | Ensign. | St. David's Parish. | Col. G. G. Powell's Regiment. | Gregg's History of Old Cheraws. |
| Daniel, Aaron | Captain. | | | Journal of Council of Safety, 21 Feb., 1776. |
| Danell, Joseph | | | | 13 Jan., " |

| Name | Rank | Notes | Command | Reference |
|---|---|---|---|---|
| Danell, —— | Captain. | | | Moultrie's Revolution, 1778. |
| David, John | Lieutenant. | | | Gregg's History of Old Cheraws, 1780. |
| Davis, David | " | Volunteer Company, St. David's Parish. | Marion Brigade. | Journal of Council of Safety, 21 Feb., 1776. |
| Davis, Henry | " | " | Col. G. G. Powell's Regiment. | " " |
| Davis, Ransom | Captain. | | " | |
| Davis, William | " | Volunteer Company, St. David's Parish. | Marion Brigade. | Gibbes's Documentary History, 1781. |
| Deal, —— | Lieutenant. | Wounded Stono, 1779. | Col. G. G. Powell's Regiment. | Journal of Council of Safety, 21 Feb., 1776. |
| DeSaussure, Daniel | Captain. | Volunteer Company, Beaufort. | | Ramsay's Revolution, 1779. |
| Dewitt, Charles | Lieutenant. | | | Harper's Memoir, 1778. |
| Dillard, —— | Captain. | | Marion Brigade. | Gregg's History of Old Cheraws, 1781. |
| Doharty, James | " | Killed near Beaufort. | | Johnson's Traditions of Revolution, 1781. |
| Dozier, John | " | Volunteer Company, St. David's Parish. | Col. G. G. Powell's Regiment. | Moultrie's Revolution, 1778. |
| Dubois, —— | " | | Marion Brigade. | Journal of Council of Safety, 21 Feb, 1776. |
| Dubose, Andrew | " | | " | Moultrie's Revolution, 1778. |
| Dubose, Elias | " | | " | Gregg's History of Old Cheraws, 1781. |
| Dupont, —— | Lieutenant. | | | " |
| Durham, Chamel | " | German Fusileers. | Charles Town Militia. | Siegling's Centennial Oration, 1776. |
| Davier, B. | | | | Ederington's Recollections, 1780. |
| Drayton, Thomas | Captain. | | | Ederington's Recollections, 1780. |
| Ederington, Francis | Lieutenant. | | Marion Brigade. | Gregg's History of Old Cheraws, 1781. |
| Ellerbee, Thomas | Cadet. | | | Journal of Council of Safety, 28 Dec., 1775. |
| Elliott, Benjamin | Quartermaster. | | | " 17 " " |
| Elliott, Samuel | Captain. | | Colleton County Regiment. | Moultrie's Revolution, 1778. |
| Ellison, —— | Lieutenant Colonel. | | | Gibbes's Documentary History. 1781. |
| Erskine, —— | Major. | | | Wallace's His. of W^msb'g Ch. Gibbes's Doc. His. |
| Ervin, John | Lieutenant. | Wounded Eutaw, 8 September, 1781. | South Carolina State Troops. | Journal of Council of Safety. 18 Jan., 1776. |
| Erwin, James | Colonel. | | Col. Rothmaler's Regiment. | " 30 Nov., 1775. |
| Eubank, John | Ensigr. | | | " 21 Feb., 1776. |
| Evans, Charles | Captain. | Volunteer Company, St. David's Parish. | Col. G. G. Powell's Regiment. | Gregg's History of Old Cheraws, 1781. |
| Evans, Enoch | Lieutenant. | Capt. Irby's Company, | Col. Hick's Reg't, Marion Brigade. | " 1780. |
| Evans, George | " | " | | |
| Elliott, Thomas | " | | | 1781. |
| Edwards, John | A. D. C, Gen. Marion. | | | |
| Elliott, —— | Judge Advocate. | | | Garden's Anecdotes, |
| Falls, —— | Captain. | Killed Ransom's Mills. | | Journal of Council of Safety, 14 Jan., 1776. |
| Farr, Thomas, Jr. | " | Commissary General and Paymaster. | | Johnson's Traditions of Revolution, 1780. |
| Farrow, Thomas | Captain. | | | Journal of Council of Safety, 1 Dec., 1775. |
| Fenwicke, Thomas | Lieutenant. | Charles Town Rangers. | Craven County Regiment. | Capt. Lining's Order Book, 1776. |
| Fitzgerald, John | " | Capt. Archibald McDaniel's Company. | Colleton County Regiment. | Journal of Council of Safety, 16 Dec., 1775. |
| Ford, George | Major. | | | Lossing's Field Book of Revolution, 1780. |
| Fletcher, —— | Lieutenant. | St. David's Parish. | Col. G. G. Powell's Regiment. | Journal of Council of Safety, 21 Feb., 1776. |
| Ford, James | Lieutenant. | Capt. Benjamin Marion's Company. | Berkeley County, Regiment. | Capt. Lining's Order Book, 1776. |
| Fogartie, James | " | Capt. Wigfall's Company. | | Journal of Council of Safety, 1 Dec., 1775. |
| Fogartie, Joseph | Captain. | | | Garden's Anecdotes. |
| Freer, Charles | Lieutenant. | Capt. Lining's Company. | | Journal of Council of Safety, 1 Dec., 1775. |
| Fuller, Nathaniel | Captain. | Indian Field Company. | Berkeley County Regiment. | " " |
| Fullerton, John | " | Capt. Postell's Company. | | " 18 Jan., 1776. |
| Futhy, William | Lieutenant. | Wounded Quinby Bridge, 1781. | | |
| Fox, —— | " | St. David's Parish. | | Journal of Council of Safety, 21 Feb., 1776. |
| Galliway, James | | | | |

Appendix to Year Book.

| Name | Rank | Notes | Command | References |
|---|---|---|---|---|
| Gamble, John | Major. | Williamsburg County. | Marion Brigade. | Wallace's History of Williamsburg Church, 1780. |
| Garder, John | Lieutenant. | Capt. Wigfall's Company. | Berkeley County Regiment. | Journal of Council of Safety, 1 Dec., 1775. |
| Garden, — | Colonel. | | Marion Brigade. | Moultrie's Revolution, 1778. |
| Gay, — | Lieutenant. | | " | Gregg's History of Old Cheraws, 1781. |
| Gee — | Captain. | Wounded Eutaw, 8 Sept., 1781. | | Ramsay's Revolution, 1781. |
| Gibbes, William Hasell | Capt., Lieutenant. | Battalion Artillery. | Charles Town Militia. | Garden's Anecdotes, 1776. |
| Gillespie, — | Captain. | Wounded Eutaw, 8 Sept., 1781. | South Carolina State Troops. | Gibbes's Documentary History, 1781. |
| Gillon, Alexander | Captain. | German Fusileers. | | Gregg's History of Old Cheraws. |
| Glover, Joseph | Colonel. | | Charles Town Militia. | Siegling's Centennial Oration, 1776. |
| Goodman, Joseph | Quartermaster. | | Colleton County Regiment. | Journal of Council of Safety, 9 Dec., 1776. |
| Godbolt, James | Lieutenant. | Capt. Peter Buckholt's Company. | | Resolutions of General Assembly. |
| Gordon, Roger | " | | Craven County Regiment. | Capt. Linng's Order Book, 1776. |
| Gough, John | Captain. | Capt. James Skirving's Company. | Marion Brigade. | Wallace's History of Williamsburg Church. 1781. |
| Gough, Richard | " | | Berkeley County Regiment. | Capt Lining's Order Book, 1776. |
| Gough, — | Lieutenant. | Volunteer Company, St. David's Parish. | Marion Brigade. | Garden's Anecdotes. |
| Graves, Joseph | Captain. | Britton's Neck. | Col. G. G. Powell's Regiment. | Gibbes's Documentary History, 1781. |
| Gregg, James | " | Battalion of Artillery. | Col. Ervin's Regiment. | Journal of Council of Safety, 21 Feb., 1776. |
| Griffith, Joseph | Major. | | | Gregg's History of Old Cheraws, 1780. |
| Grimball, Thomas | Captain. | Capt. Postell's Company. | Charles Town Militia. | |
| Grahan — | Lieutenant. | | | Jour. of Coun. of Safety. 26 Feb., 1776. Moultrie's |
| Grist — | Colonel. | | | 1781. [Rev., 1718. |
| Greer, — | Major. | | | |
| Grisset, — | | | | |
| Green, I. | | | | |
| Hall, George Abbott | Captain. | Expedition under Major Williamson. | Artillery. | Garden's Anecdotes. |
| Hamilton, Andrew | " | | | Jour. Coun. Safety, 23 Dec., '75, Gibbes's Doc. His. |
| Hamilton, Joseph | " | | | Gibbes's Locumentary History, 19 Nov., 1775. |
| Hammond, George | " | | | Johnson's Traditions of the Revolution. |
| Hammond, John | | | | Jour, of Coun. of Safety. 24 Jan., 1776. |
| Hammond, LeRoy | Colonel. | | | 23 Jan., '76. Gibbes's Doc. |
| Hammond, Samuel | " | | | Lossing's Field Book, of Rev., 1790. [His. 1781. |
| Hammond, — | Lieutenant. | Wounded Eutaw, 8 September, 1781. | State Troops, South Carolina. | Gibbes's Documentary History, 1781. |
| Hampton, Edward | Captain. | Expedition under Major Williamson. | " | Johnson's Traditions of Revolution. |
| Hampton, Henry | " | Artillery Company, Beaufort. | | " |
| Harden, William | Colonel. | Col. William Harden's Regiment. | | Jour. of Coun. of Safety, 26 Feb, '76, Gibbes's Doc. |
| Harden, — | Ensign. | St. David's Parish. | | Gibbes's Doc. His., 1781, [His., 1781. |
| Hardyman, Joseph | Captain. | | | Journal of Council of Safety, 21 Feb., 1776. |
| Hardyman, Thomas | Colonel. | | | " |
| Harleston, John | Colonel. | | | Moultrie's Revolution, 1778. |
| Hargrave, Robert | Captain. | | | Journal of Council of Safety, 9 Jan., 1776. |
| Hargrave, Samuel | Captain. | | | " 21 Feb. " |
| Harlow, Benjamin | Lieutenant. | St. David's Parish. | | Gregg's History of Old Cheraws, 1780. |
| Harrington, Wm. Henry | Colonel. | Pee Dee. | | Moultrie's Revolution, 1778. |
| Harris — | Lieutenant. | | | O'Neall's Annals of Newberry. |
| Harriss, Micajah | Major. | | | Gibbes's Documentary History, 1781. |
| Hart, Derril | Captain. | | | Mills's Statistics South Carolina. |
| Harvey, Thomas | Colonel. | Col. Richard Hampton's Regiment. | | Lossing's Field Book of Revolution, 1780. |
| Hawthorne, — | " | | | Moultrie's Revolution, 1781. |
| Hayes, — | | | | |

| Name | Rank | Company / Notes | Regiment / Brigade | Reference |
|---|---|---|---|---|
| Hayne, Isaac | Colonel. | Pon Pon Company. | | Jour. of Coun. of Safety, 15 Jan., '76. Gibbes's Doc. His., 1781. [His., 1781. |
| Hendricks, William | Captain. | | Marion Brigade. | Gregg's His, Old Cheraws, 1782. |
| Heron, — | " | | Craven County Regiment. | Capt. Lining's Order Book, 1776. |
| Heyward, Daniel, Jr. | Lieutenant. | Capt. Peter Buckholt's Company. | | Journal of Council of Sa ety, 26 Feb., 1776. |
| Heyward, John | Captain. | Volunteer Company, Beaufort. | | " |
| Heyward, Thomas, Jr. | Ensign. | " | | |
| Hicks, George | Captain. | Battalion of Artillery. | Charles Town Militia. | Moultrie's Revolution, 1776. [Old Cheraws, 1781. |
| Hill, William | Major. Colonel. | | | Jour. Coun. of Safety, 18 Feb., '76. 'regg's His. |
| Hinds, — | Colonel. | | | Lossing's Field Book of Revolution, 1780. |
| Hird, John | Lieutenant. | | | Gregg's History of Old Cheraw, 1780. |
| Hogg, — | " | Round O Company. | | Moultrie's Revolution, 1778. |
| Holding, Matthew | Major. | | | Journal of Council of Safety, 21 Feb., 1776. |
| Hollis, Moses | Lieutenant. | Capt. Robert Lide's Company. | Col. G. G. Powell's Regiment. | Gregg's History of Old Cheraws, 1783. |
| Holmes, — | " | | Col. Benson's Regiment. | Ramsay's Revoluti n, 1781. |
| Horry, Hugh | Colonel. | Killed Eutaw, 8 September, 1781. | Marion Brigade. | Lossing's Field Book of Revolution, 1781. |
| Huger, John | Captain. | Charles Town Volunteers. | | Gibbes's Documentary History, 1776. |
| Huggins, Benjamin | Lieut. and Adjutant. | | | Gibbes's Documentary History, 1781. |
| Huggins, John | Lieutenant. | Artillery Company, Beaufort. | Col. Hugh Giles's Regiment. | Gregg's History of Old Cheraws, 1779. |
| Hughes, Thomas | Colonel. | | Col. Peter Horry's Reg't Dragoons | Journal of Council of Safety, 21 Nov., 1775. |
| Hughes, — | Captain. | Expedition under Major Williamson. | | Johnson's Traditions of Revolution, 1780. |
| Hunter, David | " | | | Gibbes's Documentary History, 19 Nov, 1775. |
| Hyrne, Henry | Lieutenant. | | | Journal of Council of Safety, 23 Dec., 1775. |
| Huss, — | Captain. | | | Johnson's Traditions of Revolution, 1780. |
| Inman, S. | " | Killed Musgrove Mills. | Col. George Hick's Regiment. | Gregg's History of Old Cheraws, 1780. |
| Irby, Edmund | Colonel. | | | Lossing's Field Book of Revolution, 1780. |
| Irvine, — | " | | Marion Brigade. | Moultrie's Revolution, 1781. |
| Irwin, — | Lieutenant. | | Col. Geo. Hick's Reg't, Marion Brig. | Gregg's History of Old Cheraws, 1782. |
| Jackson, John | Captain. | | Col. Kolb's " " | 1780. |
| Jackson, Stephen | Lieutenant. | | | 1782. |
| James, Alexander | Lieutenant. | | | |
| James, John [Lake. | Captain. | | | Wallace's History of Williamsburg Church, 1776, 1780. |
| James, John, Jr., of the | " | | | |
| Jamieson, — | Major. | | | Gibbes's Documentary History, 1779. |
| Jeneret, Jacob | Captain. | Edisto Island Volunteer Company. | Colleton County Regiment. | Captain Lining's Order Book, 1776. |
| Jenkins, Benjamin | Ensign. | St. Helena Island Volunteers. | | Journal of Council of Safety, 11 Feb, 1776. |
| Jenkins, John | Captain. | Edisto Island Volunteers. | | 7 Dec, 1775. |
| Jen ins, Joseph | | | Col. Rothmaler's Regiment. | 9 Jan, 1776. |
| Jenkins, Joseph | Lieutenant. | | Colleton County Regiment. | 11 Feb, 1776. |
| Jenkins, Reuben | " | | Col. Kolb's Reg't, Marion Brigade. | Gregg's History of Old Cheraws, 1782. |
| Jenkins, Thomas | Captain. | | Col. Rothmaler's Regiment. | Journal of Council of Safety, 9 Jan., 1776. |
| Jinkins, James | Lieutenant. | | Col. Benton's Reg't, Marion Brigade. | Gregg's History of Old Cheraws, 1782. |
| Johnson, Richard | Captain. | Col. Willham Harden's Command. | Col.G.G. Powell's Reg't, Marion Brig | Johnson's Tra. Rev., '80. [Book Rev. 1781. |
| Johnson, William | Ensign. | | | Jour. Coun. Safety 21 Feb., 1776. Lossing's Field |
| Joiner, John | Captain. | | | Journal of Council of Safety, 27 Jan., 1776. |
| Jolley, — | Major. | | | Johnson's Traditions of Revolution, 1780. |
| Jones, Adam C. | " | | | Gibbes's Documentary History, 19 Nov., 1775. |
| Jones, Edward | Captain. | Artillery Company, Beaufort. | Marion Brigade. | Gregg's History of Old Cheraws, 1780. |
| Jordon, Jonathan | Lieutenant. | Expedition under Major Williamson. | Col. Rothmaler's Regiment. | Journal of Council of Safety, 2 Dec., 1775. |
| Kalteisen, Michael | Captain. | Wagon Master General. | | 23 Dec., 1775. |
| Karwon, Thomas | Ensign. | Capt. Benjamin Marion's Company. | Col. Singleton's Regiment. | |

71

| Name | Rank | | Service | Regiment / Command | References |
|---|---|---|---|---|---|
| Kee, Thomas | Captain. | | Capt. Daniel Linder's Company. | Berkeley County Regiment. | Johnson's Traditions of Revolution, 1781. |
| Kelly, Daniel | Lieutenant. | | | | Captain Lining's Order Book, 1776. |
| Kelly, James | " | | | | O'Neall's Annals of Newberry. |
| Kershaw, Joseph | Colonel. | | | | Moultrie's Revolution, 1778. |
| Kimbrough, John | Captain. | | Com'y of Volunteers, St. David's Parish Cavalry. | Col. G. G. Powell's Regiment. | Journal of Council of Safety, 30 Nov., 1775. |
| Kincaid, James | " | | | | Mill's Statistics South Carolina. |
| King, George | " | | | Col. G. G. Powell's Regiment. | Journal of Council of Safety, 21 Feb, 1776. |
| Kirkbun, — | | | | | Gibbes's Documentary History, 1781. |
| Knight, James, Sr. | Lieutenant. | | Com'y of Volunteers, St. David's Parish Round O Volunteers. | Col. G. G. Powell's Regiment. Colleton County Regiment. | Journal of Council of Safety, 30 Nov, 1775. |
| Koger, Jos. (withdrawn) | | Colonel. | | | Jour. Coun. Safety, 21 Feb. 1776. Gibbes' Doc. 11 Jan, 1776 [His. 1781 |
| Kobb, Abel | Captain. | | Killed Savannah, 9 October, 1779. | German Fusileers, Charles Town Mil. Col. Postell's Regiment. | Siegling's Cent. Oration, 1779. 1781. |
| Kinnill, Joseph | Lieutenant. | | | | |
| Kimbell, Frederick | Lieut. Colonel. | | King's Mountain. | | Lossing's Field Book of Revolution, 1780, |
| Lacy, Edward | Colonel. | | Capt. Benjamin Marion's Company. | | Captain Lining's Order Book, 1776. |
| Ladson, Abraham | Lieutenant. | | John's Island Company. | Colleton County Regiment. | Journal of Council of Safety, 2 December, 1775. |
| Ladson, Thomas | Captain. | | | Marion Brigade. | Gibbes's Documentary History, 1781 |
| Ladson, — | Major, | | | | Garden's Anecdotes. |
| Land, — | Captain. | | Expedition under Major Williamson. | | Gibbes's Documentary History, 19 November, 1775. |
| Langdon, Thomas | " | | Prisoner St. Augustine. | Charles Town Militia. | Johnson's Traditions of Revolution, 1780. |
| Lee, William | Lieutenant. | | Light Infantry Company. | " | Journal of Council of Safety, 31 Jan, 1776. " |
| Legare, Benjamin | Captain. | | | Marion Brigade. | |
| Legare, Samuel | " | | | " | Gibbes's Documentary History, 1781. |
| Lenud, — | " | | | | |
| Lesesne, — | " | | | | |
| Liddle, Moses | | Major. | St. David's Parish. | Col. G. G. Powell's Regiment, | Johnson's Traditions of Revolution, 1780. |
| Lide, Thomas | " | | | Craven County Reg't, Marion Brig. | Journal of Council of Safety, 21 Feb, 1776. |
| Lide, Robert | " | | | Berkeley County Regiment. | Capt Lining's Order Book, 1776. Gregg's His. Old '76. [Cheraws, '82 |
| Linder, Daniel | " | | | | |
| Lining, — | Colonel. | | 96 District. | | Journal of Council of Safety, 1 December, 1775. |
| Lindsey, John | " | | | | O'Neall's Annals of Newberry. |
| Lisle, — | Lieutenant. | | | | Moultrie's Revolution, 1778. |
| Lethgow, R. | Captain. | | German Fusileers. | Charles Town Militia. | Mill's Statistics South Carolina. |
| Livingston, William | Lieutenant. | | Capt. James Skirving's Company. | Berkeley County Regiment. | Siegling's Centennial Oration, 1784. |
| Lloyd, Martin | Captain. | | Expedition under Major Williamson. | | Captain Lining's Order Book, 1776. |
| Logan, Francis | Lieutenant. | | | | Gibbes's Documentary History, 19 November, 1775. |
| Logan, George | Captain. | | | | Mill's Statistics South Carolina. |
| Love, — | " | | | | |
| Lush, — | Adjutant. | | | | Johnson's Traditions of Revolution, 1780. |
| Lushington, Richard | Lieut. Colonel, | Captain. | Killed Eutaw, 8 September, 1781. | South Carolina State Troops. Charles Town Militia. | Gibbes's Doc. His., 1781. [Rev. 1784 |
| Lyles, Arramans | " | | | | Jour. Coun. Safety, 23 Dec, 1775. Johnson's Tra. |
| Lyles, James | Captain. | | | | Edrington's Recollections. |
| Lyles, John | Lieutenant. | | | | O'Neall's Annals of Newberry. |
| Lyons, Guthridge | " | | | Col. Benton's Reg't, Marion Brigade Sumter Brigade. | Gregg's History o: Old Cheraws, 1781. |
| Lyons, — | Captain. | | | | Gibbes's Documentary History, 1781. |
| Lynes, William | " | | | | 1781 |
| Lewis, W., | | | | | |
| Macauly, John | | Major. | | | Wallace's History of Williamsburg Church, 1780. |
| Marion, Benjamin | Captain. | | Wounded Eutaw, 8 September, 1781. | Berkeley County Regiment. | Jour. Coun of Safety, 22 Dec, '75. Capt Lining's |
| Martin, N. | " | | Artillery, killed siege of Augusta. | South Carolina State Troops. | Gibbes's Doc. His., '81. [Order Book, 21 April, '76 |
| Martin, William | " | | | | Lossing's Field Book of Revolution, 1781. |

| Name | Rank | Company / Note | Regiment | Reference |
|---|---|---|---|---|
| Mathewes, Benjamin | Lieutenant, | John's Island Company | Colleton County Regiment. | Journal of Council of Safety, 2 December, 1775. |
| Mathewes, John Raven | " | " | " | Johnson's Traditions of Revolution, 1779. |
| Maxwell, — | Major. | | | Garden's Anecdotes. |
| Maybank, Joseph | Lieutenant, | | Berkeley County Regiment. | Journal of Council of Safety, 30 January, 1776. |
| Mazyck, Stephen | " | Captain Ravenel's Company. | " | " 1 December, 1775 |
| Megee, or Magee, Elisha | " | St. David's Parish. | Col. G. G. Powell's Regiment. | " 21 February, 1770 |
| Middleton, Thomas, Jr | Lieut. Colonel. | Captain Smith's Company. | Berkeley County Regiment. | " 1 December, 1775. |
| Mikell, John | Lieutenant. | Wounded Eutaw, 1 September 1781. | South Carolina State Troops. | Gibbes's Documentary History, 1781. |
| Miller, John D | " | | Marion Brigade. | Gregg's History of Old Cheraws, 1781. |
| Miller, Stephen | Lieut. Colonel. | Battalion of Artillery. | Charles Town Militia. | Garden's Anecdotes 1781 |
| Mitchell, — | Captain. | | Berkeley County Regiment. | Journal of Council of Safety, 30 January, 1776. |
| Moffit, — | | | Marion Brigade. | Gibbes's Documentary History, 1789. |
| Morgan, William | Lieutenant, | Battalion of Artillery. | Charles Town Militia. | Lossing's Field Book of Revolution, 1780. |
| Moody, Charles | " | St. David's Parish. | Co.. G. G. Powell's Regim't. | Garden's Anecdotes. |
| Mone, — | | | South Carolina State Troops. | Journal of Council of Safety, 21 February, 1776. |
| Mouzon, Henry | Captain. | Kingstree Company. | | Gibbes's Documentary History, 1781. |
| Munnerlyn, James | Lieutenant. | | Marion Brigade. | Wallace's History of Williamsburg Church, 1780. |
| Murphy Maurice | Captain. | | Col. G. G. Powell's Reg't, Marion [Brig. | Gregg's History of Old Cheraws, 1781. |
| Murrell, — | Lieut. Colonel. | | Col. Hicks's Reg't, | Journal of Council of Safety, 21 Feb., 1776. |
| May, Benjamin | Captain. | | | Gregg's History of Old Cheraws, 1781. |
| Moultrie, Alexander | " | Christ Church Company. | | Gibbes's Documentary History, 1781. |
| Martin, John | " | | | |
| Milton, — | Lieutenant. | Musketeers. | Charles Town Militia. | Journal of Council of Safety, January 22, 1776. |
| Maurice, — | Captain. | Killed Strawberry. | Col. Richardson's Regiment. | 1778. |
| Muller, Albert A. | Lieutenant | | | 1781. |
| McCall, James | Brigade Major. | Expedition under Major Williamson. [Horse. | Marion Brigade. | Gibbes's Documentary History, 19 November, 1775. |
| McCall, John | Captain. | Ramsay says "Col McCall of the Li. | South Carolina State Troops. | Gregg's History of Old Cheraws, 1781. |
| McCall, Hugh | Lieutenant, | Killed Hanging Rock, —, 1780. | | Carrington's Bat. Rev., '80, Johnson's Tra. Rev., '80. |
| McClure, John | Major. Colonel. | | | Lossing's Field Book of Revolution, 1780. |
| McClure, — | Captain. | | | |
| McColtrey, William | Ensign. | Expeditton under Major Williamson. | Marion Brigade. | Wallace's History of Williamsburg Church, 1780. |
| McCreery, Robert | Captain. | | | Gibbes's Documentary History, 19 November, 1775. |
| McCullough George | " | | | Gregg's History of Old Cheraws, 1782. |
| McDaniel, Archibald | " | | Marion Brigade. | Captain Lining's Order Book, 1776. |
| McDonald, — | Lieut. Colonel. | | | Gibbes's Documentary History, 1781. |
| McDowell, — | Major. | | | Carrington's Battle's of Revolution, 1780. |
| McIntosh, Alexander | Captain. | | Col. Benton's Reg't, Marion Brigade. | Johnson's Traditions of Revolution, 1780. |
| McJunkin, Joseph | " | | | Gibbes's Documentary History, 1781. |
| McKoy, — | | Col. William Hardin's Command. | | Lee's Memoirs, 1781. |
| McLachlin, — | Lieut. Colonel. | | Marion Brigade. | Johnson's Traditions of Revolution, 1780. |
| McLidle, — | Captain. | Company of Volunt'rs, St David's Parish. | Charles Town Militia. | Journal of Council of Safety, 3 November, 1775. |
| McManess, Thomas | Lientenant, | | | Gregg's History of Old Cheraws, 1782. |
| McMuldrough, — | | The Rangers. | Marion Brigade. | Journal of Council of Safety, 1 December, 1775. |
| McQueen, John | Captain | St. David's Parish. | Col. G. G. Powell's Regiment. | " 21 February, 1776. |
| McRae, Duncan | Lieutenant, | | | |
| McCauley, — | Captain. | | | 1781. |
| McCleeland William | | | | |
| Neavill, Isaac | Lieutenant. | St. David's Parish. | Col. G. G. Powell's Regiment. | Journal of Council of Safety, 21 Feb, 1776. |

| Name | Rank | Service / Remarks | Command | Authority |
|---|---|---|---|---|
| Neil, Thomas | Colonel. | | | Journal of Council of Safety, 7 Nov., 1775, 1780. |
| Nelson, John! | Captain. | Killed Rocky Mount, —, 1780. | | Wallace's History of Williamsburg Church. |
| Neufville, Edward | Lieutenant. | Battalion of Artillery. | Charles Town Militia. | Garden's Anecdotes. |
| Newman, — | Captain. | | | Moultrie's Revolution, 1778. |
| Nichols,,, Henry | Ensign. | Stono Company. | Colleton County Regiment. | Journal of Council of Safey, 23 Jan., 1776. |
| Nixon, John | Lieut. Colonel. | | | Johnson's Traditions of Revolution, 1780. |
| Noble, Alexander | Captain. | | | Gibbes's Documentary History, 19 Nov., 1775. |
| North, Edward | " | Expedition under Major Williamson. Prisoner at St. Augustine. | Marion Brigade. | Johnson's Traditions of Revolution, 1780. |
| Norwood, John | Captain. | | " | Gregg's History of Old Cheraws, 1782. |
| Odingsell, — | " | | | Gibbes's Documentary History, 1781. |
| O'Neill, — | | | | " 1779. |
| Oswald, William | Lieutenant. | Round O Company. | Colleton County Regiment. | Journal of Council of Safety, 17 Jan', 1776. |
| Olt, Abraham | " | Capt. Daniel Linder's Company. | Berkeley County Regiment. | Captain Lining's Order Book, 1776. |
| Ottersen, Samuel | Captain. | | | Mills's Statistics South Carolina. |
| Parker, — | Lieutenant. | Wounded Savannah, 9 October, 1779. | Marion Brigade. | Ramsay's Revolution, 1779. |
| Parrott, Thomas | Captain. | Of Horse. | " | Gregg's History of Old Ch:raws, 1782. |
| Pasley, Robert | " | | | 1781 |
| Pearson, John | Major | | | Mills's Statistics South Carolina. |
| Fearson, Moses | Captain. | Wounded Eutaw, 8 September, 1781. | Col. Benton's Reg't Marion Brigade. | Gregg's History of Old Cheraws, 1781. |
| Pegee, or Pegue, Claudi-[us | " | St. David's Parish. | | Ramsay's Revolution, 1781 |
| Perkins, David | Ensign. | | Col. G. G. Powell's Regiment. | Journal of Council of Safety, 21 Feb., 1776. |
| Pickens, Andrew | Brig. General. | Killed Siege of Ninety-Six, —, 1781. | | Lossing's Field Book of Revolution, 1780. |
| Pickens, Joseph | Captain. | | | National Portrait Gallery, 1781. |
| Pinckney, — | " | | | Gibbes's Documentary History, 1781. |
| Pledger, John | Lieutenant. | Militia Rangers, Volunteers. | Col. Hicks's Reg't Marion Brigade. | Gregg's History of Old Cheraws, 1781. |
| Plowder, Edward | Captain. | Killed Eutaw, 8 September, 1781. | Col. Rothmaler's Regiment. | Journal of Council of Safety, 18 Jan., 1776. |
| Polk, Ezekiel | " Colonel. | | 10th Regiment, new acquisition. | Jour, Ccun Safety, 4 Nov., '75. Gibbes's Doc. Hist. [1781. |
| Polk, William | Lieutenant. | | " | 4 Nov. 1775. |
| Postell, James | " Major. Colonel. | | | Lossing's Field Book Rev., 1781. Moultrie's Rev. |
| Postell, John | Captain. | | | 1781. |
| Powell, Gabriel G | Colonel. | | | |
| Prince. — | Lieutenant | Wounded Stono, —, 1779. | Marion Brigade. | Journal of Council of Safety, 16 Feb., 1776. |
| Prioleau, Hext | " | Light Infantry Company. | | Ramsay's Revolution, 1779. |
| Prior, Luke | Captain. | Volunteer Company, St. David's Parish. | Charles Town Militia. | Journal of Council of Safety, 31 Jan., 1776. |
| Purvis, John | Lieut. Colonel. | | Col. G. G. Powell's Regiment. | 21 Feb., 1776. |
| Parker, John | Lieutenant. | | Col. Hicks's Reg't, Marion Brigade. | Gregg's History of Old Cheraws, 1780. |
| Price, — | | | | 1781. |
| Post, John | Captain. | | | " |
| Perry, — | Lieutenant. | Killed Quinby Bridge. | | Journal of Council of Safety, 10 December, 1775. |
| Quetch, Andrew | Captain. | Wando Company. | Berkeley County Regiment, | 1 December, 1775. |
| Ravenel, — | " | | | Johnson's Traditions of Revolution, 1780. |
| Read, Jacob | " | P-isoner at St. Augustine. | | Captain Lining's Order Book, 1876. |
| Redmund, John | " | | | Gibbes's Documentary History, 19 November, 1775. |
| Reed, George | " | Expedition under Major Williamson. | | Journal of Council of Safety, 30 November, 1775. |
| Reynolds, John | Lieutenant. | Volunteer Company, St. David's Parish. | | " |
| Reynolds, Richard | " | Captain Post's Company. | | |
| Rhodes. — | | | | Garden's Anecdotes. [1780, |
| Richardson, Richard | Colonel. General. | | | Jour. Coun. Saety, 2 Dec. '75. Johnson's Tra. Rev. |
| Richardson, Richard, Jr | Captain. Colonel. | | | 26 December, 1775. |
| Richardson, William | Colonel. | | Marion Brigade. | Gisbes's Documentary History, 1781. |

74

| Name | Rank | Notes | Command | References |
|---|---|---|---|---|
| Richardson, George | Lieut. Colonel. | | Charles Town Militia. | Gibbes's Documentary History, 1781. Journal of Council of Safety, 25 February, 1776. " 22 December, 1775. |
| Robinson, George | Captain. | | | |
| Roche, Patrick | Ensign. | | | |
| Rodgers, John | Captain. | Expedition under Major Williamson. | | Gibbes's Documentary History, 19 November, 1775. Johnson's Traditions of Revolution, 1780. |
| Roebuck, Benjamin | Co onel. | | | Journal of Council of Safety, 2 December, 1775. |
| Rothmaler, Job | " | | | Captain Lining's Order Book, 1776. |
| Rowe, Henry | Captain. | St. Mark's Parish. | | Gregg's History of Old Cheraws, 1782. |
| Rushing, John | Lieutenant. | | | Gibbes's Documentary History, 1781. |
| Rutherford, — | Major. | Killed Eutaw, 8 September, 1781. | Discharged 12 April, 1776. | Johnson's Traditions of Revolution, 1776. |
| Rutledge, Edward | Captain. | Battalion of Artillery, 2d Company. | Col. Benton's Reg't, Marion Brigade South Carolina State Troops. | Gibbes's Documentary History, 1781. Johnson's Traditions of Revolution, 1776. |
| Rutledge, Thomas | Adjutant. | | Charles Town Militia. | Journal of Council of Safety, 15 February, 1776. |
| Ryan, James | Captain. | | Granville County Regiment. | Johnson's Traditions of Revolution, 1780. |
| Rouse, A bert | Lieutenant. | | Colonel Richardson's Regiment. | 1777 1781 |
| Rogers, — | | | | |
| St John, Andeon | Ensign. | | | Journal of Council of Safety, 16 December, 1775 |
| Sanders, William | Captain. | | | Jour Coun. Safety, 27 Jan, 1776. Gibbes's Doc |
| Saunders, Nathaniel | Lieutenant. | Pon Pon Company. | Colleton County Regiment. | Gregg's His. Old Cheraws, 1781. [His, 1781. |
| Savage, John | Colonel. | Round O Company. | Col. Benton's Reg't, Marion Brigade | Tournal of Council of Safety, 7 December, 1775. |
| Sawyer, — | Lieutenant. | | | Moultrie's Revolution, 1778, |
| Scott, Joseph | " | | | Wallace's History of Williamsburg Church. |
| Scriven, — | Colonel. | The Rangers. | Charles Town Militia. | Gibbes's Documentary History, 1781. |
| Sharp, James | Lieutenant. | Killed Savannah, 9 October, 1779. | German Fusil's, Charles Town Mil'a | Journal of Council of Safety, 1 Dec, 1775. |
| Sheppherd, — | Captain. | Light Infantry Company. | Charles Town Militia. | Moultrie's Revolution, 1779. |
| Shubrick, Thomas, Jr | Ensign. | Killed Eutaw, 8 September, 1781. | | Journal of Council of Safety, 31 Jan, 1776. |
| Simons, — | Lieutenant. | | Marion Brigade. | Ramsay's Revolution, 1781. |
| Simons, Maurice | Brig. Major. | | | Garden's Anecdotes, 1781 |
| Simpkins, Ar.hur | Colonel. | | | Moultrie's Revolution, 1778. |
| Sinclair, — | Captain. | | | Mills's Statistics South Carolina. |
| Singleton, John | " | | Marion Brigade. | Moultrie's Revolution, 1778 |
| Singleton, Matthew | " | | | Johnson's Traditions of Revolution, 1780. |
| Singleton, — | Colonel. | Expedition under Major Williamson. | Berkeley County Regiment. | Journal of Council of Safety, 28 Dec, 1775 1 Dec, 1775 |
| Singuefield, Francis | Captain. | | | Gibbes's Documentary History, 19 Nov, 1775 Captain Lining's Order Book, 1776. |
| Skirving, James | Colonel. | Expedition under Major Williamson. | Berkeley County Regiment. | Moultrie's Revolution, 1778 |
| Skirving, — | Captain. | | | O'Neall', Annals of Newberry. |
| Sloan, John | " | | Berkeley County Regiment. | Gibbes's Documentary History, 19 Nov, 1775. |
| Smith, Aaron | " | | Col. G. G. Powell's Regiment. | Journal of Council of Sa'ety, 1 Dec, 1775 21 Feb, 1776 1 Dec, 1775 |
| Smith, Benjamin | Lieutenant. | Volunteer Company. St. David's Parish. | | |
| Smith, Samuel | " | St. George Company. | | |
| Smith, Thomas | " | | | |
| Smizer, — | Captain. | | Marion Brigade. Sumter Brigade. | Gibbes's Documentary His, 1781. [His, 1781 |
| Snipes, William Clay | " | Wounded Eutaw, 8 September, 1781. | Marion Brigade. | Jour Coun. Safety, 27 Jan, 1776. Gibbes's Doc 1776. |
| Snow, William | Lieutenant. | | | Journal of Council of Safety, 21 Feb, 1776. |
| Spraggins, — | Captain. | | | Gibbes's Documentary History, 1781. |
| Sparks, Daniel | Lieutenant. | St David's Parish. | Col. Benton's Reg't, Marion Brigade | Gregg's History of Old Cheraws, 1781. |
| Spivey, George | Colonel. | Wounded Parker's Ferry, 31 Aug, 1781. | Colonel G. G. Powell's Regiment. | Journal of Council of Safety, 21 Feb, 1776. [Cheraws, 1781 |
| Stafford, — | Ensign. | Volunteer Company, St. David's Parish. | Col Benton's Reg't, Marion Brigade | Gibbes's Doc. His, 1781. |
| Standard, William | Captain. | | | Jour. Coun. Safety, 30 Nov, '75. Gregg's His. Old |
| Starke, John | Captain. | | | Johnson's Traditions of Revolution. |
| Stephens, — | Lieutenant. | | Marion Brigade. | Gibbes's Documentary History, 1781. |

| Name | Rank | Unit | Reference |
|---|---|---|---|
| Stevens, Daniel | Lieutenant. | Battalion of Artillery. | Johnson's Traditions of Revolution. |
| Stevens, Jervis Henry | " | | Garden's Anecdotes. |
| Stone, Benjamin | Captain. | | Journal of Council of Safety, 21 December, 1775 |
| Steward, Chas. Augustus | Lieut. Colonel. | | Gregg's History of Old Cheraws, 1775. |
| Strobel, Daniel | Lieutenant. | German Fusileers. | Siegling's Cent Oration, 1779 |
| Strother, George | Ensign. | Charles Town Militia. | Gregg's History of Old Cheraws, 1781 |
| Sutton, John | Captain. | Capt Robt Lide's Co, St. David's Parish | Journal of Council of Safety, 21 Feb, 1776 |
| Sutton, Robert | Major. | | " 9 Jan, 1776 |
| Swinton, — | Captain. | Wounded Quinby Bridge, ——, 1782. | Moultrie's Revolution, 1781 |
| Simons, James | Lieutenant. | Col Maham's Reg't Light Dragoons. | 1782. |
| Smith, James | " | " | |
| Syders, — | | Charles Town Militia. | |
| Sinkler, — | | Col. H. Maham's Regiment. | |
| Screven, T. | Colonel. | | Johnson's Traditions of Revolution, 1775 |
| Taylor, James | Captain. | Charles Town Militia. | Lossing's Field Book Rev., '80, Moultrie's Rev., '81 |
| Taylor, Thomas | Colonel. | Marion Brigade. | Journal of Council of Safety, 21 Nov, 1775 |
| Tebout, Tunis | Lieutenant. | Colonel G. G. Powell's Regiment. | Mill's Statistics South Carolina. |
| Templeman, — | Captain. | Colonel Rothmaler's Regiment. | Gregg's History of Old Cheraws, 1782. |
| Terrell, James | " | | " 1781, |
| Terrell, Samuel | " | Col. Benton's Reg't, Marion Brigade | Journal of Council of Safety, 22 Dec, 1775. |
| Thomas, Edward | Colonel. | " | " 7 Nov, 1775. |
| Thomas, John | | Colonel Singleton's Company. | Johnson's Tra. Rev., '80, Carrington's Bat Rev, '80 |
| Thomas, John, Jr. | Captain. | Capt Benj. Marion's Company. | Johnson's Traditions of Revolution, 1780. |
| Thomas, Robert | Major. | | Gregg's History of Old Cheraws, 1781. |
| Thomas, Tresham | Captain. | Col Benton's Reg't, Marion Brigade | Journal of Council of Safety 11 Jan, 1776 |
| Thompson, Jas, (with) [drawn] | Major. | Round O Company. | Gregg's History of Old Cheraws, 1780) |
| Thornby, — | Major. | Colleton County Regiment. | Mill's Statistics South Carolina. |
| Timmons, John | Captain. | | Johnson's Traditions of Revolution, 1775 |
| Toomer, Anthony | Lieutenant. | Battalion of Artillery, | Moultrie's Revolution, 1781 |
| Toomer, Joshua | Captain. | Charles Town Militia. | Journal of Council of Safety, 26 Feb, 1776, |
| Trapier, Paul | " | | Moultrie's Revolution, 1781 |
| Turner, Sterling | " | Artillery Company, Georgetown. | Johnson's Traditions of Revolution, 1780. |
| Turner, James | " | | 1782 |
| Taylor, Samuel | Lieutenant. | Col Maham's Regiment Light Dragoons | |
| Timmacase, Henry | Surgeon. | " | 1776 |
| Theus, Perrin | Major. | | 1777 |
| Thompson, Thomas | " | | 1781 |
| Thomas, J. | Lieutenant. | | 1781 |
| Thompson, — | Colonel. | Colonel Richardson's Regiment. | |
| Tate, — | Lieutenant. | " | |
| Tenhimen, James | Captain. | Captain — Ravenel's Company. | Journal of Council of Safety, 25 Dec, 1775 |
| Vanderhorst, Arnoldus | Lieutenant. | Wounded Savannah, 9 October, 1779 | " |
| Vadeau, Peter | Ensign. | Berkeley County Regiment. | Ramsay's Revolution, 1779 |
| Waiht, Abraham | | John's Island Company, | Journal of Council of Safety, 1 Dec, 1775 |
| Wakefield, John | | Prisoner at St. Augustine. | Johnson's Traditions of Revolution, 1780. |
| Walker, — | Lieutenant. | Colleton County Regiment. Wounded Savannah, 9 October, 1779 | Ramsay's Revolution, 1779 |
| Wall, Wright | | St. David's Parish. | Journal of Council of Safety, 21 Feb, 1776. |
| Warham, Charles | Adjutant. | Col G. G. Powell's Regiment. Battalion Art'y, killed Charles Town '80, Charles Town Militia. | Ramsay's Revolution, 1780. |

| Name | Rank | Service | Command / Brigade | References |
|---|---|---|---|---|
| Waring, B | Captain. | St. George's Company | | Gibbes's Documentary History, 1781, 1775. |
| Waring, Morton | Lieutenant. | | | Journal of Council of Safety, 1 Dec., 1775. |
| Waring, Richard | Captain. | | | |
| Waters, Philemon | | | | |
| Watson, Michael | | | South Carolina State Troops. | O'Neall's Annals of Newberry, Johnson's Traditions of Revolution, 1780. |
| Weyman, Edward | Lieutenant, | Battalion of Artillery. | Charles Town Militia | Garden's Anecdotes, 1776. |
| Weyman, — | Captain. | Artillery. | Marion Brigade. | Gibbes's Documentary History, 1781. |
| White, Henry | Colonel. | | | Johnson's Traditions of Revolution, 1780. |
| White, Sims | Lieutenant, | Battalion of Artillery | Charles Town Militia. | Garden's Anecdotes, 1776. |
| Whitefield, Luke | Captain. | St. David's Parish. | Col. G. G. Powell's Regiment | Journal of Council of Safety, 21 Feb. 1776. |
| Whittington, Ephraim | Lieutenant, | | Col. Benton's Reg't, Marion Brigade. | Gregg's History of Old Cheraws, 1781. |
| Wigg, — | Captain. | | | Garden's Anecdotes, 1779. |
| Wilds, Jesse | Lieutenant. | Wounded Savannah, 9 October, 1779. | Col. Benton's Reg't, Marion Brigade. | Gregg's History of Old Cheraws, 1782. |
| Wilds, John | Captain. | Battalion Art'y, killed Port Royal, 1778. | | Gibbes's Documentary History, 1771 |
| Wilkie, — | Lieutenant. | | Charles Town Militia. | Ramsay's Revolution, 1780. |
| Wilkins, Benjamin | Colonel. | Expedition under Major Williamson. | | Moultrie's Revolution, 1778. |
| Williams, Charles | Captain. | | | Gibbes's Documentary History, 1781. |
| Williams, Daniel | Colonel. | | | 19 Nov., 1775. |
| Williams, James | Major, | Killed King's Mountain, ——, 1780. | Col. Benton's Reg't Marion Brigade. | Gregg's History of Old Cheraws, 1782 |
| Williamson, Andrew | Lieutenant, | Snow Campaign 1775, Commander. | | Carrington's Battles of the Revolution, 1780. |
| Williamson, Shadrack | Captain. Major, | | Col. Benton's Reg't, Marion Brigade. | Journal of Council of Safety, 30 Nov., 1775. |
| Williamson, Thomas | Captain. | St. David's Parish. | Col. G. G. Powell's Regiment. | Gregg's History of Old Cheraws, 1782 |
| Windham, Amos | Lieut. Major, | | | Journal of Council of Safety, 21 Feb., 1776. |
| Winn, Richard | Captain. Captain | Indian Co. of Foot Rangers or Rovers. | Col. Koll's Reg't, Marion Brigade; | Gregg's History of Old Cheraws, 1782. |
| Withers, John | Lieut. | | | Losing's Field Book of the Revolution, 1780. |
| Witherspoon, Gavin | Captain. | Capt. Thos. Port's Co., St. David's Par. | Marion Brigade- | Jour Coun. Safety, 21 Feb. 76. Gibbes's Doc. His. |
| Witherspoon, John | Lieutenant. | | | Wallace's His. Williamsburg Church, 1781. [1781. |
| Witherspoon, Robert | | | | Journal of Council of Safety, 30 Nov., 1775. 18 Jan., 1776. |
| Wright, Isaac | | John's Island Company. Expedition under Major Williamson. | | 2 Dec., 1775. |
| Wilson, William | Captain. | | | Gibbes's Documentary History, 19 Nov., 1775. |
| Warden, — | Major. | | | |
| Witherspoon, Joseph | Lieutenant. | | | Johnson's Traditions of Revolution, 1780. |
| Young, Thomas | Captain. | | | Mills Statistics South Carolina. |

77

FROM GENERAL WASHINGTON'S ORDERS AS GIVEN IN MOULTRIE'S REVOLUTION, VOL. II, p. 361:

"The Major Generals to wear a blue coat with buff facings and linings, yellow buttons, with white or buff underclothes, two epaulets with two stars upon each, and a black and white feather in the hat..Brig. Generals..one star..and a white feather..Aide-de Camps..of Maj. Generals and Brig. Generals..a green feather in their hats; those of the Commander-in-Chief, a white and green..All officers as well warranted as commissioned, to wear side arms, either swords or genteel bayonets.."

**RIBAUT MONUMENT**

Now standing on the original site of Charlesfort built in 1562 by Ribaut. Unsung and unheralded this monument in this day and age stands on what is to become one of the most hallowed spots in America. Jean Ribaut came to America to escape religious persecution in France. Charlesfort represents the first foothold of protestantism in America.

WAGONS AND CARRIAGES OF THAT TIME.

78

# MEDICAL MEN IN THE AMERICAN REVOLUTION SOUTH CAROLINA

Airs-Surg.d.1777..Alexander, Nathl.Surg.M.Axon,Saml.
Surg.M . .Brown, James . .Budd, Jno. Surg. 4th Artil.
Rgt . .Brownfield, Robt.S.M . .Carnes, Pat'k, Surg. M.
1st Cont. Drag. Aug 1777-1781 . .Carnes, Jno. Asst. D.
Apoth. . .Chalmers, Lionel. Attend. Pris. . .Clieland,
Jno. Surg. M. 3rd Rgt. . .Crane, Jno. Apothecary. . .
Dayton, Johnthan Attend Pris..DeLa Horne-At.Wounded..
Elliott, Benj. Surg.M . .Farrar, Field-Prov. Cong. . .
Fayssoux, Peter-1st. Lt. SC Rgt. 1778 . .Ferguson, Saml-
S.M. . .Flagg, Henry C.-Surg. 1st Rgt. 1775. Apoth.
Genl. 1779. . .Garden, Alex-Surg. to Pris. . .Gillett,
Abram-Surg . .Gould--Surg 1st Rgt. 1775-76. . .Haig--
Assemb . .Haley, Jno-M. Mil. . .Hart, Oliver, Surg. . .
Harris, Tucker-Surg. Mil. . .Houston, James-Phy. &
Surg . .Irvine, Wm-Surg . .Johnson, Robt-Hosp. Phy . .
Johnson, Thos . .Lockman, Chas-S.M. .Lochman, Jno -
Surg. . .Martin, Jas-Surg. . .McNeil, Danl-Surg. 2nd
Rgt. 1775-6 . .Milligan, George, Mil . .Motette, Lewis-
Surg. . .Neufville, Wm-Rgt. Surg. . .Oliphant, David-
Surg. Med. Directr, S. Div. . .Perry, Benj-Surg. . .
Poinsette, E-Surg.M . . Poyas, Jno. E-S.M. . Prescott,
James-Surg. . .Prescott, Joseph-Surg. . .Ramsay, Jos-
Surg. . .Ramsay, David-Surg. & Statesman. . .Ramsey,
Jesse-Surg. M. . . .Rasche, Isaac-Surg. M. 2nd Rgt.
1775-6. . .Rasche, Jon. H-Surg.M. . .Read, Wm-Hos.
Phy. & Surg. . .Reed, Wm-Hosp. Phy. 1780. . .Rogers,
Alex-Surg. 3rd Rgt. 1775-6. . .Rose, Hugh-Surg. . .
Smith, Robt-M. & Chap. .Smith, Danl-Dup. Md. Surv. .
Springer, Sylvester-M. 2nd Rgt. . .Stevens, Wm-Jr.
Surg. . . .Sunn, Fredk-Rgt.
Surg. . .Toomer, Anthony-
Surg. . .Tucker, Thos. T-
Hosp. Phy. & Surg. Turnbill ,
Andrw-Surg. Theus,Jeremh-
Surg. . Taliaferro, Dr. Jno. .
Vaughan-Hosp. Surg. . . . .
Vickers, Joseph-Hosp. Phy. .
Vickers, Saml-Surg. .Vidian
Saml-Hosp. Surg. .Wallace,
John-Surg. . .Weatherspoon,
J-Surg. . . .Wharry, Robt-
Surg.M. . . .Wilson, Saml—
Und. Marion. . Witherspoon,
Jno-Surg.

GENERAL NATHANAEL GREENE

# MEN OF GENERAL SUMTER'S BRIGADE, S.C.

General Sumter.

Ramsay in his history of South Carolina says that a party of exiles who had fled into N.C., as the British advanced, .made choice of Col. Sumter to be their leader, .and that he took the field against the victorious British at a time when the inhabitants had generally abandoned the idea of supporting their independence. The British had burned Sumter's home and turned his family out of doors. They also burned the home and library of the local clergyman, Rev. Mr. Simpson and all Bibles which contained the Scots translations of the Psalms. . "The people, .arranged themselves under Sumter, .with the enthusiasm of men called upon to defend not only their civil liberties but their Holy Religion.". . These men were woodsmen of the frontier up-country living mostly in the north eastern part of the state. South Carolina was no longer in a condition to pay, clothe or feed troops, therefore Sumter's men furnished their own horses and brought along their muskets and rifles. Often "iron tools of neighboring farms were worked up by blacksmiths into rude weapons, .bullets were made by melting pewter, .furnished by housekeepers. (In battles) some kept at a distance till by the fall of others, they were supplied with arms. When victorious, they rifled the dead, .of weapons." General Sumter was so daring and fearless he was called "The Gamecock."

-- ----------

LIEUT-COL. WADE HAMPTON-1st REGT. STATE TROOPS--GEN. SUMTERS BRIGADE

Rutherford, James Majr. . .Snoddy, Andrw. Adjt. . .Withers, E. Adjt. . . Harris, John Qt. Mas. . .Linton, Saml. Qt. Mas. . .Allison, Thos. Pay Mas. . . TROOP COMMANDERS: Cpts-Alexander, R. W. . .Alexander, B. Wm. . .Burns, Peter. . .Reid, John.

### CAPT. WM. ALEXANDER

Alexander, Andrw. 1st Lt. . .Gaylord, Saml. 2nd Lt. . .Hays, David Sergt. . . Wallis, Matt. Sergt. . .Alexander, David, Sergt. . .Alexander, Saml. . .Alexander, George. . .Brown, Alex. . .Barnett, Robt. . .Bruidson, Jno. . .Baker, Wm. . .Clark, James. . Cadner, Jno. . Clark, Jos. . Carothers, Wm. . Cowen, Isham. . Crawford, George. . Elliott, Wm. . .Ferguson, Moses. . .Hogshead, Saml. . .Hunter, Thos. . . Hemphill, Wm. . .Holland, Matthew. . .Johnston, David. . .Johnston, Thos. . .King, Hugh. . .Kennady, Alex. . .Linton, Saml. . .Meeks, Moses. . .McCleary, Saml. . . Millin, Jno. . .Mitchell, John. . .Ross, John. . .Robertson, Jno. . .Shelbie, Evan. . . Shealor, Wm. . .Shealor, Ino. . .Stewart, Danl. . .Williams, Jno. . .

### CAPT. ALEXANDER

Alexander, Wm. . .Albright, Simon. . .Ballings, Fredk. . .Bonds, Morris. . .Boney, Jacob. . Cammich, David. . .Chapman, Wm. . .Culpepper, Jos. . .Dobbins, David. . . Earnwood, Wm. . .Forrister, Jno. . .Forister, Wm. . .Foust, Jno. . .Foust, Wm. . . Glass, Fredk. . .Gosard, Isaac. . .Hayes, David. . .Hewet, Jno. . .Hook, Martin . . Hyde, Martin. . .Hylie, Jacob. . .Jackson, Jno. . .Jacob, Shadrack. . .James, Benj. . .

Johannes, Peter. . .Jon, Henry. . .Joyner, Wm. . .Knight, Jno. . .Legran, Oliver,
. . .Loch Alex. . Lyons, Wm., & Robt. . .Mashburn, James. . .McCloud, Donald. . .
Minich, Adam. . .Osman, George. . .Pellam, Wm. . ..Robertson, Jas. . .Rodgers ,
Majr. . .Sallers, Jno. . Tomlinson, Thos(2). . Trull, Jos. . Watson, Jno. . .Watson ,
Robt. . .Wells, Edward.

## CAPT. PETER BURNS (Pay Roll A & D)

Alexander, Abram. . .Alexander, Nathl. . .Alexander, Wm. . .Burns, Peter. . .
Black, Jos. . .Beaver, Mathias. . .Culpepper, Benj. . .Campbell, Jno. . .Campbell,
Robt. . .Caruthers, Hugh. . .Crawford, Jas. . .Cochran, Wm. . .Giles, Nathl. . .
Greer, Thos. . .Harris, Jno. . .Hayes, Jno. . .Holloway, Taylor. . .Harris, Drury. . .
Jones Jno. . . .Jackson, Ambrose. . . .Kesler, Jno. . .Lucust, Matthew. . .Miller ,
Adam. . .Maafield, Jno. . .Newell, David. . .Purvine, Jas. . .Purvine, Jno. . .Rass,
Gustavus. . .Roberts, Jno. . .Sell, Phillip. . .Smith, David. . .Smith, Jno. . Slown
or Sloan, Jno. . Shenpecker, Lawr. . .Team, Adam. . .Wilson, Humphrey. . .White,
David. . .Young, Adnrw. . .Young, Jacob.

## CAPT. JOHN REID

Archibald, Saml. . Brotherton, Wm. . .Bone, Jno. . .Bone, Wm. . .Bowman, Jas. . .
Baker, Barnabas. . .Carter, Danl 1st Lt. . .Corson, Linsey. . .Corson, Robt. . .
Campbell, Danl. . .Dickey, David. . .Gracy, Robt. . .Hill, Abram. . .Harris, Edw. . .
Love, Alex. . .Limerick, Patk. . Lawrence, Michael. . .Landsder, Robt. . .McMullen
Jno. Serg. Maj. . .McWherter, Alexr. Q. M. Serg. . .McCaferty, Jno. . .McGachy,
Jno. . .Neel, Wm. . .Nichols, Joseph. . .Potts, Wm. . .Robinson, Jno. . .Rutledge,
James. . .Rodgers, Joseph. . .Snoddy, Fergus 2nd. Lt. . .Scott, Joshua. . .Ware,
James. . .Worsley, Zacharia. . .Webb, John.

## COL. HENRY HAMPTON'S REGT. OF LIGHT DRAGOONS

Welsh, Patrick Majr. . .Foster, Jno. Cpt. . .Barnett, Jacob Cpt. . .Mills, Jno. Cpt. . .
Tate, Robt Cpt. . .Fathern, Benj. Lt. . .Rogers, Wm. Lt. . .Porter, Robt. Lt. . .
Barnett, Wm. Lt. . .Gill, Archd. Lt. . .Hamilton, James Fog. Mr. . .Andrew, Jno.
Qr. Mr. . .Wood, Thos. St. Mjr. . .Caroll, Joseph Qr. Mr. St.

## CAPT. JACOB BARNETT

Baxter, Andrw. Lt. . .Barnett, Saml. Sergt. . . .Barnett, Wm. . .Bassett, Fran
Sergt. . . . .Bourk, Robt. . .Brewster, Hugh, Jno. & Sheriff. . .Broom, Thos. . .
Caldwell, Robt. . . .Carter, Jno. . .Clark, Gideon. . .Colly, Mainyard. . .Craig,
Alex. . .Chapell, Wm. . .Bourk, Jno. . .Dennis, Isaiah. . .Flanagan, James Lt. . .
Forbes, Thos. . .Franklin, Jno. . .Gilham, Jacob. . .Gray, Jacob. . .Givens, Saml. . .
Grisham, Mjr. . .Gribble, Thos. . .Hand, Jno. . .Hargett, Jno. . .Harris, James
Sgt. . .Haws, Jno. . .Hazleton, Wm. . .Hodge, Wm. . .Howard, Wm. . .Huff, Benj.
Sgt. . . . .Humphreys, Absolom. . .Jenkins, Arthur. . .Kelly, Jno. . .Karr, Wm. . .
King, Fran. . .McCamon, Jno. . .McCurdy, Jno. . .McKinzie, Alex. . .McWherter,
Jesse Sgt. . .McWherter, Aaron & George. . .Moore, David. . .Parker, Danl. . .
Peoples, Jno. . .Porter, Hugh. . .Poston, Thos. . .Pristly, Chas. . .Rightly, Jno. . .
Roberts, Jesse. . .Shaddyn, David. . .Smith, Chas. & Ralph. . .Stewart, Jno. . .
Stinson, David. . .Tracey, James Sgt. . .Walker, Saml. . .Wallace, Levy. . .Watta ,
George. . .Wharton, Aaron. . .White, Stephen. . .Williams, Jno.

## CAPT. JOHN MILLS

Brown, Alex. . .Brown, Saml. . .Bishop, Jas. . .Bunch, Huck. . .Byrd, Jonas. . .
Cameron, Jno. . .Cougaler, Fran. . .Crosley, Saml. . .Cummins, Jno. . .Curtiss,
James. . .Dearmon, Wm. . .Deshasser, Jno. . .Duffie, Jno. . .Fibger, Lawr. . .Gill,

George. . Griffin, Gideon. . Parson, James. . Paull, James. . .Proudlove, Wm. . .
Singleton, Rich. . Taylor, Jno. . Walker, Phil. . Wallace, David. . .White, Rich. . .
Wier, Wm. . . .Wylie, James. . .Wylie, Jno. . .Hamilton, Wm. . .Hart, Jacob. . .
Hugh, Chas. . Hyatt, Jacob. . Kelson, Saml. . Kirk, Thos. . Lott, Wm. . McCammon,
Matt. . McClary, Robt. . McClure, James. . McClure, Saml. . .McFadden, Isaac. . .
Miller, Jno. . .Mills, Jno. . .Morrow, Jno. . .Off, Isaac.

## LT. COL. JOHN THOMAS REGT. LIGHT DRAGOONS--GEN. SUMTER'S BRIGADE

Moore, John Majr. . .Smith, Wm. Cpt. . .Waters, Philip Cpt. . .Lusk, James ADJT. . .
Martin, Peter Q. M. . .Johnson, Levi Cpt. . .Vanzant, Garrott, Lt. . .Glynn, David
Cpt. . .Lusk, Robt. Cpt. . .Boyer, John Lt. . .Thomson, Wm. Lt. . .Hayes, Nathl
Lt. . .Newberry, Thos. Lt. . .

### CAPT. PHILEMON WATERS

Armstrong, Jno. . .Bates, Dennis. . .Briges, Jno. Sgt. . .Calk, James. . .Calk, Wm.
Sgt. . .Chitwood, Danl & James. . .Childers, Jacob. . .Clark, James. . .Collends,
Jno. . .Crane, Wm. . .Crane, Mafeald. . .Downs, Wm. . .French Joseph. . .Jackson ,
Saml. Lt. . .Jacobs, Joshua Sgt. . .Johnston, David. . .Magruer, Elijah. . .Makentier,
Jno. . .Mode, James. . .More, Saml. . .Morrison, Patrick & John. . .Murphy, Wm.
S:M. .Noland, Shadrack. .Presnoll, Jacob. . .Pruit, Abraham. . .Rife, Cunrod. . .
Roberts, Benj. . . .Thomson, Charles. . .Tramell, Samson. . .Turner, James &
Thos. .Vaughan, Joell. .Veach, Eliza. . .Waldrop, Jno. . .Waters, West & Philip. . .
Webb, Jerry. . .Walles, Lazerus. . .Wilson, Wm. Lt. . .White, Jerry & Stephen.

### CAPT. WILLIAM SMITH

Antly; George. . . .Bearden, Richard, John & Wm. . .Bird, Nathan. . .Coldwell,
Wm. . .Chandler, Jesse. . .Dawkins, James. . .Day, Saml. . .Eliott, Chas. . .Flinn,
James. . . .Gaston, James. . . .Griffis, Thos. . .Glasgo, Robt. . .Harris, Jno. . .
Houlditch, Wm. .Herrin, Wm. .Toney, Abram & Drewry. . .Wolliston, Joseph. . .
White, Archb. . .Young, Wm. . .Jones, Jonathan. . .Lancaster, Saml. Sgt. . .Lusk.
Robt. Jr. 2nd Lt. . .Motlow, Jno. 1st Lt. . .Neal, James. . .Neighbours, Benj. . .
Pettitt, Henry. . . .Rest, Jno. . .Seagler, Wm. . .Smith, Wm. & Zopher. . .Smith,
Nathan. . . .Scott, Robt. . .Steel, Jno. . .Strother, Jas. . .Swords, Wm. . .Hughes,
Geo. . .Jeffris, Geo. & Lt. Berry & Allen. . .Jackson, Wm.

## LT. COL. WILLIAM POLK'S REGT. Light Dragoons-Gen. Sumter's Brigade.

Snipes, Wm. C. Maj. . . .Martin, Saml. Cpt. . .Martin, Nat. M. Cpt. . .Shelby,
Thos. Cpt. . .Polk, Chas. Lt. . .Long, Jno. Lt. . .McCurby, Archd. Lt. . .Clarke,
Jno. Adjt. . .Conner, James Q. Mas.

### CAPT. NATHL. M. MARTIN

Adams, Thos. . .Beryhia, Alexr. . .Black, Wm. . .Bryan, Henry. . .Clarke, Jonas
1st. Lt. . .Clarke, Jesse Sgt. . .Cooke, Nathl. . .Dunn, Andrw. . .Davis, James. . .
Dickson, James. . .Evance, James. . .Farson, Jno. Sgt. . .Frizell, Jno. . .Forden,
Jno. . . .Freeman, Michl. . . .Grimes, Wm. . .Hayes, Adam, Hugh, John, Moses,
Wm. .Haynes, Barthw. .Harris, Wm. .Hughes, Saml. . Irwin, Robt. . .McGwigin,
Danl. . . .McDowell, Thos. . .Mitchell, Wm. . .Miller, David. . .Jenny, James. . .
Rhodes, Jacob. . .Ried, Jno. . .Rogers, Seth. . .Rodgers, Nathl. . .Russell, Jno. . .
Robineff, Jesse. .Smith, Thos. .Sandford, Saml. .Short, Abram. . .Smith, Wm. . .
Stuart, Thos. .Smith, Saml. .Saxton, James. . .Simons, Ishml. . .Sample, Wm. . .
Shelby, Moses. . .Thomson, Wm. . .Walker, Robt. 2nd Lt. . .Witherspoon, Wm.
Sgt. . .White, Benj. Sgt. . .Walker, Robt. . .Woods, Wm. . .Wyatt, James.

## CAPT. SAMUEL MARTIN

Adams, Joseph Sgt. . .Allen, Wm. . .Alexander, Joel. . .Baker, Peter. . .Benson, Thos. . .Barr, Will. . .Bonner, Will. . .Barron, James. . .Carruth, Alex. Sgt. . . Carson, Jno. . . .Cumpton, Thos. . .Crayton, Chas. . .Cazza, Henry. : .Coleman, Chas. . . .Clendening, Mattw. . .Clendening, Wm. . .Cress, Phil. . .Cunningham, Robt. . . .Deepnest, Wm. . . .Dupriest, John. . .Eliott, Jno. Sgt. . .Furman, Benj. Sergt.M. .Frazer, San. . .Fitten, Isaiah. . .Huffman, Jno. . .Gray, Jno. . .Gillaspi, James Sgt. .Garrison, Isaac. .Hemphill, Sam 2nd Lt. .Hager, Cymon. . .Houston, Geo. . . .Irwin, Jno. . .Jack, James 2nd Lt. . .Johnston, Matt. . .Kline, Michl. . . Knowls, Abram. . .Logan, Hugh. . .Lessonbury, Reuben. . .Linn, Alex. . .Lisse, Leonard. .McCain, Hans & Hugh. .Merneal, Jno. . .McCallaster, Jno. . .McFalls, Jno. .Mitchell, James. .McCracken, James. . .McEntire, Robt. . .Moyer, Elias. . . McDonald, Pat. . .McCracken, Hugh. . .McCoy, Mechd. . .Nelson, Robt. Sgt. . . Nelson, James. . . .Oliphant, Robt. . .Osborn, Robt. . .Pendleton, Jno. . .Philips, Wm. . . .Polk, Thos. 1st Lt. . .Rogers, Alex. Q. M. S. . .Rea, Robt. . .Russell, Thos. John. . .Robinson, Wm. . .Scot, Wm. Sgt. . .Sloan, Robt. . .Shield, Thos. . . Shield, Robt. .Stoner, Peter. . .Sadler, Jno. . .Sullivan, Dan. . .Savage, Henry. . . Walker, James. . .Wells, Wm. . .Wilson, Joseph. . .Williams, Thomas.

## COL. WILLIAM HILL'S REGT. Of State Troops

Buford, Wm. Majr. . .Giles, James Cpt. . .McGay, Wm. Cpt. . .McKenzey, Will. Cpt. . .Neely, Sam Cpt. . .Reese, Chas. Lt. . .Camil. Jno. Lt. . .McDowl, James Lt. . .Reed, John Lt.

## CAPT. JAMES GILES

Brian, Matt. . . .Calhoon, Davd. . .Clark, James. . .Cohorn, Hugh. . .Cummens, Jon. . . .Cunngham, Miles. . .Curry, Robt. . .Davies, Joseph, Lt. . .Davies, Jon. Sgt. . .Dowall, Jno. . .Denny, Jas. . .Graham, George Lt. . .Gerret, Wm. . .Green, Wm. . .Hains, Davd. . .Hall, Sam. . .Hill, Wm. . .Hutchison, Sam Q. Mst. Sgt. . . Inis, Martin & Wil. . .Knox, Sam. . .Liveston, Henry & Abram. . .Liddy, Jno. Q. Mst. .McCall, Jon & David. .McGibenay, Hugh. . .Moor, Jno. . .Nicleson, Jon. . . Nicles, Thos. . .Reed, Geo. & Thos. . .Smith, Wil & Jon. . .Waker, Jon Sgt. . . Wilson, James Sgt. .Wilson, Wm. . .Wilson, Jon. . .Williams, Thos... .Ward, Wil.

## CAPT. WM. McKINZEY

Adams, Jno. Carrol Arm. . . .Alexander, Abram. . .Armstrong, Nathen. . .Baty, Simon. . .Bowell, Thos. . .Bryan, James. . .Cobb, Abrous. . .Collins, Jo. . Con, Wm. .Davis, Sneed. .Dowell, Geo. Elkins Jno. . .Fortinberg, Jno. . .Green, Isaac & Thos. . .Gules or Jiles, Wm. . .Hodgiss, Saml. . .Humberger, Josua. . .Hunt, Jo. . . .Hunter, Edw. . . .Hunter, Jno. . .Hutson, Drury. . .James, Rollen. . .Jiles, Wm. . . .Lequeare, Jno. . .Mattock, Wm. . .McCain, Jos. . .McCracken, Wm. . . McGuinis, Andrw. . . .McMichea, Davd. . . .McGlane, Jno. . .McKenzie, Wm. . . Mullinax, Mathea. . .Rackley, Francis & Parson. . .Rackley, Jos. . .Rhinehardt, Prunen. .Rhinehardt, Coonrad. . .Robertson, Israel. . .Robertson, Jas. . .Sallins, Jas. .Shope, Peter. .Smith, Thos. . .Starnes, Jno. . .Templeman, Aron. . .Twitty, Wm. . .Whitehead, Geo. . .Withers, Valentine.

## COL. CHARLES MYDDLETON'S REGT - 2nd Regt. State Dragoons

Boykin, Francis Mjr. .Reid, Wm. Cpt. .Adams, Godfrey, Cpt. . .Moore, Francis Cpt. .Ross, Isaac Cpt. . .Willson, Jno. Lt. . .Lloyd, Joseph Adj. . .Hayes, Andrw Qm. . .Sharp, James QM. . .Gosling, Geo. Sgt. Mjr.

## CAPT. FRANCIS MOORE

Abshaw, Jacob. .Anthony, Jno. .Baker, Demion. . .Baker, Jehu. . .Barns, James. . .
Brown, Richard & Geo. . .Brandon, Matt. . .Brazeel, Richard. . .Croft,˙ Jno. 2nd.
Lt. . .Deal, Michl. . .Evance, Jno. . .Forbes, Jno. & Robt. . .Harison, Constn. . .
Hart, Jos. Sgt. . . .Hart, Jas. Sgt. . . .Huston, Jno. . .Hood, Jno. . .Kerr, Jos. . .
Mathews, Rowld. . .Miller, Robt. . .Murray, Davd & Josh. . .McNeely, Davd. . .
McWaters, Jno. .McDowell, Thos. .McCree, Wm. . .McGoch, Jno. . .McCormick,
Robt. . . .McCamon, James. . .Neele, Wm. . .Owens, Jno. . .Reed, Wm. . .Roney,
Maurice Sgt. . . .Richards, Jno. . .Saylor, Michl. . .Sloan, Jas. . .Steele, Jas. . .
Suthmyer, Jacob. .Spencer, Benj. .Scott, Rich. .Smith, Phil. .Thomson, Moses. . .
Wadle, Robt. .Wilson, Jno. .Wenkler, Conrad. .Wilson, Ezekel. . .West, Leond. . .
Campbell, Miss Robt. 1st Lt.

## CAPT. ISAAC ROSS

Akins, Wm. .Bell, Jas. . .Boyce, Wm. Sgt. . .Bowders, Jno. Sgt. . .Brannan, Danl
Sgt. . .Boyd, Ed. . .Carick, Adam. . .Carter, Jno. Sgt. . .Campbell, Geo. Sgt. . .
Cooke, Burrill Sgt. . .Disto, Jesse Sgt. . .Duggin, Leo Sgt. . .Dash, Jno. . .Ezell,
Jno. Sgt. . . .Flint, Jno. Sgt. . .Graham, Alexr. . .Gatam, Jno. . .Gregory, Thos.
Sgt. . .Griffin, Jno. Sgt. . .Hayes, Jas. Sgt. . .Hill, Lodwk. Sgt. . .Hatfield, Saml.
Sgt. .Hardgrove, Jno. Sgt. .Harris, Mason Sgt. . .Harris, Griffin Sgt. . .Howser,
Andrw. .Henson, Jesse. .Irish, Martin. . .Jackson, Thos. 2nd Lt. . .Jones, Britton
Sgt. . .Jenkins, Shadk. . .Jackson, Jno. . .James, Henry. . .Keer, Hance. . .Kitts,
Martin. . .Laws, Matt. . .Miller, Abram. . .Martin, Martin. . .McGrew, Wm. . .
Murchey, Wm. .Outson, Jonth. . .Pullam, Wm. Sgt. . .Pennington, Kinchin Sgt. . .
Pone, Davd. Sgt. . .Pawling, Wm. . .Swetman, Stephen Sgt. . .Sellers, Jacob. . .
Smith, Henry. . .Tayley, Jno. Sgt. . .Whitaker, Jno. 2nd Lt. . .White, Jon. Sgt. . .
Wilkinson, Wm. Sgt. .Wilkinson, Jno. Sgt. .Wilkinson, Thos. Sgt. . .Watts, Thos.
Sgt. . .Ware, Wm. . .Winingham, Jas. . .Kelly, Miss Jas. . .Yates,Thos.

------------

## STAFF OFFICERS AND ARTIFICERS OF STATE TROOPS

Alexander, Chas. . . .Dysert, Corn. . .Dickson, Will. . .Jinkens, Jno. . .Lipham,
Fred. .Mee, Geo. . .Murrell, Wm. . .Miller, Chas. . .McClerath, Wm. . .Provoe,
Mr. . . .Price, Isaac. . .Shields, Mr. . .Simpson, Wm. . .Tenell, Wm. . .Taylor,
Saml. . .Withers, Enoch. . .White, Jno. . .White, Henry. . . White, Hugh. . .White
Jno. . .

## THOS. SUMTER

A list of "Sundry Persons who received pay for cloathing-who are not included in Sumters List," and Special Bounty:

Adams, Richard. .Bordin, Richard & Wm. .Bryant, Henry. .Cardock, George. . .
Crawford, Saml. .Chitwood, Jno. . .Curweethus, Wm. . .Caruthers, Wm. . .Clark,
Joseph. .Edmaston, Jno. .Gardner, Wm. & Jno. .Gill, Jno. . .Gilbraith, Joseph. . .
Heran, Jno. . .Harris, Drury. . .Hunter, Saml. . .Jeffers, Littlebury. . .McClery,
Saml. . .McDaniel, Wm. . .Sadler, Jno. . .Shield, Wm. & Jno. . .Elliott, Wm. . .
Ziegler, William.

# *Charleston* GATES

In Charleston we find the outstanding work of artists who designed in iron. Some of the wrought-iron gates certainly antedate the Revolution, as those before the Brewton Houses. The Gates of Saint Michael's Churchyard are believed by many to be the lovliest of their kind in America. Among others are: Simonton's, known as the "Sword Gates" (house prior to 1776); The Pineapple Gates at Geo. Edward's House (1770); Sass Gates; John Rutledge House; Lesne Gate.

GATES OF ST. PHILIP'S          Sword Gates

The Lesesne Gate,

ST. MICHAEL'S CHURCHYARD GATES.

SMYTHE HOUSE—14 Legare. Built 1770.

HARRIETTA PLANTATION

The Waring Gateway

MEMORIAL To The Four South Carolina Signers Of The Constitution of The United States (Courtesy of D.A.R. Mag.).

THE FOUR FUNDAMENTAL DOCUMENTS OF THE U. S. GOVERNMENT ARE: The Articles of Association 1774; The Declaration of Independence 1776; The Articles of Confederation 1778; The Federal Constitution 1787. South Carolina Signers of the Declaration of Independence were: Thomas Lynch Jr., Thomas Heyward Jr., Edward Rutledge, Arthur Middleton...Signers of The Constitution were: John Rutledge, Charles Cotesworth Pinckney, Charles Pinckney, Pierce Butler.

# SOME REVOLUTIONARY WAR PRISONERS OF SOUTH CAROLINA

The Historian Ramsay says that some of the first prisoners were confined in vaults with the dead, and later, crowded on prison ships in such numbers there was only standing room. In thirteen months of captivity about a third had perished. The following data is taken from the South Carolina Historical and Genealogical Magazine, and checked with Ramsay and other sources.

On Sunday 27 Aug. 1780, following persons, prisoners on parole in Charleston, were suddenly taken from their homes by armed British Troops and conveyed to the ship, SANDWICH, moored near Ft. Johnson, and in a few days transported to St. Augustine:
Budd, Dr. John. . .Blake, Edward. . .Cochran, Robert. . .Edwards, John. . .Flagg, George. .Fayssoux, Dr. Peter. . .Gadsden, Christopher, Lt. Gov. . .Gibbs, Wm. Hasel. . .Hall, Wm. & Thos. . .Heyward, Thos. Jr. . .Holmes, Isaac. . .Hutson, Richard. . . .Johnson, Wm. . . .Lewis, Rev. John. . .Livingston, Wm. . .Loveday, Jno. . .Lushington, Cpt. Richard. . .Moultrie, Alex. . .McCrady, Edw. . .Mouatt, Jno. . . .Neufville, Jno. . . .North, Cpt. Edw. . .Parker, Maj. Jos. . .Poyas, Jno. Earnest. .Ramsey, Dav. .Read, Cpt. Jacob. . .Rutledge, Hugh & Edw. . .Sansum, Jno. . . .Savage, Thos. . .Singleton, Thos. . .Smith, Josiah Jr. . .Thompson, Jas. Hamden. . . .Timothy, Peter. . .Todd, Jno. . .Toomer, Anthony. . .Massey, Col. William.

On Nov. 15, 1780 the following persons joined the above group:
Bee, Joseph. .Beresford, Rich. . .Berwick, Jno. . .Bordeaux, Daniel. . .Cudworth, Benj. . . .Crouch, Henry. . .Cripps, Jno. Splatt. . .Darrell, Edw. . .DeSaussure, Daniel. . .Hall, Geo. Abbott. . .Grimball, Thos. . .Jones, N. W. . .Lee, Wm. . . . Logan, Wm. . .Middleton, Arthur. . .Peters, Chris. . .Postell, Benj. . .Prioleau, Saml. . . .Smith, Philip. . . .Waller, Benj. . .Wakefield, Jno. or Jas. . .Weyman, Edw. . .Morton, Wilkinson. . .Masters, Vendue. . .Savage, Thos. . .Isaacs, Col. Elijah. .Rutherford, Gen. Griffith, N. C. Mil., Rich. H. Thomson. .Mrs. Moultrie & daus. . .Jno. Morrell.

On 17 May 1781, the following persons were sent on board the prison ship TORBAY and the schooner PACKHORSE:
Arthur, Geo. . .Atmore, Ralph. . .Axson, Wm. . .Ash, Saml. . .Anthony, Jno. . . . Blake, Jno. .Baddely, Jno. .Barnwell, Jno., Edw., Robt. . .Bounetheau, Peter. . . Bambridge, Henry. .Branford, Wm. . .Blundel, Nathan. . .Baskins, Wm. . . .Bayle, Jos. .Bricken, Jas. .Bellamy, David. .Bonniot, Jno. . . .Cummins, Rich. . .Cochran, Thos. .Clarke, Jonathan. . .Cray, Jos. . . .Conyers, Norwood. . .Cox, Jas. . . .Cooke, Thomas. . .Cohen, Jacob. . .Calhoun, Jno. . .DeSaussure, Wm. . .DeWar, Robt. . . Dunlap, Jos. .Dorsius, Jno. .Edmonds, Rev. Jas. . .Elliott, Thos. O. . .Edwards, Warren Jr. & Jno. Jr. . . .Eberly, Jno. . .Eveleigh, Thos. . .Evans, Jno. . .Egan, Jno. . .Elliott, Wm. & Thos. Jr. & Jos. . .Gadsden, Philip. . .Girraud, Peter. . . Graves, Jno. & Wm. . .Grayson, Thos. .Glover, Jos. . .Gibbons, Jno. . .Guerrard, Benj. . . .Gaskie, Michael. . .Grott, Francis. . .Geer, Christian. . .Holmes, Bee Jno. & Wm. .Hughes, Thos. .Hews, Thos. .Hamilton, David. . .Heyward, Jas. . . . Harris, Thos. .Henry, Jacob. .Harvey, Wm. H. .Hornby, Wm. . .Jacobs, Danl. . . Jones, Geo. . . .Keowin, Thos. . .Kent, Chas. . .Kennon, Henry. . .Kean, Jno. . . Lebby, Nathl. .Lesene, Jno. .Lever, Abram. . .Legare, Thos. . .Liston, Thos. . . .

Lee, Stephen. .Lybert, Henry. .Lockhardt, Saml. .Layle, Wm. .Legare, Benj. ..
Michael, Jno. . .Meyer, Philip. . .Minot, Jno. Sr. & Jr. & Abram. . .McDonald,
Chas. .Moss, Geo. . .Moncrief, Jno. . .Milner, Solomon. . .Monk, Geo. . .Morgan,
Jonathan. . . .Miller, Saml. . .Moore, Stephen. . .Murphy, Wm. . .Neufville, Jno.
Jr. & Wm. .Owen, Jno. . .Prioleau, Saml. Sr. & Philip. . .Poyas, Jas. . .Palmer,
Job. . . .Pinckney, Chas. Jr. . . .Robertson, Jos. . .Rhodes, Danl. . .Reid, Geo. .
Singleton, Ripley. . .Skottowe, Saml. . .Shrewsberry, Stephen. . .Snyder, Paul. . .
Smith, Saml. . .Sanders, Jno. . .Stephenson, Jno. Jr. . .Scott, Jno. Sr. . .Snelling,
Wm. .Troussiger, Jas. . .Taylor, Paul. . .Waring, Thos Jr. . .Waties, Jno. Jr. . .
Wigg, Wlm. . .Wilkins, Jas. . .White, Sims. . .Waring, Rich. . .Warham, Chas.&
David. . .White, Isaac. . .Wrighton, Jos. . .Wilkie, Wm. . .Welch, Geo. & Jno. . .
Wheeler, Benj. . .Wilcox, Wm. . .Yeadon, Rich. . .You, Thomas.

The following were sent on the PACKHORSE:
Baird, Jonas. .Boquet, Peter. .Bordeaux, Nathl. . .Durham, Charnell. . .Fowles ,
Oliver. . .Hancock, Clement. . .Kilgore, Benj. . .Sarrazin, Jon'a. . .Ryan, Jno. . .
Turpin, Jos. . .Sudre, Peter. . .Wyatt, William.

On 31 Dec. 1781, the Edict of Col. Balfour Commandant of Charleston,
BANISHED all who would not take protection from the British. The heads of
families of these persons are hereby given. (Except the women who are given
in a separate list)
Arthur Geo. . .Atmar Ralph. . .Axson Wm. . .Anthony Jno. . .Anderson Rich. . .
Butler Pierce. .Baldwin Saml. . .Blake, Edw. . .Budd Jno. Dr. . .Bouequet Peter
Jr. .Bremar Francis. .Berwick Jno. . .Bricken Jas. . .Berrisford Rich. . .Bonnist
Jno. .Bee Jos. . .Ball Jos. . .Bourdeaux Danl. . .Bourdeaux Nathl. . .Blake Jno. . .
Burke Adinus. .Cudworth Benj. .Conyers Norwood. .Cox Jas. . .Crouch Henry. . .
Costeng Jno. . .Cochran Robt. . .Cochran Thos. . .Cripps Wm. . .Cripps Splatt
Jno. .Crawley Chas. . .Crawford Bellamy. . .Dewar Robt. . .DeSaussure Danl. . .
Darrell Edw. .Eveleigh Thos. .Edwards Jno. .Edwards Jno. Jr. . .Elliott Thos. . .
Elliot O. Thos. .Edmonds Jas. Rev. . .Ford Benj. . .Fisher Jas. . .Fuller Wm. . .
Ferguson Thos. . .Flagg Geo. . .Garkey Michael. . .Gross Francis. . .Grimball
Thos. Jr. .Graves Jno. . .Graves Wm. . .Gadsden Christopher. . .Guillaud Jas. . .
Gibbons Jno. .Gibbes Hazel Wm. .Guerrard Benj. . .Gaze Noel. . .Harvey Henry
Wm. .Hall Abbott Geo. . .Harris Thos. . .Hart Oliver Rev. . .Hart Oliver Jr. . .
Hutson Rich. .Hall Thos. Jr. .Holmes Wm. . .Hamilton David. . .Hughs Thos. . .
Holmes Isaac. .Heyward Thos. . .Heyward Jas. . .Holroy Turpin. . .Hall Wm. . .
Johnson Wm. . . .Kean Jno. . .Kennan Henry. . .Legare Benj. . .Lee Stephen. . .
Lesesne Jno. .Logan Wm. .Lee Wm. . .Lybert Henry. . .Lebby Nathl. . .Loveday
Jno. . .Livingston Wm. . .Lewis Jno. Rev. . .Legare Thos. . .Lushington Rich. . .
Lochman Jno D. . .McBride Jas. . .Mey Florian Chas. . .Mercer Rich. . .Mayret
Abram. . .Massey Wm. . .Miller Saml. . .McDonald Chas. . .Monk Geo. . .Minot
Jon. Jr. . .McLean Jane. . .Michael Jno. . .Moultrie Alex. . .Mouat Jno. . .Moore
Thankful. .Moultrie Wm. Cpt. . .McCall Hext. . .McCrady Edw. . .Moultrie Wm.
Genl. .Neufville Wm. . .Neufville Jno. . .Neufville Jno. Jr. . .North Edw. . .Nones
Benj. . . .Owen Jno. . .Pinckney Cotes. Chas. . .Pinckney Thos. . .Poyas Ernest
Jno. .Prioleau Saml Jr. . .Peters Christopher. . .Postell Benj. . .Parker Jos. . .
Palmer Job. .Prioleau Philip. .Pillans Robt. . .Parker Wm. . .Pickering Wm. . .
Pinckney Chas. Jr. .Righton Jos. . .Rooks Wm. . .Read Jacob. . .Robinson Jno. . .
Rutledge Thos. .Rutledge Hugh. . .Rutledge Edw. . .Ramsay Dav. Dr. . .Robinson
Jos. . . .Shrewsberry Stephen. . .Singleton Thos. . .Stone Chas. . .Stiles Edw. . .
Stone Wm-Pilot. .Starnes Danl Jr. . .Smith Thos-Pilot. . .Sansum Jno. . .Stafford
Arthur. . . .Stevens Danl. . . .Smith Josiah Rev. . .Smith Josiah Jr. . .Sararazin
Jonathan. . . .Stinson Jas. . .Synder Paul. . .Smith Robt. Rev. . .Smith Saml. . .
Threaderaft Bethel. . .Todd Jno. . .Tousiger James&c. . .Tufts Simon. . .Toomer
Anthony. .Thomson H. Jas &c. .Taylor Paul. . .Turpin Jos. Jr. . .Timothy Peter

Peter &c. . . .Thomson Andrw. . .Welch Geo. . .Wilkie Wm. . .Waller Benj. . ..
Warham Dav. . .Wilkinson Morton. . .Way Robt. . .Welch Jno. . .Wilkins Jas. . .
Wheeler Benj. .Wakefield Jas. .Weyman Edw. . .Waring Rich. . .Waring Thos. .ᵣ
White Isaac. .Wil Philip. . .Yeaden Rich. . .Cattell Benj. . .Henry Jacob. . .Jones
W. Noble Dr. . . .Savage Thos. . .Oliphant Dav. Dr. . .Brown Dennis. . .Dunlap
Jos. . .Gadsden Thos. Cpt. . .Kirk Jno. . .Cooke Thos. . .Dacosta Isaac Sr.

"Besides the Persons mentioned...a number of Men, both Officers in the
Continental Line, and Militia Men of S. Carolina, were landed from Cartel
Vessels at Jamestown in Virginia..." This data and above list of names  was
copied from the Josiah Smith Diary as published in the S. C. Histl. & Geneal.
Magazine of April 1933.

------------

## LIST OF MILITARY PRISONERS AT PLYMOUTH

Ashton, Lt. Jno. .Ball, Thos. .Duff, Andrw. . .Kennedy, Jas. . .Markham, Jas. . .
M'llahany, Wm. .Pitts, Wm. . .Russel, Danl. . .Ripley, Paul. . .Singleterry, Jos.
& Jno. . . .Steele, Wm. . . .Stobo, Lt. Jacob. . .Vestals Jas. . .Wells, Andrw. . ..
Wilkes, Hardy (From S. C. Histl. Mag. Vol. 10)

----------

## PRISONERS BUTCHERED AT HAY'S STATION, LAURENS COUNTY, S. C.

Cook, Jno. . . .Feris, Jas. . .Goodman, Benj. . .Hays, Col. Joseph. . .Hardy, Lt.
Christopher. . .Hancock, Clement. . .Irby, Joseph Sr. & Jr. & Greaf. . .Milvern,
Jno. . .Neel, Lt. John. . .Williams, Cpt. Daniel & Joseph. . .Saxon, Yancy. . .Hays,
Danl. . .Leonard, Lock.

Ramsey says that in the summer of 1780...20 or 30 citizens of most re-
spectable character...were shut up in prison...and loaded with irons, among them
were: Alexander, Col. . .Bradley, Jas. . .Boykin, Cpt. . .Chesnut, Cpt. Jno. . .
Few, Col. .Kershaw, Mr. .Hunter, Col. .Irwin, Mr. . .Strother, Mr. . .Winn, Col.

"Near Camden (the following with others whose names are unknown) were
taken out of goal and hung without ceremony: Andrews, Saml. .Gayle, Josiah. .
Miles, Jno. . .Smith, Eleazer. . .Tucker, Richard."

ONE OF MORGAN'S
RIFLEMEN.

CAYCE HOUSE, OVERLOOKING CONGAREE RIVER, NEAR WHERE "LIGHT HORSE HARRY" LEE AND HIS REVOLU-
TIONARY TROOPS CAPTURED FORT GRANBY FROM THE BRITISH MAY 15, 1781.

Original church
built in 1684

Only Huguenot church
in America adhering
exactly to the liturgy
of the French
Protestant Church.

FRENCH PROTESTANT (HUGUENOT) CHURCH, CHARLESTON, S. C.

Commemorative services of the two hundred and fifty-fifth
Anniversary of the Revocation of the Edict of Nantes were held
on October 20th, 1940, in the Huguenot Church in Charleston.

Medway, built in 1687, home of one of the landgraves, the
oldest house standing in South Carolina.

# SOME SOUTH CAROLINA HEROINES
# OF THE REVOLUTION

(These names were abstracted from D.A.R. records, newspapers, family records including Bible and cemetery data and county histories.)
Adair, Mary. . .Arnett, Hannah White. . .Arnold, Mrs. Anne Hendrick. . .Arnold, Temp. .Allen, Judith. . .Beale, Unice. . .Barry, Marg. C. Moore. . .Bradley, Mrs. Elizabeth. . .Bratton, Martha. . .Butler, Behethland Foote. . .Dillard, Mrs. Mary W. of Cpt. Jas. .Dunklin, Mary. .Ervin, Mrs. Elizabeth James. .Ervin, Elizabeth Ellison. . .Ervin, Jane Witherspoon. . .Elliott, Susanna. . .Elliott, Jane. . .Elliott, Anne. .Farrow, Rosannah Waters. . .Gaunt, Hannah (Mooney). . .Geiger, Emily. . . Gibbes, Sarah, R. . .Gilliam, Elizabeth C. . .Gordon, Margaret Gregg. . .Hay, Ann Hawks. .Heyward, Mrs. Thomas. .Holtzclaw, Catherine R. . .Hopton, Mrs. Sarah & Daus. . . .Jackson, Mrs. Elizabeth. . .James, Mrs. Sarah. . .Kennedy, Anne. . . Lee, Nancy. . . .Leonard, Mrs. Mary G. . . .Leitner, Maria Beard. . .Langston, Laodicea. .Lindley, Elizabeth Hall. .Motte, Rebecca. .Musgrove, Mary. . .Morris, Anne E. . . .Mclean, Jane. . .Moore, Thankful. . .Noot, Mrs. Angelen. . .Pickens, Rebecca C. .Philips, Mourning. . .Moultrie, Mrs. & Daus. . .McDowell, Margaret O'Neal. . .Otterson, Mrs. Saml. . .Scott, Joyce Callahan. . .Steele, Elizabeth. . . Sullivan, Mrs. Mary Charlton. . . .Thomas, Jane Black. . . .Richardson, Dorcas Nelson. . .Waring, Elizabeth Grace. . . .Watson, Martha. . .Walker, Esther. . . . Wilkerson, Eliza Younge. . . .Listed on the roll of Cpt. Jno. Irving's Co., Col. Williamson, are: The widows-Thomas, Forbes, Brown, Parker. .On roll of Cpt. Francis Moore, Myddleton's Regt is-Miss Robt. Campbell. On the roll of Cpt. Ross, Myddleton's Rgt. is-Miss Jas. Kelly. On the roll of Cpt. Phil. Waters, Col. Thomas, Sumter's Brigade is Eliza Veach. At Hist'l Commission, Lib. U, is Mary Richie, N. 342.

----------

The names listed next are taken from the S.C. Historical & Genealogical Magazine of April 1933. "Dec. 31, 1781. The Cruel Edict of Lieut. Col.Balfour Commandant of Charleston, for BANISHING from thence the Wives, Children & others dependent on those Virtuous Citizens, that wou'd not Sully their honour by taking protection...hereunto inserted their Names..." (I give only the women in this list who were heads of families):
Moore Thankful. . .McLean Jane. . .Anderson, Rebecca. . .Baker, Mary. . .Beale, Unice. . . .Brewton, Mary. . .Campble, Elizabeth. . .Dubertas, Widow. . .Dewees, Sarah. . . .Eldsworth, Susannah. . . .Glaze, Ann. . .Guerraud, Elizabeth. . .Gillon, Mary. . .Gleadow, Mary. . .Maltby, Elizabeth. . .Main, Rachel. . .Noles, Mary. . . Owen, Elizabeth. .Springer, Margaret. . .Tobias, Elizabeth. . .Melvin, Martha. . . Dickerson, Sarah. .Sheed, Eleanor.  There were 186 men, 120 women (including wives of heads of families) and 264 children.

"The distressed Situation of the familys that were ordered to leave Charleston by the first of August...occasion'd...in Congress...a Loan of $30,000 for the support of such citizens...as have been driven from their Country...(&) relief of said Sufferers."

----------

# SOUTH CAROLINA WOMEN WHO RECEIVED REVOLUTIONARY INDENTS

----------

This list has been compiled from the records in the nine volumes of STUB ENTRIES TO INDENTS and the three volumes of ACCOUNTS AUDITED of Revolutionary Claims against South Carolina, issued by the Historical Commission of South Carolina. Some of these women loaned money to the state, some furnished supplies or rendered other services.

A ********************** A

Indents Bk. I: Annas Mrs. Elizbth p.65. . . .Bk. B: Anderson Mrs. Ann 68. . . . Atchison Mary 62. .Axson Elizbth 3,42. .Accts. Aud. Vol. 1: Abney Martha 34. ... Aberlay Mrs. Ann 13. .Adams Mrs. Mary 66. . .Addison Mrs. Mary 103,105. . . Akin Mrs. Ann 120. . .Alcorn Mrs. Catherine 128. . .Allen Mrs. Agnes 175. . . Accts. Aud. Vol 2: Anderson Mrs. Rebecca 72. .Anderson Ruth 66,67. .Anderson Mrs. Margt wid. of Cpt. Geo. 64,65. . . .Anderson Mrs. Margt wid. of Thos. of Camden 112. .Allison Dorothy 4,5. .Allison Mrs. Sarah 10. .Allison Rachel 7,9. . Allston Elizbth 32. . . .Allston Mrs. Rachel 34. . .Altman Mrs. Sarah 35,37. . .. Andrews Mrs. Jane 127. . .Accts. Aud. Vol 3: Ayer Mrs. Frances 13. . .Ayers Mrs. Margt 15. .Bk. L-N:Altman Mrs. Sarah 3. . .Bk. R-T Adair Mrs. Elizbt h 101. . .Adair Mrs. Sarah 162. .Andrews Mrs. Jane 57. . .Arnett Mrs. Jane 56. . . Bk. U-W: Adams Mrs. Sarah 25. . .Arnst Mrs. Maria 203. . .Atkins Mrs. Elisha 205. . . .Austin Mrs. Elizbth 204. . . .Bk. Y-Z: Aberly Mrs. Ann 161. . .Alcorn Catherine 161. . . .Allison Rachel 319. . .Anderson Mrs. Ann 104. . .Attoy Mrs. Mary 111. . .Bk. O-Q: Altman Mrs. Sarah 273.    Anderson Sara 89.from Bk. B

B ********************** B

Indents Bk. I:  Bails Mrs. Elizbth 66. . .Bair Mrs. Barbara 66. . .Barber Mrs. Mary 66. . .Barron Mrs. Rebecca 66. . .Beard Mrs. Mary 104. . .Bk. U-W:  Box Mrs. Margt 248. . .Boyls Mrs. Martha 152. . .Bk. Y-Z:  Baxter Mary 313. . .. Baynard Eliza 210. . .Berwick Mrs. Ann 217. . .Bolton Agnes 12. . .Brice Mrs. Margt (Lockhardt) 206. .Budd Susannah 62. . .Bugg Elizbth 126. . .Burke Elizbth 217. . .Bk. X. Pt. 1:  Bayley Mrs. Lucy 145. . .Brandon Mrs. Agnew 142,196. . . Breed Mrs. Briscilla 142. . .Brown Mrs. Grizell 143. . .Bk. O-Q:  Benbow Mrs. Martha 114. .Beverly Mrs. 309. . .Booth Mrs. May 179. . .Bowers Mrs. Sylvana 273. . .Bradley Mrs. Margt 46. . . .Brumfield Mrs. Elizbth 48. . .Bk. X. Pt. 2: Buzzard Elizbth 27. .Bk. L-N: Bagwell Mrs. Jane. .Brazell Hannah 6. . .Bridges Mrs. Mary 265. . .Brown Mrs. Sarah 262. . .Bryant Mrs. Sarah 264. . .Bk. R-T: Babb Mrs. Mary 164. . . .Babilitman Mrs. Zaba 9. . .Bonneau Mrs. Ann 106. . . Bowman Mrs. Sarah 165. .Box Mrs. Mary 163. .Boyd Mrs. Martha 9. . .Brazzel Mrs. Hannah 8. .Burns Mrs. Mary 166. . .Accts. Aud. Vol. 3:  Babb Mrs. Mary 17. . .Bacot Mary 32. . .Ball Mrs. Elizbth 96. . .Bails Mrs. Elizbth 50-2. . .Bair Mrs. Barbara 52. . . .Baird Mrs. Winifred 55. . .Baker Charlotte Bohun 71. . . Bampfield Mrs. Rebecca 127-30. . .Barber Mrs. Mary 142. . . . .Bare Mrs. John Christopher 143. .Bk. B: Bacot Mrs. Mary 27. . .Baker Charlotte B.59. . .Baker Elizbth E. 137. . .Ball Elizbth 44. . .Bampfield Mrs. Rebecca 162,208. . .Barron Mrs. Sarah 127. . . .Batchelor Mrs. Mary 22. . .Bancart Mary 137. . .Beresford Dorothy 34. .Beresford Sarah 18,105,110. .Berwick Mrs. Ann 90. . .Boobe Sarah 56. . .Bounetheau Mrs. Mary 220. . .Bower Mrs. Katherine 139. . .Boyd Elizbth 153. . .Broughton Ann 20. . .Burrington Elizbth 127. . . .Butler Sarah 36. .Butler Jane 87.

## C ************************ C

Bk. B: Caesar Mrs. Hannah 116. . . .Campbell Lady Sarah Izard 152. . .Camon (Cannon) Mrs. Mary 102. . . .Cardin Judith 161. . .Cardy Mrs. Ann 40. . .Cattell Mrs. Sabina 159. .Chalmers Ann 130. .Chalmers Elizbth 80. . .Chalmers Martha 130. .Cockfield Mrs. Mary 140. . .Cook Margt 67. . .Cook Rebecca 67. . .Cooper Mrs. Mary 95. . .Cordes Mrs. Ann 80. . .Cowen Jane 190. . .Accts. Aud. Vol. 3: Colleton Mrs. Margt Swainton 162. . . .Bk. U-W: Caldwell Mary 65. . .Cottheen Mrs. Charoty 226. . .Bk. Y-Z: Campbell Elizbth 13. . .Carr Mrs. Jane 172. . . Carroll Mrs. Mary 173. . . .Clyatt Hannah 173. . .Corben Elizbth 212. . .Creech Ann 12. . .Creighington Mrs. Elizbth 253. . .Crouch Mary 126. . .Bk. O-Q: Caw Mrs. Rachel 178. . . .Clyatt Mrs. Hannah 172. . .Cottheen Mrs. Charity 223. . . Crosby Mrs. Hannah 278. . .Bk. L-N: Connell Mrs. Mary 268. . .Cooper Mrs. Elizbth 269. .Concil Mrs. Elizbth 271. . .Conturier Martha 9. . .Bk. R-T: Cason Mrs. Rosey 12. .Castellaw Mrs. Ann 70. . .Cobb Mrs. Judith 106. . .Collins Mrs. Mary 106. . .Craig Mrs. Eleanor 170.

## D ************************ D

Indents Bk. I: Davis Mrs. Agnes 38. . .Bk. B: Dart Mrs. Amelia 117. . .Darrell Mrs. Frances 17. .Dawney Mrs. Sarah 81. . .Daws Margt 239. . .Delaney Elizbth 18. .DeWar Mrs. Elizbth 11. .Donnom Mrs. Susan 183. . .Doughty Elizbth 78. . . Doughty Mrs. Mary 78. . . .Dunlap Mrs. Margt 17. . .Accts. Aud. Vol 3: Darby Elizbth 28. . .Dawkins Mrs. Elizbth wid. 57. . .Bk. L-N: Daughtery Mrs. Mary 275. . .Bk. R-T: Davis Mrs. Mary 70. . .Bk. U-W: Durn Elizbth 261. . .Bk. Y-Z Davis Mrs. Mary 15,215. . .DeSaussure Mrs. Jane 130. . .Dick Mary 76. . .Droze Mrs. Mary 114. . . .Bk. X. Pt. 1: Davidson Mrs. Sarah 65,152. . .Dawkins Mrs. Chloe 151. .Bk. O-Q: Davis Mrs. Jane 106. .DeSaussure Mrs. Jane 310. . .Dobin Mrs. Elizbth 173. . .Bk. X. Pt. 2: Darling Mary 56. . .Dawkins Elizbth 127. . . DePre Mrs. Mary Elizbth 128.

## E ************************ E

Bk.L-N: Elliott Mrs. Sabina 288. . .Evans Mrs. Elizbth 12. . .Bk. R-T: Edwards Mrs. Elizbth 189. . .Bk. U-W: Ellison Elizbth 67. . .Bk. O-Q: Elkins Mrs. Ann 280. . . .Ellis Mrs. Elizbth 310. . .Bk. B: Edwards Margt 185. . .Edwards Mary 185. . .Edwards Rebecca 100. . .Edwards Sarah 52. . .Ellington Amarinthia 85. . . Elliott Mrs. Mary 35. . .Elliott Mrs. Sarah 117. . .Ellis Mary 30. . .Ellis Mrs. Mary 45. . .Entelwein Martha 23. . .Eikester, Mrs. Mary 71.

## F ************************ F

Bk. I: Ferguson Mrs. Mary 45. .Ferguson Mrs. Elizbth 45. .Fogle Mrs. Barbara 72. .Bk. B: Frazer Elizbth 92. . .Freer Mrs. Ann 224. . .Frierson Mary 156. . . Fripp Mrs. Elizbth 30. .Fuller Mrs. Judith 127. .Bk. L-N: Flanagan Mrs. 279. . Bk. R-T: Fisher Mrs. Sarah 22. . .Bk. Y-Z: Frashers Ann 52. . .Bk. O-Q:Faust Mrs. 311. . .Felder Mrs. Sarah 228. . .Fonches Mrs. Catherine 281. . .Fox Mrs. Mary 71.

## G ************************ G

Bk. B: Gardner Lucy 243. .Gignilliat Mrs. Mary Magdalen 11. . .Gignilliat Susan 12. .Gillon Mrs. Mary 150. .Griffis Mrs. Barbara 6. . .Bk. U-W: Gardiner Lucy 268. . . .Bk. Y-Z: Gaddis Mrs. Christana 175. . .Gest Sarah 52. . .Gordon Mrs. Margt 150. . . .Gore Margt 41. . .Graham Mrs. Sarah. . .Bk. O-Q: Griffin Mrs. Mary. . .Greenwell Mrs. Mary 233. . .Grimball Mrs. Sarah 284. . .Gupbell Mrs. Elizbth 283. . .Bk. L-N: Gore Mrs. Rachel 14. . .Gray Mrs. Mary 253. . .Accts. Aud Vol. 1: Gloster Margt 141.

## H ************************ H

Bk. I: Hartzog Mrs. Catherine 74 (Hartsuck). . .Hoffman Mrs. Catherine 76. . . Hutto Mrs. Ann 76. .Bk. B: Haley Mary 18. .Hall Mary 217. . .Hall Susan 43. . . Hall Mrs. Susana T. 84. .Hart Mrs. Ann 112. .Hill Mrs. Hannah 221. . .Hodsden Mrs. Mary 97. .Hoyland Mrs. Anna M. 102. . .Huger Mrs. Martha 193. . .Huger Mary E 11. .Huntingdon Lady Selina Countess 11. . .Hyrne Mary 37. . .Bk. U-W: Heath Ethel 168,174. . . .Hill Mrs. Mary 153. . . .Howe Mrs. Jane 153. . .Howell Martha 69. . .Bk. Y-Z: Hadden Mary 128. . .Hall Mary Ann 42. . .Hamilton Mrs.

Rachel 122. . .Harden Mrs. Elizbth 177. . .Harleston Mrs. Ann (Ashby) 121. . .
Hilton Amey 164. .Howell Mrs. Martha Eppes 177. .Hyrne Sarah Ann 53,168. . .
Bk. X. Pt. 1: Holcomb Mrs. Lucy 159. . .Bk. O-Q: Hadden Mrs. Jennett 78. . .
Heyward Mrs. Elizbth 288. . .Hopkins Mrs. Sarah 285. . .Howell Mrs. Martha
288. . .Huggins Mrs. Mary 106. . .Accts. Aud. Vol. 2: Haddick Sarah 82. . .Bk.
L-N: Hayne Mrs. Susan 255. . .Hicks Mrs. Jane 325. . .Hodges Mrs. Rebecca
324. . .Hubbard Mrs. Manoah 322. . .Bk. R-T: Haddock Mrs. Sarah 108. . .Hanby
Mrs. Jeremiah 220. . . .Hanby Mrs. Susannah 220. . .Heap or Heays Mrs. Sarah
29. . .Hill Mrs. Milly 202. . .Hubbard Mrs. Abigail 200.

I **************J************** K

Bk. B: Izard Mrs. Charlotte 108. .Bk. R-T: Inabinet Margt 211. . .Bk. B: James
Eliz Ann Mrs. 103. . .Bk. L-N: James Mrs. Sarah 328. . .Johnson Mrs. Grissett
330. . .James Mrs. America. .Bk. Y-Z: Johnston Mrs. Martha 122. .Bk. X. Pt. 1:
Johnston Mrs. Sarah 162. .Bk. O-Q: Jenkins Mrs. Phoebe 3. .
Bk. X. Pt. 2: Jackson Amey 134. . .Bk. L-N: Keith Mrs. Margt 331. . .Bk. R-T:
Kelley Mrs. Margt 224. .Kessel Mrs. 212. .Bk. U-W: Keith Margt 115. . .Knight
Catherine 71. . . .Knox Sarah 70. . .Bk. O-Q: Kettle Mrs. Elizbth 290. . . Bk. I:
Kennelley Mrs. Elizbth 78. .Kibler (Keebler) Mrs. Lucretia 79. . .Kirkland Mrs.
Susannah 79. .Bk. B, Kelsal Mary Elizbth 137. .Kennan Mary Ann 101. . .Kinloch
Mrs. Ann 11. . .Knap Mrs. Mary 35. . .Knox Elizbth 4.

L ************************ L

Bk. B: LaRoche Mrs. Elizbth 71. .LaTour  Mrs. Susan 126. .Ladson Eliz 217. .
Lance Mrs. Ann M. 116. . .Lane Mrs. Catherine 139. .Lesesne, Mary 54. . .Lind
Agnes 138. .Lining Mrs. Sarah 15. . .Liston Martha 44. . .Logan Elizbth 147. . .
Logan Martha 4. . . .Bk. R-T: Lesesne Mrs. Mary 148. . .Lewis Mrs. Eleanor
225. .Bk. U-W: Lance Ann 184. .Lowry Mrs. Jane 155. .Bk. Y-Z: Lenud Elizbth
5. .Little Mary 264. . .Lipton Mary. . .Bk. X. Pt. 1: Lesesne Mrs. Mary 225. . .
Bk. O-Q: Linn Mrs. Mary 5. . .Lootholts Mrs. Sarah 176. . .Accts. Aud. 1: Lee
Sarah 66.

M ************************ M

Bk. B: Marion Catherine 69. .Mazyck Mrs. Mary 155. .McWharter Mrs. Elizbth
221. . .Melvile Mrs. Jane 91. . .Mercer Mrs. Grace 133. . .Bk. 1 Maid Mrs Ann
65. .Moorer (Morreau) Mrs. Mary 83. .Myers Mrs. Mary 82. . .Bk. L-N: Mason
Mrs. Martha 341. . .McClwur Mrs. Mary 40. . .Morgan Mrs. Elizbth 337. . .Bk.
R-T: Mallard Mrs. Susan 45. . .Martin Mrs. Mary 213. . .McElveen Mrs. Mary
151. .Miller Mrs. 213. .Miller Mrs. Mary 158. . .Miller Jane 90. . .Minter Mrs.
282. .Minnich Mrs. Rebecca 213. .Bk. U-W: Magdalen Mrs. Mary 210. .Maxwell
Mrs. Sarah 284. . . .Marshall Sarah 72. . . .Mason Eleanor 286. . .McCord Mrs.
Sophianisba 283. .McKelveen Mrs. Mary 146. . .Miads Mrs. Sarah 224. . .Moore
Sarah 73. . . .Bk. Y-Z: Marr Elizbth 169. . .Marshall Mrs. Mary 134. . .McKay
Mrs. Cabton 135. . .McPherson Sarah 192. . .Melvill Mrs. Jane 82. . .Mucklewain
Mrs. Mary 132. . .Bk. X. Pt. 1: McKendrick Mrs. Catherine 173. . .McInSmith
Mrs. Catherine 173. .Mixon Mrs. Frances 14. .Bk. O-Q: McDonald Mrs. Rachel
11. . .Mann Mrs. Susanna 183. . .Marshall Mrs. Mary 3. . .Martin Mrs. Susanna
261. .McGill Hannah 184. .McIlveen Mrs. Mary 183. . .Moore Mrs. Dolley 41. . .
Bk. X. Pt. 2: McCarty Martha 158. . .Murphy Sarah 136.

N ************************ O

Bk. R-T: Newton Mrs. Jane 46. .Bk. U-W: Nieley Sarah 187. .Bk. Y-Z:Novelton
Mrs. 207. . .Bk. O-Q: Nance Mrs. Elizbth 294. . .Bk. R-$^T$: Odom Margt 289. . .
Bk. Y-Z: O'Bannon Mrs. Abigail 176. .Olephant Catherine 315. .Bk. L-N: Oswald
Margt 26. . .

P ************************ P

Bk. L-N: Pagan Mrs. Jennett 53. . .Parsons Mrs. Susan 26. . .Patton Mrs. Jane
304. . . .Pitman Mrs. Priscilla 27. . .Powell Elizbth 304. . .Bk. R-T: Pon Mrs.
Elizbth 51,214. .Printer Mrs. Margt 294. .Bk. U-W: Pelot Mrs. Frances 150. . .
Pelot Mrs. Mary 150. .Penney Ann 77. .Petty Elizbth 189. . .Potts Mrs. Eleanor

132. .Pratt Mary 79. .Prescott Mrs. Esther 131,149. .Priggs Mrs. Eliza 155. . .
Bk. Y-Z: Patton Mrs. Sarah 158. .Pearson Tabitha 200. .Pendarvis Sarah 44. . .
Powell Mrs. Sarah. .Punch Mary 192. . .Bk. X. Pt. 1: Pyatt Mrs. Mary 186. . .
Bk. O-Q: Philips Mrs. Elizbth 16. . .Accts. Aud. : Paggett Mrs. Sarah 35.

### R ************************* R
Bk. I: Reeves Mrs. Ann 86. . .Rickenbacker (Riconbaker) Mrs. Ann 86. . .Bk. B:
Robinson Nancy 102. .Roulain Mrs. Susan 163. .Bk. L-N: Ravenal Elizbth 29. . .
Reiley Mrs. Ann 30. .Ross Mrs. Elizbth 58. .Bk. Y-Z: Ravenal Mrs. D. Elizbth
275. . . .Rhodes Mrs. Elizbth 96. . .Rouse Mrs. Deberah 95. . .Bk R-T: Roberts
Mrs. Mary 208. . .Bk. U.W: Reading Mrs. Hannah 149. . .Ravenal Mrs. Elizbth
153. .Ritchie Mary 51. .Rowdus Elizbth 79. . .Rushing Sabrina 294. . .Bk. X. Pt.
1: Ravenal Mrs. Demaris Elizbth 24. .Ravenal Elizbth 23. . .Reggs Mrs. Elizbth
104. . .Robinson Mrs. Ann 83. . .Rows Mrs. Deborah 25.

### S ************************* S
Bk. I: Seigler Mrs. Mary 88. . .Smith Mrs. Catherine 70. . .Snider Mrs. Mary
89. . . .Sucuck Ursala 91. . .Spurlock Mrs. Elizbth 89. . .Syfrett (Suffrett) Mrs.
Rebecca 88. .Bk. B: Saunders Mrs. Ann 20. . .Savage Martha 85. . .Savage Ruth
100. .Scanlan Deborah 129. .Scott Mrs. Frances 118. . .Screven Rebecca 162. . .
Simmons Mrs. 45. . .Simmons Mary 46. . .Skirving Elizbth 233. . .Skirving Mrs.
Sarah 87. .Smith Anna M. 237. .Smith Elizbth 196. . .Smith Mrs. Elizbth 236. . .
Smith Mary 205. . .Stanyarne Ann 83. . .St. Julien Susan 181. . .Stanyarne Mrs.
Elizbth 203. . .Stoll Mrs. Phoebe 219. . .Stone Mrs. Ruth 63. . .Bk. L-N: Smith,
Mrs. Mary 355. .Spring Mrs. Dorothy 315. .Bk. R-T: Saltus Mrs. Mary 154. . .
Sanders Mrs. 111. .Saylor Mrs. Elizbth 217. . .Shinholster Mrs. 296. . .Simpson
Mrs. Sophia 216. .Slappy Mrs. Isabella 216. . .Swan Mrs. Mary 155. . .Bk. U-W:
Shilley Mrs. Drewsella 157. . . .Singleton Ann 107. . .Snow Mrs. Hannah 139. . .
Sweet Keziah 140. .Bk. Y-Z: Simpson Sophia 182. .Smith Mrs. Catherine 103. . .
Smith Mrs. Janet 184. . .Stoll Rebecca 32,103. . .Suss or Surs Mrs. Susan 97. . .
Swan Mary 33. .Bk. X. Pt. 1: Saller Elizabeth 31. .Sanders Margt 51. . .Simpson
Mrs. Isabel 178. . .Simpson Mary 52. . .Singley Mrs. Rachel 83. . .Smith Mrs.
Christopher 181. .Smith Susan 29. . .Snellgrove(Swillgrove) Sarah 86. . .Steen Mrs.
180. . .Stuart Isabel 53. . .Stuart Mary 48. . .Bk. O-Q: Shoemaker Mrs. Elizbth 92,
248. .Singleton Mrs. Ann 131. .Smith Mrs. Mary 132. . .Summerford Mrs. Sarah 95.

### T ************************* T
Bk. I: Tanseller Mrs. Mary 91. . .Bk. B: Tennent Mrs. Catherine 91. . .Thomas
Mrs. Ann 53. . . .Thomas Mrs. Mary 22. . .Trezevant Charlotte 78. . .Bk. L-N:
Tennant Mrs. Susan 313. . .Terrell Mrs. Sarah 34. . .Tyson Mrs. Sarah 35. . .
Bk. R-T: Teague Mrs. Alee 157. . .Toller Mrs. Mary 218. . .Bk. U-W: Thomas
Mrs. Mary L. 162. .Thompson Mrs. Sarah 161. . .Bk. O-Q: Thomas Mrs. Mary
Lambel 250. . .Bk. Y-Z: Taylor Sarah 9. . .Trapier Mrs. Elizbth 145. . .Bk. X.
Pt. 1: Taylor Jane 35. .Thompson Mrs. Elizbth 185. .Thorn Mrs. Elizbth 185. . .
Bk. O-Q: Taylor Mrs. Ann 194. .Terrell Mrs. Elizbth 96. .Bk. X. Pt. 2: Tebout
Mrs. Sarah 56,82.

### U **** V ********* Y **** Z
Bk. U-W: Undean Mrs. Mary E. 196. . .Bk. Y-Z: Underwood Mrs. Naomi 60. . .
Bk. Y-Z: Vaux Mrs. Ann 201. . . .Verre Mrs. Mary 208. . .Bk. O-Q: Vanbibber
Mrs. Margt 134. .Bk. R-T: Young Elizb 250. .Bk. U-W: Zimmerman Mrs. Mary
151. . .Zuber Mrs. Rachel 142 in X,. Pt. 2. . .Bk. B: Villepontoux Mrs. Jane 5. .

### W ************************* W
Bk. I: Walker Mrs. Bersheba 14. . . .Weaver Mrs. Hannah 92. . .Williams Mrs.
Elizbth 93. .Williams Mrs. Mary 15. .Winckles Mrs. Elizbth 13. . .Wisher Mrs.
wid. 38. . . .Accts. Aud 3: Wilson Mrs. Winifred 55-7. . .Bk. B: Walker Elizbth
245. . .Walker Susan 31. . .Walter Mrs. 88. . .Warham Mrs. Mary 187. . .Waring
Dorothy 14. . .Waring Juliet 14. . .Waring Mary 61. . .Watson Mrs. Mary 107. . .
Watts Mrs. Rachel M. 183. .Wilkins Rebecca 61. .Williams Mrs. Elizbth 163. . .

Wood Mrs. Ann 101...Wood Martha 101...Bk. L-N: Walters Mrs. Mary 35...
Watson Mrs. Mary 318...Watsone Mrs. Catherine 36...Wheeler Mrs. Mary 70...
Wilson Mrs. Mary 37...Williamson Mrs. Celia 37...Bk. U-W: Williams Mrs.
202...Williams Mrs. Henry 148...Winkler Mrs. Mary 149...Withers Mrs. Mary
200...Wright Sarah 60...Bk. Y-Z: Walker Eleanor 222...Walker Mrs. Elizbth
177...Welch Mrs. Eleanor 129...Wilson Mrs. Martha 241...Bk. X. Pt. I: Watson
Mrs. Margt 58...West Mrs. Jane 188...Williams Elizbth 38...Williams Mary.
58...Wilson Martha 40...Wilson Mrs. Winired 100...Wood Mrs. Mary 87...
Wood Catherine 42...Wragg Henrietta 108...Wright Elizbth 107...Bk. O-Q: Ward
Mrs. Susan 252...Watts Mrs. Rebecca 196...Weston Mrs. Barbara 195...Weston
Mrs. Sarah 195...Whitfield Mrs. Christy 100...Williamson Mrs. Mary 104...
Wooters Lilly 254.

Mrs. Rebecca Motte giving the
soldiers fire arrows with which
to burn her home.

PIONEER WOMAN

Arrest of Emily Geiger.

From D.A.R. Magazine, April 1937

## Some Women of South Carolina in the Revolution

| | | |
|---|---|---|
| Mary Adair | Sarah Reeve Gibbes | Mrs. Samuel Otterson |
| Mary Alexander | Mary Anna Gibbes | Sarah Overstreet |
| Kate Barry | Mrs. Thomas Heyward | Rebecca Pickens |
| Mrs. John Beckham | Mrs. John Jolly | Eliza L. Pinckney |
| Mary Booth | Nancy Jackson | Dorcas Richardson |
| Martha Bratton | Dicey Langston | Joyce Callihan Scott |
| Behethland Butler | Esther Marion | Isabella Sims |
| Cateechee | Elizabeth, Grace and Rachel | Jane Thomas |
| Mrs. Dillard | Martin | Jane Elliot Washington |
| Anna Elliot | Mary McClure | Martha Watson |
| Susannah Smith Elliot | Jane McJunkin | Jane White |
| Sabina Elliot | Rebecca Motte | Eliza Yonge Wilkinson |
| Esther Gaston | Jane Morrow | Isabella Wylie |
| Emily Geiger | Mary Musgrove | |

94

Rosemont, Home of Ann Pamela Cunningham, Savior of Mt. Vernon.
(Laurens County)

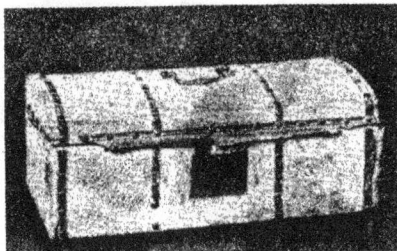

MARY MUSGROVE'S TRUNK. PRESENTED TO THE SOUTI
CAROLINA STATE CONFERENCE BY MRS. W. S. ALLEN,
TO BE PLACED IN THE D. A. R. MUSEUM, OLD EX-
CHANGE, CHARLESTON

THIS BRIDGE HONORS MARY MUSGROVE, REVOLUTIONARY HEROINE, WHO RENDERED CONSPICUOUS SERVICES
TO PATRIOTS DURING THAT PERIOD. BRIDGE SPANS ENOREE RIVER AT MUSGROVE MILL BATTLEGROUND.

# WORLD'S "MOST BEAUTIFUL SPOT"

Glimpses of the Beauties and
Glories of Magnolia Gardens

St. Michael's Episcopal Church—S. E. corner Broad
and Meeting. Corner stone laid in 1751. Occupied
1761. Its bells have crossed the Atlantic five times.

## A ☆ A

Abercrombie, Charles, Major
Abney, Paul
Abney, Nathaniel, Captain
Abney, Samuel
Adair, James Jr.
Adair, James, Sr.
Adair, John, Major
Adair, Joseph, Jr.
Adams, David
Adams, David, Jr.
Adams, Joel
Adams, Jonathan
Adams, Jonathan, Jr.
Adams, Thomas
Adams, Timothy
Adams, William
Albergotti, Anthony
Alexander, Adam, Colonel
Alexander, Abram, Lieutenant
Alexander, Elias, Jr., Colonel
Alexander, Dr. Isaac
Alexander, Jno. McKnitt
Alexander, Samuel
Alford, Jacob
Allen, Charles, Jr.
Allen, George
Allen, James
Allen, John, Captain
Alston, John Captain
Alston, William, Captain
Anderson, David, Major
Anderson, David
Anderson, Denny
Anderson, James, Captain
Anderson, Joseph
Anderson, Robert, Colonel
Anderson, William, Captain
Andrews, Sylvester, Captain
Archer, John, Lieutenant
Arnett, Hannah White
Arnold, William
Askins, William
Atwood, Joshua
Austin, William, Colonel
Avlett, William
Ayer, Thomas, Captain
Ayers, Thomas

## B ☆ B

Bacot, Samuel, Lieutenant
Baer, Jacob, Lieutenant

Bailey, John, Colonel
Bailey, Samuel
Bailey, Thomas
Baker, Richard Bohun, Captain
Baker, William
Ball, William
Ballenger, James
Barker, William, Captain
Barkley, John, Major
Barnett, Joel
Barnwell, Edward, Major
Barnwell, Robert Gibbes
Barr, Martin
Barre, Jacob, Lieutenant
Barron, Archibald
Barry, Andrew, Captain
Bartlett, Josiah, Colonel
Baruch, Rufus
Baskerville, William, 2nd Lieutenant
Baskin, Andrew
Bates, Zealous, Sergeant
Baxter, Andrew, Major
Baxter, Daniel
Baxter, John, Captain
Beaty, John
Beatty, Thomas, Colonel
Beck, Jeffery
Bedford, Thomas, Sr., Lieutenant
Bedford, Thomas
Beers, Gresham
Belk, John
Bell, Samuel, Jr.
Bellinger, Edmund
Bellinger, John
Benan, James, Colonel
Benton, Felix
Benton, Lemuel, Lieutenant-Colonel
Bentham, James, Lieutenant
Berdsall, Benjamin, Lieut.-Col.
Berrian, John, Major
Berry, Hendson
Bethea, John, Jr.
Bethea, John, Sr.
Bethea, John
Bethea, William
Bethel, William, General
Billen, Stephen
Bird, Mark, Lieutenant-Colonel
Bissell, Ebenezer Fitch, Captain
Black, John, Sr., Lieutenant
Black, Joseph
Blackburn, Ambrose, Captain
Blackensderfer, Christian
Blackstock, William, Jr.
Blackwell, Samuel

Blair, James, Colonel
Blake, Isham
Blakely, William
Bland, Robert
Blassingame, John
Bledsoe, Bartley
Blythe, Samuel, Lieutenant
Boevie, Rhoda, (Rhody or Rhodi)
Boddie, Nathan
Boggan, Patrick
Boggs, Aaron
Bolling, Samuel
Bolling, William, Colonel
Bolton, Matthew
Bolton, Robert
Bonham, Absolone, Captain
Booth, John
Bostwick, Littleberry, Colonel
Botsford, Reverend Edmund
Bouchellon, Joseph, Captain
Bounethran, Peter, Lieutenant
Bowen, Robert, Captain
Bowers, David
Boyce, John
Boyd, David
Boyd, John
Boykin, Burwell
Boys, Nathan
Bracey, Sackfield M.
Bracket, Samuel
Bradford, John, Colonel
Bradford, Joseph B.
Bratton, William, Colonel
Brent, James, Major
Brewster, William
Brian, James
Brock, Reuben
Brockman, John
Browne, Henry
Brown, Archibald, Colonel
Brown, Bartlett
Brown, Bernard
Brown, Charles, Lieutenant
Brown, Daniel, Surgeon
Brown, John
Brown, John, Jr.
Brown, John, Sr.
Brown, Samuel
Bruce, Donald
Bryan, Nathan
Bryan, Simon
Bubier, John, Corporal
Buck, Jonathan, Colonel
Buddin, James, Second Lieutenant
Buford, William, Major
Bugg, Sherwood, Captain

Bull, John, Sr.
Bullock, Hawkins
Burkhalter, David
Burn (Burns), John
Burnley, Henry
Burress, Solomon
Bush, Daniel
Bussey, Edward, Lieutenant
Butler, James
Butler, Thomas
Butler, Thomas, Sergeant
Butler, William, General
Butterick, Joseph
Byrd, George, Second Lieutenant

# C ☆ C

Cade, Drewry B. (Drunery) Captain
Caldwell, David, Reverend
Caldwell, James, Captain
Caldwell, John, Captain
Caldwell, William, Lieutenant
Calhoun, John
Calhoun, Patrick
Calloway, John, Major
Calmes, William, Jr. Lieutenant
Calvert, John
Camp, John
Camp, Thomas, Sr.
Campbell, David, Major
Campbell, Whittaker, Captain
Campbell, William, Colonel
Cannon, Daniel
Cannon, Isaac
Cantey, James, Captain
Cantey, Samuel
Cantrell, Thomas
Capers, William, Captain
Carey, (Cary), James
Carey, (John), Captain
Carothers, Andrew, Lieutenant
Carr, Dabney
Carroll, James
Carson, James, Lieutenant
Carswell, John, Lieutenant
Carter, Abraham
Carter, Churchwell
Carter, Dale
Carter, Giles
Carter, John, Captain
Carter, Samuel, Corporal
Carter, Thomas A.
Cartwright, Robert
Carwile, Zachariah
Casey, Levi, General

Cater, Thomas, Captain
Cave, John
Chambers, John
Chandler, Matthew
Chandler, Mordecai
Chapin, Benjamin, Surgeon
Chaplin, William, Jr.
Chaplin, William, Sr.
Chappell, Hix
Chappell, James
Chappell, Robert
Chappell, Thomas
Chase, Nathaniel Low
Cherry, Samuel, Lieutenant
Childs, Abraham
China, John
Chivesman, Samuel
Chloe, Michael
Clapp, Earl, Captain
Clark, James, Lieutenant
Clark, Timothy
Clark, William
Cleveland, Benjamin, Colonel
Cleveland, Robert, Capt
Cline, Michael
Coalter, Michael
Cobb, Jesse, Captain
Coe, Ebenezer, Sergeant
Coffin, William
Colbertson, Robert
Colburn, James, Brigadier General
Coles, John, Colonel
Coleman, John H.
Coleman, William
Collier, Joseph, Lieutenant
Collins, John, Captain
Collins, Joseph
Collins, Thomas
Connor, James
Conrad, Steven, Captain
Converse, Amos
Conyers, John
Cook, Burrell, Sergeant
Cook, James
Cookley, Benjamin, Lieutenant
Cooner, Jacob, Sr.
Cooper, Ezekiel
Cooper, George, Lieutenant
Cooper, James
Cooper, John
Copeland, John
Cornwall, Benjamin
Corrigan, William
Corry, Nicholas
Cosnahan, Joseph
Council, Henry, Captain

Covington, Benjamin
Cowen, Henry
Coxe, Samuel
Craig, James, Captain
Craig, John
Craig, Isaac, Major
Craighead, Alexander
Crane, Stephen
Crawford, James, Captain
Crawford, James
Crawford, Patrick
Creswell, James
Crittendon, Nathaniel, Second Lieut.
Cropper, John, Lieutenant-Colonel
Crossland, Edward
Culler, Benjamin
Culp, Benjamin
Cunningham, Arthur, Lieutenant
Cunningham, John
Cureton, William, Jr.

# D ☆ D

Dalrymple, John
Daniel, James
Daniel, John
Daniel, William, Sr.
Dantzler, Jacob
Darby, Asa
Darnall, Joseph
Darrant, Charles, Sr.
Davenport, Jas. M.
Davenport, William, Captain
Davis, Amos, Captain
Davies, Samuel, Colonel
David, William, Captain
Davidson, John, Major
Davidson, William, Major
Davies, Myrick
Davis, Andrew
Davis, George
Davis, John
Davis, T. Joseph
Davis, William, Lieutenant-Colonel
Davis, William, Colonel
Davis, William, General
Dean, Joel
DeGraffenried, Techarner, Sergeant
DeLeon, Jacob
DeLoach, David
Dennis, John
deSaussure, Daniel
Devlin, James
Dew, Thomas
DeWitt, William

Dial, Martin
Dickson, Matthew
Dillard, James, Captain
Dobson, Coillion
Doby, John
Dodge, Oliver
Dominick, Henry
Donelson, William, Captain
Dorn, George
Dorsey, Basil
Doty, Silas
Douglas, John, Lieutenant
·Douthit, John
Dowling, Robert
Dowling, William
Downes, William, Adjutant
Dozier, John, Captain
Drake, Albrittain
Drake, Alberlain
Drake, Augustus Matthew
Drake, Oliver
Drayton, William Henry
DuBose, Samuel, Lieutenant
Duckett, Joseph
Dudley, Ambrose, Captain
Dunbar, William
Duncan, James
Dukes, Joseph
Dukes, Thomas
Dunklin, Joseph
Dunlap, George
Dunlap, William
Dunn, Jeremiah
DuPuy, John, Captain
Durant, Henry
Durham, Charnel, Captain
Durkins, John
Dusenburg, Charles

E ☆ E

Earle, Baylis
Earle, John, Captain
Earle, John, Colonel
Earle, Samuel
Easterling, William
Edings, Benjamin
Edwards, Richard
Edwards, Thomas
Elam, William
Eldridge, Christopher
Ellerbe, Thomas, Captain
Ellerbe, William
Ellison, Robert, Captain
Ellsworth Charles, Captain

Emerson, John, Captain
Ensign, John, Captain
Epes, Peter
Epting, Adam
Ervin, John, Colonel
Erwin, James, Lieutenant
Erwin, William
Espey, Samuel, Captain
Estill, William
Evance, Thomas
Etheredge, Henry, Sergeant
Evans, Batte
Evans, Ezekiel
Evans, John
Evans, Nathan
Evans, Nathan, Lieutenant
Evans, Roland, Captain
Evans, William, Lieutenant
Everett, Thomas
Ewell, James, Lieutenant

F ☆ F

Fain, William, Second Lieutenant
Farquhar, Robert
Farr, William, Captain
Farrow, Rosanna Waters
Faust, Burrell
Fayssoux, Peter Dott, Surgeon
Fearn, John, Second Lieutenant
Feaster, Andrew
Felder, Henry, Captain
Felder, Henry, Sr., Captain
Felder, Jno. Henry
Ferguson, Samuel
Few, William, Sr.
Finlay, James, Reverend
Fishburne, William, General
Fishburne, William, Lieutenant
Fisher, Adam
Fisher, Samuel, Captain
Fitts, John, Captain
Fladger, Charles
Fladger, Henry
Fleorl, John, Captain
Flewellyn, Abner, Captain
Flinn, William
Flood, Thomas
Flornay, Matthew
Floyd, John, Lieutenant
Foard, John
Folger, Frederick
Folger, Reuben
Forney, Peter, General
Forsythe, Robert, Captain

Foster, Abiel
Foster, James
Fox, William
Frasier, Alexander
Frazier, Thomas
Friday (or Fridig,) Gabriel, Captain
Frierson, John
Fripp, John
Fuller, John
Fullerton, John, Captain
Furman, Wood

# G ☆ G

Gabeau, Anthony, Sergeant
Gadsden, Christopher, Brigadier General
Gaillard, Charles
Gaines, Joseph
Gaither, Burgess
Gale, Matthew
Gamble, Robert, Colonel
Gardner, William
Garry, John
Gary, Thomas
Gaston, John
Gaston, Joseph
Gaston, William, Captain
Gause, William
Gayle, Matthew
Geiger, Jacob John, Major
Geiger, John
George, Gotleib
Gervais, John Lewis (Louis)
Gibbes, William Hasell, Captain
Gibson, Erasmus
Gilbert, Amos Alling
Gilbert, Asabel
Gilchrist, John
Gile, Noah
Gilder, Reuben, Surgeon
Giles, James
Giles, William
Gilkey, William
Gill, Archibald, Colonel
Gillespie, George
Gillian, Robert, Major
Gillian, Robert, Sr., Major
Gilliland, James
Girardeau, John
Givens, Samuel, Captain
Gladney, Samuel
Glasgow, Robert
Glazier, John
Glenn, David, Lieutenant-Colonel

Glenn, James
Glenn, William C.
Glover, Joseph, Colonel
Godbold, Stephen, Captain
Goforth, Preston
Goggans, David
Goldsmith, William
Goldwire, James, Captain
Golson, John
Golson, Lewis, Major
Gooding, John
Gordon, David
Gordon, Roger, Lieutenant
Gordon, William, Captain
Gough, Richard, Captain
Grady, John
Grady, William
Graham, William, Colonel
Graham, William, Qm. Sergeant
Grant, James
Grant, William, Lieutenant
Gray, James
Grayson, John, Lieutenant
Green, George, Captain
Green, John, Colonel
Green, Isaac
Greene, Peter
Gregg, James, Captain
Gregg, Joseph
Gressett, William, Colonel
Grier, Thomas
Griffin, Charles, Sergeant
Griffin, James, Corporal
Griffin, Joseph
Griffin, Richard
Guin, John Nicholas
Gumeas, Elias
Gutekunsh, Frederick

# H ☆ H

Hailey, William
Halbert, William
Hall, Jesse
Hall, William, Captain
Hall, William
Haltiwanger, John
Hambright, Frederick, Colonel
Hambright, Frederick, Lieut.-Col.
Hamett, Thomas
Hamilton, Andrew, Major
Hamilton, Ann Kennedy
Hamilton, David
Hamilton, John, Sergeant
Hamilton, John, Lieutenant
Hamilton, Thomas

Hamilton, William
Hammond, Abner, Captain
Hammond, Charles, Lieutenant
Hammond, LeRoy, Sr., Colonel
Hammond, Samuel, Lieutenant-Col.
Hampton, Thomas
Hanson, Walter, Captain
Harchfield, Henry
Hardin, Henry, Second Lieutenant
Hardy, John, Captain
Hardy, Thomas
Harnsberger, Conrad
Harrell, Lewis
Harrington, Henry W., General
Harris, Arthur
Harris, Hugh
Harris, John, Captain
Harris, Matthew
Harris, Robert, Colonel
Harris, Sherwood, Sr., Captain
Harris, Walter
Harrison, Benjamin
Harrison, James
Harrison, Richard, Maj.
Harvey, Arnold
Harwell, Landson
Harwood, Thomas, Captain
Haselden, William
Hatch, Benjamin
Hatch, Joseph
Hatcher, Benjamin, Captain
Hatcher, Josiah
Houser, Andrew
Hay, Ann Hawkes
Hay, Melchior, Captain
Hayes, John
Hayes, Joseph
Hayne, Isaac, Colonel
Haynes, John, Captain
Haynesworth, Henry
Hazel, Henry
Hazzard, William
Heath, Jordon
Hempsted, Stephen
Henderson, Samuel
Henderson, Thomas, Lieutenant
Henry, William, Sr
Heriot, Robert, Colonel
Herndon, Benjamin, Lieutenant-Col.
Herrick, Ebenezer
Herrick, Israel
Heyward, Nathaniel
Heyward, Thomas, Jr., Captain
Hickman, William
Hicks, George, Colonel
Higgins, John
Hill, Joshua

Hill, Lodowick, Sergeant
Hill, Squier
Hill, William
Hinds, Bartlett, Captain
Hinman, Elisha
Hodges, Joshua
Holbrook, Nathan
Holland, Reverend Moses
Holland, Thomas
Hollingsworth, Enoch
Hollingsworth, Jeptha
Hollister, Deacon Elijah
Holman, Conrad
Holmes, Orsamus
Holtzclaw, Catherine Russell
Hook, Martin, Sergeant
Hopkins, David, Lieutenant
Hopkinson, Francis
Horlbeck, John
Houseal, William, Captain
Houser, George, Lieutenant
Houston, Samuel
Howard, Groves
Howard, Seth
Howe, Daniel
Howe, (How), Samuel
Hubbard, William
Hudgens, Ambrose
Hughes, Joseph, Captain
Hughes, Thomas
Huggins, John, Captain
Hunt, Samuel
Hunter, Andrew
Hunter, Henry
Hunter, James, Colonel
Huntington, James
Hutchins, Drury, Captain
Hutson, Thomas, Captain
Hyde, Jedediah

I &#9734; I

Inabinet, John
Ingles, William, Major
Ingram, Edwin, Captain
Ingram, John
Irby, Joseph
Izard, Ralph

J &#9734; J

James, Benjamin
James, Daniel
James, Elias
James, John

Jarvis, Nathaniel
Jeffries, Nathaniel, Captain
Jenkins, Benjamin, Jr.
Jenkins, Benjamin
Jenkins, Reverend James
Jenkins, Joseph, Lieutenant
Jernigan, Jesse
Jeter, James
Jeter, Henry, Lieutenant
John, Thomas
Johnson, James, Captain
Johnson, Noble
Johnson, William
Johnston, John
Johnston, Nathan, Captain
Jolly, Joseph
Jones, Abraham Parman, 2nd Lieut.
Jones, Adam Crain, Jr.
Jones, Charles
Jones, Daniel
Jones, Jeremiah
Jones, John
Jones, John, Lieutenant
Jones, Peter, Lieutenant
Jones, Samuel
Jordan, Henry E.
Jordon, John

# K &#9734; K

Keeler, Jeremiah
Keels, John
Keith, Alexander
Keith, Cornelius, Captain
Kendrick, John
Kendrick, Samuel
Kennedy, James, Lieutenant
Kennedy, John
Kennedy, John, Sr.
Kennedy, Samuel, Surgeon
Kennedy, William
Kennerly, James
Kent, Phineas
Kershaw, Joseph, Colonel
Kerr, Daniel
Ketchen, Joseph
Kilgore, Benjamin, Captain
Kilpatrick, Reverend Robert
Kinard, Michael
Kincaid, James, Captain
King, Benjamin
King, Charles
King, John M.
Kirby, James
Kirk, Lewis
Kirkland, Reuben

Knight, John
Knotts, Benjamin
Knox, James, Jr.
Knox, Sara
Koger, Joseph, Captain
Kolb, Abel

# L &#9734; L

Lake, Thomas
Lamar, Thomas, Jr.
Land, William
Lane, Jessie
Lane, Job
Langston, Laeodicia
Langston, Solomon, Lieutenant
Langston, Solomon
Lanier, Burwell
Larray, Michael
Lawrence, Benjamin, Second Lieut.
Lazarus, Marks, Sgt.-Major
Lea, Gabrielle
Lea, James, Sr.
Leach, James
Leach, Nehemiah
Leary, Cornelius
Lecesne, Charles Frederick, 2nd
    Lieutenant
LeCompte, John, Lieutenant
LeConte, John Eaton
Lee, Andrew
Lee, Joseph
Lee Joshua
Leech, David, Captain
Leeland, John, Jr., Captain
Leeland, John, Sr.
Leonard, Laughlen, Captain
Letcher, William, Colonel
Lewis, Andrew, General
Lewis, Anne Montgomery
Lewis, John, Major
Lewis, William, Colonel
Libby, Nathaniel
Lide, Robert, Major
Lide, Thomas, Colonel
Liddell, Andrew
Lindley, Ziba
Lipscomb, Thomas
Lipscomb, William, Major
Little, James, Colonel
Livingston, Henry
Livingston, John
Livingston, Thomas
Locke, Richard
Lockwood, Joshua
Logan, Hugh, General

Logan, John
Logan, William
Long, Felix
Long, Henry
Long, Jacob
Love, Alexander
Love, Andrew, Colonel
Love, David, Lieutenant-Colonel
Love, Robert, Lieutenant
Lovell, James, Sr.
Lowell, James, Jr.
Lowell, James, Sr.
Lucas, John
Lunsford, Swanson, Captain
Lyne, William
Lymme, John, Colonel
Lyles, Aramanus, Captain
Lynn, David, Captain
Lynn, John

# M ☆ M

Machen, Henry, Sergeant
Mack, John
Mackay, James, Sergeant
Manning, Lawrence
Manson, Frederick
Marbury, Thomas
Marion, Joseph
Marques, Isaac
Marsh, William
Marshall, James
Marshall, Thomas, Colonel
Martin, David
Martin, Edward
Martin, Gatlop, Lieutenant
Martin, Isaac
Martin, James
Martin, Kitchen
Martin, Matthew
Martin, Richard
Mason, David
Mason, George
Massey, William, Sr., Lieut.-Col.
Matlock, Timothy
Mattison, James
Matthews, Sampson, Colonel
Mauldin, Rucker, Preacher
Mauney, Valentine
May, John, Captain
Maybank, Joseph, Colonel
Maxwell, William T.
Means, James
Meetze, John Yost, Reverend
Mellichamp, St. Lo.

Mengel, Adam
Merchant, William
Meredith, Elisha, Captain
Meredith, Samuel, Colonel
Merrill, Benjamin, Sr., Captain
Merriwether, Thomas
Mershimer, Sebastian
Metze, John
Meyers, John F., Major
Mikell, John, Major
Milledge, John
Miller, Charles
Miller, David
Miller, Jacob
Miller, James, Colonel
Miller, Robert, Sr., Captain
Milner, John, Captain
Mills, John, Captain
Mims, Drury
Mitchell, Nazarath
Mitchell, Wm. Wilbur
Mobley, Jeremy, Captain
Moffatt, John, Captain
Monday, Jeremiah
Monroe, Malcolm
Montague, John
Montague, Peter
Montague, Thomas
Montgomery, Hugh, Lieutenant
Montgomery, James
Montgomery, John
Moore, Alexander
Moore, David
Moore, Eliab
Moore, James, Major
Moore, Phillip
Moore, Stephen, General
Moore, William, Lieutenant
Moorehead, William
Moorer, John
Mordecai, Samuel
Morehead, Charles, Captain
Morgan, Benajmin
Morgan, David
Morgan, George, Colonel
Morgan, Spencer
Morris, John
Morris, Joseph
Morrow, John
Morrow, Samuel
Morton, John, Captain
Morton, Oliver
Mosely, Azariah
Mosely, Benjamin, Lieutenant
Mosely, Samuel
Moses, George
Moses, Myer

Mosse, George, Doctor
Most, George, Doctor
Moultrie, William, Major-General
Moye, George
Muckenfuss, Michael
Mullin, James
Mulloy, Edward
Munnally, John
Murff, John
Murray, William
Myers, Jacob, Lieutenant


## Mc ☆ Mc

McArthur, Daniel
McBee, Vardy, Captain
McCain, William
McCants, Nathaniel
McCants, Thomas
McCalla, David
McClendon, Travis, Captain
McClung, John, Lieutenant
McClure, John, Colonel
McColl, George
McCord, Charles, Corporal
McCord, Mark
McCormick, John
McCoy, John
McCoy, William
McCravy, Thomas, Sr.
McCrea
McCurdy, John, Jr.
McDavid, James
McDonald, Daniel
McDowell, Charles, Brig.-General
McDowell, Joseph
McDowell, Margaret O'Neal
McElwee, William, Lieutenant
McFadden, Robert
McGarrough, Joseph, Major
McGee, Michael
McGill, Samuel
McGregor, John, Lieutenant
McGrew, William
McIntosh, William
McIver, Evander
McJunkin, Joseph, Major
McJunkin, Samuel, Captain
McKinsey, William
McLean, Ephriam
McMaster, Hugh
McMaster, Hugh
McMaster, James
McMorris, William
McNeil, Hector

McNeill, Hector, Captain
McRaw, Francis
McWhorter, John


## N ☆ N

Nason, Joshua, Captain
Natch, Edward
Neal, Henry, Captain
Nelson, Samuel, Sr.
Nesbitt, Jonathan
Nesmith, Robert
Nettles, George
Nettles, William, Captain
Nettles, Zachariah, Lieutenant
Neufrille, John
Neville, Jessie
Newcomb, Daniel
Newton, Younger
Nicholson, Wright, Lieutenant
Nimmons, William
Nims, Ariel, Sergeant
Nixon, Hugh Alexander
Norris, John, Sergeant
Norris, William, Sr
Norton, Ichabod, Captain
Norwood, George W.
Nuckolls, John
Nuckolls, John, Sr.


## O ☆ O

Oakes, Daniel
Odill, Thomas
Ogier, Lewis, Captain
Ogletree, William
Oliver, Alexander
Orr, James
Osborne, Ephram, Jr.
Osborne, Ephram, Sr. Sergeant
Otis, Ephriam, Doctor
Ott, Abraham, Lieutenant
Outz, Peter
Outze, Peter
Overall, Nathaniel
Owen, Jesse, Captain
Owens, James


## P ☆ P

Pace, Newsom, Sergeant
Page, John, Colonel

Paine, David
Palmer, John
Palmer, Jonathan
Parcival, Benjamin, Corporal
Parham, Drury
Parker, David
Parker, John
Parker, Moses
Parkinson, John
Parks, Samuel
Parrott, John, Sr.
Pate, John, Lieutenant
Pate, Matthew, Lieutenant
Patrick, Cain, Jr.
Patterson, Josiah
Patterson, William Joseph
Patton, Matthew
Paulling, William
Payne, John
Payne, Josiah
Payton, John, Lieutenant
Pearce, Joshua, Jr.
Pearman, William, Sr., Sergeant
Pearson, John, Major
Pearson, Moses, Lieutenant
Pech, Bela
Peeples, Henry
Pegues, Claudius, Captain
Perse, Silas
Perry, Benjamin F.
Peters, John
Pettigrew, Alex
Pettigrew, James, Sr.
Pettigrew, James
Petty, Absolom
Phelps, Elijah
Phillips, John
Phillips, Jonas
Phillips, Hugh
Phillips, Levi
Phillips, Mourning
Pickens, Andrew, Brig.-General
Pinckney, Charles
Pinckney, Hopson
Pitman James,
Pocher, Samuel
Poindexter, Joseph, Captain
Polk, John, Captain
Polk, William
Pollard, Robert
Pool, William
Pope, Barnaby
Pope, Folgu
Pope, Solomon
Pope, Solomon, Captain
Porcher, Peter
Porter, William, Lieutenant

Postell, Benjamin
Postell, James, Colonel
Postell, John, Lieutenant
Potter, John
Powell, Absolem, Sr., Captain
Powell, James
Powell, Sevin, Lieut.-Colonel
Poyas, Jean Ernest
Poyas, John Ernest
Preston, Walter
Price, Charles
Prior, Seth
Pritchard, George
Protho, Evans
Pruitt, Joshua
Purser, William
Purvis, George
Putman, Israel, General
Pyles, Reuben

# Q ☆ Q

Quarteman, Robert

# R ☆ R

Raeford, John
Ragsdale, John
Ragsdale, Peter, Sergeant
Rainey, Samuel
Rall, Thomas, Reverend
Ralston, John
Ramsburgh, James, Sr.
Rankin, Thomas, Captain
Rasor, Christian
Ravenel, Daniel
Redding, Anderson
Reed, Benjamin, Corporal
Reed, Samuel
Reese, Joseph, Reverend
Reeves, Enos, Captain
Reid, Francis
Reid, Joseph, Lieutenant
Reid, William, Jr.
Renfro, Mark Ensign
Rice, Aaron
Richards, Amos
Richardson, Amos
Richardson, John Richard
Richardson, Richard, Captain
Richardson, Richard, General
Richardson, William, Captain
Richardson, William, Colonel
Riddick, Joseph

Rinker, Jacob
Ripley, Jeptha
Risher, Benjamin
Rivers, Samuel
Roberts, John
Roberts, Reuben
Robertson, Thomas
Robertson, William
Robinson, Isaac
Robinson, Peter
Robinson, Thomas, Colonel
Robinson, William
Rogers, Benjamin, Colonel
Rogers, Lot
Rosa, Petru
Roseboom, Garrett
Ross, David, Sergeant
Rothmahler, Erasmus, Lieutenant
Rouse, William, Colonel
Rowe, Christopher, Lieut. Colonel
Roy, Beverly, Captain
Royal, William
Ruff, David
Rumph, Abraham
Rumph, David
Rush, David
Russell, Thomas, Lieutenant
Russell, William, Brig. General
Rutherford, James, Major
Rutherford, Robert, Colonel
Rutledge, George, General
Rutledge, Robert, Colonel

# S ☆ S

Sadler, David, Sr.
Salley, John, Captain
Salter, Edward
Sanders (Saunders), Peter
Sartor, William
Sass, Jacob, 2nd Lieutenant
Saunders, Nathaniel, Lieutenant
Scott, John
Scott, Joseph James, Captain
Scott, Joseph, Lieutenant
Scott, Joyce Jane Callahan
Scott, Samuel
Scovell, Elisha, Lieutenant
Seddall, Stephen
Sellers, Gordan
Setgreave, John
Sevier, John, Lieutenant Colonel
Sevinton, Hugh, Sr.
Shackleford, John
Shakleford, William, 2nd Lieutenant

Sharp, William
Sheldon, Whiting
Sheppard, James, Sr.
Shingler, George
Shiving, James, Captain
Shubirch, Richard, Captain
Shuford, John, Sr.
Simons, Keating, Asst. Brig. Maj.
Simonton, John
Simmons, James
Simmons, John, Lieutenant
Simpkins, Arthur, Captain
Simons, James Col.
Simpson, John, Commander
Simpson, John, Reverend
Sims, Charles, Lieut. Colonel
Singletary, Ebenezer
Singleton, John, Captain
Singleton, Matthew
Singleton, Ripley Nicholson
Singleton, Thomas
Skirving, James, Jr., Captain
Sloan, David, Captain
Smith, Aaron
Smith, Annanias
Smith, Charles
Smith, John, Colonel
Smith, John, Lieutenant
Smith, Jonathan, Jr., Reverend
Smith, Joshua
Smith, Merriwether
Smith, Roger Moore, Lieut. Colonel
Smith, Samuel
Smith, Samuel, Colonel
Smith, Stephen
Smith, Thomas, Lieutenant
Spann, James, Lieutenant
Sparks, Daniel, Captain
Spencer, Calvin, Lieutenant
Spencer, Thomas, Colonel
Spigner, Frederick
Spofford, Joseph
Sprague, Joseph, Captain
Spratt, Thomas, Captain
Spootswood, Alexander, General
Stackhouse, William
Stanley, Samuel
Starr, Daniel
Steadman, John
Steedman, John
Steele, Elizabeth
Steel, Francis
Steele, John, Captain
Steele, Joseph, Captain
Steen, James, Lieut. Colonel
Sterns, Josiah
Stevens, John, Lieutenant

Stevens, Simeon, Lieutenant
Stiles, Benjamin, Captain
Stillwell, John
Stock, John
Stokes, Jeremiah
Stone, Jacob, Sr.
Stone, John
Stone, Jonathan, Lieutenant
Stoncipher, John
Stoney, John
Storrs, Joseph, Major
Stratton, John
Streit, Christian, Chaplain
Strickland, Jacob
Strobel, Daniel, Lieutenant
Stroman, Jacob
Stroman, John Jacob
Stroman, Paul
Strong, Christopher
Strother, George, Lieutenant
Stuart, David
Stubbs, Lewis
Stubbs, William
Sullivan, Hewlett, Sr., Lieutenant
Summer, Francis
Summer, John Adam
Summer, John Adam, Lieutenant
Sumner, David
Swearingen, Van, Captain
Sweedy, David
Swink, John Little
Swinton, Hugh
Switzer, Henry

## T &#9734; T

Talbert, Richard, Lieutenant
Talbird, Thomas, Captain
Taliaferro, John, Doctor
Tarver, Absalom
Tatnall, Joseph
Taylor, Eldad
Taylor, Francis, Colonel
Taylor, George, Lieutenant
Taylor, James, Colonel
Taylor, Othneil, Sr., Adjutant
Taylor, Samuel, Major
Taylor, Thomas, Colonel
Taylor, Thornton, Lieutenant
Teer, William, Captain
Tennant, William, Reverend
Terrell, George, Major
Terry, Nathaniel, Major
Thatcher, Obediah
Thomas, Jane Black
Thomas, John, Colonel

Thomas, John, Sr., Colonel
Thomas, Jonathan
Thomas, Stephen
Thomas, William
Tompkins, Stephen, Captain
Thompson, John, Captain
Thompson, Matthew
Thomson, William, Colonel
Threewitz, John, Brig. Major
Thelkeld, John
Tillman, Frederick
Tillotson, Daniel, 2nd Lieutenant
Tinsley, Golden
Townes, William
Tozer, Julius
Treadwell, Reuben, Lieutenant
Trent, Thomas
Treutlin, John Adams
Trezevant, Theodore
Trott, Benjamin, Sergeant
Tucker, Harbert
Turner, James
Turner, John, Captain
Turner, Zadoc

## U &#9734; U

Ulmer, John Jacob
Underwood, Joseph

## V &#9734; V

VanAuken, John
Vance, Nathaniel
Vance, Samuel, Colonel
Vandiver, Edward
Varden, Steven
Vaught, Matthias
Venable, Nathaniel
Verner, John, Jr.
Vince, Joseph, Captain

## W &#9734; W

Waddill, Edmund
Wade, George
Waldo, Samuel
Walker, Adam
Walker, Alexander
Walker, Daniel, Jr.
Walker, Esther
Walker, John, Sr.
Walker, Nathaniel, Sr.

Walker, Samuel
Walker, Thomas
Walker, Thomas, Doctor, General
Wall, Wright, 2nd Lieutenant
Wallace, James
Wallace, John, Sr.
Waller, George, Major
Waller, John
Waller, Thomas, Sergeant
Wannamaker, Jacob, Lieutenant
Wannamaker, Jacob, Lieutenant
Wansley, John
Ward, Enoch, Captain
Ward, William
Warren, Josiah, Captain
Warriner, James, Captain
Waters, Boardwine
Waters, Philemon, Captain
Watson, David
Watson, Hezekiah
Watson, Michael, Captain
Watts, James, Lieutenant
Watts, James, Sr., Lieutenant
Watts, John, Colonel
Way, Moses, Captain
Weed, Reuben
Weedere, Augustine, Sergeant
Welch, Thomas, Sergeant
Wells, Richard
Wells, Robert, Lieutenant
Wertz, George Henry
Wertz, John
West, William, Colonel
Westbrook, Samuel, Captain
Whaley, Thomas
Wharton, Samuel, Colonel
White, Anthony
White, James
White, John
White, Vassel
White, William
Whitfield, Needham
Whitfield, William, Sr.
Whitner, James
Whitner, Joseph
Whitney, James, Rex
Whittaker, Thomas
Wideman, Adam
Wilfong, George, Major
   nkie, Lieutenant
Wilkie, William, Lieutenant
Wilkins, William, Captain
Wilkinson, Morton
Wilks, Thomas
Willard, Jonathan, 2nd Lieutenant
Williams, Benjamin
Williams, Elijah

Williams, James, Colonel
Williams, John, Major
Williams, Stephen
Williams, William
Williamson, Samuel
Wingo, John
Wilson, James P., Surgeon
Wilson, John, Captain
Wilson, John
Wilson, John Robert
Wilson, William
Winslow, John, Captain
Winston, Peter
Witcher, William, Sr., Major
Withers, Elisha
Witherspoon, David, Captain
Witherspoon, David, Captain
Witherspoon, Gavin, Corporal
Witherspoon, James, Captain
Witherspoon, John, D. D.
Witherspoon, John
Witherspoon, John
Withrow, James, Captain
Wofford, Joseph, Captain
Wood, Benjamin
Wood, Reverend Henry
Wood, John
Wood, Leighton, Jr.
Woodward, John, Lieutenant
Woodward, Thomas, Captain
Woodward, William
Wooten, Shadrack
Wooten, Shadrack (Patriot)
Warnock, Joseph
Wright, Joseph
Wright, Issac
Wright, Nicholson, Lieutenant
Wyatt, William, Jr.
Wyles ,William, Sergeant


# Y  ☆  Y

Young, James
Young, Thomas


# Z  ☆  Z

Zackary, John A., Sergeant
Zane, Isaac
Zenn, Jacob, Lieutenant
Zubers, John

ADDITIONAL ANCESTORS TAKEN FROM THE SUPPLEMENT TO THE
ROSTER OF S.C. D.A.R. COMPILED BY THE STATE REGISTRAR
MRS. JAMES T. OWEN IN 1944

Arnold, Jonathan
Anthony, James
Ayers, John
Adair, Jasper
Boykin, Maj. Francis
Bridgeman, Erasmus
Bennett, Reuben
Blount, Charles W.
Blanding, Capt. Wm.
Boozer, Henry
Bartlett, Capt. Wm.
Blassingame, Julien
Burris, Wm.
Beverly, Capt. Ray
Bowie, Maj. John
Brumbaugh, Jacob
Brush, John
Corley, Caleb
Cantalou, Capt. Louis
Chappell, Laban
Crosby, Thomas
Carruth, Robert
Conyers, Charles
Conyers, James
Crawford, Robert
Carmichael, Jno. Duncan
Cole, Capt. Abram
Cox, Henry
Cosnahan, Joseph
Croom, Major
Dick, William
DePriest, Wm.
Dorland, Garrab
Dukes, William
Deyo, James
Epperson, David
Fambrough, Thos.
Finley, Paul
Fayssoux, F.
Fullton, Jasper P.
Farrabe, Caleb
Gunnungust, Fred
Gray, John
Gaines, Richard
Gause, John
Grigsby, E
Graham, Michael
Garvin, Thomas

Gunnell, Henry
Gough, Capt. Richard
Gay, James Jr.
Goodman, William
Haselaw, Wm.
Hodges, John
Halbert, Wm.
Hayes, James
Hope, James Sr.
Hough, Joseph
Hilton, James
Huske, John
Hutto, Henry
Harris, Tucker
Hopson, Capt. Henry
Hoyle, John
Hearst, James
Johnston, Dr. Thos.
Johnston, Charles
Jarvis, Solomon
Knight, James
Kirkland, Francis
Kershaw, Jasper
Kirkpatrick, Jno.
Kennamer, George
Koger, Capt. James
Lewellyn, Capt. Abram
Lowe, Jno. Peter
Lowe, Robert
Lathrop, M
Lampkin, Stephen
Lowe, Basil
Lewis, Col. Fielding
Lennart, Wm.
Lee, Arthur
Lipscomb, James
Little, Col. James
McCalla, David
McKeown, Alexander
Messenger, David
Masters, David
McAbley, Wm.
Mackey, Thomas
Massey, Henry
Mosher, John
McMurray, Wm.
Morris, Julien
Moorer, James

McCattry, Robt.
McMullen, John
Nagel, Philip
Neel, Vol. Thos.
Orr, G
Oliphant, John
Orr, Jehu
O'Heak, James
Parsons, Wm.
Phelps, Capt. David
Pyron, Wm. C.
Pugh, Elijah
Query, Alexander
Rister, Benj.
Rose, Russell
Richards, Richard
Royse, Solomon
Scott, David
Sanders, Thomas
Sexton, Chap. O.
Sharp, Col. Starkey
Sweargengen, Capt. D
Springs, Richard
See, John Daulbit
Taliaferro, Jack
Tousinger, James
Tillingast, Col. D.
Twitty, Wm.
Ulmer, Jacob
Van Meter, Abram
Vance, Capt. David
Vaughan, John
Vigneron, Charles
Warren, Isiah
Watson, Col. Saml.
Waddle, William
Webb, Francis Jr.
Willis, Richard
Wilkinson, David
Windley, Maj. Thos.
Williams, Maj. Jno
Wings, John Sr.
Whitaker, Hudson
Wooten, Shadrach
Yancey, Capt. Thornton
Young, Capt. William

MONUMENT AT SITE OF ANDREW
JACKSON'S BIRTHPLACE

FORT MOULTRIE. On Sullivan's Island. This fort, originally called Fort Sullivan, has played a great part in two wars. From here the first decisive victory of the Revolution was won when the British fleet was repulsed in the engagement which made Sergeant Jasper nationally famous.

Jasper Replacing the Flag.

MAIN BUILDING (1828), COLLEGE OF CHARLESTON
The Oldest Municipal College in America

Williamsburg County Court House, Designed by Robert Mills who
designed the United States Treasury Building and the Washington
Monument.

# GENERAL FRANCIS MARION

One of the great Partisan Leaders in South Carolina, was of Huguenot descent. He was known as THE SWAMP FOX, because he operated in the swampy forests of the Pedee region and lower part of the state. His strategy was to dash out quickly with his superbly mounted men, surprise and cut the enemy's supply lines, kill their men and release American prisoners, then swiftly back again to "the thick recesses of the deep swamps." Ramsay says of his equipment that "the pruning hook was converted into a spear; and the saw, under the hands of a blacksmith, became a terrible sabre." Marion's ORDERLY BOOK, 1775, has this item: "Every officer to provide himself with a blue coatee, faced and cuffed with scarlet cloth, and lined with scarlet; white buttons; and a white waistcoat and breeches...also, a cap and black feather..."

Below I list a few of Marion's soldiers that were connected with my family or else lines that I have worked on as a genealogist:

Arnold, Wm...Adair, Jas...Boyd, Jno...Conyers, Jas., Jon., Chas...Dickey, Jno...Ervin, Col. John, Col. Hugh, Saml...Ellerbe, Thos. & Robt...Fleming, Jno., Jas., Wm....Frierson, Philip, William, John, George, Robert, William, Gordon, John, James, Wm...Gillespie, Andrw...Hamilton, James, John, Wm...Knox, Hugh, Robt...McGill, Saml, Jno...Patton, Matt, Jacob...Nelson, John Saml, Thomas, Robert, Wm....Wilson, John, Hugh, Wm....White, John....Witherspoon, Gavin, David, James, John, Robert...James, Major Jon, Alex, Geo, Robt., Wm.

Also the women: Dunklin, Mary. .Ervin, Mrs. Eliz. James...Ervin, Eliz. Ellison....Ervin, Jane Witherspoon....James, Mrs. Sarah....Wilson, Mrs. Mary...

**OLD STONE CHURCH**
A few miles south of historic Pendleton. It was here that General Robert Anderson and General Andrew Pickens attended services and served as elders. Completed in 1802, this structure of rough native stone still stands as one of the oldest landmarks in upper South Carolina.

**"HALCYON GROVE"**—Historic Home of Gov. Andrew Pickens

St. David's Church at Cheraw, used as a hospital during the Revolution.

112

# MISCELLANEOUS NOTES AND DATA

One hundred and forty-six actions were fought in the state during the Revolution and for almost three years, South Carolina was a battleground. This is stated in an article published in the D.A.R. Magazine of April 1937, by A.S. Salley, State Historian of South Carolina. Quoted in the article is General Knox, first Secretary of War, and the Historian, George Bancroft, neither of whom were South Carolinians and had no reason to be partial to this state, - Knox as saying that South Carolina furnished more troops to the general cause in proportion to population than any other state, and more money, regardless of population. Bancroft is quoted as saying that South Carolina suffered more and achieved more than the men of any other state. For almost three years civil war raged and there was no constituted government. Chapman in his History of South Carolina says that General Greene's Army outside Charleston, was for three months, half-naked and over 700 of them had no clothing except a small strip of cloth about the waist. In Johnson's Life of Greene we read, "...hundreds...were naked as they were born...the bare loins of many brave men...were galled by their cartridge boxes, while a folded rag or tuft of moss protected the shoulders...from injury (of) ...muskets." Chapman says that "after Charleston...had fallen, and the men who so bravely defended it had become prisoners of war, the British soon overan the whole state; for after the loss of Lincoln's Army, there were no Americans in arms in the state, except a few small detached bodies..." Quoting White, The Making of South Carolina, "...the region of the waters of Broad and Saluda...filled with companies of armed patriots...(they) planned attacks upon the enemy in their own way, captured forts in a manner not spoken about in books...did more than any other people of equal numbers to win freedom for America." Simms, History of S.C. states that "vapacious plundering and outrages (were the order of the day) ...volunteer bands...sprang up like mushrooms...officers without commissions, pay or provisions or necessary clothing (for their men) were leading (them) daily to little victories...many leaders...not mentioned in history, with troops of volunteers, achieved the salvation of South Carolina." Again, "after the battle of Eutaw Springs...William Cunningham (Tory leader) took advantage of the absence of any large American force, penetrated the interior, broke his force into small bands...gave no quarter..." Ninety-Six District alone had "1400 widows and orphans."

Chapman tells us that "Major Cunningham...led (a band) ...sole object... seemed to be to plunder, burn, murder. In the dead of night... they entered the solitary farm homes and sacrificed to their revenge the heads of families... these and other cruelties, compelled parties to arm and associate in self-defense." The Colonial and Revolutionary History of Upper S.C., by Landrum, states that "the unexpected appearance of Cunningham and the consternation that spread rapidly over the country on account of his cruelties, caused small parties here and there, to get together and take up arms in self-defense." Simms says that "soon small parties headed by outraged fathers were upon the heels of the marauders." Among the best known of the Partisan Leaders were Generals Francis Marion, Andrew Pickens, Thomas Sumter, Colonel & Brig-Genl. Williams. of Ninety-Six District, hero of Musgrove Mills and who fell at Kings Mountain. Major James was a well-known leader in Williamsburg county and organized the battalion that became the nucleus of Marion's Brigade. There were many other local leaders throughout the state. Ninety-Six District, embraced what is known as the Up-Country or Piedmont section and in 1785 was composed of what was later the following counties: Laurens, Edgfield, Abbeville,. Newberry, Spartanburg, Union. This district claims 30 Revolutionary battles within her borders and 7 more on the Cherokee Indian lands which later became Up-country counties.

----------

## MISCELLANEOUS LIST OF S.C. SOLDIERS

Andrews Saml. . .Arnold Wm. . .Arnold Benj. . .Anderson Jno. . .Bolling Wm. . . Burton Jno. . .Choice Wm. . .Craig Jno. . .Cureton Jno. . .Gayle Josiah. . .Giroud David. . . .Holley Rich. . . .Kilgore Henry, Benj. . . .Knight Jno. . .Lewis Chas. Crawford. . . .Mahaffey Martin. . .Miles, Jno. . .McCauley Jas. . .Moore, Gully, Jeremiah, Chas, Jno. . .Moon, G--- . . .Paine Thos. . .Perrin Theus. . .Patton, Jacob. . .Pinson, Moses. . .Rodgers, Edward, John, Robt. . .Ridgeway, John Jr. & Sr. . .Susack Adam. . .Smith Eleazer. . .Simons, Cor. Jas. . .Sullivan, Moses, George, Patrick, Johnathan, John, Daniel, Hulet, Charles. . . .Tucker Rich. . . Waller Benj. . .Watson, Michael, David, James, Joh, Robert, Gavin.

----------

## LIST OF SOUTH CAROLINIANS WHO CAME TO RELIEF OF BOSTON

The historian Ramsey says that people from every part of the state met in Charleston on 6 July 1774 to consider plans to support Boston. For the following list see D.A.R. Mag. Mch. & Aug. 1945. Also, McCrady, Under the Royal Gov; Gregg, Hist. of Old Cheraws; Drayton, Memoirs of Revo. South Carolina was the first to minister to the need of Boston. "By account pub. by Comm. appt. by Boston to receive donations...July 18, 1778, it appears that (those of) S.C. exceeded both in money & supplies, any other, not excepting Mass. itself":

Alston, Joseph, John, Joseph, William, Josias, Francis. .Andrews, Jno. .Barnard, Noble. .Bingham, Thos. .Butler, Thos. .Bonneau, Anthony. . .Boykin, Burrel. . . Buchanan, Peter Simons. . . .Clyf, Saml. . . .Cuttino, Wm. . .Council, Henry. . Corgill, Magnus. .Downs, Walter. .Donaldson, Jno. . .Dwight, Nathl. . .Edwards, Abel. . .Ellerbe, Thos. . .Godfrey, Thos. . .Gordon, Jas. . .Gillespie, Francis. . . Hazel, Thos. . .Hennery, Saml. . .Henry, Futhy. . .Hart, Arthur. . .Harrington, H. W. . .Huger, Ben. . .Horry, Alex. . .Hardwick, Wm. . .Hariot, Robt. . .Hicks, Geo. . .Lide, Thos. . .Lessenee, Peter. . .Mitchell, Anthony. . .Murfee, Malachi Jr. .Parks, Abram. .Pledger, Philip. .Pyatt, John. .Pegues, Wm. & Claudius. . . Pawley, Col. George, Memb. Prov. Cong. & Benj. & Wm. . .Roche, David. . . Rogers, Ethelred. . . .Reed, James. . . .Sparks, Danl. . .Scriven, Benj. . .Smith, Saml. . .Saunders, Jas. & Nathl. . .Trapier, Benj. . .Williams, Thos. . .Wright, Thos. . . .Wragg, S. . .White, Arthur. . .Warden, John. . .Wright, Geo. . .Young, William. . .Withers, Jno. . .Young, Benj. . .Hennery, Thos. . .Wright, Thomas.

----------

## MISCELLANEOUS

Soon after Battle of Lexington, following men chosen a COUNCIL of SAFETY: Henry Laurens, Chas. Pinckney, Rawlins Lowndes, Thos. Ferguson, Miles Brewton, Arthur Middleton, Thos. Heyward Jr., Thos. Bee, John Huger, James Parsons, Wm. H. Drayton, Benj. Elliott, Wm. Williamson, David Oliphant, Thos. Savage. Also Henry Middleton & John Rutledge were on a Council in 1775.

DELEGATES TO FIRST PROVINCIAL CONGRESS, JAN. 1775, from the DISTRICT BETWEEN THE BROAD & SALUDA, were: Jonathan Downs, James Williams, Maj. Jno. Caldwell, John Colcock, Rowland Rugely, John Satterwhite, John Williams, John McNees, Chas. King, George Ross. On DISTRICT COMMITTEES were: James Creswell, Saml Savage, John Satterwhite, John Ford, John Thomas, John Gordon, John Prince.

PROVINCIAL CONGRESS voted themselves the GENERAL ASSEMBLY 1776 and elected the following members a Legislative Council: Thos. Beem, Stephen Bull, Thos. Ferguson, John Kershaw, LeRoy Hammond, Wm. Moultrie, Henry Middleton, Rawlin Lowndes, Chas. Pinckney, Richard Richardson, David Oliphant, Thos. Shubrick, Gabriel Powel.

MEMBERS OF THE PRIVY COUNCIL: Jno. Edwards, Wm. H. Drayton, Jas. Parson etc...ORDINARY: Wm. Burrows...ASST; JUDGES: John Matthews, Henry Pendleton, Thos. Bee. ATTY. GEN'L: Alex. Moultrie. PRESIDENT: John Rutledge and VICE-PRES., Henry Laurens.

## THE S.C. LEGISLATURE MET IN JANUARY 1782 at JACKSONBOROUGH
----------

Members from the Districts named were as follows:

NINETY-SIX----Senator: John Lewis Gervais. Representatives: Robt. Anderson, LeRoy Hammond, Patrick Calhoun, Jno. Ewing Calhoun, John Murray, James Moore, Hugh Middleton, Andrew Simkins, Andrew Pickens.

LITTLE RIVER, between Broad & Saluda rivers----Senator: Col. Levi Casey. Representatives: Benj. Kilgore, Dr. Ross, Cpt. Wild Montgomery.

LOWER DISTRICT, Broad & Saluda----Senator: Maj. Gordon. Representatives: David Glynn, Philemon Waters, Michael Leirner, George Roof.

SPARTAN DIST.------Senator: Simon Berwick. Representatives: Col. Wm. Henderson, Col. Thos. Brandon, Col. John Thomas Jr., Saml McJunkin.

ST. JOHN, BERKELEY-----Senator: Francis Marion. Representatives: John Frierson, Thos. Giles, Richard Gough, Alex. Broughton, John Cordes, Gabriel Gigailliat.

(Taken from Diary of Josiah Smith Jr.)
----------

Provisional Articles of Peace between Great Britian and the United States were signed in Paris 15 Nov. 1782 but war was not legally terminated until 1783. Under an Act ratified 12 March 1783 the Governor of South Carolina was authorized to appoint an auditor for each judicial district to adjust all claims arising out of the Revolution. These were for fol. Dists:

NINETY-SIX, Robt. Anderson; CAMDEN, Wm. Tate; GEORGE TOWN, Peter Horry; BEAUFORT, Wm. Hazard Wigg; ORANGEBURG, Wm. Arthur; CHERAW, Thomas Powe.            ----------

## PETITIONERS TO COMMON HOUSE ASSEMBLY FOR RELIEF BECAUSE OF STAMP ACT 7 May 1776

Ash Jno. . . .Ash Cato. . . .Andebert Philip. . .Atkinson Jos. . .Bruce Donald. . . Boone Wm. & Thos. . .Baker Jon. & Wm. . .Blake Wm. . .Bedon Jno. . .Bothwell Jon. . .Banpfreed Wm. . .Bounetheau Peter. . .Berwick, Simon. . .Bocquet Peter Jr. .Banbury Wm. .Butler Peter. .Cope Brian. . .Chapman Jon. . .Carson Jas. . . Cannon Danl. . . .Crington Jos. . .Crosby Timothy. . .Capers Chas. . .Dawson & Dudley. . . .Dodd Jon. . .Dill Jos. . .Downs Arthur. . .Farr Thos. . .Fitzsimmons Christpr. . .Grimke Jon. P. . .Godfret & Gadsden. . .Grimke Fredk. . . .Gibbes Wm. . . .Guern & Williamson. . . .Harvey Robt. . .Hinds Patk. . .Horn Alex. . . Hartly Thos. .Hopton Wm. . .Holson Christpr. . .Hutcheson & Elfe. . .Hall Wm... . Holiday Wm. . .Hutchins Jos. . .Hogan Jas. . .Ingles Lloyd. . .Kinlock Francis. . . Jones Edw. . .Logan Wm. . .Lyford Wm. . .Lightwood Edw. . .Legaree Danl. . . Learmouth Alex. . .Legaree Sol. . .Legaree Jas. . .Marr Andrew. . .McCall Jon. Jr. .Morris Mark. .Mill Thos. .Marley Jon. .Martin Edw. .Matthews Edmund. . . . McGilivray Robt. . .Rutherford Robt. . .Neufvill Jon. . .Poyas Jas. . .Prue Jon. . . Odingsell Chas. . .Pockron Jon. . .Pike Thos. . .Perdriau & Fabre... .Pendergrass Darby. . .Prioleau Saml Jr. . .Smith Thos. . .Scott Jno. . .Stockton & Jackson. . . Richardson Rich. . .Savage Wm. . .Robinson Thos. . .Sarrazin Jonathan. ...Roberts

Benj. .Scott Nathl. .Tebout Tunes. .Sharp Jas. . .Tufts Simon. . .Trustler Wm. . .
Theus Jeremiah. .Toux Villepou. .Townsend Paul. .Tidyman Phil. . .Vanderhorst
Elias. . .Ward Jon. . .Warley Melchoir. . .You Chas. . .Wagner Jon. . .Wish Jon. . .
You Thos.

# First 'Tea Party' Was Held Here

The Old Exchange building at East Bay and Broad streets in Charleston was the scene of the first tea tax revolt against the British before
the Revolution and here also was where the Provincial Congress met in
July, 1774, to set up the first independent government in America.

Historical Prince George Winyah church, built
1742-46.

CHARLES BREWTON HOUSE
(BUILT BEFORE 1733)

The Funeral Procession of the Stamp Act
From an old print

HAMPTON (1735), NEAR McCLELLANVILLE

116

# MISCELLANEOUS RECORDS

A Muster Roll of the Grenadier Company in the Second Regiment of South Carolina Infantry, on The Continental Establishment, commanded by Colonel Isaac Motte.

August 25, 1778.

| Names | Date of Commissions |
|---|---|
| *Commissioned Officers* | |
| Thomas Dunbar, Captain | November 9, 1777 |
| Albert Roux, 1st Lieutenant | December 15, 1777 |

*Staff-Commissioned Officers*

| | |
|---|---|
| John Downs, Adjutant | March 12, 1778 |
| Rev. Henry Purcell, Chaplain | May 7, 1776 |
| John Hall, Quarter-Master | July 1, 1776 |
| Henry Gray, Pay-Master | December 16, 1777 |
| Jeremiah Thews, Surgeon | August 2, 1777 |
| John Henry Rusche, 1st Mate, do. | June 11, 1778 |
| Silvester Springer, 2d Mate, do. | June 27, 1778 |

*Staff Non-Commissioned Officers*

| | |
|---|---|
| Lewis Coffer, Sergeant-Major | June 16, 1778 |
| John Wickom, Sergeant-Major | October 5, 1778 |
| William Fletcher, Qr.-master Sergeant | July 15, 1778 |
| Daniel Simpson, Qr.-master Sergeant | During the war |
| James Arnold, Drum-Major | September 16, 1779 |
| Hugh Campbell, Fife-Major | June 16, 1778 |

| Non-Commissioned Officers | Enlistment Time | Time of Service |
|---|---|---|
| **Sergeants** | | |
| William Jasper | July 8, 1775 | July 8, 1778 |
| John Marlow | June 26, 1775 | June 26, 1778 |
| John Gemmell | July 18, 1775 | July 18, 1778 |
| Robert Watt | Aug. 5, 1777 | During the war |
| William Brown | July 6, 1778 | July 6, 1781 |
| **Corporals** | | |
| Samuel Butler | July 7, 1775 | July 7, 1778 |
| John Roberts | Nov. 26, 1776 | Nov. 26, 1779 |
| Robert Watt | Aug. 5, 1777 | During the war |
| Frederick Simons | July 27, 1777 | During the war |
| **Drummers** | | |
| John Wheeler | July 1, 1775 | July 1, 1778 |
| Peter Uptegrove | July 18, 1778 | Jan. 18, 1780 |
| **Privates** | | |
| William Ashford | July 11, 1777 | During the war |
| William Arnold | July 8, 1775 | July 8, 1778 |
| Barnaby Bryan | Aug. 5, 1777 | During the war |
| John Cook | July 13, 1775 | July 13, 1778 |
| Charles Cox | July 1, 1778 | Mar. 1, 1779 |
| John Baptist DeLaney | June 25, 1775 | June 25, 1778 |
| Owen Griffin | July 11, 1777 | During the war |
| Silas Gibson | July 16, 1778 | July 16, 1781 |
| Loami Husbands | Aug. 2, 1775 | Aug. 2, 1778 |
| John Humphreys | June 18, 1775 | June 18, 1778 |
| Aaron Harris | Jan. 31, 1777 | Jan. 31, 1780 |
| James Hooper | Aug. 5, 1777 | During the war |
| William Jones | July 7, 1777 | During the war |
| Robert Ivey | July 8, 1775 | July 8, 1778 |

| | | |
|---|---|---|
| Charles Lucas | July 19, 1775 | July 19, 1778 |
| Joseph Martin | July 10, 1775 | July 10, 1778 |
| Martin Moore | July 8, 1775 | July 8, 1778 |
| Jacob Murphy | July 8, 1775 | July 8, 1778 |
| John McCaid | Aug. 5, 1777 | During the war |
| John McDowell | June 16, 1778 | During the war |
| James McClean | Aug. 5, 1775 | Aug. 5, 1778 |
| Archibald McDonald | | During the war |
| James Oliver | | During the war |
| Edmund Penrice | July 2, 1775 | July 2, 1778 |
| David Parsons | Aug. 1, 1775 | Aug. 1, 1778 |
| Richard Richardson | Aug. 3, 1777 | During the war |
| William Roberts | Aug. 7, 1775 | Aug. 7, 1778 |
| Frederick Simmons | July 27, 1777 | During the war |
| Thomas Stafford | Jan. 4, 1777 | During the war |
| John Steele | July 9, 1778 | During the war |
| Anthony Uhthoff | July 6, 1775 | July 6, 1778 |
| John Whitely | July 11, 1777 | During the war |
| Robert Whiley | Mar. 11, 1778 | During the war |
| Shadrack Williamson | July 8, 1775 | July 8, 1778 |
| Richard Williamson | July 9, 1777 | During the war |
| John Kelly | | During the war |

We do swear the above Muster Roll is a true state of the Company, without fraud to the United States or any individual, according to the best of our knowledge.

THOS. DUNBAR, Captain
ALBERT ROUX, 1st Lieutenant

Sworn before me this 25th August, 1778.
FRANCIS MARION, Second Colonial Regiment
Then mustered, as certified by

THOS. JERVEY, Deputy Muster Master.

\* \* \*

A Muster Roll of Capt. Richard B. Roberts' Company of the South Carolina Continental Corps of Artillery, Commanded by Col. Owen Roberts.

Head Quarters, Purysburgh, March 19, 1779.

| Com. Officers' Names | Rank | Date of Commission |
|---|---|---|
| Richard B. Roberts | Captain | June 4, 1777 |
| John Gorgan | Capt.-Lieut. | May 30, 1778 |
| Frederick Von Plater | 1st Lieut. | October 28, 1778 |

| Non-Commissioned and Private Names | Date of Enlistment | Time of Service |
|---|---|---|
| John Smith, Sergeant | June 3, 1777 | 3 years |
| Brice Mathews, do. | Nov. 24, 1777 | 3 years |
| Joseph Hull, Corporal | June 25, 1777 | The war |
| John Sessions, do. | June 29, 1778 | 3 years |
| Edward Conner, do. | June 29, 1778 | 3 years |
| Robert Goodall, Gunner | Sept. 17, 1777 | The war |
| Benjamin Williams, do. | June 2, 1777 | 3 years |
| Alexander McMullan, do. | Feb. 3, 1779 | 16 months |
| Aaron Baroth, do. | June 3, 1777 | 3 years |
| David Cunningham | June 3, 1777 | 3 years |
| John Driver | July 14, 1778 | 3 years |
| Joseph Johnson | June 2, 1777 | The war |

| | | |
|---|---|---|
| John Causey | Sept. 5, 1778 | 3 years |
| John Murrow | July 16, 1778 | 3 years |
| Samuel White | Sept. 25, 1777 | The war |
| Jacob Paul | June 2, 1777 | The war |
| John Porter | June 19, 1777 | The war |
| Aquilla Sing | July 18, 1778 | 3 years |
| John Colby | Aug. 10, 1778 | The war |
| James Roe | July 22, 1778 | The war |
| Lewis Cornyorck | | The war |
| Charles McIver | Aug. 2, 1778 | 3 years |
| James Hughes | June 1, 1777 | 3 years |
| John Conner | | The war |
| Nicholas Glossom | | The war |
| James Lewis | | 3 years |
| Michael Lewis | Sept. 17, 1778 | The war |
| Isaac Garrick | Feb. 16, 1779 | 16 months |
| Wm. Maloy | | 3 years |
| James Causey | Sept. 5, 1778 | 3 years |
| Denis Choloque | | The war |
| Joseph Antonio | Sept. 17, 1778 | The war |
| Samuel Hickman | July 21, 1778 | 3 years |
| Robert William | May 28, 1778 | The war |
| Hill Hewet | June 2, 1777 | 3 years |
| Nicholas Prince | Aug. 3, 1778 | 3 years |
| Samuel Jefft | July 16, 1778 | The war |
| William Read, Drummer | Sept. 21, 1777 | The war |
| Wm. Fleming, Fifer | | The war |

I do swear that the within Muster Roll is a true state of the Company, without Fraud to the United States, or to any individual thereof, according to the best of my knowledge.

R. B. ROBERTS, Capt. Artillery.

Sworn before me this 19th March, 1779.

J. WISE.

Then mustered as certified by

F. BREMAR, Deputy Muster Master.

\* \* \*

From Documentary History of American Revolution from originals in possession of the Editor—by R. W. Gibbs, Maryland, 1857.

Appeared in the D.A.R Magazine.

CONTINENTAL PAPER MONEY.

------------

# CPT. WM. BUTLER'S COMPANY OF VOLUNTEERS, EDGEFIELD DIST., S. C.

Allen Jas. .Berry Jno. .Butler Jno. . .Butler Wm. Lt. . .Bledsoe Bartlett. .Bledsoe Berryman. .Butler Jas. Sr. . .Corley Abner. . Corley Sherod. . . .Corley Jno. Lt. . . .Corley Nathl. . .Corley Zacheus. . .DeLoach Saml. . .Davis Robt. . .Davis Thos. . .Davis Zachariah. . .Douglas Jno. . . .Edson Jas. . .Edson Jno. . .Fort Dunn. . .Foy Peter. . .Eskridge Burdett. . .Jones Danl. . .Jones Matt. .Jones Danl C. .Mason Bledsoe. .Nuun Joseph. . .Nicholson Gideon. .Laggett Josiah. . .Padgett Joel. . .Richardson Amos. . . Sissoin Fredk. . .Sison Wm. . .Smith Jno. . .Smith Smallwood. . . Turner Starling. . .Troop, James. . .Wilson Russell. . .Warren Josiah. . . .Wilson Jno. . .Watson Zakiah. . .Watson Richman. . . Watson Willis. . . .Williams Saml. . . .Webb Handley. . .Watson Hesekiah. .Cate. .two Harrisons. .Humphreys. .Whittle Burrows.

# SOLDIERS OF OTHER STATES
## INCLUDING LISTS OF MANY FROM SOUTH CAROLINA

### REVOLUTIONARY SOLDIERS BURIED IN MISSOURI

Allen, Jno. .Boles, Saml. .Boyd, Thos. .Burks, Saml. .Berry, Wm. .Brann, Wm. .Casey, Christopher. .Chambers, Jno. .Cooper, Col. Benj. .Conway, Saml. .Dodd, Abel. .Finnell, Chas. . .Franklin, Maj. Thos. .Goodson, Wm. .Harding, Geo. .Hawkins, Jno. .Headlee, Elisha. . .Hill, Abram. . .Jamison, Robt. .Kennedy, Thos. .Kirkpatrick, Robt. .Leake. . Lemon, Robt. .Lumbley, Wm. .Majors, Jno. .Martin, Lewis. .Moore, Maj. Zechariah. . Musick, Elder T. R. .Overly, Henry. .Parks, Jas. .Paul, Jno. .Peers, Maj. Valentine. . Quarles, Maj. Robt. .Ramsey, Capt. Wm. .Reading, Geo. .Robertson, Edw. .Scruggs, Timothy. .Russell, Robt. S. .Sewell, James. .Sims, Richard, .Sims, Rodem. .Steele, Saml. . Snowden, Jas. .Stuflebeau, Jno. .Taylor, Benj. .Thomas, Edw. .Talbot, Haile. .Taylor, Danl. .Tomb, David. .Truesdale, Nathan. .Wells, Jas. .Woolfolk, Jno. .Walker, Jesse. . Walton, Wm. Ward, Col. Wm. .Watson, Saml. .Wells, Col. Saml. .Brock, Uriah. .Nicholson, Wm. .Miller, Geo. .Wyatt, Thos. .Baylis, Cpt. Wm. .Lambley, Wm. .Mason, Benjamin.

### REVOLUTIONARY SOLDIERS BURIED IN TEXAS

Jas. Wilson Henderson, bur. at Shilo Cem. Wife drew a pension. .John Abston, bur. in Lavon, Collins Co. Applied for pension. .James Thompson, bur. Peacock Cem. .Stephen Williams, bur. near Jasper. .Alexander Hodge. .John Archer Elmore, bur. New Waverly. . Jonas Chaison, bur. near Beaumont.

### REVOLUTIONARY SOLDIERS WHO EITHER LIVED, DREW A PENSION OR BURIED IN IOWA

Bell, Benjamin. .Bean, Danl. .Breese, Timothy. .Brown, Nathan. .Brown, Timothy. .Bell. Timothy. Baine, Danl. .Crockett, Wm. .Scarrem, Richard J. .Caldwell, Saml. .Dow, Danl. . Fellows, Nthl Sr. .Garricks, Wm. .Harry, Chas. .Kincaid, John B. .Leeper, Jno. .Linn, Martin. .Morgan, Jno. .Kincaide, Wm. J. .McDonald, Jno. .Lewis, Saml. .Osborn, Jno. Perkins, Geo. .Poole, Sherman I. .Price, Samson, .Price, Saml. .Rogers, Achilles. . Rhodes, Thos. .Shepard, Chas. .Stubbs, Chas. .Smith, Joseph W. .Ware, Fredk. .Wiley, Jacob. .Winton, Nathan. .Woody, James. .Woody, Jonathan. .Woody, Wm.

### SOUTH CAROLINA SOLDIERS WHO REMOVED TO ALABAMA

Arnold, Thos. .Barnet, Thos. .Barton, Jno. .Brown, Hamilton, Dav. .Broughton, Thos. . Bussey, Zadoc. .Campbell, Geo. .Casey, Wm. .Clement, Thos. .Clements, Culliver. . Chandler, Jno. .Crenshaw, Stephen. .Darden, Geo. .Day, Wm. .Dickey, Geo. .Du Bais. . Eddins, Benj. Elliot, Elizbth Knox. .Embrey, Jos. .England, Wm. .Files, Abner, Jeremiah. Franks, Marshall. .Gill, Jas. .Garrett, Thos. .Gary, Thos. .Gayle, Matt. .Godbold, Zach. . Graham, Jno. .Green, Jacob. .Holland, Jacob. .Hamilton, Thos. .Hanna, Robt. .Harrington, Drury. .Hill, Hiram, Lewis. .Hogg, Thos. .Holloday, Danl. .Houston, Saml. .Howard, Jos. . Hughes, Jos. .Johnson, Wm. .Kelly, Gresham. .King, Jos. .Kirkland, Wm. .Lofton, Thos. . Lavender, Hugh. .Lipscomb, Joel. .Littlejohn, Chas. .Lynn, Jas. .McCutcheon, Jno. .Mc Gaughey, Saml. .Majors Benj. .McGuire, Elijah. .Malone, Cornl. .Mangum, Jno. .Morgan, Jas. .Morrow, Saml, Davis. .McWhorter, Jno. .Norris, Patk. .Nollen, Stephen, Geo. .Oden, Alex. .Outlaw, Alex. .Owen, Jno. .Pettigrew, Jas. .Poe, Jas. .Pool, Jno. .Queen, Thos. . Randolph. Abram. .Reese, Geo. .Robertson, Jas. .Rolison, Wm. .Ross, Isaac. .Roy, Jos.. Russell, Thos Sr., Wm. .Sample, Jno. Sr. .Sawyer, Jos. .Scott, Jas. .Stone, Reuben, Wm. . Storey, Henry. .Strothers, Wm. .Sutton, Jacob. .Stephenson, Hugh. .Tarrant, Jas. .Tribble, Jas. .Tubb, Jno. .Turner, Lewis, w. Nancy. .Walton, Wm. .Vaughan, Joel. .Ware, Robt. .

Weston, Robt. .Winn, Gallenus. .Witherspoon, Mary. .Wright, Danl. .Wylie, Wm. .Wynee, Williamson. Susp. Claims: Duncan, Jno. .Hawkins, Thos. .Hollis, Wm. .McFerrin, Archb. . Murcer, Jas. .Petty, Theop. .Riley, Jno. .Robuck, Jno. .Sterling, Silas C. .Thompson, Wm. . Williams, Thos. . .Walker Matthias. .Covington, Susan wid. Jno. .Hart, Martha wid. Henry. .Ponder, Violet wid Amos. .Turner, Nancy wid. Lewis. .(Above abstracted from : Ala. Histl. Quart. Winter Issue 1944. Editor Marie B. Owen, Pub. by State Dept. Archives & Hist; also recds. from D.A.R. Magazines; DaA.R. Lineage Books.)

## SOUTH CAROLINA TO GEORGIA

Addington, Wm. .Bryan, Jonth. .Buchanan, Benj. .Buckhalter, Marion. .Baker, Jon. .Brown, Jno. .Bullock, Hawkins. .Brown, Bartlett Jr. .Boykin, Fran. .Barnet, Wm. .Butler, Jno. . Bratton, Martha R. .Cante, Jas. .Cook, Jno. .Clark, Thos. .Craps, Jno. .Crawford, Joel Sr. .Bugg, Sherwood. .Brisbane, Adam. .Daniel, Jno. .Dickson, Dav. .Davis, Wm. .Ezell, Hartwell. .Edenfield, Dav. .Edwards, Wm. .Elbert, Sam. .Floyd, Chas. .Farrow, Rosanna W. .Garrard, Jacob. .Griffin, Jno. .Garrison, Jed. .Gillham, Ezek. .Gibson, Jno. Jas. . Graves, Lewis. .Howard, Jno. .Hardwick, Wm. .Hatton, Fran. .Hardin, Wm. .Hartwell, Ezell. Hames, Jno. .Harvey, Thos. .Jackson, Dan. .Jeter, Levi. .Jones, Jas. .Kelly, Lloyd . . Lindsay, Jno. .Lamar, Basil, .Martin, Wm, Elijah. .McCall, Jas. .Middleton, Hugh. . Montgomery, Jas. .Milner, Jno. .McMullen, Jas. .Matthews, Jas. Moses. .McClure, Mary G. .McCalla, Sara. .Morris, Thos. .Mallette, Gideon. .Newton, Moses. .Oliver, Jas. B. . Pittman, Jas, Jno. . .Prothro, Evan. . .Quarterman, Rob. Thos. .Randall, Robinson. . Rutherford, Jno. .Rushin, Jno. .Stevens, Jno. .Slappy, Henry, Saml. .Scott, Walter Jr. . Strickland, Jacob. .Storey, Anthy. .Stutstill, Jno. .Sparks, Danl. .Spann, Jas. .Taylor, Wm. . Tharp, Vincent. .Watson, Jno. .Winn, Jno. .Williams, Isaac. .Young, Jas. .(From: Memb. Roll & Reg. Ancestors Ga. Soc. D.A.R; D.A.R. Lin. Bks; D.A.R. Magazines.)

## SOUTH CAROLINA SOLDIERS WHO REMOVED TO FLORIDA

Bessent, Jno. .Bird, Jno. .Brown, Jno. .Bozeman, Ralph. .Edwards, Henry. .Fletcher, Jno. . Harbison, Geo. .Hudson, Hall, r. .Liles, Jno. .McCall Sherrod. .Osteen, Sol. .Rawls, Wm. . Singletary, Jos. .Taylor, Jeremiah. .Snowden, Aaron & Ester. .Weeks, Levi. .Wood, Dempsey. .(From: D.A.R. Lin. Bks. & Mag; Pen. Recds. of Sold. removed to Fla., By Jessie Robinson Fritot, Jacksonville Chpt. D.A.R. 1946.)

## SOUTH CAROLINA--MISSISSIPPI

Brown, Jno. .Buckholtz, Abram. .Brent, Jno. .Crane, Mayfield. .Chambers, Jos. .Downes, Wm. .Davis, Saml. .Farrar, Thos. .Fitzpatrick, Thos. .Hillhouse, Wm. .McBee, Silas. . May, Jos. .McCaleb, Wm. .Murphy, Jno. .Neely, Saml. .Portman, Jno. .Purvis, Gilbert. . Raley, Chas. .Turner, Noel. .Smith, Chas. .Wigington, Geo. & sons. .Whittington, Grief. . Wilson, Jas. .(D.A.R. Lin. Bks. & Magazines.)

## SOUTH CAROLINA--ILLINOIS

Gaston, Wm. .Gill, Thos. .Woods, Jno. .Means, Wm. .McClurkin, Thos. .McMillian, Danl. . Lusk, Jas. .Gilliham, Issac. .Land, Moses. .Warnock, Jos. .(From: D. A. R. Lin. Bks. & Magazines.)

## SOUTH CAROLINA SOLDIERS BURIED IN OHIO

Barr, Christopher. .Berryhill, Alex. .Campbell, Jno. .Caldwell, Wm. .Cunningham, Jas. . Dickey, Robt. .Farley, David. .Hale, Wm. N. .Morton, Jno. .McGaw, Wm. .Stephenson, Jno. .Stewart, Wm. Sr. .Stone, Benj. .Strain, Dav. .Williamson, Rev. Wm. .(From: "Offic. Roster Sold. Amer. Revo. Bur. Ohio"; D.A.R. Lin. Bks. & Magazines.)

## SOUTH CAROLINA SOLDIERS TO TENNESSEE

Armstrong, Robt. .Barnett, --. .Bostic, Jno. .Blair, Jno. .Burns, Laird, .Carter, Danl. . Davis, Andrew, Absolom, Fredk. .Dial, Jeremiah. .Frierson, Wm. .Franks, Marshal. .

Fenner, Rich, Robt. .Goggans, Wm. .Houston, Jno. .Kennedy, Wm. .Kaigler, Andrew. .
Lee, Thos. .Love, Hezek. .Mayes, Saml. .McClosky, Jos. .Miller, Adam. .McDearman,
Thos. .Meek, Adam. .Martin, Matt. .McGowan, Wm. .Pickens, Wm. .Pinckney, Chas. G . .
Queen, Thos. .Sample, Jesse. .Suddoth, Benj. .Thomas, Jas. .Teague, Wm. .Taylor, Geo. .
Wilson, Jno. .(D.A.R. Lin. Bks. & Mag.)

## SOUTH CAROLINA SOLDIERS TO KENTUCKY

Adair, Jno. .Brothers, Jno. .Connall, Jesse. .Clinton, Jas. .Ford, Wm. .Jeffries, Nathl,
Wm. .Lynn, Jas. .Love, Wm., Mark. .McDougal, Alex. .Prince, Wm. .Pickens, Wm. .
Petrie, Peter. .Ringo, Corn. .Renick, Jas. .Ramsey, Jno. .Scott, Wm. .Tanner, Josiah. .
(D.A.R. Lin. Bks. & Mag.)

## SOUTH CAROLINA SOLDIERS TO INDIANA

Abney, Geo. .Adair, Jas. .Alcorn, Geo. .Archer, Robt. .Bell, Thos. .Benbow, Edw. .
Brown, Matt. .Cain, Jno. .Campbell, Wm. .Cannon, Jas. .Culbertson, Josiah. .Dowell,
Geo. Evans, Jno. Floyd, Abram. .Garretson, Jno. .Gibson, Wm. .Griffin, Ralph. .Hammond,
Job. Hanna, Robt. Harrel, Jeremiah. Horton(Hooten) Thos. .Irvin, Saml. .Kever, (McKever)
Jas. .Kellar, Devault. .Lanman, Jas. .Lawrence, Isaac. .Lipperd, Wm. .Logan, Wm. .
Martindale, Wm. .Moore, Wm. .McCammon, Matt. .McClure, Robt., Wm. .McMillom,
(McMullen), Rowley. .Palmer, Jno. .Parr, Arthur. .Sample, Thos. .Sanders, Henry. .
Shores, Christian. .Still, Murphy. .Tramel, Sampson. .Veale, Jas. Carr. .Williams, Isaac. .
Young, Jaret. .Youngblood, Jacob. .(Abstracted from "Roster Sold. of Amer. Revo. Buried
in Ind" by Mrs. Roscoe C. O'Byrne -- 1938; D.A.R. Lin. Bks.)

## SOUTH CAROLINA REVOLUTIONARY ANCESTORS OF ARKANSAS D.A.R.

Arnold, Thos. Adair, Jno. Addington, Wm. .Bennet, Thos. .Brown, Sims. .Bobo, Sampson. .
Blakeney, Jno. Sr. .Bullock, Hawkins. .Casey, Randolph. .Collins, Jno. .Crawford, Joel. .
Carroll, Saml. .Cowan, Andrw. .Cherry, Lamuel. .Darby, Benj. .Evins, Alex. .Felder,
Henry. .Hawthorne, Jos. .Harrison, Reuben. .Haile, Benj. .Hamilton, Paul. .Hall, Wm. .
Hallam, Jno. .Holcombe, Phil. .Knight, Jno. .Kalb, (Kulp) Benj. .Lining, Chas. .Longmire,
Wm. Moores, Henry. Maxwell, Edw. Mayson, Jas. McIntosh, Wm. .Moss, Jno. .Martindale,
Wm. Jr. Nisbit, Wm. Nicholson, Wright. .O'Neall, Wm. .Pickens, Andrw. .Prothro, Evan. .
Russell, Wm. .Strobel, Danl. .Snoddy, Jno. .Shirley, Thos. .Saxon, Lewis. .Smith, Aaron. .
Sloan, Alex. .Thomas, Jas. .Trammel, Thos. .Ward, Jno. .Williams, Moses, H. .White, Wm.
(From: D.A.R. Year Bk. State of Ark. 1948-9; D.A.R. Lin. Bks.)

## SOUTH CAROLINA REVOLUTIONARY ANCESTORS OF OKLAHOMA D.A.R.

Adams, Dav. Alexander, Jnl, Elias. .Barnett, Jno. .Benson, Thos. .Barry, Andrw. .Bonner,
Jas. .Butler, Wm. .Bobo, Sampson. .Bumpass, Jno. .Bryan, Jas. .Black, Jos. .Cannon,
Henry. .Choice, Tully. .Coleman, Jas. .Cooper, Geo. .Davis, Surrey. .Dunklin, Jos. .Dodd,

Jesse, Jno. Sr. .Drewery, Fletcher. .Findley, Jno. .Felder, Henry. .Foster, Wm. .Gamble,
Jno. .Gough, Rich. .Gowan, Jno. .Gilliam, Robt. Sr. .Gaston, Wm. Robt. .Hall, Wm., Thos. .
Harrel, Zach. .Hamilton, Wm. .Henry, Malcolm...Howle, Wm. .Head, Jas. .Irby, Jos. .
Jaudon, Jas. .Jaggers, Nathan. .Kilgore, Benj. .Kennedy, Jas. .Keith, Corn. Jr. .Know, Jas .
Knox, Jno. .LaGroue, Adam. .Liddell, Wm. .Lee, Wm. .Lucas, Jno. .Martin, Salathiel. .
McAbee, Vardrey. .McKinney, Jno. .McIntosh, Wm. .McDaniel, Edw. .McDill, Thos. H. .
Michau, Jacob. .Milner, Sol. .Miller, Mordecai. .Mitchell, Sol. .Marion, Jos. .Moore,
Henry. .Moberly, Edw., Saml. .Nicholson, Dav. .Neal, Thos. .O'Neall, Wm., Saml. .
Patton, Jno. .Pinckney, Chas. .Pittman, Philip. .Polk, Ezek. .Reynolds, Saml. .Salmon,
Geo. .Simmons, Maurice. .Selman, Jeremiah. .Sibert, Jno., Dav. .Stone, Jas. .Switzer,
Henry. .Tandy, Archilles. .Tennant, Wm. .Terrell, Geo. .Tisdale, Jno. .Tracey, Nathl. .
Walker, Alex. .Winn, Rich. .Wilson, Dav., Jas. .Weyman, Edw. .Wingo, Jno. W. .Walkup,
Jno. .Van Arsdale, Simon. .(From: N.S. D.A.R. of Okla. Year Bk. 1948-9; D.A.R. Lin.
Bks.)

The records of many S.C. Revolutionary soldiers have never been published.
Some of the lines have not been proved by descendants. Consent has not been given
to publish others.

The first State House, built in
Charles Town in 1753-1760.

**St. Philip's Episcopal Church—**        Churc
Founded 1670. First church corner Broad and Meetir
(where St. Michael's now stands), built in 1681. Mov
to present site, 1723.

REVOLUTIONARY
POWDER-HORN AND
CANTEEN.

Middleton Place Gardens, Oldest Landscape Gardens in America

General Pickens.

# GENEALOGIES OF FAMILIES DESCENDED FROM S. C. REVOLUTIONARY SOLDIERS

JAMES ABERCROMIE md. twice. ISSUE, viz: Isabel md. a Blackwell in Va. . . 2-Mary md. a Dial in NC. . .3-Thos. md. Mrs. Rucket SC. . .4-Isaac, grant in Laurens SC 1769(wit. by Jas. & Jno. A-) to NC. . .5-JOHN of Laurens had-Jas. Jr., Alex, Jonathan, Wm. . .6-James of Laurens b. abt. 1740. . .7-Alex. . .8-Chas. NC-Ga. . .9-Colvill. . .10--Rebecca 1738-1825 md. Hastings Dial. . .11-Crystie md. Martin Dial. . . .ALEXANDER SR. of Laurens had w. Susan & sons-John, Alex, Henry, Hugh, Lewis, Jonathan; drts-Hannah, Susan, Polly. . .COLVILL, abv. CHN: Harriet Nash, Mary Sims, Rebecca Babb, Elizbth Campbell, Christy Ridgeway, Ruth Sims, Jonathan, Lindley, Colvill, James to Ga., John. . .Colvill Abercromie Jr., md. Sara Mahaffey. . . .JAMES ABERCROMIE of Laurens, no. 6 abv. md. twice. CHN: (1) Mary md. 1st Benj. Williams: 2nd Wm. O'Daniel. Had-Josiah, James, Abercromie, Mary, Rhoda, Lucinda, Pamelia, Elizbth (2) Isabella md. Josiah Blackwell, is in Tex. (3) Rebecca md. 1797 Gabriel Jowell to Miss. (4) Susannah Matthews (5) Hannah md. Elias Brock (6) Elizbth Andrews (5) James had w. Cynthia.

JAMES AGNEW settled abt. 1737 in Pa. md. twice. ISSUE, viz: John, Janet Scott, David**Saml**James**, Martha, Margt, Rebecca, Sara, Anna, Abram. The son David md. Mary Irwin. The son James md. Mary Ramsey & was 1st to SOUTH CAROLINA. I- Samuel abt. 1770 md. Elizbth Seawright & had-Mary, Andrew, Jane, Elizbth, Saml, James. The son Samuel had-Elizbth, James, Andrew, Joseph, Alfred, Malinda, William, Dr. Wash who md. Elizbth Sullivan, Dr. Enoch who md. Letitia Todd of Laurens to Miss. . .JAMES AGNEW, s. of Saml & Elizbth, md. Mahala Dodson. ISSUE five: Saml, Elizbth, Mahala, Andrew, & Dr. Enoch who md. 3 times. 1st-Sara Sullivan, 2nd-Jane Waters, 3rd-Ella Waters. Had-Anna Smith, Jennie McCarley, Ena Sullivan James.

BENJAMIN ARNOLD & w. both**. He b. Va. d. SC 1796. ISSUE to maturity, viz:. . . 1-Wm. md. twice & left-Benjamin, Anderson, William, Polly. . .2-Edward to Ky & left chn. . .3-Charity Martin had-Nancy Townsend, Temperance Smith Gunnels. . . 4-Hendricks of Laurens, SC had-Mary Townsend, Nancy Taylor, Ira who md. Polly Saxon; William who had-Jeff, Hendrick, Billy. . .5-Temperance md. Thos. Hamilton** 6-John from Laurens to Tenn. Chn: Benjamin, Rickerson Lem. . .7-Thomas** had-Temperance Ross, Ann Dunklin, William, Thos. H., Sally. . .8-BENJAMIN JR.** d. in SC. ISSUE: Alston, Martin, Benjamin, Ann H. Sullivan, Temperance Sullivan, Winifred Camp, Clara Grace, Sara Pinson, Malinda Arnold.

CHARLES ALLEN SR. md. Lucy Bacon Va-SC. ISSUE, viz: CHARLES JR** md. Susan Garner; Lyddall md. Milly L. Downs; Sara K. md. 1st Lewis Saxon; Cynthia Catherine md. Jno. Williams; Isiah & possibly Mary, Drury, Richard, Joel. The son Lyddall Allen of Laurens, SC had Issue: Isaac md. twice, to Ga; Jonathan, Milly Frances Atkin; Lucy Bacon Arnold; Chas. Walter, Mary Drury, Sara Jane(Nancy). Four Revo. S. in this line.

ANDERSON--JOHN, WM, JAS, & THOS. ** filed Revolutionary claims, Camden Dist., later Chester. James & Thos. appeared to be bros. James Anderson Sr. & sons-John, James, William & prob. Quinton, moved from Chester area to Greenville, lands on Horse creek, while William had lands on Rabun & Lick cks. JAMES ANDERSON who d. 28 Oct. 1807 md. Nancy Ewing. ISSUE 9, viz: Robt. Quinton d. 1852, Jane d. 1857 Mary, John, Anny, Elizabeth, William, James, Ewing. . .I.-James Anderson II (s. of Jas & Nancy) md. Martha Young (Fulton) & had 4 sons, viz: Thomas, Daniel, Robert Quinton, George. (1)Thos. md. Jane Williams (2)Danl md. 1st Lucinda Smith, 2nd . Fanny Miller. Had-Emmie, Cora, Lizzie, Mattie, md. Albert Todd. (3) Robt. Quinton md. Frances Louise Smith. Had 11 chn: Nan, James, Oscar, Walter, Mary, William, Alice, Thomas, Clara, Louise, Sally. Of these (a) Nan md. Martin (b) James md. Minnie Williams & had-Ruth; Ann md. Dr. H. A. Pruitt; Lois md. W. W. Sullivan Jr., Maj. Saml (c) Oscar md. Ida Williams (d) Walter md. Zella Campbell (e) Sally md. Sam

Bowen (f) Louise md. Cape McPhail (7) Thos. unmd. (8) Mary md. 1896 Edw. H. Anderson, desct. of Maj. Dav. of Nazerath community, had-John, Frances. . .II.-MARY ANDERSON, drt. of Jas. I & Nancy, md. Austin Williams. ISSUE; 5: Nancy J. md. Thos. F. Anderson; Jno. Lewis md. Helen Featherstone & had 8 chn; Jas. unmd; Saml md. Ann Archer; Harriet md. W. S. Blake. . .III.-JOHN ANDERSON, s. of Jas. I Nancy, 1784-1837, md. Mary Terry (drt. Thos. T. &-w. a Harrison. 2 md. w, Rebec. McDowell) ISSUE, 10, viz: Anna G., William, James, Thomas, Ewing, John, George, Robert, Mary, David. (1) Anna Gibson md. Hewlett Chapman, had-Bill, John, Mary (2) Wm. of Ala. had-Thomas, John, Cassy, others (3) James of Fairview, Grv Co. SC md. Rachel Stenhouse. Had 11: (a) Geo. C. md. Hattie Sprouse (b) Margt L. md. J. Wister Stewart & had-Leila, Mrs. Cath Rachel Peden; Anderson H. Stewart (c) Lawrence md. Evelyn Thornberry of Ala. Had 4: Forest M. of NY City md. 1915 Grace F. Barnum & had-Eleanor, Virginia, Mary; Marvin s. of Lawr. of Okla. has 2 chn; Mrs. Julius Bujol of Baton Rouge, drt. Lawr. (d) Sara J. drt. Jas. & Rachel, md. Lawrence Garret. Had-Jody A. md. Geneva West; Talmadge Miles Garret md. Lila Cameron Witherspoon & had: Talmadge (e) Ann md. Charlie Smith. . .(4) Thomas, s. of Jno. & Mary, md. Carrie Gray, Woodruff, SC. Had-Pierce, Mittie, Ida, Berry, Lillian, Jeff (5)-John d. 1865 bur. Fairview md. Sara Blakely. Had 4: Chas who md. Anna Knox; Lina md. M. Prince; Mattie md. Jno. Savage; Wm. P. md. Carrie Peden (6) Ewing d. 1842 bur. Fork Shoals (7) George s. Jno. & Mary, bur. Williamston, SC md. Nancy N. Nesbitt. Had 10 chn. viz: (a) Geo. L. md. Ida Holland (b) M. Jane md. W. D. Hutto (c) Dr. James Nesbitt of Univ. Fla. md. Janie drt of Cpt. C. W. Sullivan of Williamston (d) Jno. L. d. 1928 (e) Mary N. (f) Annie (g) Bertha md. D'Arcy P. Gray (h) Wm. (i) Albert (j) Lillian Andrea md. Dr. Jno. W. Parker Jr. . .(8) Robert, unmd. . .(9) Mary Jane, drt. of Jno & Mary, md. Wm. L. Hopkins. Had-(a) Robt. md. Mattie Ramsey & had-Wm, David, Fred, Ethel (b) Jas, unmd. (c) Jno. H. md. Minnie Wright. . .(10)-David Quentin, md. Parnecia Griffith. Had-John, William, S. Griffith of Woodruff, SC. David md. a 2nd time, had chn.

ANDERSONS of Laurens, SC: George, William, Andrew & probably Joel, bros. GEORGE ANDERSON 1740-1808, Capt. of Militia Co. raised in Laurens, pro. to Major. His 12 yr. son David served with him & recvd Pen. 1838. Maj. George md. 3 times, 1st Miss Anderson; 2nd Miss Lewis (mother of D. Lewis A- who served as Prob. Judge of Laurens 30 yrs) 3rd-Molly Saxon 1773. By her 13 chn. viz: Chas 1774, Margt 1775, Judith 1778, James 1780, Geo. 1783, Wm. 1785, Tabitha 1787, Lewis 1789, Jno 1791, Molly 1794, Saxon 1797, Elizbth 1797, Sally 1802. The son JAMES md. 1801 Nancy Saxon & had 11 chn: Parmelia, Joshua, Geo. David (Ga. descts) Wm. C. Saxon, Lucinda, Jno. Saml, Jas. M., Sara Ann, Saxon Mills, Mary C.

WILLIAM ANDERSON**bro. of Maj. George, d. 1795, md. Elizbth Cobb. ISSUE, 9-viz: Margt md. Jno. Middleton, s. of Ainsworth M-of Laurens; Mary md. Robt. Stevens; Sara Ann; Saml md. Mary Hinton, drt. Robt. H-of Laurens; Ambrose; James md. Elizbth Middleton, s. of Jno. & to Mo; Andrew; Joel; Robert. The son SAMUEL ANDERSON & wife Mary Hinton, had 10 chn. Viz: Robt. W. 1812; James md. Nancy Wilson Poole; John, Malinda, Nellie, Rachel, Margt, Larkin, Samuel.

NATHAN & SAMUEL AUSTIN among first Greenville county settlers, near Enoree & Gilder's ck 1761. Nathan High Constable, but later he & 10 sons in Revo. One was Col. Wm. . .Dr. Thos. C. Austin had son, Hon. J. Thos. Austin, rep. Grv. 1876 in "Wallace House". . .Dr. Manning Austin had s. Jno. W.

THOMAS BELL md. abt. 1744 Jane-ISSUE, viz: Adam, Robert, William, Thomas. REVO. claims filed for last three. ADAM BELL d. bef. 1805, Laurens, SC w. Mary, Chn: David, John, Adam, James, Robert, Mary, Isabel, Esther, Elizbth. . .JAMES Bell of Laurens d. bef. Sept. 1824, w. Sara, CHN: John, Robert, Adam, James, Elizbth Milan, Susan. . .WILLIAM BELL** Laurens, SC md. Rachel Waters & had-Thomas, Peter, md. Lucinda Eddins, Jane md. Mr. Vandiver, William md. Mary Crews, David to Ga. . . The William Jr. lived first in Laurens then Ala. His chn. were- Francis M. to Miss; Mary Warton, Martha Henry, Dorothy Gann, Benjamin, Jonathan, Jas. William, Thomas, Joseph N.

JOHN BETHEA** md. Mary Pearce. ISSUE, viz: 1-William md. 1st Olivia Pearce, 2nd Sara Hargrove. .2-Tristram md. 1st Mrs. Ann Pearce Bethea, 2nd Margt McCall. . 3-John md. Hannah Walker. .4-Cade md. Kitty Bethea. .5-Martha md. John Bradley. . 6-Sara md. Timothy Rogers. .7-Betsy md. Jerry Walter. The above John's son, DAVID md. Sara Manning. . .WILLIAM BETHEA** 1725-1799 md. Sara Goodman. ISSUE, viz: 1-John md. Mary Hanagan & had-Elizbth. .2-Goodman md. Mary Council. . 3-Philip md. Ann Bethea. .4-Jesse md. Celia Harrelson. .5-Charity ,md. Henry H. Hybert. .6-Martha md. Athneil Trawick. .Members of our D. A. R. chapt. on this line-Mrs. Cornelia Bethea Harris*, Mrs. Evelyn Peele Sullivan*.

WILLIAM BLACKSTOCK SR. 1720-1799, w. Euphemy, had-Wm. Blackstock Jr.**1750-1841 md. Mary Yarborough b. Laurens Co. Chn: Polly md. Berry Poole; Jane md . Mr. Foster. . .D. A. R. on this line: Ruth Todd Waldrop*.

WILLIAM BOLLING OF VA.** ISSUE, viz: Samuel**, Archibald, John, Amelia, Matoaka (Mata). The son SAMUEL BOLLING b. Va. d. SC Laurens county. ISSUE, viz: Nancy Sullivan, Elizbth Dunklin, Lucinda Johnson, Mary Perritt, Mehitabel Tarrant, Robert md. Rachel Tarrent, Tully md. Mary Ann Smythe Mimms, John md. Sara Rabun, Thornberry unmd. The dau. NANCY md. James Sullivan II & had-(1) Edny Cunningham (2) Lucinda (3) Henderson Whitlow md. Grace Downs (4) Tully Francis md. Sara Berry & had-James, Robert, Sara Ann. The son James Bolling Sullivan md. Elizbth Griffin & had-Arthur, Ann. Descts in Ga. . .D. A. R's this line: Lee Hunt Pinson*, Cecile Moore Mallory*, Patti Willis*, Florence Trapp Smith*.

BOYD the bros-Jame, Samuel & William    settled in Laurens Co., SC bef. Revolution. JAMES BOYD I md. Bonnie Luray & had-John 1753-1827 md. Rebec. Amelia Watson. Had 9 chn. viz: 1-Abram md. Annie Gray, to Tex. .2-John D. 1775-1859. .3-Wm. II md. Fannie Bullock,. to Va. Had Alfred. .4-Edney. .5-Mary md. John H. Boyd. Had-Louella, Rebecca W., Jno. Abram. .6-Martha md. Joel Allen. Had 10 chn. .7-Nancy md. Frank Ross. .8-Sallie md. Raymond Fuller. .9-Rebecca-----WILLIAM BOYD(bro. of Jas.) wife Eva(says one recd). . .A Wm. Boyd is bur. abt. 2 mi. w. Madden Station, Laurens Co., stone marked 1738-9. He said have md. 1st Miss McClanahan & had 2 drts, one of whom md. Mr. Brock. William md. 2nd Miss McClurkin. ISSUE, nine, viz: 1-Catherine md. Isaac Pinson, had-Lucinda, Elizabeth, Gabriel, others. .2-James md. Elizbth Parks, had-David, William, Isaac, Sara K. Simpson, Nancy, Catherine Pitts, Jane Peden, Elizbth Hipp, James F., Margaret. .3-David was gr-father of the two "Todds". .4-Samuel md. Nancy Henry. .5-Eleanor Henderson. .6-One to Tex. no heirs. .7-Isaac. .8-Bradford md. Margt Watkins. .9-Prob. Jane, 2nd. w. Jno. Henry-----SAMUEL BOYD(one of the 3 bros) md. Nancy Valentin Mace or Macey. Had chn: Samuel II, Bradford...The son Saml II md. Miss Henry of Laurens Dist, SC. Had-David, Jno. Bradford, Sanford, Harrison (These data from Miss Hitt, a Boyd desct). . .The following Boyd data from Rev. T. S. Mosely. . .A Boyd b. abt 1762 had chn: William b. 1787, Joseph 1791, Mary 1793, Hugh 1797, Jennet 1799, James 1802, Robt 1805, Rosannah 1807, David 1810, Frances 1812, Jeff 1817, John 1795-1872. Later md. Elizbth Blackburn, to Ala. Had chn: Nancy Canon, Rosanna Tramill, Emily Tubb, Mary Hall, George, Rachel Ellis Hurley, William, Matilda Mackey, Sara Mackey Turner.

ELIAS BALL founder SC family, md. Elizbth Harleston. Had-Bartholomew, w. Elizbth. ISSUE, viz: Bartholomew II b. 1736, Edward 1744**, Sampson, William, Sara Giles 1754, drt. md. Thomson, drt. md. Mikell. Wm. Ball md. 1769 Sara Martin(He s. of Wm. Ball** 1750-1805, d. in Laurens Co.)

ROBERT BOLT**, will 1795, had-John, Lewis, Peggy, Sally, Polly. SQUIRE JOHN BOLT & wife Nancy had-Samuel md. 1848 Ellen Kennedy. . . .JOHN BOLT & Nancy of Va. Had-Asa, Robert. .Asa Bolt md. Hannah Crombie. ISSUE 13, viz: William, Toliver, John H., Thomas, Crombie, Abram, Lewis, Martin, Edmund, Oliver, Elizbth, Mary C., Theresa. The son Abram b. LAURENS 1839, d. 1909 md. 1856 Mary M. Clark. Had-Martha, Lawson A., Thos. L., Dolphus J.

JOHN COOK** from Va. to SC 1770 md. 1st-Betty Brown; 2nd-Martha Pearson. ISSUE , viz: Elizbth McCrellis, Mary Hutchinson, Burrell, John md. Ellen Hampton,, Nathaniel P., Phillip to Ga; Isaac, & several drts. The son BURRELL** md. Mary Pope & had among others, Burrell md. Mary Kirkland.

JEREMIAH COOPER from Pa. to SC abt. 1774, Indian Trader, md. Charity Clark. (Clark, Columbus, Micajah, Saml-bros.) Clark was b. in Laurens 1818, youngest of 11 chn., md. 1847 Alice Reed. ISSUE, viz: Samuel P., Marion, Georgey md. Robt. G. Center, Jerome, William S., Eliza Clark, Julia D., Alice, Lillian. The son, Wm. S. md. Augustus Faust.

THOMAS CAMP SR.** 1717-98 md. twice. ISSUE 24. Of these, Nathan & Thos. settled in Laurens, SC; John & Benj. in Grv., SC. .1-Edmund md. twice & had 21 chn. d. in Ga. .2-Joseph md. Miss Rountree. .3-John md. Mary Tarpley. .4-Nathl md. Winifred Tarpley, had Hosea md. Elizbth Jordan. Desct in La. .5-Thomas md. Nancy Tarpley. One child, Sara Calhoun. .6-Starling. .7-Hosea. .8-William, descts. Spartanburg, SC. . 9-Alfred NC-SC. .10-Benjamin md. Elizbth Dykes, had-Joseph, John, Benjamin, Winifred Ackins. .11-Elizabeth md. Reuben Brock. .12-Joel NC. .13-Crenshaw NC. .14-James md. Sara Jennings. .15-Daniel md. Sara McKinney NC. .16-Adam, bach. .17-Lewis md. Joanna Neel. .18-Stephen. .19-Larkin. .20-21--Uriey & Ruth no is. .22-Aaron md. 1st Miss Terrill; 2nd Sara Suttle. .23-George md. Mary Norman. .24-Joshua md. Nancy Gregory NC-SC. THE SON JOHN CAMP**bur. in SC. ISSUE nine, viz: 1-Thos. had-Nancy Smith, Violet Stroud, Patience Thompson, Elizbth Camp, William. .2-Abner md. Miss Ragsdale (drt. of Revo S) to Ga. had-Edmond, Russell, Arthur, Hiram, Satira, Martha, Mary, Thomas, John. .3-Starling. .4-Wm. .5-John. .6-Kizziah md. Benj. Arnold & had is. .7-Sara Grayson. .8-Winifred Kinman. .9-Annie Hill. (Sullivan-Dunklin D. A. R. on this line-Mrs. Sara Ervin*, Mrs. Albert Stephens*, Mrs. Thos. Baldwin*, Mrs. Jack Agee*, Mrs. Jno. Allbritton*, Mrs. Wm. Horton*, Miss Mary Jean Knight*.)

REV. THOMAS CRAIGHEAD died 1739 Pa.The Rev.Alex Craighead 1705-1766, had ISSUE: Rachel Caldwell, SC., Nancy Richardson SC., Jane Calhoun SC., Margaret Carruth, Mary Dunlap, Elizbth Crawford, Agnes Alexander, Thomas.

COL. JOHN CRAWFORD had sons-Robert, James, Joseph from Pa. to Waxhaws, SC abt. 1760. Joseph or Joel said to have settled in Edgfield, SC but moved to Ga. & father of William H. Crawford. . . .2-ROBERT CRAWFORD** md. Jean White. ISSUE: Sara Donnon, Mary Dunlap, Isabel, Martha Williams to Ala., Elizbth Vaughan, James, William, John. . . .3-JAMES CRAWFORD; w. at Charleston, SC., d. 1779, md. Jennett Hutchinson. ISSUE: James; Alex md. Elizbth Craighead; George; drt. md. Jno. Martin; drt. md. Isaac Smith; drt. md. Wm. Henderson; drt. md. Jno. Parton (drts. were-Mary, Jean, Martha, Margt); John md. Miss Snead, Thomas.

JOHN CURETON** 1731-1803 from Va. 1788 to SC. He md. in Va. 1st w. Winifred Heath. Appears 1790 census SC. Records at Newberry & Laurens Courthouses. Will, Laurens prv. 1803. Bur. Beaverdam church-yard, grave marked. ISSUE(all wives): John, Louisa, Susanna, Frances, Martha, Charles, Nathl, David, George W., Heath, Jinny, S. Hunter, E. Sheppard, Danl, Thos. T. . . .The Son JOHN (1757-1821) named in will, md. in Va. 1778 (Bond no 113) Sarah Moon. Sells out in Va. 1797 (Lunenburg recds). Wife dying, he follows relatives to SC with two sons, John Moon age 18 & Abner Heath, 12. They settle near county line Spartanburg-Greenville, Enoree river & were associated with the LESTER family in the old factory there. (The son Abner, md. Matilda Lester) The newspaper, The Greenville News (Oct. 1948) had article on early cotton mills in US, which says in part: "Wm. Bates b. R. I. came to this county 1819. BY THAT TIME, Spartanburg county already had a small textile manufacturing plant-LESTERS- at which Bates worked until he & associates were able to establish BATESVILLE on the Greenville county side on the Enoree riv. . ." Here at Lester Factory, on the Spartanburg side of the Enoree river, lived John Cureton (1757-1821) & sons, Jno. Moon & Abner Heath.About a mi. away, in prv. cem. the fath. John is buried. The two sons later removed to Sandy Springs Section of Greenville county, lived adjoining plantations & Abner bur. Sandy Springs. John Moon Cureton md. Mary Adkins Dacus & both bur. on plant(still owned by desct), graves marked.

126

ISSUE: M. Layfatte, Mary E., Harriet D., Claudia C., John M., David T., Pascall, Sarah, Ann, William...CHN. OF ABNER(md. 2) were: Thos. Jeff, George W., David, William, John M., Sally, Mary, James, Pascal, Tandy, Robert, Abner, Walker, Lizzie, Caroline.

CAPT. HENRY ARTHUR DIAL md. Isabella Hastings. ISSUE, viz: Hastings, James of NC., Isaac, Isabella, Albert, John, Martin. .The son, Col. Hastings Dial, d. in Laurens, SC md. Rebecca Abercromie. ISSUE: 1-Hastings md. Miss Allen. .2-Isaac md. 1st Amanda Coker, 2nd Mary Coker. Had 15 chn. Most of whom to Tex. .3-James md. Elizbth Stallworth. .4-Rebecca md. Jas. Johnson. .5-Isabella md. Jno. Woody. .6-Jane md Abram Madden. .7-Mary md. Mabra Madden (These two had bro Wm. Madden md. Sara Pinson). . . .MARTIN DIAL (s. of Cpt. Henry Arthur) d. in Laurens Co. md. 1st Christy Abercromie: 2nd Hannah--ISSUE, viz: 1-John md. Chrystie Thomason. .2-Hannah md. Cpt. Jno Armstrong. .3-Colvill md. Lidia Eastwood. .4-Isaac md. Sara Thomason.. 5-James md. 1st Sara Stoddard; 2nd Jane East. .6-Martin Jr. md. Jane Eastwood. .7-Jonathan unmd. .8-Wm. md. Hannah Hellams. Members of our chapt. who joined on this line: Mrs. Marcelle Babb Quillen*, Sara Frances Abercromie*, Mrs. Lucile Baldwin Hellams*.

JOSEPH DUNKLIN of South Carolina** md. Jean Warthen** (variously spelled) ISSUE, 7-viz: Joseph, Elizabeth, Nancy Ann, John, Mary, William, James. .1-Joseph II md. Sara Margt Sullivan. Had-Mary Gregory, Jane C. Hicks, Joseph who md. in SC Sara Parkins to Miss; Stephen T. md. Rachel McGuire to Mo: Gov. Daniel of Mo.. .II-ELIZABETH DUNKLIN md. Mr.Sweeny in Ky.. .III-NANCY ANN DUNKLIN md. 1st Wm. Shipp** Had-William, Joseph, Harriet. She md. 2nd Nat Sullivan to Ala.. .IV-JOHN DUNKLIN** md. Polly Bowman from SC to Ky-Mo. Had-William, Nancy, Jeff, Madison. . . .V-MARY DUNKLIN**md. Hewlett Sullivan**(See Sullivan). . . .VI-WILLIAM DUNKLIN md. Anne Hendricks Hamilton, from SC 1819 to Ala. Had-Hance, John, Dr. Wm., Dr. James, Thos. W., Temperance, Caroline, Elizabeth, Mary, Margaret. Of these, Hance md. Miss Arnold, some descts to Tex; Dr. William md. in Miss., moved Tex; Thomas had 7 chn. Three descts members our D. A. R., viz: Joyce Dunklin*, Patricia Smith*,Mrs. OlenDelany*. .Temperance abv. marr. Wm. B. Haralson Ga-Ala. ... Thomas of Ala. Had-Mary Rast, Elizbth Hardy, Martha Dudley, Emma Rast, Frank, Wm. John CA. .Caroline md. Hugh Caffey, Ala. Had-Hugh, Thomas, Mary Dunklin of Tex; Irene Caffey. .Elizabeth md. J. A. Pierce, Ala. Had-Dr. Dunklin, Dr. Wm., Annie, John. .Mary & Margt unmd. . . .VII-JAMES DUNKLIN, s. Jos. & Jean, lived on Reedy River near Laurens-Grv. line, md. four times, 1st in Laurens, Elizbth Bolling; 2nd in SC., Marjorie Law; 3rd Martha Irby; 4th Catherine Lee Gafford. He moved to Ala. 1819. ISSUE, ten, viz: John, Joseph, Abigail, Nancy Ann, Lucinda. By 2nd w: James Law, Caroline, Turner. By 3rd w: Dr. Irby Dunklin of SC. By 4th w: Daniel Gafford. . .1-JOHN DUNKLIN to Ala. ISSUE: James H., Joseph, Dock, Nord, Thomas, Lucinda, Caroline, others. . .2-JOSEPH DUNKLIN SC-Ala., md. Mary C. Judge. ISSUE: James H., Elmira, Abigail. (1) Gen. James Hilliard Dunklin, C. A., had Revo. ancestors in Cook, Hutchinson & Bolling families. He md. 1st Abbie Reid; 2nd Mary Jane Reid. ISSUE: Mollie, Elizabeth, Anna, Jas. H., Joe, Jennie, Erin, Lora, Judge. .(2) Elmira md. Judge Fletcher Johnson, M. C. Had-Jennie Whittington, Fletcher Jr., Mary May. .(3) Abigail md. Capt. Holden Wade, Montgomery, Ala. . .3-Abigail md. Dr. Hillory Herbert SC-Ala. ISSUE: George, James, Elizabeth, Lucinda, Martha, Fannie, Cornelia, Abigail, Margery Catherine. . .4-Nancy Ann Warthen md. Dr. George Herbert in Ala. ISSUE: Richard, Nancy, Curtis Burke, M. D.. .5-LUCINDA md. Ennis McDaniel. ISSUE: Two. . .6-JAMES LAW DUNKLIN md. Mary Amanda Burnett. ISSUE: William Turner, Catherine, Susan Florence, Daniel Edward, Almira, Ida, Caroline F., Irby J., Ellen Reid. The dau. Susan Florence md. 2nd 1869 Joel Flanagan Thames & had-Ruby Florence* md. 1899 Levy John Beeland & had-Florence Perdue* & Marjorie Steele*. Ellen Reid, drt. of Jas. Law Dunklin md. 1882 Thos. Wm. Peagler & a drt. Myra W.* md. 1921 Wm. S. Blackwell. .7-Caroline md. S. A. Mears. . .8-William Turner md. Mary H. Cook, had-James, Ella, Margery, George, Herbert, Irby. . .9-Dr. Irby Dunklin md. late in life, Harriet F. Montgomery. He was for many years a prominent physician in Laurens, S. C. Had chn. (1) Mary M. (2) James W. who md. Zelene, drt. of Hugh E. Gray & wife Susie (drt. of Hon. Chas. P. Sullivan & wife Zelene Boyd)...

10-Daniel Gafford Dunklin C. A., md. 1st Susan C. Burnett. Had-Walter unmd. He md. 2nd Hannah Pickett Patton. Had-Patton, d. unmd.

I.---JAMES IRVINE (Ervin), md. Elizbth, drt. Capt. John William James. ISSUE, viz (known): Rebecca, Jean, Robert, Elizbth Shaw, Hugh Sr., John. . .1-The son Hugh md. 1st Mary Ellison; 2nd Elizbth James & his chn. were-Susannah md. 1st Cooper, 2nd Jos. Wilson. . .2-Elizbth McClure. . .3-Mary Cannon. . .4-Isaac. .,.5-Jane, md. cous. Robt. Ervin. . .6-Sara. . .7-Margt. 2nd w. Col. Jno. Ervin. . .8-James md. Elizbth Witherspoon. . .9-Wm. to Miss. . .10-Col. Hugh md. Drt. Gavin Witherspoon & had-Robert, Mary Wilds. . .II.---JOHN IRVINE SR., md. Elizbth, drt. Robt. Ellison Esq. ISSUE, viz: 1-Elizbth md. Jno. Fulton & had-Elizbth md. Robt. s. of Col. Hugh Ervin. Descts in Darlington,SC. . .2-Robert md. Jane, drt. Hugh Ervin Sr. . .3-Sara Dobbins. . . 4-Jeane Matthews. . .5-Mary James. . .6-James. . .7-Col. John. . .8-Margaret. . . .III.-COLONEL JOHN ERVIN** md. 1775 Jane Witherspoon; md. 2nd 1791 his cous. Margt Ervin. Colonel John Ervin commanded Britton's Neck Regiment under General Francis Marion. ISSUE to maturity, viz: 1-Samuel 1776-1823 md. 3 times. . .2-Elizbth md. Mr. Ford of Miss. Had drt. md. Mr. Cooper, parents of Tim Cooper, Chief Justice of Miss. . .3-James Robt, next in line. . .4-Hugh 1792-1815. . .5-John md. Harriet Glenn Pope. . . .IV.-COLONEL JAMES ROBERT ERVIN md. 1813 Elizabeth Powe, drt. of Genl. Erasmus Powe & wife Esther Ellerbe**(Erasmus s. of Thos. Powe**, Father of Esther was Wm.) ISSUE, viz, 8: 1-Saml James md. twice & had-James Robert, Erasmus Powe, Elizbth, Samuel J., Clarence. . .2-Erasmus Powe md. 1847 Mary McCollum & had-Nellie, Gavin, Robert James, Maxy Gregg, Thomas Powe, Jane, Mary, Erasmus. . .3-Elizbth 1819-22. . .4-John Witherspoon, next in line. . .5-Jane md. 1851 Wm. S. Harris & had-Ervin, Everard, Charles, Jane, Brevard. . .6-Jas. Robert killed battle 1864. . .7-Mary Caroline md. cous. John Fulton Ervin, Lt-Gov. of SC. Had-(among others) Mary md. Colonel Evander McIver. Darlington, SC. . .8-Anne Davis by Col. Jas. Robert Ervin's 2nd wife, md. 1851 Dr. H. K. W. Flinn. . . .V.-JOHN WITHERSPOON ERVIN removed from Manning, SC to Morganton, NC md. 1844 Laura Catherine Nelson (drt. of Jared Nelson & wife, Susanna Magill Conyers & gr-drt. "Fighting Capt John Nelson** who lived on Black river, now Clarendon Co., SC) ISSUE, nine, viz: 1-Lawr. Nelson, next in line. . .2-Rev. Erasmus Ellerbe md. 1st Lillias Blair McPhail; 2nd Mary Guthrie. Had-Lilly Blair, John Witherspoon, Belle Walker. . .3-John Conyers Ervin md. Louisa Morgam. . .4-Donald McQueen Ervin md. Sue Barr. . .5-Susan Elizbth md. James E. Kennedy. Had-Katie, Louisa, Crawford, Harry, Thomas. . .6-Samuel J. Ervin md. Laura T. Powe & had-Laura W; Catherine E; Margt T; Edw. Powe; Saml James; Hugh Tate; Joseph Wilson; Eunice Wood; John W; Jean C. . .7-Louisa Nelson md. Wm. C. Ervin & had-Flora, David W; Eliza; Dorothy C; Mary W. . .8-Annie D. md. James L. Michie & had-Margt, Mamie, Elsie, Donald McQueen. . .9-Henry Flinn, inf. . . .VI.---LAWRENCE NELSON ERVIN b. Clarendon Co., SC. d. Indiantown, SC. Confederate Soldier, wounded in battle, md. 1871 Elizbth Gotea Wilson (drt. of Harvey Wilson & Jeannette Witherspoon who had chn: Clara md. F. E. Taylor 1868 of Charleston, SC; Mary, Emma, Harvey, Gotea) ISSUE of Lawr. Nelson Ervin, viz: Mary, Jno. W., Robt. W., Laurie N., Clarendon, Annie Louise, Eras. Powe, Samuel J., Jane W. . . .Descendants in Laurens county, S. C., are: Houston S. Ervin; E. Felicia Ervin Stephens*.

SAMUEL FLEMING, est. settled 1805 in Laurens, SC. Sons-Robert, Saml. Big Robert Fleming 1771-1826 md. Elizbth McClintock, had among others, Mary. . .SAMUEL FLEMING JR., 1763-1843 md. Rebecca Hall. One child was Joseph H. md. Elizbth Jane Bryson.

WILLIAM FULLER md. Jane Griffin, had 14 chn. . .CALVIN L. FULLER b. 1848 Laurens md. Carrie Philips. ISSUE five, viz: Benj. R. md. Mrs. Antho Watt Dial; Calvin M. md. EffieWinebrener;Clementine md. Dr. J. H. Teague; Rosa md. J. H. Motes; William P.

CHARLES GARY OF VA. had sons: Thomas, Absolom, West. 1-THOMAS md. Rebecca Jones, SC-Ala. Had-Thomas, William, Arthur, Isaac, Dr. Martin, Jesse, Charles (last three of SC). Jesse had a son Dr. Thos who had-Gen. Martin W. Gary. . .2-Absolom of SC md. Hetty Griffin, had-Some descts in Tex. . .3-West of SC md. Frances Griffin, had-Charles, Wash, Dr. John K.

JOHN GWIN(Guinn), Va. to SC as wid'r, d. aft 1756, md. 2nd 1739 Catherine Ricketts. ISSUE (known) 7, viz: Jno. Nich., Richard, Mary, George, Roger, Catherine, Elizbth An. . .The son, Jno. Nicholas Gwin(Guinn)** md. Mary Elizbth Bland. Known ISSUE: Jno. Lancelott Bland Guin md. Mrs. Eliza Ann(Moore) Henderson; Jos. Maurice Guin md. twice, 1st w. d. in SC. He migrated to Tenn-O. . .D. A. R: Dorothy Humbert*, Louise Humbert Milburn*, Emma L. H. Nash*.

JOHN HARRIS** b. Md. 1763 md. Mary Pickens. ISSUE: 7 sons, 4 drts. One son was John Jr., had a gr-son Benjamin md. Orpha Harris. Had 5 girls, 4 boys, two served CA. Bonneau Harris md. Nannie Hudgens of Laurens. Had-8 sons, 3 drts.

LT. THOMAS HERBERT, settled Old Dutch Fork, SC by 1772, md. Jemima Dawkins. ISSUE: 1-John b. abt. 1760/3, had-William, John Thomas, Amanda. . .2-George. . .3-Hardy who Bishop Abury ments as accomp. him from Charleston to Ga., to Finches ck 1794. Had-drt Alice Dameron. . .4-Thos. Sharp md. Elizbth Hampton. ISSUE, 10: Harriet Cook, Elizbth McDaniel, Nancy Hampton, Mary Wade, Hardy, John, Thos. S., Edward, Richard, ?Preston. . . .GEORGE HERBERT (no 2 abv) md. 1787 Elizbth Finch, to Ala. Had-Martha Page, Ann Cook Oliver, Dr. Hillary who md. Abigail Dunklin; Geo. who md. 1st Anne W. Dunklin; Thos. E. md. Dorothy Teague Young & had-Aurelia Calhoun d. in Miss; Theodora Adams Royal; Flora A. Buel; HILLARY b. in LAURENS, SC., M. C., Secretary Navy, md. Ella Smith. They had three chn. but only Ella Micou left issue.

TIMOTHY KELLY & sons, Saml, John with drt. Abigail, set. in SC near Camden. John md. abt 1755 Mary Evans, lived in 1762 on Bush riv. ISSUE: Isaac md. Merrie Gaunt; Anna md. Abijah O'Neal; Saml d. 1851 aged 91 md. 1788 Hannah Pearson. They had-Mary Whitacre, John, Timothy, Saml, Moses to Ohio, Anna.

JAMES WILLIAM KILGORE md. Elizbth Jack in Pa. had 19 chn. of whom nine believed in Revolution. The son BENJAMIN moved to NC & later SC md. Ann McCreary, land deed recd, Laurens. ISSUE, viz: James, & fol. to Ala-Miss: David, William, Martha Elizbth, Anna Isabel, Saml. The drt. Martha Elizbth md. John Walker. . .JAMES, s. of Benj. Kilgore, md. Kizziah Greer. ISSUE: 1-Elizbth Stone SC. . .2-Mary Brockman SC. .3-Dr. Ben had-9 chn. .4-Margt. Barry to Miss. . .5-Jesse. . .6-Malinda Barry. . . 7-Lavinia Borum to Miss. . .8-Dr. James. . .9-Josiah. . .JOSIAH KILGORE md. Harriet Benson. ISSUE, seven: Dr. Benjamin; Mary Stokes, Harriet Hunter, William C., James B., Jesse, Isabel. . . .CHARLES KILGORE (one of the 19) md. 1st. Winnie Clayton; 2nd Martha McIllhaney. He d. in Tenn. 1823. ISSUE: 1-Chas. Jr. md. Avirilla Simpson. . .2-Rev. Robt. md. Jane P. Green. . .3-William md. Va. J. Osborn. . .4-Mary Culbertson. . .5-Hiram md. Rebecca Renfro. . .6-Ralph md. Miss Gray. . .7-James. . . 8-Jno. . .9-Martha Walker. . .10-Rebecca Shirl. . .11-Sara Henderson.

WILLIAM KENNEDY** md. Ann Brandon. ISSUE, 11. Two drts. Letitia, Ellen, md. Brandons; James md. Mary Snowden; Ann md. Thos. Hamilton; Elizbth md. Saml Clowney; Mary md. Wm. Hamilton; Jesse md. Mary Hughs; Benjamin md. Lucy Gilbert; William Jr. . .The Rev. John Brandon Kennedy md. Rebecca Ross, Laurens County, S.C.

HENRY LAURENS b. 1724 Vice-Pres. of SC 1776 & Pres. Continental Congress of U.S. He signed Preliminary Peace in Paris 30 Nov. 1782 in conjunction with Jno. Adams, Dr. Franklin, Jno. Jay. "One of the Founding Fathers of this Nation." Was sent to borrow 10 million from the Dutch, ship captured by British & he confined in Tower London 1780. He md. Elinor Ball. ISSUE 4: John killed in Revo; Henry; Mary Pinckney, & a dau. md. Dav. Ramsey.

LIDE: John, Thos., Robt** bros. abt. 1740 to Cheraw Dist. SC. . .Robt. md. Hannah Hart, had 5 sons; one was Hugh who had sons: Rev. Thos. P. & Jno. M. Latter had Jno. Miller md. Eliza Edwards; Rev. Thos. md. Martha Hawkins, & a s. was Robt. Lide of Greenville.

129

WILLIAM LIPSCOMB** from Va. bef Revo. to Cherokee Co., SC(Sptg) had s. John. Had Edw. md. Melissa Littlejohn & had-Hamlet S. md. Alice Wood. . .Nathan, CA 1842-1918 md. Mary Wilkins.

ALEXANDER LOVE of York Co. Pa. md. Margt Moore, to SC. abt 1765. Set. near old Yorkville & memb. Prov. Cong. 1775. A desct was: Robt. Mitchel Love who had s. Dr. Robt., md. Jane Hemphill.

PATRICK MARION md. Jane McNeel, had-Jno. Alex Marion md. Margt. J. Sterling, had-James Taylor Marion 1845-1911 CA md. Jane A. Hardin, had-Hon. Jno. Hardin Marion md. Mary P. Davidson (drt. Col. Wm. D.-& Ann Irvin Pagan. Col. Wm. Davidson was gr-son of Maj. Jno.**) GENERAL FRANCIS MARION** 1732-1795, the "Swamp Fox" was son of Gabriel & Esther Cordes Marion & youngest of six chn. Gabriel was son of Benjamin Marion & Louise d'Aubrey, French Huguenots, to S. C.

JAMES MARTIN 1723-1792 md. 1745 Amy Holt. Their son, KINCHEN MARTIN** 1762-1841 md. Chloe Hough. ISSUE: 1. William md. twice,-Parker, McBride. . .2. John md. twice,-Parker, Boswell. . .3. Jas. H. md. Charlotte Kirby. . .4. Lucy md. three times,-Morton, Ingram, Kendred. D.A.R: Lena J. Abercromie*.

JOHN MATTISON McDAVID, w. Anna, had (known) chn: 1-John Allen md. Nancy Acker & had 11 chn. . .2-Patrick** descts Ky-O. . .3-Rosannah md. McKay, SC. . .4-David** of SC. . .5-Jennie md. Mr. Rutledge. . .6-JAMES md. Penelope Rodgers. ISSUE to maturity: (1) Abner (2) Hiram (3) William to Miss. (4) Anny Shumate, (5)Nancy Mattison Graham (6) John md. Miss Davenport (drt. & gr.drt. of Revo. S.) Chn: James, William Jackson, Richard, John, Adeline Roberts to Tex., Robert, George, Mary, Andrew, Nancy, Benjamin, Rosannah Williams, Nancy Graham to Ga., Mary Arnold, SC. (7) Jas.

JESSE McGEE located in Anderson Co, had s. Elias md. Sara Landrum, had s. Julius F. md. Mattie J. Jones. . .One Michael McGhee**. Desct. Hon. Saml Hodges McGhee of Cokesbury md. Laura Harrall of Bennettsville.

WILLIAM, JOHN & JAMES McGOWAN filed Revo. Claims in S.C. . .William McGowanjmd. Jane McWilliams, Laurens County. They had a son, SAMUEL McGOWAN who md.Susan Caroline Wardlaw. He was Brig-General 1863 in command of McGowans Brigade ISSUE: Lewis, Samuel, Sara E., William C., Alex M., Lucia R. . . .Capt John Jackson McGowan md. Mary Wells. Had-Franklin Pierce, b. Laurens Co. md. 1887 Mattie Calhoun.

ROBERT MOSELEY 1725-1796, b. in SC md. 1st Mary; md. 2nd Penelope Talley. Fol. Moseleys filed Revo. Claims in SC: Robert, John, Thomas, Benjamin, William, James. Robert by 1st w. had-Rachel Davis, Elizbth Vann, Sara Hagood, Martha Stallings, Susan Adams, Mary Holsonbacke, Edward 1771-34 md. in SC Miss Butler, John. . .Robt. Moseley Sr. had by 2nd w. issue: Anna Jeter, Lydia Williams Moseley, Robert J., Jesse, Daniel, Grace, Thomas, Penelope Copeland. The son, EDWARD MOSELEY md. 1793 in SC. Miss Butler, d. in Ala. . . .A GEORGE MOSELEY** of Laurens from Va. md. 1st Lucy Moore; 2nd Mary Moore.

THOMAS NEAL SR, md. Susannah Harrell, had-SAMUEL NEAL** md. Patty McCormick 1786 in SC. ISSUE: Polly Pruitt, Betsy, John, Sara, Thomas, James who md. 1st Elizbth Beal, 2nd Elizbth Rawlings Davenport.

WILLIAM O'NEALL Va-SC 1766, Mudlick Ck. Laurens. Son Hugh b. 1767 was father of Judge O'Neal, historian.

RICHARD OWINGS** & wife Ann, Laurens Co., SC. ISSUE with descendants: 1-Richard** & wife Sara, had-Richard, William, Archibald, John. . .2-Edward to Tenn. . .3-Butler md. in Laurens abt. 1787. . .4-Archibald to Kershaw Co. . .5-William to Va-Ky. . .5-Jonathan of Laurens County.

WILLIAM PARSONS** md. in Va. Mary Goolsby. ISSUE: Samuel, Joseph,, Archibald, Isiah, others. D.A.R. members: Margaret Brockman Fowler*, Rosemary Fowler*.

HENRI PATRICK, M.C. & REVO. Patriot, Orangeburg Dist. HAD-Mary & twin sons, George, Lewis. Geo. md. Hannah Lee of Edgfield (drt. Andrw Lee** & Nancy drt. Russel Wilson & Susan Rutherford.)

PHILIP PENDLETON of New Kent, Va. ISSUE: Elizbth Clayton; Rachel Vass; Cathryn Taylor; Henry. Latter md. Mary Taylor & had-James, Philip, Nathl. Latter md. in Va. dau. of Philip Clayton. They had-Henry b. 1750 d. in SC 1789; descts in Pendleton Dist.

GENERAL ANDREW PICKENS** b. Pa. d. SC. md. Rebecca Calhoun. ISSUE, viz: 1-Mary md. John Harris & had-Andrew, Rebecca, John, Ezekiel, Mary, Nathl, Thomas, Joseph, Eliza, Benjamin. . .2-Ezekiel Pickens had(by 1st w. Elizbth Bonneau): Ezekiel Saml, Elizbth. by 2nd w.(Eliza Barksdale): Thomas, Mary, Andrew. . .3-Ann md. Jno. Simpson, Ala. Had-Leah, Andrew, Rebecca, John, Ezekiel, James. . .4-Jane, 2nd of that name, md. Dr. John Miller. Had-Robert, Eliza, John. . .5-Margaret md. George Bowie, had-Louisa Smith. . .6-Andrew md. 1st Miss Wilkinson, had-Frances W., Susan Calhoun. . . 7-Rebecca md. Wm. Noble. Had-Andrew, William, Ezekiel, Samuel, Joseph. . .8-Catherine md. Dr. Jos. Hunter, had-Margt-Eliza, Maria, Ezekiel, Andrew, Joseph. Res. Ark. . . 9-Joseph md. Miss Henderson. Had-Sara McQueen, Joseph, Rebecca Green, Anderson, Andrew.

COL. CHAS. PINCKNEY 1731-1782 md. Frances Brewton. A son was Chas. (2nd cousins: Chas. Cotesworth Pinckney & Thos. P.) The son Chas. md. 1788 Mary Eleanor Laurens: "It is believed that at least 31 of Chas. Pinckney's ideas went into the Constitution of U.S." [Every time we are reminded of the Constitution under which we live in freedom & independence, we might remember this great South Carolinian who did so much to bring about that freedom, which makes of us the most fortunate people in the world.] (Hennig)

AARON PINSON of Va. left w. 1758. He md. twice. Some of his chn. migrated to NC. Aaron Pinson left w. in NC naming wife Delilah. his chn. were: Thomas, Joseph, Zachariah, William, Aaron, Isaac, Ann Cunningham, Mary Evans, Elizbth Campbell, Dorcas Austin, Sara Head. Descts of Thomas to Ga. . .Both Aaron & Joseph Pinson belonged to Rabun Creek church, St. Marks Parish, Craven Co., SC in 1771 (the present Mt. Pleasant section of Laurens Co) AARON had land grant 1766. This Rev. Aaron Pinson of Laurens, w. Elizbth, had chn. 10, viz: Aaron, Joseph, Marmaduke, John, Moses, Isaac, Mary Cole, Jemima Henry, & drts. who md. Thos. Shirley, Joseph Fowler of Tenn. There is Revo. Service for 3 this family. . . .JOSEPH PINSON md. Mary Omehundro. He appears 1790 census, 7 in family, one being the son, MARMADUKE PINSON SR, will at Laurens, SC 1820. Chn: Abijah md. an Arnold, all to Ark. except youngest son to Ala; Isaac J. to Ga; Edith McDaniel; Huldah Cunningham; Polly Strain; Jerusha (Ruchey); Ruth; Sallie Madden; Marmaduke Jr. . . .The Rev. Marmaduke Pinson, w. at Laurens, md. Elizbth Sullivan 1805-1847. Had 8 chn, viz: 1-Mary Harris of Waterloo, had 6 chn. . .2-Louisa Brown. . .3-Dr. Washington. . .4-Elizbth Blain. . .5-Virginia Dora Edwards. . .6-Martha Charles. . .7-Joseph who md. 1871 Mary Luana Cox. Had 8 chn, viz: James Abner, John S., Mildred E., Joseph C., Washington, Clincie W., Clara M., Corrie L. . .The son JOSEPH ABNER PINSON md.1895 Emmie Shirley. Had 6 chn. Of these, following members our D. A. R. chapter: Annie Laurie Pettus*, Lydia Pinson Thomas, Shirley Perry, & a gr.drt. Vera Higeria*, dau. in-law, Lee Hunt Pinson*.

RAZOR, CHRISTIAN of Va. Had-Ezekiel Razor, CA md. Pamela Barmore & had 11 Chn: James C., E. B., others. JAMES CHRISTIAN RAZOR of Laurens Co., md. Lucy Ann Agnew. Among their chn. were: Elizbth, Maggie, Emma, Ida, Wm. C., Ella, James, Samuel, Sally, John B. The son, William Christian Razor of Laurens Co., md. 1884 Ella L. Clardy of Laurens. . .E. B. Razor, md. Eliza, drt. of Dr. Harrison Latimer.

131

AMOS RICHARDSON** 1741-1815 md. Mary Elizbth Peterson. ISSUE: (1) David md. Fannie Williams (2)Susanna md. Mr. Allen (3)Rush md. Amanda Boulware. . .D. A. R. Louise Holmes Motes*.

JOHN RIDGEWAY** had a son JOHN** md. Fanny Ragsdale (drt**) ISSUE: 1-John had a son John. . .2-Betsy Lindley. . .3-Richard, had-David, Elijah, John. . .D. A. R. member-Agnes Ruth Babb.*.

DR. JOHN RUTLEDGE & ANDREW RUTLEDGE, bros. to SC. 1730-5. ANDRW md. Sarah Boone Hext. No chn. ment. will. . .DR. JOHN RUTLEDGE md. 1738 Sarah Hext (her mother md. Andrw) ISSUE, 7 viz: (1)Com.-in-Chief & Pres. of SC John md. 1763 Elizbth Grimke. .(2)Edward, SIGNER Declaration Independence md. Henrietta Middleton. . (3)Andrw. md. Elizbth Gadsden. . .(4)Thos. md. Margt Deveaux. . .(5)Sara md. Gov. Jno. Matthews. . .(6)Hugh md. Ann Smith. . .(7)Mary md. Roger Smith. . .Pres. of SC Jno. Rutledge had ISSUE, viz: Martha Kinlock; Sarah; Gen. John md. 1791 Sara Motte; Edw. md. Jane Harlestone; Fred'k md. Harriet Pinckney Horry; Chas. md. Caroline Smith; Elizbth md. Henry Laurens; Thos. d. young; Wm. md. Ann Coslett; States md. Julia Haskell.

CHARLES SAXON d. 1816** Cpt. Revo. Will at Laurens. Chn: Polly Anderson, Sally Rodgers, Lewis. . .The son, CAPT. LEWIS SAXON** md. Sally Allen. ISSUE, viz: 1-Clarissa Downs who had-Phoebee Farley, Mary Grace Sullivan, Susan T. Griffin, S. Caroline Downs. . .2-Charles md. twice-Pierce, Wolf. Had-J. F. W., Lewis, G. W., Robt. C. . .3-Mary Arnold. . .4-Joshua had-John, Sara Craig, Dr. Charles A., Mary E. Dorrah, others. .5-Lydall P. Saxon to Ala. .6-Tabitha Cleveland. .7-Susannah Thurston. . 8-Samuel. . .9-Allen. . .Others unmd. Following Saxons of Revolution granted Bounty Lands: Samuel, James, Wm. Following filed Revo. Claims: Joshua, Charles, Hugh, Lewis, John, Archille, Yancy, Thomas & Edmond Sexton. D. A. R. members: Bernice Abercromie George*, Ruth A. Cain*.

I.--OWEN SULLIVAN II(s. Owen I, s. Jno) md. 1721 Mary Margt. Hewlett (Hughlett) ISSUE 5 to SOUTH CAROLINA; viz: James, Oen, Margt, Charles, Pleasant. . .I-JAMES OF LAURENS, SC** md. 1st Meta Bolling; 2nd Sara Harrison Choice. Had 10 chn: Sara Godfrey; Elizbth Burton to Ga; Larkin; Harrison; Delphy Osborne; John to Ga; Priscilla Moore; Jas. Jr; Rebecca Roland; Nancy Vaughan. . .2-OWEN III**, grant SC 1773, d. 1797 SC md. Sallie O'Dell Nelson. Had-(1)Fanny md. a Gore, Grv. Co, had 2 drts. One was first per. bur. Lebanon. Other md. a Lowe (2)Sallie md. a Croft, had Dr. Geo. of Ala. (3)Elizbth Jackson to Ky (4) (5)Wm & Nelson to Ky. (6)Charles md. 1816 Jane Ressell to Ala. 1824, had 6 chn: Abigail md. Thos. A. Lanford; Caroline md. Henry Harte; Dr. Oen md. 3 times, d. 1897, Waterloo, Ala. Had-Jane, Hewlett, Mary, James, Lizzie, John & Charles. Latter prac. medicine with father. . .3-MARGT or MAUDLINE md. Col. Saml Wharton b. 1740 d. SC. Had: (1)Betsy Burts (2)Patsy Grimes (3)Lottie Davenport (4)Nancy Lowe (5)Sam who had Edw & Geo. (6)Pleasant who had Wm. . .Wm. Nelson md. Leanna Fuller & had-Wm. & Jno. of Laurens. . .Jno. md. 1869 Laura Harris & had 8 chn. . .4-PLEASANT** ancestor Anderson, SC branch, md. Milly Kelly. Pen. papers give chn, viz: Kelly, Nimrod, Hudson Berry, Mary J., Sara, James, Maria, Mosby, Frances. The son Kelly had: Nimrod b. 1829 md. Emily K. Mattison & had 5, viz: James M. b. 1855 md. Mary A. Wannamaker; Nimrod B. 1863 md. Lila Simpson; Charles S. b. 1868 md. 1890 Lutie Bewley; William W. md. Anne Patrick; H. K. . .5-CHARLES.

II.--CHARLES SULLIVAN** md. 15 June 1749 wid. Mary Charlton (Johnson)** b. Va. 1722, d. SC. 1837. ISSUE 5 to South Carolina, viz: Moses, Sara, Claiborne, Stephen, Hewlett. . .1-MOSES** d. abt 1810 SC md. Milly Chandler d. 1832 Ala. Had-Joel md. a Johnson; Martha md. Joel Ferguson; Matilda md. Jas. Webb; Agnes md. Vardy Bonds; Nancy md. Isaac Littleton; Mary md. Robt. Scott. All to Ala., except Mary. . .2-SARA MARGARET md. Joseph Dunklin in SC**. Aft. his d. she to Ky. with bros. Stephen & Claiborne & bro-in-law Jno. Dunklin. ISSUE 5, viz: Mary H. md. David Gregory in SC to Ala; Jane Caroline md. Isaac Hicks in SC to Ky; Governor Daniel md. Emily W. Haley in Ky. to Mo. 1810; Joseph Jr. md. Sara Parkins in SC to Miss. 1834 & wid. to

La-Tex; Stephen Tomplat md. Rachel McQuire to Ky. 1816. . .3-CLAIBORNE to Ky. 1806 to Mo. d. 1860 very old, md. Mary Harvey in SC. He with bro. Stephen & sister Sara Dunklin, helped blaze trail across mts, belongings on pack-horses, joined Danl Boone. Had 10 chn. viz: (1)Rev. James who had 4 (2)Mark had 6 .chn (3)Stephen b. 1795 md. Dorcas Pinell & had 13 chn. viz: Claiborne to Ohio; Blassinggame md. Elizbth Burton & lived Phelps Co. Mo. & had-Herbert, Blassinggame Jr., Mary, Lily, Fanny; Anna, drt of Stephen & Dorcas, d. in Cole Ridge; Sara md. a Mitchell to Miss; Elizbth md. a Magee & had 3 boys & 1 girl; Lettie of Crawford Co. Mo. md. J. Huitt & her drt. Elizbth md. N. W. Gibbs; Mary md. a Huit or Hewitt & a drt. md. Thos. Tune. . . Claiborne Sr. md. 2nd a Davis. A gr.son was Saml b. 1813 md. sister of Genl. Geo. Crook, Indian Fighter & had a son Thos. C. (Genl. Thos. C. Sullivan USA). Going to Ky-Mo. with Sullivans & Dunklins was Joseph Shipp & other relatives. . .4-STEPHEN to Ky. 1806 had a s. Charles md. a Hammett. . .5-HEWLETT;

III.--HEWLETT SULLIVAN(s. Chas. s. Owen II)** md. 19 Dec. 1787 Mary Dunklin**, drt. Jos. D-**. Hewlett entered army age 15. With father's assistance some 4 yrs. later in fall 1781, he organized a company of Scouts or Rangers, composed of relatives & neighbors. They caught & hung many Tories & cleared their section of Red Coats. He d. Grv. Co., SC. 1830. ISSUE 12, viz: Judge Dunklin, Dr. John C., Joseph P., Hewlett Jr., George W., T. Jefferson, Dr. James M., Jane, Elizbth, Frances, Mary, Charles P. . . .1-JUDGE DUNKLIN SULLIVAN 1791-1837 md. Mary Mayberry, lived Perry Co. Ala. Member Convt. organized State Gov. One of founders Judson Col. Had 6 chn: (1)Mary Jane md. E. G. Byrne of Selma, Ala. & had Edw. md. T. King & had-Emma Harris*, Mary, Gonzella, Ida, Edw. (2)Lumley md. Jos. P. Walker & had 2 daus. She md. 2nd Elam Parrish. Chn: Maud & Ida Walker; Emma, Lona & Elam Parris (3)Hewlett md. Eliza Reid, Leon Co., Tex. Had-Dunklin, Lumley. Dunklin md. & had-Terrell, Marion, Harold, Herman; Lumley md. a Davidson & had- Wm., Lewis, Arthur, Dunklin, Ira, Clyde. (4)Dunklin md. Margt Griffin, Ala. Had-Dunklin, Jeff, Griffin, Bessie, Mary (5)Monroe md. Mary Griffin to Miss. Had-James, Tolbert. . . .2-DR. JOHN C. SULLIVAN, s. of Hewlett, 1793-1864 md. 1828 Anne Hendricks Arnold, Fork Shoals, Grv. Co., SC. Had 7 chn, viz: (1)Jno. D. md. Penelope McDavid & had-Allen md. Lula Garrison; Benj. md. Mabel Mendenhall; Caroline* md. H. H. Newton; Mark md. Elizbth Frierson; Mary md. F. M. Royall (2)Sara md. Dr. Enoch Agnew of Abbv., SC & had-Janie; Anna md. Chas. Smith (3)Jane md. Capt. Jno. McFall & had-Mary Elizbth md. Lt. H. L. Odiorne USN & drt. was Mabel* md. Hugh S. Macglashan; Rachel* md. J. R. Shannon & had-Marjorie Lawry*, Lilou McLane* (4)Elizbth md. Dr. W. Agnew (5)Emma md. Col. Mark Hardin, had-Blanche McCoslin*, Mattie Garner*, Virginia* (6)Martha md. Adam Eichelberger (7)Clara md. Dr. I. Cannon. Also descd. through this line: Mrs. Henry White* of Chester, SC; Jean McFall White*, Mrs. Ann White Leith*, Mrs. Jno. Edwards* of Seneca. . . .3-GEO. W. SULLIVAN, s. of Hewlett, of Sullivan Township, Laurens Co. 1809-1887, md. Jane Washington Brooks of Edg. Co. Had 6 chn, viz: (1)Addie md. J. C. Featherstone & had-Judge C. C. Featherstone of Greenwood (2)Mary md. Robt. Goodgion & had-Maida*, Geo., Brooks (3)Jane md. Saml. Todd of Laurens & had-Rev. Charlton (4)Lizzie md. Chas. Garlington. One drt. is Janye Pruitt* (5)Geo. Jr. md. Mary E. Chiles of Abbv. One son, Wash, md. L. Moseley & had among others, Mary Louise* (6)Joseph md. Mary Pelham, Laurens, SC. . . .4-JOSEPH PINCKNEY SULLIVAN, s. of Hewlett, 1796-1820 md. Temperance Hamilton Arnold, Laurens Co. Had 8 chn. viz: (1)Jno. Hewlett md. Mary D. Cureton (2)Milton CA. Bach (3)C. Pleasant, md. Mary E. Gilkerson & had-Be Pure, Linda M. Wood* (4) Keziah J. md. Col. Jas. McCullough (5)Mary Ann md. James M. Eppes. One son, Jas. md. Emma Davenport & had-Jesse Goode*. Others: Temp. md. Capt. James L McCullough; Mary Ann md. Wash Sharp; Lina md. Saml Dent; Lucia md. Saml Eppes (6)Malinda C. md. 1st Dr. Wm. C. Kilgore; 2nd B. D. Kay (7)Temperence md. 1853 Jesse C. Kilgore & had-Mary, Jesse, Josiah, Frances. Fol. descts this branch, charter members Sullivan-Dunklin D. A. R: Mrs. Mary L. Leonard*, Mrs. Frances Wood*, Mrs. Edna Hodges*, Mrs. Mary Hassell*, Mrs. W. M. Melton*, Miss Clara Kilgore*, Mrs. W. C. Smith*, Mrs. W. E. McKamy*. . .(8)William Dunklin 1838-1931 Laurens Co. md. 3 times, 1st Elizbth Humbert & had-Elizbth Johnson, Gainesville, Ga; Zelene Wells* who had-May Smith*. He md. 2nd Harriet G. Humbert & had-(1)Joseph Giroud of Laurens md. Lidie Miller. Had-Bob, Herbert, Cecil, Hattie, Anna, Dunklin (2)Felicia A. md. 1884 Thos.

133

J. Sullivan II & had 6 chn. WDS. md. 3rd Mary E. Quarles & had-Anges West, Margie Culberson, William, Richard, Keziah McKelvy, Thomas, Milton. ,5-HEWLETT SULLIVAN Jr-. bach. . . .6-ELIZABETH (drt. of Hewlett Sullivan Sr.) md. Marmaduke PINSON (see Pinson Geneal). . . .7-FRANCES (drt. of Hewlett Sullivan) md. SQUIRE CALHOUN. ISSUE, viz: (1)Dr. John of Summerville, Ga. (2)Thos. of Crackett, Tex. (3)Jane md. Judge Glenn of Laurens (4)Elizbth md. Dr. E..C. Ragsdale of Grv. Co. SC to Tex. (5)Lucinda md. Jos. Beavers, Houston Co., Tex. (6)Hewlett md. Miss Smith, Cook Co., Tex. (7)Fanny unmd. . . .8-JANE (drt. of Hewlett Sullivan) md. SAMUEL L. MOORE; Grv. Co., SC. Had-(1)Hewlett md. Esther Benson & had Saml. Then he md. Temp. Shepherd & had-Hewlett, Maggie, Annie Fanny, Shepherd, Orph (2)Dr. D. D. Moore md. Eliza Barber & had-Mrs. H. H. Blalock, Charlton D., J. H. S., Claud (3)Mary Jane md. Jno. D. GRAY & had-Mrs. Ransom, Oscar, Thomas, Jane (Chapt. D. A. R. members: Mrs. Ann W. Gray*, Mrs. Alice M. Taylor*). . . .9-MARY (drt. of Hewlett Sullivan) 1813-83 md. Jas. M. Latimer of Abbv. ISSUE: (1)Helen md. Wm. Shumate of Grv. Co. & had-Albert, Lillie, Frank, William, Helen. .D.A.R. Helen Fawcette*. (2)Amanda md. Dr. Jno. Groves of Ga. & had-Sallie, James, Bessie (3)Frances md. Jno. Jordan & had-Isabel, Lallah (4)Elizbth md. Thos. Cosby of Atlanta (5)Emma md. Capt. Jno. Austin of Grv. & had-Joseph, William, Hattie, Gertrude (6)Dr. Joseph P. md. Hattie Mooney of Grv. & had-Annie, Lullie, Jos. Jr., Jean (7)Jno. Henry md. Molly Lites, near Troy, had-Jno. H., Mary (8)James H. md. 1884 Mary L. Ramsey, Grv. Co. Had-Mary, Andrew, DeWitt, Charles, James, Frances, David, Jno. Austin. . . .10-THOS. JEFFERSON SULLIVAN (s. of Hewlett) 1807-1866 md. 12 Sept. 1833 Sara Cureton of Grv. Co. 1817-82. Res. Sullivan Township, Laurens Co., SC. ISSUE, 8 viz: (1) Henrietta md. Capt. C. H. Parkins 1866. Res. Grv., SC. Had-Paul C; Elizbth Norris; C. Allen; Mark D; H. Jeff; Cora; John H. (2)Frances A. md. 1880 Capt. J. W. Goodgion (3)Adelaide md. 1865 Pascal D. Huff & had-Dr. Junius of Hodges; Agnes Childers; Swan B. of Grv. Co; Vilonia Garrison; Warren; Corrie Bozeman (4)Sarah md. 1868 L. T. Mahaffey, Laurens Co. Had-Sara md. 1895 R. L. Mears & had-Dr. G. M; Carrie E; Prof. Jeff md. Ruth Harrelton; Walter md. Rosa Wham 1897 & had-Margt, Sara Grace, Bonnie; Claudia was 2nd w. R. L. Mears & had-Robt, Herman, Edw;' Pauline* md. 1897 W. M. Nash & had-Sara, Hortense Ropp had-Helen*; J. W. Walter md. Mary Austin; Lois Parsons, Alfred, Pauline Corden, Annett Hellems, Ellen* md. Robt. C. Wasson. (5)John D. Sullivan md. 1st Ellen Clinkscales & had-Florence md. W. W. Smith & had-Dr. David; Jno. S; Ellen Rippy, William, Thomas. JOHN D. 2nd w. Florence Allen 25 Feb. 1880 & had-(a)Ella md. Izzy Gray (b)Allen J. md. Mary T. Humbert & had-A. Carlisle, Lois W. (c)Jno. D. Jr. md. Sidney Harris & had-Jno. D. Elliott H. (d)Grace md. Rev. J. H. Brown & had-James H; Grace, Ella, Rebecca, Annette, Elizbth. . . .(6)CLAUDIA C. md. 1877 Aug. Huff & had-Ernest A. md. Catherine Blake. . . .(7)Chas. Pascal McLeod md. 1882 Arrah J. Watts. . .(8)THOMAS J. Sullivan II b. 24 Dec. 1853, d. 5 Nov. 1923 md. 11 Nov. 1884 Felicia Arnold Sullivan b. 1 Aug. 1865, d. 26 May 1927, drt. of Wm. D. Sullivan & Harriet Humbert. ISSUE 6 to maturity, viz: (a)Jos. Giroud, bach. (b)Claudius A. Vet. WWI (c)Sara Lucile* md. 6 Mch. 1907 E. P. Ervin & had 2 chn: Houston S. Vet. WWII; Elizbth Felicia* md. 24 May 1935 Albert Stephens, Laurens, SC. Chn: Sara, Albert E., Robt., John (d)Rev. C. H. Sullivan, Meth. Conf. SC & Vet. WWI & Chap. & Cpt. WWII md. Grace Pitts & has-Joan, Jack (e)Dr. Charlton H. Sullivan md. Evelyn Peele* & had-Giroud, Earl (f)M. Catherine' b. 1899 md. A. F. Holley. Has-Linda Frankie* & adopted son Billy. . . .II.--CHARLES P. SULLIVAN, s. of Hewlett, 1811-1876, md. 1st Sara Smith of Newberry d. 1845. He md. 2nd Zelene Boyd of Laurens. His chn. were, viz: Jno. M.; Warren P.; Jarred D.; James; Charles, Hewlett, Arthur, Addison, Alice, Zelene, Susan. The son Jared md. Rosalie Moore & some of chn. were: Blanch Bostic, Sara Milan, James H., Rosalie Burnside. The son Charles to Miss. Arthur md. Cornelia Herndon. Susie md. Hugh E. Gray & had-Zelene md. J. W. Dunklin & others. Hewlett was father of Mrs. Joe Sparks of Grv; Mrs. H. A. Jennings of Grv. & others. Alice md. John Grier. The descendants of CPS not complete. . . .12-Dr. JAMES M. SULLIVAN, s. of Hewlett, 1816-75, Res. Grv. Co., SC. md. 1st Sara Mimms of Abbv. Had-(1)M. Frances md. Peter A. McDavid (2)Sara md. Mack Harrison (3)Harriet md. Wm. Holland (4)Capt. Mimms md. Mary Stokes (5)Joseph md. Emma Earle (6)Jane md. John W. McCullough. One ch. was Sara md. John J. McSwain, M. C. . .DR; JAMES M. md. 2nd Lizzie Vaughan of Fla. Had-(7)Paul of Honea Path, SC. md. Ena Agnew (8)Marion md. J. Agnew (9)Elma md. 1st

Hankins, 2nd Martin (10)Belton md. Jane Walsh (11)Virginia md. W. M. Waterfield (Some branches of this family more complete because we had the cooperation of members of Sullivan-Dunklin D.A.R.)

Among SIMPSONS who filed Revo. Claims are: John, William, James, Hugh. .Dr. John Wells Simpson of Laurens had two sons: John Wister 1821-1893 md. Ann Patillo Farror; Governor Wm. D. Simpson & Chief Justice Supreme Court. There was also a drt-Cornelia F. md. Henry P. Farrow. John Wister & Ann Simpson md. 1847. Chn: John md. Annie Knox; Wm. Wells md. Francis Jane Kilgore of Laurens; Stobo J. md. Elouise, drt. of Gov. Simpson; Elizbth md. Chas. W. Zimmerman; Paul md.Flora Cates; Richard & Casper unmd; Dr. Frank.

WILLIAM SPEER** 1747-1830. (Mother was drt of Wm. Houston) 1776 moved to Abbeville, md. 1784 wid. Mrs. Eleanor (Little) Norris, had 4 chn: John, Alex, Margt md. Jos. Rucker, Wm. He md. 1811 Mary S. Gill. Had 8 chn. One was Dr. Andrw, surg. C. A. md. Sophia Verdell.

WM. THOMAS SUMTER & w. Patience of Va., had: THOMAS SUMTER 1734-1832, Landowner in SC 1763 md. 1767 the wid. of William Jameson (Polly). ISSUE: Mary. . . . THOMAS b. 1768. Two of Gen. Sumter's gr.sons were: Charles & Etienne de Fontenay. Sumter built his home at Statesburg which he hoped would be the state capital. He owned 150,000 acres land. Sumter District named for him. He was one of South Carolina's famous Partisan Leaders.

THOS. TAYLOR of Culpepper, Va. w. Johanah, will 2 Dec. 1787. Thos. Taylor Jr's will names w. Elizbth; Daus: Mary Ann Burress, Sara Obriant, Johannah S. Campbell, Frances & a son Edw. A Thos. Taylor sold land on Horse ck to Wm. Arnold 1822 & to Jas. Riley 1825. . . .NANCY (sd to be dau. of Thos. Taylor Sr) 1782-1856 md. James Riley, lived near Tumbling Shoals, Laurens County.

JAMES THOMAS** 1757-1803, SC, md. Elizbth Calaham. Had 1-John C. to Miss.-Ala. abt. 1816. . .2-Joyce md. Thos. Williams to Miss. . .3-Silas unmd. . .4-Wm Shepperd, w. Mary. . .5-Elizbth md. 4 times, to Miss. . .6-James, w. Lucy. . .7-Sara md. Wm. Brunson.

BARRETT TRAVIS md. Elizbth Deloach. Res. Edgfield, SC. Two known sons, Mark, Alex. I--Rev. Alex 1790-1852 md. Polly Williams. ISSUE: (1)Jno. D. md. Mary Stallworth (2)Martha md. Nich Stallworth (3)Jas. md. Mary Ann McCreary (4)Philip md. Adriane Calloway, Ala-Tex. . .II. MARK TRAVIS 1783-1836 SC-Ala. md. 1808 Jemima Stallworth. ISSUE: (1)Col. Wm. B. perished at the Alamo 1836, md. Rosanna Cato. Had-Chas E., Susan I. (2)Mark B. md. Louise A. Bradley. Had-Pierce, Butler, Mason (3)James C. md. 1st Saphronia Davis; 2nd Mary E. Green. Had-Louise, Mark (4)Sara A. md. Francis Brantley (5)Emily C. md. Jos. Brantley (6)Nancy md. Rufus Kilpatrick. Others were: Jemima, Calloway, Alex & a dau.

NATHANIEL VANCE SR.** Laurens Co., SC. md. Mary Dunbar McTier. ISSUE who left descts: 1-Samuel md. 1st Mrs. Elizbth Kincaid Armstrong & had-Mary Simms; Major James. The latter md. twice & had some 15 chn. A drt. Mary A. Dorrah had-Griffith V. who md. Richard Mimms Sullivan Jr. . .2-Frances md. Wm. Greer. . .3-John md. Nancy Wright Watson. . .4-Mary Caroline. . .5-Allen. . .6-William md. Elizbth Edington. Had-Mary, Sara, William, Martha, Eliza, N.W., Susan. . .7-David md. 1st Sara Eddington, 2nd Matilda Tinsley. Had-Mary Rivers, Sara Godbold, Eliza Copeland, Permelia, Martha Ferguson & 3 sons to La., viz: Dr. Roseborough, Dr. Samuel W. and Harrison.

ALEXANDER VERNON to Spartanburg Co. SC 1755, md. Margt Chesnee. ISSUE: James, had-(1) Dr. Jas. J. md. drt. of Judge Jas. Jordon. . .(2)Judge Thos. O. P. Vernon 1818-1877 md. drt of Elisha Bomar, had chn: 7. . .Was holding court when LAURENS RIOT occured, Writ of Habeas Corpus suspended, to give prisoners hearing.

JOHN WATTS** b. Va. d. Laurens, SC md. 1788 Margt (Peggy) Pollard (She drt.)**

ISSUE, viz: Beaufort, Matilda, William, Eliza K., Braxton, Richard, Louisa, Narcissa who md. 1829 John Ball, John, Cornelia, Elvira, Peggy. . .The son JOHN WATTS md. 1841 Elizbth Cannon (Drt.**) & had Chn: 1-William A. of CA. . .2-Arrah md. 1882 Chas. M. P. Sullivan. . .3-Richard, Chief Justice SC md. 1st Alline Cash; 2nd Lottie (drt. of Chief Justice Henry McIver) He was surv. by drts: Mrs. Bessie Royal, Mrs. J. D. Sullivan, Mrs. Frank Stokes. . . WILLIAM DENDY WATTS md. 1828 Miss Young; md. 1837 Sara Speake Cannon. ISSUE: Nancy, Phoebe, William, John W., Laurens, Susan Young, Lucy Nance, Eliza who md. B. W. Ball, Lucy Boyd, William Mills, Arrah N., James Dunklin, Rhoda B., W. D. . .The son James D. Watts md. Harriet Frierson. The unmarried drt. Betty made her home with niece Mrs. M. L. Copeland.

COL. JAMES WILLIAMS** 1740-1780, settled Laurens Co., 1773. Hero of Up-country, fell at Kings Mt. md. Mary Wallace 1762. Had among others-Washington Williams 1777-1829 md. 1797 Sara Griffin (drt.**).

WILLIAM WYATT JR.** md. twice, 1st Frances Newton. Had 6 chn. viz: Frances Mattison, SC; Macajah, Va; Lettice Smith, SC; William, Elizabeth English, Elijah. . . Wm. Wyatt Jr. md. 2nd Elizbth Snoe. Had-Talitha Payne, Malinda Dumington, Frances Wyatt, Mahala Rosser to Mo., Malissa Rosser. . . .The son ELIJAH WYATT md. 1793 Mary Grigsby Foster, to SC 1800. ISSUE 9 chn. viz: Eliza Mattison, Esther Mitchell, Jas. F., William N., Redmond G., Mildred Cox Susan C. Kay, Harriet Mauldin, Malinda Alexander. . . .MILDRED LUANI WYATT became 2nd w. of Abner Cox. They had, among others, Mary Cox md. Joseph D. Pinson. From this line 4 D. A. R. members, Sullivan-Dunklin chapter.

In these brief genealogies,** signifies Revolutionary service, and *, D. A. R. member. There are no doubt some errors, but in every case, the data was obtained or checked by a member of that family or a family connection. No attempt has been made to give all the descendants of any family, but only the ones that were available through the cooperation of members of the Sullivan-Dunklin D. A. R. chapter. These data should furnish enough "clues" so that further research can develop many new D.A.R. and S.A.R. lines.

GRAVE OF GENERAL THOMAS SUMTER, WITH SMALL CATHOLIC CHAPEL BUILT FOR HIS WIFE, IN THE BACKGROUND

136

# ABSTRACTS OF WILLS----1775-1855
# LAURENS COUNTY, SOUTH CAROLINA,
# PART OF OLD NINETY-SIX DISTRICT

In the early days, all courts were held at Charleston, so the oldest records were filed there. However in 1768 by Act of the South Carolina Assembly, seven Judicial Districts were created for the province, one of these being Ninety-Six. The old log Court-house was located at the town of Old Ninety-Six (about 2 1/4 miles south of the present town) and here in the summer of 1783, from the steps of this building was read "the Treaty of Peace between his Brittanic Majesty and the United States of America." At the Court of General Sessions held there on Nov. 20, 1784, the Treaty was duly recorded. It appears that no courts were held at Ninety-Six during the Revolutionary Period of July 1776 to the Spring of 1783. The Court of General Sessions convened there 1783-1799 and Courts of Equity, continued for some years. In 1785 the twenty-six counties were formed from the Judicial Districts. County courts of limited jurisdiction, were now held and continued for fourteen years. Members of the Court were drawn from among the leading citizens. In 1799 the counties were called Districts and were not again called counties until "Reconstruction." About 1800 the General Assembly abolished Old Ninety-Six Court and formed Equity Districts. Division two of the Western District included Laurens and Newberry with Court being held at Laurens. At the Court House, rooms of Clerk of Court, is found the first written record of a court for Laurens in Book I, page 1, dated 12 Sept. 1785. The gentlemen Justices were: Jonathan Downs, James Montgomery, Silvanus Walker, William Mitchelson, Charles Saxon. On 15 May 1792 Samuel Saxon sold four acres to "the Judges of the County Court of Laurens, to wit: Jonathan Downs, John Hunter, Thomas Wadsworth Esquires, for the use of the County Court of said county," also the right to use a certain spring. The price paid was two guineas.

----------

ABBETT, Abbott-Daniel--"I have soldier claims for lands in the western state of Pa., & 850 A. in Laurens Co., S.C.--all to wife during widowhood or until oldest ch. Betsy be lawful age or marry.." Chn: Lewis M., Wm. McClanahan, Danl. Marshall, James Smith youngest, Betsy Pagett...EXR: Wife Ailsey, Danl. Wright, Reuben Kelly...30 Oct. 1800--16 Mch. 1801...Bk. A, p. 285...WIT: Austin Moore, Nelson Kelly, M. E. Stallard.

ABERCROMIE Alexander--Chn: Martha Jane, Susannah S., Lucretia, Elizabeth, Richard A., Hugh, Robert, Wingfield B...EXR: John Woods, R. Alex. Abercromie son...28 Apr. 1852--25 Mch. 1853...Bk. A...WIT: M. P. Evins, Arthur Roger, Thos. A. Saden.

ABERCROMIE Alexander Sr.--Wife Susannah...Sons: Lewis, John, Alex, Henry, Hugh, "Unfortunate son Jonathan".."other sons already recv'd share"..Daus: Hannah, Susannah, Polly...EXR: Sons John, Alex...28 Dec. 1830--16 Apr. 1831...Bk. F, p. 344...Wit: John Harris, Jno. Woods, Matthew P. Evins.

ABERCROMIE Calvin, Colvin--Wife Mary & at her death prop. div. bwt. fol. chn: Harriet w. of Jno. W. Nash; Mary w. of Hiram Sims; Rebecca w. of Kellet Babb; Calvin Jr; Elizabeth w. of Halway Campbell; Christy w. of Wm. Ridgeway; Ruth w. of Alfred Sims. John dec'd & wid. Elizabeth & heirs; Johathan; James; Lindley to take care of mother...EXR: Sons Johathan, Lindley...21 Sept. 1837--Bk. A, p. 96...Wit: Asa Garret, Isham Bolt, William F. Davis.

ABERCROMIE James-Son James..Step-son Archibald McDaniel,.gr. son Jas. Abercromie... Daus: Mary wife of Wm. Odaniel (?McDanl); Isabella Blackwell; Rebecca wife of Gabriel Jewell; Susannah Mathews; Hannah Brock; Margaret Blackwell; Elizabeth Andrews...

EXR: Son James, Elias Brock Jr...29 Nov. 1819--8 Feb. 1820Bk. E, p. 56...WIT: E.L. Rowling, David Bell, John Neel.

ABRUMS Abrams, Martha--Chn: Thomas, Joseph, James, George, William, John, Mary Montgomery, Elizabeth Jones, Margaret?Siddar, Anna, Lucky or Leah...EXR: Friend John Whitmire, Whitmore..4 Apr. 1840--8 Nov. 1842..Bk. A, p. 24..WIT: Thos. Whitmore, Geo. Young Jr; Byrd B. Allen.

ADAIR Hannah---Living Chn: Eleanor Ramage, Hannah Meadows, Nancy Langston, Susannah wife of Wm. Castle, James Adair...Gr. ch: Patsy Gamble, Jinny Beavors... EXR: James Adair...25 Oct. 1826--4 Dec. 1826...Bk. F, p. 65...WIT: Thos. Leek, Isham Milan, Susannah Prater.

ADAIR Joseph--Wife Susannah...Sons: Joseph, Benjamin, James "my cooper's tools be- longing to my trade"...Daus: Sarah, Jean Ramage, Mary & hus. John Owins...S.L. Robt. Long...EXR: Sons Joseph & James...9 Jan. 1788...Bk. A, p. 19...WIT: Jas. Montgomery, Wm Bourland, Jas. Greek.

ADAIR Joseph--Sons: John, James, Robert, Elisha & Gr. son Joseph Adair...Daus: Jane & hus. Thomas Holland; Elizabeth & hus. John Hutson; Casey & hus. ThomasMcCrary; Charity & hus. David Little...EXR: Elisha & John Adair...20 Jan. 1812--15 Jan. 1813... Bk. D-1, p. 105...WIT: Richard Holland, Wm. Adair, George McCrary.

AKINS Lewis--Sons: John, Ezekiel, Archer, Frank...Daus: Sally, Patty Petty...Two Gr. sons; Wm. & Thos. Petty...16 July 1791...Bk. A, p. 40...WIT: Joel? Leagill, Thomas Feevil, John Meadon...EXR: Son Ezekiel & S.L. Benj. Feevil.

ALLISON James--Wife Nancy, home place dur. widowhood...Son James, land with grist & saw-mills...Daus: Polly, Elizabeth...EXR: Son James...10 Nov. 1788--9 Mch. 1789... Bk. A, p. 9...WIT: R. R. Bowen, Saml. S. C. Campbell, Joseph Lyon.

ALLISON Robert--Sons: James, Robert, William, Joseph, Samuel, Francis, Watson, Moses Lewis "land on n. side Beaverdam," Joseph...Daus: Margaret, Mary, Ann & her son William Hellans...Gr. S. James Allison...EXR: Wife Frances, son Joseph.... 5 Jan. 1791...Bk. A, p. 53...WIT: Wm. Turner, Emanuel York, Wm. Higges.

ANDERSON Philip--Wife Elizabeth...Sons: Allen, Reuben, Lewis...Daus: Elizabeth, Ann Davis, Lucy Davis..."Three youngest chn"...EXR: Son Allen & friends Joseph Jones, Moses Whitten...27 Mch. 1814--19 Apr. 1814...Bk. D-1, p. 152...WIT: John B. Bennett, Moses Whitten, Joseph Dunkin (Dunklin?).

ARMSTRONG John--Wife Elizabeth...Daus: Artemesus wife of Saml. Austin; Cresy Ann wife of Wm. Owens. Syntha wid. of Isaac Hollingsworth; Mary w. of Edward Martin; Haney or Hannah "place where I live provided she does not marry John R. Fuller son of Solomon & Phoebe Fuller," Elizabeth, wid. of John Fuller & apparently wife of Dr. Robert Austin...TRUSTEES for dau. Artemesus, Edmond Martin & Wm. Owens...EXR: Wife Elizabeth but in case of her death or marriage, friends: John & Henry Burton, Travis Hill...Prv. 26 Apr. 1845...Bk. A, p. 39...WIT: John & A. C. Garlington, W. D. Watts, R. Campbell.

ARMSTRONG Joseph--Wife, land on Mudlick ck...Two sons minors...Dau. Mary Ann... Also named, John Williams & James Burnside...EXR: Wife Rebecca & friend Robt. Gilliam Sr...30 Jan. 1790...Bk. A, p. 37...WIT: James & Andrew Burnside, Jno. Butler.
ARNOLD Hendrick--Wife Ruth (Cash)...Sons: William, Ira...Daus: Mary, Nancy.."my living chn. & their heirs"...15 July 1795...Bk. A, p. 142...(Note: Ira md. a Saxon; William was father of Jeff, Hendrick & Billy).

ARNALL (Arnold) Joshua--Wife Leanna...Only dau. Martha...200 A. div. bwt. Joshua Arnall & Joshua Franks...Gift to Joshua Millenor...EXR: Joshua Franks, Charles Smith.. 5 Mch. 1792...Bk. A, p. 34...WIT: Robert, Poley & N. Franks.

ARNOLD Zachariah--Sons: Lewis, William minors...Daus: Rebecca Flynn, Sara Arnold, Nancy Arnold, Juda West & chn: Georgeberry West & Mary West...Bequest to Jim B. Moseley...EXR: Wife Mary, John West...15 Nov. 1826--11 Mch. 1829...Bk. F, p. 210...

WIT: Reubin Powell, Reubin Arnold, Mark Moseley.

ATKINSON Henry--Wife Mary "all until oldest son John is 21"...Youngest chn: William, Alexander...EXR: Wife Mary & John Dacus...22 Apr. 1799...Bk. A, p. 199...WIT: John Davis, Mansfield Walker, Barthlomew Craddock.

ATWOOD James--Son William..Son-in-law Wm. Ball..EXR: Wife Polly, William Atwood, Wm. Ball...17 Jan. 1816--Bk. D-1, p. 257...WIT: John Clemons, William Pollard, Tobias Cook.

AUSTIN Alexander Sr--Wife Agnes...Chn: Alexander, Samuel, Robert, John, James, William, Jennet, Henrietta, Sarah...Gr. Chn; David & Agnes Whiteford...EXR: Sons James, ?Alexander, Samuel...18 Sept. 1826--28 Nov. 1826...Bk. F, p. 59...WIT: Alsey Fuller, John Cook, F. D. Cook.

AUSTIN James--Wife Henrietta...Son James..."my children"...EXR: Alex Austin...30 Mch. 1832--14 Apr. 1832...Bk. F, p. 416...WIT: R. C. Austin, John Moore, Thos. Austin.

AUSTIN Samuel--Sons: James, Thomas, Alexander, William...Daus: Elizabeth Munro, Mary Caldwell, Nancy Carter, Nelly Streight...EXR: Major James Austin, John Moore Sr., Son Thomas Austin...10 Nov. 1826--21 Apr. 1827...Bk. F, p. 106...WIT: John Moore, James Carter, Daniel Downmond.

AVARY Joseph--"Joseph & Cynthia as much as others had when they left me"...balance "bwt. all my chn. except Joel who has his"...EXR: Wife Rhoda, son Joseph,..27 Sept. 1848...Bk. A, p. 108...WIT: E. B. Gambrell, A. McKnight, Joseph Sullivan.

BABB Sampson (Simpson?)--Chn. of dau. Polly who md. Wm. Boyce...Balance "bwt. all chn"...EXR: Sons Alston, Martin & Simpson Babb...30 Oct. 1847--Bk. A, p. 145... WIT: Hosea Mahaffey, Thomas A. Peden, John Woods.

BAILEY James--Sons: William, Zachariah, James, Silas...Daus: Polly Brown, Sally Ducker, Winifred, Betsy, Levicy or Givety...William's part div. bwt. his chn: Madison, Susanna, James, Broth...EXR: Benj. Brown, James & Silas Bailey...19 Jan. 1826-- 14 Nov. 1826--Bk. F, p. 51...WIT: John Snead, James Nickles Jr., Wm. Bailey.

BAILEY William (Revo. S.)--Wife Ann...Chn: John, Zachariah, Margery, Mary, William, James, Lucy..Gr. chn: Wm. son of David Bailey..EXR: Sons Zachariah, William, James... 27 Jan. 1787...Bk. A, p. 48...WIT: A. Rodgers Jr., Thomas & John Rodgers.

BALL George--"Children"...EXR: Wife Memima, John Ball, Lewis Ball Sr...28 Dec. 1807--10 Mch. 1817...Bk. D-1, p. 359...WIT: James Ball, Jas. Neely, Henry Hitt.

BALL Jeremiah--Sons: Stephen, Harris, John, ?Minyard, Young..Daus: Elizabeth Garrett, Nancy Abercromie, Frances Owen's chn...EXR: Son John...18 Nov. 1850--8 Mch. 1856... Bk. A, p. 180...WIT: S. Knight, Z. C. Garrett, James A. McDowell.

BALL John--Father...Bros. & Sisters: Martin, Reubin, James, Katherine, Peter...20 Dec. 1824--7 Mch. 1825...Bk. E, p. 480...WIT: Ben & Reubin Martin, Thos. Garrett.

BALL Martin--Wife Hannah...EXR: Thos. Garrett...4 Sept. 1827--4 Mch. 1828...Bk. F, p 172...WIT: Jeremiah Ball, Benj. Martin, Reubin Ball.

BALL William--Wife "estate that came with her"..Chn: John, George, William, Jeremiah, Elizabeth Stephens, Frances Hitt, Martin Peter, James Lewis, Mary Sadler, Pamelia & heirs (names not separated)...EXR: Wife Lillian, Reubin Martin...23 July 1805--5 Apr. 1806...Bk. C-1, p. 169...WIT: Reubin Martin, Stephen Garrett.

BARKSDALE Nathan--Sons: Allen, John, Nathaniel, Colyar (Collier)....Daus: Nancy, Leannah...EXR: Wife Mary, sons Colyar & Allen...8 Sept. 1812--17 Nov. 1812...Bk. D-1, p 92...WIT: L. Saxon, Charles Allen, Sam Dason.

BARKSDALE John--Bros. & sisters: Nancy, Martha, Polly, Lennah, Nathaniel, Collyar... EXR: Allen Barksdale, Thos. F. Jones...14 Apr. 1830--4 Oct. 1830...Bk. F, p 283... WIT: Andrew Kennedy, Francis Ross, John Garrett.

BAUGH William--Sons: John, William, David, Jonathan...Daus: Elizabeth, Margaret, Mary, Agnes & "rest of chn"...Wife Agnes & son John EXR...4 May 1787-Rec. Bk. A, p. 21...WIT: James Abercromie, Wm. Obannon, John Pinson.

BEASLEY Thomas--Wife Patsy - At death wife, est. div. bwt. 5 daus, eldest Polly Ferguson; Nancy w. of Abram Holland & son Edmund; Elizabeth Ferguson; Jinsey Williams; Dolly Chambers & Dr. Alex. Chambers...EXR: S.L. Dr. Alex. Chambers, Maners Williams...23 Feb. 1831--27 Mch. 1832...Bk. F, p. 407...WIT: Perry Jeans, Elizabeth W. Ferguson, Cary Bell.

BELL Adam--Sons: David, John, Adam land purchased of Saml Erving..."if my son Robert ever returns..." Daus: Isabel, Mary, Esther, Elizabeth...EXR: Wife Mary... 16 Dec. 1801--18 Nov. 1805...Bk. C-1, p. 180...WIT: Robt. Long, Jas. Bell, Thos. East.

BELL James--Sons: John, Robert, Adam, James...Daus: Elizabeth Milan, Susanna: EXR: Wife Sarah...27 Mch. 1824--5 Sept. 1824...Bk. E, p. 413. (Note-These Bells evidently descendants of Thos. B. Ire abt. 1726 to S.C. 1762. Descendants in Laurens, Abbeville, Greenville cos.)

BENNETT Richard--Wife Sarah...Chn: Anna, Miles, Jennette...EXR: Thos. Hendrick, Lewis Jones...3 Dec. 1820--4 June 1821...Bk. E, p. 165...WIT: Jesse Prater, Jenes Jones, John B. Bennett.

BLACKWELL Richard--Wife Margaret....Sons: James, David, Joel, Richard...Daus: Nancy, Elizabeth, Rebecca, Hannah, Margaret, Caroline, Susan Frances...EXR: Charles Brook Jr...25 July 1832...Bk. F, p. 427...WIT: J. Abercromie Sr., John Coats, John Morgan.

BLAKELY William Sr---Chn: Jonathan, John, William, James, David, Thomas, Samuel, Catherine, Isabel...EXR: Wm. Blakely...13 Dec. 1845...Bk. A, p. 82...WIT: James L. Young, F. N. Folker, Henry M. Bryon.

BOBO Absolum--(Revo. S.) Wife Amey...Dau. Betsy Gaines...S.L. Wm. Powell & fol. Powells: Fanny, Sarah, Ann, Belinda, Milly, Virginia...Roddy Waits...? Perady Posey... Polly Delph...EXR: Friends David Anderson, Lewis Graves...8 July 1808...Bk. D-1, p. 159...WIT: John Golding Sr., Andrew & James Anderson, Wm. Anderson.

BOBO Dr. E. M.--Chn: C. D., Mary Ann, Susan Jane Springs...EXR: C. D. Bobo & S.L..R. A. Springs...3 May 1853...Bk. A, p. 313...WIT: Thomas W. Holloway, Drayton Nance, James A. Graham.

BOLLING Samuel (Revo. S.)--Sons: Robert, John, Tully, Samuel, Thornberry...Daus: Elizabeth Dunklin, Lucinda (Johnston), Polly (Perritt) youngest, Nancy Sullivan, Mehitabel (Tarrant)...EXR: Wife Abigail, sons Robert, Tully, John, Saml...9 May 1808--5 Sept. 1808...Bk. C-1, p. 318...WIT: William, Mary, Tully Choice.

BOLLING Thornberry--Mother Abigail..."to Thornberry (s. of Saml. Jr) my share & interest in the Fork Shoals Library Society...to Samuel Perrit (son of Alfred & Polly)... to Saml. Bolling (son of John) land in Ala.",...4 bros: Robert, Tully, John, Samuel... 4 sisters: Nancy (Sullivan) Strange, Lucinda Johnson, Polly Perritt, Elizabeth Dunklin... balance to Henderson Sullivan & Joseph N. Johnson...EXR: Tully Bolling, Henderson Sullivan, Jos. N. Johnson...13 June 1822--3 Sept. 1827...Bk. F, p. 125...WIT: Micajah Berry, Tully Bolling, Sophia Choice.

BOLT Robert Jr--Sons: John, Lewis...Daus: Peggy, Sally, Polly & "if wife be with child"...EXR: Neighbor Joseph Downs...20 Oct. 1795...Bk. A, p. 143...WIT: James & Thomas Parker, Susanna McHarg.

BONDS James--Daus: Jinny Welsh & son James; Mary Welsh; Nancy Murphy & dau. Mary...Sons: James, son Colvin's chn...EXR: Sons John & Richard...22 June 1820--3 Sept. 1820...Bk. E, p. 87...WIT: Robert Long, James Bell, Sarah Bell.

BROCKMAN, Borockman, Backman John--Chn: Anny Parks, Mary Deen, Franky Mullens, Henry "lands on Enoree riv"...Dau. Lucy Dec'd w. of John Owens Sr. left chn: Betty,

Amely, John H; Dau. Frankey w. of Thomas Mullins, no issue as yet...Son Henry & his son John Brockman...EXR: Wife Ameley, Son Henry...27 Nov. 1800--13 Feb. 1801... Bk. A, p. 274...WIT: Daniel Wright, Robt. Burton, Asa Wright.

BOULAND, Bourland, Bowland John--Wife Mary...Sons: John, Thomas James...Daus: Mary Scott, Martha Ramage, Sarah, Jane, Charlotte..EXR: John Ramage, Robert Bouland.. 10 Jan. 1820--17 Apr. 1820...Bk. E, p, 70-72...WIT: Robt. Ramage, Samuel Young, Edward Wasson.

BOURLAND William Sr--Chn: John, William, James, Andrew, Ruby ?Welburn dec'd; Elizabeth Ramage & dau. Jennet; Rebecca Fowler; Peggy Harper; Sara Grace; Jennet Dooland; Mary Odle; Nancy Whetford...EXR: Son John...6 Jan. 1804--6 Feb. 1804...Bk. C-1, p. 95...WIT: Robert Long, John Wilson, Elizabeth Langston.

BOWLEN, Bolen Martha--Sons: William H. & Albert D..Daus: Elizabeth, Patsa, Matilda, Nancy, Polly...EXR: Son William, Bro. Wm. Green...25 Aug. 1834...Bk. A, p. 4...WIT: Elisha Watkins, Franklin Glen, John C. Watkins.

BOX John--Wife Rachel...Sons: Shadrack, Robert, Abraham, Benjamin...Daus: Nelly South, Rachel Banks, Jemima Sneid..Gr. chn; Rachel & Louisa Box, Elisha Williamson... EXR: Elisha Williamson...22 Nov. 1815--5 Feb. 1821...Bk. E, p. 137...WIT: William Arnold, Robert Nabors, Joseph M. Ewen.

BOYCE Drury--"all my chn"...Sons: Drury, James...Daus: Nancy, Polly..."to Anderson Arnold as his share of his father's est., which came to me in consequence of my marriage with Adminstrx. of said est.",..EXR: Wife, or at her death, Dempsey Nesbitt... 1 July 1830--20 Dec. 1830..Bk. F, p. 311..WIT: John Anthony, Nathan & Thomas Nesbitt.

BOYCE John--"Present wife, Nancy E. Boyce"...Chn. by present wife equal share... other chn. recv'd from est. of their dec'd Gr. father John Robertson...Gr. chn: Sarah I. & John B., chn. of Elizabeth Craig dec'd...8 Sept. 1841--7 Aug. 1843...Bk. A, p. 36...WIT: Rowland Jennings, John F. Kern, A. R. Boyce.

BOYD Isabella--Sons: William H., Samuel A...EXR: Gr. son Abram Miller Johnson... 25 July 1842--16 Dec. 1850...Bk. A, p. 135...WIT: William W. Floran, Archilles Dendy, Elihu Watson.

BOYD Margaret--Dau. Jane w. of Samuel R. Todd...EXR: Saml R. Todd...4 Nov. 1843-- 3 Apr. 1860...Bk. A, p. 329...WIT: John W. & S. D. Simpson, W. E. Templeton.

BRADEN David--Wife Peggy...Sons: William, Isaac, Reubin...Daus; Betsy, Margaret, Peggy, Susan, Polly Ann, Sary...EXR: Sons William, Isaac...11 Aug. 1822--10 Sept. 1822...Bk. E, p. 234...WIT Benjamin F. Tearce, James Wardlaw, Jesse E. Clardy.

BRADY Charles--Wife Eleanor...Sons: William, John, Alexander "land on Reedy riv," Charles & George youngest sons...EXR: Wife Eleanor, friend John Cochran...3 Oct. 1793...Bk. C-1, p. 167...WIT: Anna Wadkins, Deborah Barns, John Cochran.

BRAMLETT Nathan--Wife Elizabeth....Sons: James, Billy...TRUSTEES, William H. Kennedy, Henry Bass, David Derrick...EXR: Thomas Brownlee, William Henderson... 11 Mch. 1839...Bk. A, p. 12...WIT. James B. & D. Higgins, Washington French.

BREAZEALE Enoch--Wife Ruth..Daus: Hulda Johnson, ?Hamutal Hall or Hill, Caroline.. EXR: S.L. Wiley Hill, George W. Johnson...10 Apr. 1826--2 Oct. 1826...Bk. F, p. 45... WIT: Zachariah Bailey Jr., Tobias Cook, Robt. Campbell.

BREAZEALE Ruth---Dau. Hulda w. of George W. Johnson...Gr. daus: Frances & Hemital Johnson, Frances & Caroline Hill...EXR: James Davis...30 Aug. 1831--17 Nov. 1831...Bk. F, p. 420...WIT: Matthew Gamble, James Davis, Barbara Casey.

BROWN Benjamin--Wife Polly...Dau. Ann...Gr. son Thomas Jeff Tygart...EXR: Wife & in case of death, friend J. M. Young...19 Feb. 1847...Bk. A, p. 84...WIT: J. M. Young, Ross Benham, A. C. Young.

BROWN James (Revo. S.)--Wife:..Daus: Rachel, Elizabeth, Jane, Peggy, Mary...Son

141

William & friend Robert Creswell EXR...17 Feb. 1822--15 Apr. 1823...Bk. E, p. 280...
WIT: William & James F. Wright, R. Creswell.

BROWN Roger--"gave all my chn. that's married..." Daus: Lydia, Annie, Judy, Rebecca, Mary, Ferebe, Matty, Bexee, Cennee, Fanny, Genney youngest & Rachel a min., Elizabeth Gill...Sons: William & Roger minors, "in case son James never settles here"...EXR: Wife Bexey...Dec. 1818--20 Mch. 1826...Bk. F, p. 11...WIT: William Adair, Joseph Hitch, L. Hitch Sr.

BROWN William (Revo. S.)--Wife Frances..Chn: John, William, Joseph, Ursley Thompson, Mary Wood, Frances Brook, Susannah Nix, Sara Gilbert...EXR: Son Joseph...16 July 1811--5 Jan. 1818...Bk. D-1, p. 426...WIT: Wm. Gilbert, John Meadows, Thos. Jones.

BROWNLEE Esther, Easter--Dau. Alsey Babb..TRUSTEE & EXR: James B. Brownlee... 19 Nov. 1828--6 Apr. 1829...Bk. F, p. 212...WIT: John Martin, Mary & F. Richardson.

BRISON William--(also Bryson)--Sons: John, James, Robert...Daus: Jean, Sarah "the watch I fetched from Ireland"...EXR: William Blakeley, Charles Little...7 Dec. 1807... Bk. C-1, p. 285...also Bk. D-1, p. 411.

BRYSON John--Wife Martha...Dau. Margaret & hus. Wm. Fleming...Bro. Wm. Bryson & chn...EXR: Col. John Simpson, William Fulton...27 Mch. 1804--Apr. 1804...Bk. C-1, p. 110...WIT: Archibald Lewis, John Fakes, Agnes Boyd.

BURGESS Joel--Wife Ellen...Sons: Elijah, Walter, Thomas, William, Roland, Joel, John "to be schooled"...S.L. Wm. Hendrick & dau. Tabitha min...Daus: Jenny, Sally, Nelly, Tatty (Tabitha?) ...EXR: Wife, sons Roland, Joel...11 Feb. 1803--2 Mch. 1803...Bk. C-1, p. 32...WIT: E. S. Roland, Thomas Babb, William Nelson.

BURNSIDE Ann Jane--Bros: William, Thomas...Sisters: Elizabeth, Martha, Hannah... EXR: William & George Burnside (sons of Andrw)...29 Jan. 1827--18 Nov. 1828...Bk. F, p. 185...WIT: James Hollingsworth, Daniel & Nancy Jones.

BURNSIDE Elizabeth--Sisters Esther, Martha, Ann Jeane, Hannah...EXR: William & George, sons of Andrw. Burnside...7 Nov. 1828--4 Feb. 1829...Bk. F, p. 203...WIT: James & Anna Young, Mary Burnside.

BURNSIDE James--Sons: John, William T., James "lands in Laurens Dist"...Wife Anna to "school & settle younger chn."...EXR: Wife & son James...10 Dec. 1801--Mch. 1803... Bk. C-1, p. 34...WIT: Joseph & Goerge Hollingsworth.

BURNSIDE James Sr--Sons: James, William, Thomas, Andrew (Revo. S)..Daus: Jennet Anderson, Margaret, Elizabeth, Martha, Ann Jane, Hannah...EXR: William & Thomas Burnside, Margaret Burnside...17 Aug. 1797...Bk. A, p. 179...WIT: Wm. & A. Rodgers, James Cook.

BURNSIDE Martha--All est. to 3 sisters: Elizabeth, Ann Jean, Hannah...EXR: William son of Andrew Burnside, Geo. A. Burnside...29 Jan. 1827--18 Nov. 1828...Bk. F, p. 186...WIT: Daniel & Nancy Jones, James Hollingsworth.

BURNSIDE Thomas--4 youngest sisters: Elizabeth, Martha, Ann Jeane, Hannah...neph. Thomas son of Andrew Burnside...EXR: James Hollingsworth, Thos. Burnside...7 May 1826--16 Oct. 1826..Bk. F, p. 47..WIT: James Young, Mary Burnside, Andrw. Rodgers.

BURNSIDE William--4 youngest sisters: Elizabeth, Martha, Ann Jeane, Hannah...EXR: Bro. Thomas & friend John Kennedy...14 Nov. 1808--23 Mch. 1826...WIT: Wm. Black, Enos Cook, James Moore...Bk. F, p. 12.

BURTON John--Chn. of dau. Edny Wells dec'd; dau. Susannah w. of Wiley Hardy; S.L. James Henderson...19 Dec. 1853...Bk. A, p. 344...WIT: W. D. Watts, H. R. Shell, J. H. Rose.

BURTON Thomas--Wife Rachel...Sons: William, Charles..."all my chn"...EXR: Sons William & Charles...12 Feb. 1827--13 Feb. 1630...Bk. F, p. 257...WIT: Isaac Pinson,

James Lowery, Augustin Marshall...the two sons named "had by me in the evening of my life."

BURTON Thomas--Chn: Samuel, Robert, Benjamin, Ann, Rebecca Ford, Judah youngest. Last two "until of age or marry"...EXR: Wife Lillian, Sons Benj. & Henry Box...4 May 1802--28 June 1802...Bk. C-1, p. 2...WIT: Jno. Puckett, Jno. Garlington, Thomas Grace.

BYRD Benjamin--Wife Jane Downs....Sons: William, (md. a Barksdale), George (md. a Kern), Purnelly...Daus: Leah (md. Benj. H. Allen & had Benj); Sarah, w. of Wm. Hill; Mary Jane..Wm. Hill & son Purnelly or Purnall, trustees for Sarah & also EXR... 14 Nov. 1828--21 Mch. 1831...Bk. F, p. 338...WIT: John Cargill, R. Freswell, Robt. Anderson.

BYRD Elizabeth--Dau. Hannah w. of Danl. Cook (&David Cook named); Martha Mitchell; Eliza Coleman; Dorothy Blum (all apparently daus); part to James C. Lasley or Lesley for his family & heirs, one being the dau. Elizabeth...EXR: Henry, Austin & Edmond Lesly (?sons-in-law)...9 Dec. 1844--9 Jan. 1845...Bk. A, p. 42...WIT: Wm. & Jemima Cook, Daniel Carter.

CABANESS, Cabiness Amey--Neph. Elijah Cabiness & he EXR...4 Oct. 1823--18 Nov. 1823...Bk. E, p. 331... WIT: John G. Viern Jr; P. D. Dern or Dorn; John Davis.

CABANESS Elizabeth--Son Elijah EXR...4 Oct. 1823--18 Nov. 1823...Bk. E, p. 332... WIT: John B. Kennedy, John Henderson, John David.

CALDWELL James (Revo. S.)--Bro. David Robert Caldwell, min...EXR. Bro. George Forrest Caldwell, friend Dr. John Simpson...24 Apr. 1827--3 Sept. 1827...Bk. F, p. 126...WIT: Drayton Nance, R. C. Caldwell, C. D. B. Higgins.

CAMPBELL Angus--Son & dau-in-law Angus & Milly Campbell & their chn., the Jones Plantation; son Robert, place where I live & books; dau & S.L. Sarah & Robert Cunningham; S.L. & dau. Jonathan & Jane Johnston; dau. & S.L. Polly & Jesse Paine; son Sullivan Campbell....1 Aug. 1809--17 Aug. 1809....Bk. C-1, p. 358...WIT: John Nickles, Wm. F. Burnside, James Ward.

CAMPBELL John M.--Sister Mary Aikin two chn. viz: John & Elizabeth...EXR: James Aiken...26 Apr. 1848...Bk. A, p. 85...WIT: John R. Spearmand, Wm. Hitt. H. Carter.

CARGILE, Cargill William--Mother Sally...Sisters: Elvira, Rebecca, Rachel, Nancy... EXR: M. T. Evins Esq....20 Jan. 1844-27 June 1844...Bk. A, p. 26...WIT: Arch I. Owings, Amelia Owings, M. P. Evins.

CARLISLE Coleman--Chn: James J., Thomas A., Gideon N., Sarah H., Elizabeth L., William H., Jonna...EXR: Wife Sarah, John Abel, Thos. A. Carlisle...11 Jan. 1824-- 6 Dec. 1824...Bk. E, p. 440...WIT: William Wright, James Leake Sr, John Able.

CARTER John--Wife Rachel...Son William...S.L. Wm. McCrary & his sons John & James...EXR: Wife, sons Wm. Carter & Wm. McCrary...14 Apr. 1798...Bk. A, p. 180... WIT: John Rowland, J. Johnson, Robert Carter.

CARTER John--Sons: Joel, Benjamin...Daus: Elizabeth Garner, Mary Nelson, Ruth Brown, Margaret Bailey...EXR: Son-in-laws Benj. Garner, Andrw. Nelson...3 Apr. 1818...Bk. D-1, p. 120...WIT: John Johnston, Howard Pinson, Elizabeth Brown.

CARTER Robert--Wife Betsy...Sons: Robert, Richard, Zimry, James...Daus: Patsy Osborn, Polly Perkins, Sarah Riley, Elizabeth ?Bagley...EXR: Sons Zimry & Robert... 6 Dec. 1825--4 Feb. 1826..Bk. F, p. 3..WIT: Nancy Carter, Mary Pinson, Jonah Johnson.

CARTER William--Wife Martha, "the Cross Hill tract"..."all my surv. chn. as they come of age or marry"...EXR: B.L. Daniel Ligon & bro. Henry N. Carter...20 Nov. 1845--27 Nov. 1845...Bk. A, p. 65...WIT: J. H. Coleman, Wm. Lindsay, Jno. Watts.

CASON (?Carson) Mary--Bros: William, Thomas...Latter's chn: William, John, James,

Samuel...EXR: Sister Sarah Miller, friend David Green...15 Jan. 1812--5 Feb. 1821, Bk. E, p. 136...WIT: John & Wm. Miller, Anderson Hill.

CHANDLER John--Wife Mary & son Asey EXR: Son ?Wiltt...Daus: Elizabeth Leek, Patsy Griffin, Polly Clardy, Nancy Martin...8 Sept. 1820--2 Sept. 1822...Bk. E, p. 229...WIT: William & John Dunlap, Thomas Stone.

CHARLES John--Prop. div. bwt. wife & chn...EXR: Wife Margaret, William Fulton... 14 Mch. 1808--10 Aug. 1808...Bk. C-1, p. 316...WIT: Wm. & Andrew Burnside, Jas. Donald.

CHEEK Ellis--Chn: William, Richard, Sally Sentall, Mary Rhodes, Jane Rhodes, Casey ?Farrow, Willis D., Linvey Riddle...EXR: Willis Cheek & Friend William Ross...12 Jan. 1838--17 Sept. 1838...Bk. A, p. 115...WIT: James B. & Benjamin B. Higgins, Samuel Willis.

CHEEK Willis--Wife Eliza & her two chn: James William & Willis Abram Cheek... First wife Jemima's chn. viz: Randal, Silas, Austin, Ellis, Anna Garret; Rebecca Hammond & her 4 chn; Dau. ?Levi, Levy Riddle's pt. in trust...EXR: Friend Wm. M. Dorrah...7 Nov. 1845...Bk. A, p. 154...WIT: Joseph Sullivan, Hastings Johnson, Andrew McKnight.

CHEEK Willis D--Wife Priscilla..."Small chn. & all my chn"...EXR: Wife, son John... 5 Oct. 1849...Bk. A, p. 113...WIT: James Nesbitt, W. W. Hitch, Wm. A. Todd.

CHILDRESS Richard--Wife Martha...Sons: Richard, John, Robert, Abraham...Daus: Nancy, Sarah, Patsy, Melinda, Betsy, Lucy...23 Mch. 1825--15 Nov. 1830...Bk. F, p. 301...WIT: George Fuller Sr. & Jr., Robert Tuater.

CLARDY James--Wife Sarah...Sons: Jesse E., James, Michael..."have given to heirs of son William dec'd"...Daus: Nancy Wright, Suky Tierce...EXR: Sons Jesse, James, Michael...2 Sept. 1830--14 Oct. 1846...Bk. A, p. 37...WIT: Philip Waite, Jeremiah Bailey, James Daniel.

CLARDY Jesse E.--Wife Rachel...Chn: Michael, William, Katy, Sarah, ?Mahaby, Jesse Ellis James Andrew Jackson, Zachariah, Derrock Smith, John Wesley, Zedikiah Henry (names all run together)...EXR: James & Michael Clardy brothers of Jesse E...29 July 1832--17 Sept. 1843...Bk. A, p. 32...WIT: Philip Wait Sr., John C. Wait, William P. Delph.

COKER Drury--Wife Betsy...Son Joseph & wife & chn...Daus: Menice Coker, Polly Dial...EXR: Dau. Menice or Mencie...Prv. 21 Dec. 1830...Bk. F, p. 312...WIT: Samuel & William F. Downs, James Bruster.

COKER Joseph--Wife...Sons: Drury, Colvin, Thomas, youngest John...EXR: Sons Drury &Colvin..20 Mch. 1792...Bk. A, p. 71...WIT: Wm. Hellams, Thomas Coker, Martin Dial.

COLEMAN Absolom--Sons: John, Larkin, Alfred, Alsey...Guardian for John is Bro. William & Zachariah Bailey...Dau: Decorah Ann...EXR: Wife Sarah, friend Parson Fuller...17 Nov. 1814--10 Dec. 1814...Bk. D-1, p. 179...WIT: James Young, William Bailey, W. Walker.

CORLEY, Coley Charles--Wife Henrietta...Sons: James, John, Spencer, Jackson...Dau. Sally Smith...EXR: Wife...25 July 1818--5 Sept. 1818...Bk. E, p. 4...WIT: John & Elijah Walker, Samuel Boyd.

COOK Abraham--Wife Henrietta...Son William...Daus: Martha E., Henrietta Frances, Mary Louise...EXR: Friend Alsey Fuller...30 May 1843--11 Oct. 1843...Bk. A, p. 19 ...WIT: John Young, Silas M. Bailey, Henry Miller.

COOK George--Chn: James, Joshua, Nancy, Allen B., John, William E., Mary Martha Abram, George (no commas bwt) Elizabeth Knight...EXR: Sons Joshua & James with wife Polly...23 July 1845--15 Aug. 1845...Bk. A, p. 58...WIT: J. J. Atwood, R. Thomas, William Rose or Ross.

COOK James--Wife Ursula & Sons Mitchel & Daniel...EXR: Sons Clayton & his son James a min; John, Tobias, William...Gr.chn: Emily, Matilda, Eliza, Mary Teague... 28 Feb. 1815--15 Aug. 1816...Bk. D-1, p. 330 ...WIT: Agner Pyles, Wm. Black, Allen Pitts.

COOK John--Wife Catharine Sons: James, William, Franklin...Daus: Edny Ligon dec'd; Mary Ann Babb...EXR: s.l. Alsey Fuller, son William...16 July 1835--24 June 1844... Bk. A, p. 19...WIT: David Owen, John Hitt, A. C. Griffin.

COOK William--Chn. of sister Ann Fuller viz: Franklin G., Anthony C., Mary Smith, Edny Richardson, Augustus, ?Lalessie, John C., Edward P...EXR: Wife Jamima...19 May 1850...4 Oct. 1853...Bk. A, p. 197...WIT: Henry W. Pasley, Duke Goodman, Jones Loyd.

CROUCH Isaac--Wife Susannah...Chn: Samuel, Becky w. of John Stroud; Susannah w. of B. Roberson...EXR: Son Samuel...Bk. F...22 Mch. 1817--2 May...WIT: William, Nancy & John Young.

CROCKER James--Dau. Sarah dec'd wife of Meredith Brison & gr.chn: Henry & Whitefield Brison...Sons: James, John, Joseph, ?Athenion...EXR: Wife Elizabeth & sons William, James, Atharion...12 Jan. 1808--12 Oct. 1822...Bk. E, p. 238-9...WIT: David Anderson, John Cruz, Ebenezer Starnes.

CRAGE(Craig) Eleanor--Sons: John, William, James, "balance div. bwt. chn. not herein named"...EXR: Thomas Logan, James Craig...17 Oct. 1785...Bk. A, p. 79...WIT: Robert Hanna, James Craig, Thomas Logan. (An Eleanor wid of Jno. Craig, filed a Revo. claim.)

CRAIG James--"my chn"...EXR: Wife Elizabeth. Bro. William, Dr. George Ross...2 July 1813--2 Nov. 1813...Bk. D-1, p. 132...WIT: Jno. Briggs, Danl Long, Jno. Craig.

CRAIG John (Revo. S.)--Niece Jane dau. of Joseph Harland...Neph. George Craig...Also ment. fol. Craigs: Wm. Perry, Saml G., William W., Thomas, Robert, William; also Thomas Little...EXR: Thomas & Robert Craig...18 Oct. 1843--30 Oct. 1843...Bk. A, p. 31...WIT: Thos. B. Rutherford, N. C. Nance, W. D. Byrd, Samuel H. Murell.

CRAIG William--Sons: John, William, Thomas, James...Dau. Eleanor...Gr.son: William C. Harlen; Gr.dau. Jane E. Harlen...EXR: Sons John, James & Rev. Wm. Alexander... 10 Oct. 1824--3 Jan. 1825...Bk. E, p. 480...WIT: James & John Craig, John Templeton.

CRAWFORD John--Son: John, James...EXR: Friends John Young, John Black...4 Aug. 1824--3 Dec. 1826...Bk. F, p. 66...WIT: G. W. Young, George Teague, Daniel Cargill.

CREECY John (Creece)--Wife Elizabeth & "her chn. by Zachariah Sims dec'd"...Son of wife, James Sims...Joel Sims...Son Zachariah S. a min...Fanny w. of Jacob Clemmans...John Wait...EXR: Friends David Anderson, Robert Cunningham...15 Jan. 1812...Bk. D-1, p. 64...WIT: John & Frances Wait, John Midleton.

CROSSEN(Croson) Thomas--Dau. Mary w. of Zimry Carter...Son Thomas, wife Martha EXR...5 May 1800--30 July 1800...Bk. A, p. 243...WIT: John Wiseman, Joseph Hollingsworth, J. Reed.

CUNNINGHAM James--Sons: Thomas, James, John, William, George, Samuel...Daus: Margaret, Dorcas, Catherine, Ann Allison & chn: Mary, Saml...Named also David Allison, William Hall, Joseph Dean (prob. son-in-laws)...EXR: Sons John, Thomas, wife...15 Oct. 1788...Bk. A, p. 17...WIT: David Dunlap, James Dorroch or Dorrah.

CUNNINGHAM John--EXR: Wife Nancy, James & Wm. Cunningham, Joseph Dean...8 Mch. 1814...Bk. D-1, p. 172...WIT: John D. & Thos. Cunningham, Hannah Dean.

CUNNINGHAM John--Wife Mary Louise..."all my bros. & sisters"...son Samuel James Cunningham...EXR: Bro. Thomas...27 June 1832--6 Aug. 1832...Bk. F, p. 422...WIT: H. G. Young, R. C. Campbell, A. Kennedy.

CUNNINGHAM, John D.--Wife Mahala..."All my chn. as come of age": Thomas,Mary, Elvery, Sintha, Margaret, Laursay, Nancy...EXR; Wife...13 Dec. 1832--10 Aug. 1833... Bk. F, p. 495...WIT: Philip Wait, I. Culberson, Allen Johnston.

CUNNINGHAM Patrick--Wife Ann...Sons: William land on mid. fk. br. of Reedy & Saluda; John tract on Beaverdam ck; Robert home place...EXR: Sons John & William... 22 Oct. 1796...Bk. A, p. 153...WIT: Lewis Graves, M. Walker, Sarah Clarey.

CUNNINGHAM Sally--Bros: Elihu & Jacob Cunningham...Sisters: Jane, Mary, Elizabeth, sister Margaret Norris' chn; sister Anna Bolt, Wm. Bolt & 8 daus; neph. Franklin Cunningham...EXR: Elihu Cunningham & neph. James Hudgins...Prv. 30 Jan. 1855... Bk. A, p. 184...WIT: M. Madden, Benjamin Yeargin, Sarah C. Ray.

CUNNINGHAM Thomas--Sons: Thomas, Samuel, John Dean & "each of my chn. as come of age"...EXR: Wife Mary, bro. Samuel, Joseph Dean...2 Apr. 1796--3 Feb. 1806...Bk. C-1, p. 201...WIT: James S. Dorrah, John & William Cunningham.

CUNNINGHAM William--Sons: John, William...EXR: Martha Cunningham, son John...1 Sept. 1822--2 Dec. 1822..Bk. E, p. 242..WIT: Wm. Pitts, L. Cunningham, Henry Marzen.

CURETON David--Neph. Elihue & his 4 chn. viz: James G., Richard, Levington, Mary A....EXR: Elihue Payne, George Wells...29 Dec. 1846...Bk. A, p. 95...WIT: Wm. H. Adams, James A. Foshee, David F. Foshee.

CURETON John (Revo. S.)--Sons: John, Nathaniel, David, George Washington, Thomas, Daniel...Daus: Jinny Paine, Elizabeth Barnette, Heath...EXR: Wife Hannah, Edward Cureton, Thos. Taylor Cureton, David Cureton...31 Aug. 1802--9 Jan 1803...Bk. C-1, p. 19...WIT: James Young, Blagrove Glenn, Stephen Jones (Note: John Cureton is buried at Beaverdam Church, Laurens Co., grave marked. He md. (1) Winifred Heath.

DALRYMPLE Ann--Chn: Benjamin C., John, Henry H., Ephraim, Susanna Jones; Mahala Benjamin & dau. Anna; Lucinda Hitt dec'd & dau. Susanna; Lucretia Jones dec'd... EXR: Lewis D. Jones...3 Feb. 1846--15 Nov. 1852...Bk. A, p. 246...WIT: John Jones, Thos. W. & Thomas Dalrymple.

DALRYMPLE John G.--Wife Sarah.."Bros. & sisters"..EXR: Friends-Dr. James Dillard, Joshua Saxon, George Byrd, John Craig, John F. Kern, John Henderson, W. D. Byrd & wife...22 Sept. 1842--6 Nov. 1843...Bk. A, p. 22...WIT: David Templeton, Berry C. Beasley, W. D. Byrd.

DANDY, Dendy Daniel--Dau. Irene..."Equal div. when youngest chn. of age"...EXR: Marcus & William Dendy...9 Sept. 1829--20 Nov. 1829...Bk. F, p. 239...WIT: John W. Smith, Jack S. Godfrey, J. Chapman.

DANDY, Dendy Thomas Sr.--Sons: Cornelius, Thomas, William...Daus: Elizabeth w. of Samuel Powell, Sarah w. of James Young, Molly w, of William Mitchell, Patsy w. of M. Walker...EXR: Wife Mary, son William...20 Sept. 1797--3 Mch. 1800...Bk. A, p. 229...WIT: John Hunter, William Dendy, Samuel Leek.

DANDY, DENDY William--Wife Clary..Sons: John, Joel, William, Thomas, Daniel, James H...Daus: Priscilla, Sally Motes, Betsy...EXR: Sons John, William, Joel, Daniel...12 Aug. 1800--9 May 1801...Bk. A, p. 294...WIT: D. Hill, Wm. Smith Jr., Jeremiah Sadler.

DAVENPORT John--Sons: John Ransom, Thomas, William, Richard, David,.Wife Mildred. EXR: John Roberson, Frederick Purty...5 Feb. 1806--19 June 1807...Bk. C-1, p. 268... WIT: Jonathan Johnston, William Roberson, Howard Pinson.

DAVENPORT Thomas--First wife Sally, "present wife Lathee"...Son Burket...Dau. Lucy Harris...14 Sept. 1812--25 May 1816...WIT: William Nelson, Nathan Sims, Stephen Wharton...Bk. D-1, p. 295.

DAVIS John--Wife Ann...Sons: John H., James...Daus: Mary Creswell, "unfortunate dau. Elizabeth" & trustees for her viz: Robt. Creswell, Dr. James Davis, John McClellan, Benjamin James...Son John to have "land in Kentucky conveyed from Littleberry Sullivan to me"...EXR: Sons John, James, Robt. Creswell, Dr. James Davis...22 Apr. 1823--7 Nov. 1823...Bk. F.

DAY Jemima--All to Charles Simmins, Pamela his wife & their chn: Pamela Adeline & Charles Young Lafayette Simmons...23 Aug. 1850...Bk. A, p. 134...WIT: William Graves, Wm. W. Graves, Wm. E. Caldwell.

DAY Philip--Wife Frances...Chn: William, John, Philip, Daniel, Benjamin, Nathaniel, Mary, Elizabeth, Jemima, Nancy, ?Amy...EXR: William Cason Jr. of Bush riv., John Watts...9 Jan. 1793...Bk. A, p. 118...WIT: Robt. I. Smith, Thos. W. & Margaret Fakes.

DEAN Easter--Lands on Indian ck. bounded by John Mason, David Martin...Sister Polly Dean & aft. her death, bros. Thomas Sr. & Job Dean to have all est. because "they lived near us & saw to us in old age"...Other bros. & sisters: Isham & Wm. Dean, Dan Dean's heirs, Sarah Dalrymple's heirs...EXR: Friend John Mason...28 Mch. 1844--7 June 1844...Bk. A, p. 44...WIT: William Hutchinson, H. R. Metts, C. James.

DENDY John--Chn: Elizabeth Tinsley; Nancy w. of Branch Ligon; Posey w. of Langford Power; Sally w. of David Craddock (Craddoah); ?Youngsets Dendy; Share to Daniel I. Dendy...EXR: Son Thos. N. Dendy...24 Sept. 1847...Bk. A, p. 73...WIT: Charles & L. G. Williams, James A. Hood. (See also Dandy)

DIAL Hastings--Wife Rebecca (Abercromie)...Sons: Hastings, Isaac, James & his chn. Hastings & Joseph...3 sons-in-law, Mabra & Abraham Madden & John Woody...EXR: Wife, Sons Isaac, Hastings...17 Apr. 1809--5 June 1809...Bk. C-1, p. 349...WIT: John Godfrey, Asa Turner, John Cochran (Note: Chn. not named: Isabella, Mary, Rebecca, Jane)

DIAL Martin--Wife Hannah...EXR: Son Jonathan...30 June 1827--5 Feb. 1844...Bk. A, p. 14...WIT: Elihu Abercromie, Jonathan Abercromie, J. G. Sims.

DIAL Rebecca--Sons: Hastings, James, Isaac...Sons-in-law: Mabra Madden, Abraham Madden, John Woodie, James Johnson...EXR: Isaac Dial, Robert McNees...16 Apr. 1825--18 July 1825...Bk. E, p. 511...WIT: Samuel H. Lockhardt, David Hellams.

DILLARD Ann (Hus. Samuel)--Prop. div. bwt. surv. chn: George, John, Polly w. of Capt. N. C. McCrary; Nancy wid. of William Parks; Mildred w. of Reubin Jordan; Sarah...Gr. son Thomas McCrary...the plant. orig. granted Jas. Dillard 1784 & from him went to Saml of Laurens...EXR: Sons John, George...20 Dec. 1821...Bk. E. p. 201...WIT: John B. Bennett, Charles Thuber, John Dillard.

DILLARD George--Wife Martha...Chn: Susan Johnson, Elizabeth, A. I. Dillard, Elvira, J. B., ?Sebran...Gr. son Samuel Packer...Wife to keep amt. recv'd from est. of Susan Dillard dec'd...Dec. 16, 1846...Bk. A, p. 69...WIT: James Hill, L. T. Rhodes, N. Harris.

DOLLAR, Doller Sarah--"husband"...Chn: Susan Colley, Rhoda Biges, Elizabeth Baker, John dec'd., William, Reubin...EXR: Charles G. Franks...26 Oct. 1841...Bk. A, p. 11...WIT: J. D. Hopper, Joshua Burns, Thomas Luvens.

DONAHOE John--"her children & my children"...EXR: Wife Eleanor, Peter Roland...25 Dec. 1801--23 Mch. 1802...Bk. A, p. 316...WIT: Peter Roberts, Mary Kellett, Eliza Sarah Donahoe.

DORROH, Dorrah James--Wife Jane...Son James EXR...23 Apr. 1810--2 Oct. 1820...Bk. A, p. 12...WIT: John Taylor, George Pearce, A. Downs.

DORRAH James--Sons: William M., John F., Lewis C...Daus: Margaret, Nancy, Martha, Mary..."7 oldest chn"...EXR: Wife Sarah & son David...25 Jan. 1840--5 Mch. 1842... Bk. E, p. 94...WIT: John B. Simpson, Daniel & Samuel Todd.

DORROH James--Wife Martha EXR....17 Oct. 1850--6 Oct. 1857...Bk. A, p. 288...WIT: W. D. Simpson, Alexander McCarley, H. M. Young.

DOWNS Jonathan--Daus: Jane w. of Benj. Byrd; Milley (Mildred Lucy) w. of Lydell Allen; Frances w. of William Kelly; Phoebe w. of James Bruster (Brewster); Louisa w. of John Bruster...Son William F. Downs...(md. Clarissa Saxon)...Gr. son Jonathan Allen...EXR: Wife Sarah (Gary), son William F...18 Aug. 1818...Bk. E, p. 9...WIT: John F. Wolf, C. Saxon, D. T. Saxon.

DOWNS Joseph--Wife Jane (Alexander)...Daus: Arrabella Lewis, Rebecca Alexander, Sarah Gary, Nancy (Anne) Barksdale, Mary L. Downs (md. Mr. Alexander)...(Note: Joshua not named but he set. in Miss.)...EXR: Sons Samuel, Jonathan, neph. William F. Downs...26 Dec. 1818--5 July 1819...Bk. E, p. 32...WIT: E. A. Saxon, G. F. Wolf, J. Allen.

DOWNS Sarah--To Wm. Byrd in trust for dau. Phoebe Brewster wife of James & for gr.son Jonathan D. Brewster...to trustees for dau. Claricy (Clarissa) Brewster...to Wm. R. Farley & Dr. Hugh Saxon, trustees for family of Wm. F. Downs...EXR: William D. Byrd, Allen Barksdale...17 Aug. 1842--27 Dec. 1844...(the gr.son Jonathan died bef. 14 Feb. 1844)...WIT: N. D. & C. Barksdale.

DREW William Sr.--Ninety-Six Dist., S. C...Sons: Langston, William 300 A. on forks of Beaverdam by Wharton's cabin...Daus: Lucy, Polly, Sarah, Elizabeth...Rem. div. bwt. "all chn. males at 21, fem. 18"...Wife Sarah EXR...14 Feb. 1777--15 Mch 1786... Bk. A, p. 1 (part of p. 1 destroyed)...WIT: A. Rodgers Jr. John Lucas, Edw. Philpot.

DUNCAN James--Sons: Joseph, Jonathan, chn. of dec'd son David...Daus: Elizabeth w. of Whitman Jones; Margaret w. of John Jeans; Sarah w. of Fred Jones...Aft. abv. beq. rem. est. div. bwt. "all my chn"...20 May 1820--5 Sept. 1828...Bk. F, p. 174...WIT: Mary, Reubin & James Flanagan...EXR: Benj. Ducket, Bardywin Roberts.

DUCKET Sarah--6 chn: Martha, Alcey Robertson, Liday Dillard, George Young, John, Thomas (names all run together)...EXR: John & George Duckett...13 Jan. 1832--3 Dec. 1832...Bk. F, p. 455...WIT: John Whitmore, Joseph Garrett, George Dillard.

DUNLAP David--Sons: James, Brill, Mitchell, Robert, David, John..Daus: Mary, Christen, Jane, Martha, Elizabeth...2 gr. sons David Bishop, Robert Green...S.L. Caleb ?Earp... EXR: Wife Jane, Wm. Miller, James Dunlap, James Powell...26 July 1805--15 Apr. 1807...Bk. C-1, p. 262...WIT: John McDavid, Mary Dunlap, Leanna Powell.

DUNLAP Samuel--Wife Nancy...Sons: James, Samuel, John land on Rabun ck...Daus: Catherine, Susannah, Sarah, Nancy, Mary ?Jeather...EXR: John Dunlap, Wm. Hellams, Martin Dial...5 Feb. 1791...Bk. A, p. 43...WIT: Martin Dial, John Dunlap, Wm. Hellams.

EAGERTON Charles--Wife Frances "not allowed to dispose of prop. to Benj. Holt & wife Amelia & chn; nor to Nathan Chapman & wife Sophia & chn"...adopted son & neph. John Edw. Jones...to John Joseph, Frances & Matison chn. of Robert Gates dec'd.. "my sisters: Clarissa Scott, Elizabeth Oliver dec'd & her chn"...EXR: Friend Anthony Y. Golding...26 June 1846...Bk. A, p. 91...WIT: Patrick & Wm. Todd, Sarah Wright.

EAKINS Lewis--Sons: John, Ezekiel, Anker, Frank...Daus: Sally, Fannie...S.L. Benj. Kevel...2 gr. sons: William & Thomas sons of Patty Petty...EXR: Son Ezekiel, Benj. Kevel...16 July 1791...Bk. A, p. 60...WIT: Joel League, Thos. Kevel, Jno. Medder.

EAST Josiah--Daus: Sarah Drake, Nancy East...EXR: Son Langston, Sarah Drake...27 Aug. 1818--16 Nov. 1824...Bk. E, p. 434...WIT: William Neil, Richard Davis.

EAST Shadrack--Wife Mary...Chn: Kesiah, John, Thomas, Ann "as they marry or come of age," oldest son Allen, min...EXR: Thomas East Sr., James Cook...12 Nov. 1792... Bk. A, p. 78...WIT: Samuel Henderson, William Young, Thomas Wordsworth.

EVANS John--Wife land on Cane ck...Sons: Josiah, William, John...Daus: Mary Edwards, Frances & Rachel mins...rem. to chn. living or their heirs at death of wife...EXR: Wife Sarah...16 Feb. 1779--8 Feb. 1785...Bk. C-1, p. 141...WIT: Mary Edwards, Martha & James Puckett.

FAIRBURN, Fairbern Alexander--Of Durkin's ck...Wife Crissey...Dau. Geney Wood...

EXR: Son James...2 June 1798...Bk. A, p. 197...WIT: Roger Brown, Samuel Laid, B. Holland.

FARLEY Mary--Son Thompson...18 Dec. 1817...Bk. E, p. 133...WIT: John Wallace Sr., William Ross, Benjamin Griffin.

FARROW John--Everything to Eupemia Brown & William Winder Hitch...EXR: Joshua Saxon, William C. Byrd, Dr. James H. Dillard...23 July 1841--22 Jan. 1844...Bk. A, p. 21...WIT: Joshua Saxon, Isaac B. Henry, James J. Newman, T. F. Murphy.

FARRAR, Farrow Patillo--Wife Jane S...Sister Mrs. Nancy Farrow to have judgment on late Dr. Samuel Farrow...My chn: James, Susan W., Thomas, Henry P., Rosannah, Lilly, Anny w. of Wister Simpson...John L. James is named...EXR: Sons James, Thomas, S.L. John W. Simpson...16 Oct. 1849--19 Nov. 1849...Bk. A, p. 104...WIT: Samuel R. Todd, William Anderson, John Garlington.

FARROW Thomas F.--Wife Sophia EXR.,"my chn"...29 Mch. 1852--23 Jan. 1855...Bk. A, p. 185...WIT: J. H. Thomson, John R. Lyons, W. H. Langston.

FELTS John--Wife Mary...Daus: Mary J. Finley; chn. of dec'd dau. Susannah Houlditch viz: Wm. H. & Jno. F...EXR: Son John, s.l. Wm. T. (?J) Finley...11 Dec. 1852...Bk. A. . . WIT: Alsey Fuller, James F. Coleman, Matthew Bryson.

FERGUSON Nehemiah--Sons: John, William, Jeremiah, Joseph, James, N. B...Daus: Elizabeth, Margaret, Sarah, Mary...EXR: Sons Joseph & James...9 Sept. 1787...Bk. A. p. 16...WIT: Joseph Wood, R. Roland, John Dalrymple.

FERGUSON Richard--Sons: Miles, John & his chn., Charles, ?Wara...Daus: Tabitha Motley, Mary Vaughan, Franky McCravey, Elizabeth...EXR: George McCravy, Samuel Ferguson...25 July 1807--6 June 1808...WIT: T. A. Elmore, N. T. Martin, Turner Richardson...Bk. C-1, p. 315.

FILLSON Alexander--Cousin Robert Fillson & his son...EXR: Henry C. Young...8 Oct., 1842 prv...Bk. A, p. 14...WIT: Milton Pyles, M. I. Lockhardt, W. Leak.

FINLEY John--Wife Polly....sons Hampton, his w. Susan & dau. Mary Frances;Dau Elizabeth w. of Larkin Coleman & gr. ch. James T. & Nancy Elizabeth Coleman; Gr. ch: Sara Frances Tyler...At death wife, est. div. bwt. son James, Margaret Miller, Jane Walker, James F. Coleman, Sara Frances Tyler, Nancy Elizabeth Coleman... Mary Frances Finley equal with chn...EXR: Son James, in case death, Albert Miller, Azariah Walker, James F. Coleman...20 Feb. 1851--30 Aug. 1852...Bk. A, p. 148... WIT: John Wharton, Moses Griffin, J. H. Coleman.

FINLEY Paul--Wife Mary...Chn: Hampton, John, Margaret, Nancy Hank, Anne Coleman, Lettice Coleman, Jane Houlditch, Elizabeth Cargill dec'd; Sarah Wait dau. of Nancy Arnold a legacy...EXR: Son Hampton...15 June 1843--12 Sept. 1843...Bk. A, p. 25... WIT: Larkin Coleman, Alsey Fuller, F. G. Fuller.

FINNEY John--Wife Nancy...Daus: Elizabeth, Ann, Polly, Sarah, Peggy, Martha...Son John...24 Jan. 1820--19 Apr. 1825...Bk. E, p. 494...WIT: Jason & Polly Meadows, Wm. Copeland.

FORGY, Forgey, Forgie, Peggy--Sons: Menoah, Ase...Dau. Rachel McPherson...EXR: George Anderson...9 June 1828--11 Apr. 1829...Bk. F, p. 216...WIT: Elijah Elmore, Rachel & D. Anderson.

FOSHEE Benjamin--Wife Susannah, son Benjamin EXR...Chn: Nancy, Sally Turner, Abby Turner, Jancy Turner, Benjamin, Daniel...25 Nov. 1807--14 Aug. 1824...Bk. E, p. 409...WIT: H. Walker, Ephraim Knight, Daniel Foshee.

FOWLER John--Chn: James, Wade, Millicent, Wesly, Linsa, John, Jesse a min; William & his chn; Nancy Thomas; Elizabeth Gowesy (names all run together)...14 Jan. 1790-- 4 June 1791...Bk. A, p. 32...EXR: Wife Elizabeth, friend John H. Henderson, son William...WIT: G. Thomas, William B. Boyd, Moses Williams.

FOWLER John--Wife Elizabeth...Chn: William, Wade, Wiley Y., John, Wesley, Jesse, Elizabeth w. of James ?Lawry, other daus...EXR: Son William, friend John Henderson... 16 Aug. 1851...Bk. A, p. 112...WIT: Wm. B. Gary, Henry H. Watkins, Wm. Burgess.

FOWLER Josiah--Wife Sarah...Sons: Thomas, Newton...EXR: Sons Richard, Thomas, Alhanan Crocker, Alsa Fuller...21 Feb. 1817--7 Apr. 1817...Bk. D-1, p. 370...WIT: Abner Pyles, Thomas Burnside, Isaac Mitchell.

FOWLER Nathan--Wife Martha...Dau. Sarah Ann...EXR: Thomas Owins, George Young Jr...8 Apr. 1827--17 Sept. 1827...Bk. F, p. 127...WIT: Thomas Young, John Whitmore, John Addington.

FOWLER Richard--Wife Elizabeth...Chn: Joshua, Richard land on Durbin ck; Ann Neuel, Elizabeth Flannigan, Rebecca ?Barton...EXR: Sons Richard, Joshua...5 Oct. 1790...Bk. A, p. 42...WIT: Hudson Berry, Joseph Burchfield, John Armstrong (Descts. claim also William & John as sons.)

FOWLER William--Wife Agnes...Sons: John, James, William, David, Charles...Daus: Nancy, Peggy Parks & her son William...EXR: Wife Agnes & son John...22 June 1800-- 5 Sept. 1803...Bk. C-1, p. 68...WIT: James McClintock, Jas. Hutchins, Jas. Fowler.

FRANKLING, Franklin Mathew--"wife, negro woman Dinah & her chn"...EXR: Friends Stephen & Jesse Garret srs...30 June 1821--7 May 1822...Bk. E, p. 215...WIT: W. F. Downs, G. F. Wolf, Mary Wolf.

FRANKS Joshua--Wife Prudence...Sons: Robert P., Niles, Joshua S., Abner C., George... Daus: Mary Hellams, Nancy Bolt...six Saxon gr. chn. named: Samuel, Joshua, William N., John W., Mary, Thomas L...EXR: Sons Joshua, William...17 Nov. 1847--30 Jan. 1848...Bk. A, p. 102...WIT: William Clardy, Lewis Saxon, Arch Henderson.

FULLER Avent--Nieces: Rebecca A. & Delphy Fuller...Son John T...EXR: Delphy Fuller, Henry ?One...31 Aug. 1838--6 Sept. 1841...Bk. A, p. 9...WIT: James Leaman, Justiman Henderson.

FULLER Henry--"chn"...EXR: Wife Charlotte, worthy friend Zachariah Bailey Esq... 28 Sept. 1813--3 Sept. 1814...Bk. D-1, p. 167...WIT: James Fuller, John Holt, Sarah Holt.

FULLER John--EXR: Elizabeth G. Fuller wife...12 Sept 1842--29 Oct. 1842...Bk. A, p. 25 WIT: Abraham Thompson, Anthony F. Golding, I. I. Brownlee.

FULLER Solomon--Sons: Solomon, William, John ?Avent, Ransom, Alsey...Daus.: Charlotte, Sarah Coleman...S. L. William Green & gr. dau. Gilley A. Green...EXR: Wife Gilley, son Solomon...26 Feb. 1816--19 Nov. 1821...Bk. E, p. 191...WIT: David Stephens, Joseph Hodges, Richard S. Drake.

FULLER Solomon--Wife Phoebe...Chn: Ellison I., John R., Harrison M., Solomon T., Mary--two sons-in-law & their chn. & "those that have already recv'd their pt."... EXR: Bro. Alsey Fuller, sons John & Harrison...27 Aug. 1844--2 Sept. 1844...Bk. A, p. 48...WIT: Henry W. Pasly, William Fuller, George Robert.

FUNK George--Wife Nancy...Chn: Hampton, Elizabeth Ann Watson, Albert W., Ann Wood...EXR: Sons Albert, Wade...17 Dec. 1842-7 Jan. 1843...Bk. A, p. 37...WIT: J.A. Coleman, John Wood, Robert Brady.

GAMBLE James--Son John...Wife...EXR: William Fulton, John Williamson...20 Apr. 1799—13 Oct. 1800...Bk. A, p. 250...WIT: Charles Witson (?Wilson), John O'Neel; also Bk. D-1, p. 107.

GARLINGTON Edwin--Wife Eleanor...Son Johnny Motes..."all my chn"...EXR: Son John Garlington...31 Oct. 1823--7 Jan. 1824...Bk. E, p. 341...WIT: John Cook, Wm. Ball.

GARNER Thomas--Sons: John 640 A. at Rocky Mt.,Benjamin min...Daus: Molly Roberts, Sarah ?Laffold, Elizabeth youngest & min...niece Sally Garner...EXR: David Anderson, Joseph Downs...13 July 1791--Bk. A, p. 44...WIT: Jonathan Downs, James Floyd, J. F. Wolff.

GARNETT (?Garrett) Ambrose--"Chn"...EXR: Wife Nancy, friend Fountain Martin...
9 May 1840--9 July 1840...Bk. A, p. 3...WIT: Stephen Garrett, Jesse Davis, B. Davis.

GARRETT Hannah--Sons: Elisha, Charles, Jesse...EXR: Elisha & Chas. Garrett...3
Dec. 1818--4 June 1821...Bk. E, p. 166...WIT: Joseph & Nathan & Wm. Harris.

GARRETT Jesse--At death of w. Elizabeth, div. 7 pts...Sons: John, Thomas H., Edward,
Jesse, Stephen & wife Polly, William...Daus: Polly Cook; dec'd dau. Fannie Martin ;
Betsy Ashley...EXR: Thomas & Jesse Garrett...22 Sept. 1847--30 Oct. 1853...Bk. A,
p. 161...WIT: Willis Wallace, William Clardy, Calvin Abercromie.

GARRETT John--Sons: Joseph, Henry, Elisha, Jesse, Charles (last 3 youngest)...Daus:
Abby, Sarah Prude, Rebecca, ?Minorah..EXR: Wife Hannah, son Joseph...12 Aug. 1805--
4 Apr. 1806...Bk. C-1, p. 215...WIT: John & Rachel Carwell (Caldwell).

GARRETT Silas--Wife Ann..Sons: Enoch, Joab, John, Silas..Daus: Mary, Martha Harris,
Elizabeth Yarborough, Margaret....EXR: Son Enoch...3 May 1796--7 Jan. 1805...Bk
C-1, p. 140...WIT: Roger Brown, John Garrett, William Doller.

GARRETT Edward (Garrot)--Wife Anny..Sons: James (no pt. until he reforms), Stephen...
S.L. Stephen Mullins...a dec'd dau. had md. Pleasant Sullivan & her ch. Garret
named...Will in the form of statement...EXR: Nelson Kelly, Stephen Mullins, Stephen
Garrett...23 Aug. 1794...Bk. A, p. 102.

GAREY Charles--Friend Milly Coker..."my natural dau. Cason Coker to have est.
at Milly's death or marriage"...EXR: Bro. David Garey, friend Drury Coker......22
Feb. 1805--5 Feb. 1806..Bk. C-1, p. 202...WIT: John Armstrong, John Coker, Wm. Gary.

GARY David--Sons Joseph, Warren...EXR: Wife Sarah...23 Sept. 1832--3 Dec. 1832...
Bk. F, p. 456...WIT: Samuel Downs, Henry R. Brewster, William F. Downs.

GARY Newman--Wife Elizabeth...to Daniel Mangum one-third as trustee for my dau.
Mary R. wife of Thomas McDowell; gr. dau. Elizabeth dau. of dec'd son Jesse R.
Gary; chn. of dec'd dau. Pamela C. Pyles...EXR: Addison T. Martin...25 Nov. 1848...
Bk. A, p. 119...WIT: Daniel & Belsa Magnum, Asa B. Davis.

GILBERT William--Wife Sarah....Dau-in-law Catherine Gilbert...Sons: James, John,
William, Jeremiah, Joshua, Harvey Austin..Daus: Elizabeth ?Collins, Mariah Wilson,
Rebecca Burchfield...EXR: Son William Jr...29 July 1822--7 Oct. 1822...Bk. E, p. 237...
WIT: Hartwell Lester, Joseph Gilbert, Isaac Liedham.

GILBERT William--Chn: William H., Edward, Matilda Austin, Lucinda Atkins, Nancy
Cooper...EXR: William Gilbert...30 Apr. 1842--22 Mch. 1843...Bk. A, p. 23...WIT: G.
B. Teague, W. H. Hughes, J. P. Sarett.

GLENN Alexander--Dau. Nancy T. Rice & her chn...EXR: Dr. Hezekiah Rice, James
Young, Richard F. Simpson...5 Jan. 1826--5 June 1826...Bk. F, p. 28...WIT: Langdon
East, James Crawford, James Young.

GLENN David--Chn: Anna, Rebecca, Elizabeth, James, George, John, David...EXR:
Wife Elizabeth & bro. Francis....28 Feb. 1821--3 Sept. 1821...Bk. E, p. 176...WIT:
John Stuart, J. T. Citch, James Fleming.

GLENN James--Sons: Francis, James, John...Daus: Catherine...EXR: William Cowan,
David Glenn...17 Apr. 1815--17 June 1816...Bk. D-1, p. 313...WIT: Alexander Mills,
Francis & Elizabeth Glenn.

GLENN Jeremiah--Sons: Blagrove, Jeremiah, William, Tire...Daus:Frances Craighead,
Sarah Garland Walker, Martha Newstep Moon, Mary Williamson, Elizabeth Walker;
"rest to all my chn"...EXR: Wife Anne, sons Jeremiah & William...22 Dec. 1807--
5 June 1809...Bk. C-1, p. 347...WIT: John Davis, Richard Shackleford, Robert Pasley.

GLENN Reuben--Wife Elizabeth all prop...EXR: Alexander Glenn...26 Oct. 1808--11
Nov. 1808...Bk. C-1, p. 327...WIT: John Caldwell, Michael Frantman, Wm. Wright.

GOFF Hugh--Son Thomas...Dau. Christeen Mears...EXR: Wife Rebecca, Ira Arnold...

22 Jan. 1823--7 July 1823...Bk. E, p. 293...WIT: J. L. Maddox, Wm. Arnold, Joel Ellison.

GOLDING Anthony--Wife Isabel...Sons: James, John, Anthony Foster, Thomas min... Daus: Elizabeth, Rachel, Permelia Nancy...EXR: Friend Charles Griffin, neph. Jacob Crastwhite...27 Dec. 1800...Bk. A, p. 282...WIT: James Tinsley, James Williams, John Leonard.

GOLDING Anthony F.--Wife...Trustees: Dr. R. E. & A. C. Campbell...Daus: Caroline Matilda Elizabeth Golding, Pamela Cunningham Golding, Clemintine B. wife of Dr. Wm. Philips...Sons: John Brown Golding, chn. of dec'd son Anthony R. Golding....gr. son Calvin Foster...EXR: Nephs. B. R. & A. C. Campbell, wife Caroline Matilda.... 27 Sept. 1853--23 Apr. 1858...Bk. A, p. 303...WIT: H. G. Dean, O. P. Vernon, E. I. Henry...Named in codicil: Son-in-law Dr. Wm. Philips, neph. Dr. Robt. E. Campbell... A. C. Campbell died bef. Oct. 1857.

GOLDING Temperance--Hus. James...3 sons: Foster, John Franklin a min...EXR: Dr. Wm. Philips friend..24 July 1845...Bk. A, p. 60...WIT: Wm. & Christina Philips, Anthony Golding.

GOODGION Joseph--"chn"...EXR: Wife, Micajah Berry...4 Aug. 1837--7 Dec. 1840... Bk. A, p. 5...WIT: Garland Lewis, Thomas Pedero, Jonathan Downs.

GOODMAN Duke--Place stones at graves of father, mother, bro. Bluford, sister Sally Goodman & all my other bros. & sisters...sister Kitty Goodman named, also sister Rebecca w. of Humphrey Willis & their heirs--25 Oct. 1851...Bk. A, p. 147...WIT: James Parks, J. J. Atwood, W. D. Watts.

GOODMAN Samuel Sr.--Wife...Sons: James, Samuel, Gilliam, David...Daus: Rhoda w. of James Nickles; Maria w. of James Cook; Jamima w. of Wm. Cook; heirs of my chn. that may be dec'd...EXR: Friend John D. Williams...9 Oct. 1829--3 Jan. 1831... Bk. A, p. 61...WIT: M. W. Cristman, James G. Williams, E. D. Williams. Also Bk. F, p. 314.

GOODMAN William--Wife Mary...Bro. Claborn, all prop. at death wife...Bro. James... 28 Sept. 1793...Bk. A, p. 86...WIT: Mary Goodman, Nicholas Vaughan, Saml. Warthis.

GORDON Ann I.--Daus: Catherine Alexander, Charlotte Fulton, ?Join...EXR: William Dunlap..9 May 1823--3 Apr. 1826...Bk. F, p. 15...WIT: Joseph Griffin, William Milligan, Sarah E. Saxon.

GORDON Jane---Sisters: Charlotte Fulton, Catty or Cetty Hannah ?Maxleds, & to William Dunlap in trust for Charlotte...29 June 1832--10 Sept. 1832...Bk. F, p. 428... WIT: Edward Jones, Robert Johnson, James Lip.

GRANT Isaac--Wife Jane...Son Marion...Dau. Ariahah..."prop. been given chn. married & left me"...EXR: Son Marion, William A. Sten...6 Sept. 1832--22 Oct. 1832...WIT: John Boyd Sr., Thomas Salmon, Sally Golding...Bk. F, p. 452.

GRANT John--Wife Mildred...Son Milton two-thirds & if he leave no heir, to the daus. of Robert Whiteford...Bk. A, p. 151...WIT: Henry Whitmire, C. D. Smith, Wm. S. Shell.

GRAY Isaac--Dau. Sally Roundtree...Gr. chn: Bethia w. of Thomas Meadows; Jenny w. of John Gray; Mahala dau. of Abraham Gray; Melepa w. of John Taylor...other Gray gr. chn: Eliza, Lesly, Josiah, Polasky, Abelina, Mekona, Madison, Archer, Tallson...EXR: John Taylor...26 Mch. 1829--1 Mch. 1830...Bk. F, p. 261...WIT: Starling Tucker, Samuel Parsons, Elias Cheek.

GRAY James--Dau. Elizabeth's 2 chn; dau. Sarah's chn. viz: Agnes ?Rearnaghan; dau ? Phelu & her son James Cochran...rest div. bwt. 4 chn. viz: Andrew, John, Robert, Mary ?Lewers & heirs...EXR: Sons Andrew & John, S.L. Thos. Lewers...23 Apr. 1824-- 9 Jan...Bk. A, p. 267...WIT: William Hobody, Joseph Downs.

GREEN James--EXR: Friend Mary Nisbett, Richard Blackwell...19 Apr. 1818--6 July 1818...Bk. E, p. 2...WIT: Robert & Sally McNeer, Elizabeth N. Pool.

GREEN William--Wife Agnes...Daus; Sarah Rogers, Elizabeth Motes, Martha Boling... EXR: Son William...5 Oct. 1823--4 Dec. 1824...Bk. E, p. 439.

GREEN William--Wife Frances...Sons: N. A., E. B., J. F., Wm. W., Washington, S. R., S. C...Daus: Nancy Simms, Gilly A. Pasley...14 June 1847...Bk. A, p. 140...WIT: Wm. C. Nickles, Willis Dendy, Benj. M. Wells.

GREEN Zachariah--Chn: James, Elizabeth Eastwood...neph. Elisha Casey...EXR: Gr. son James Green, Elisha Casey...11 Feb. 1793...Bk. A, p. 73...WIT: William Hellams, Elizabeth Atkins.

GRIFFIN Anthony--Sons: Asa, Abia, James...Daus: Betty Butler, Caty Cook, Suky Griffin...EXR: Wife Mary, Richard Griffin, John Cole...20 Aug. 1798...Bk. A, p. 178... WIT: Robert Russell, Robt. Cleland, John Armstrong.

GRIFFIN Anthony--Chn: Dr. W. H., Richard F., Frances Amanda, Jane L. Fuller, Martha F. Higgins, Mary W. Watts, Sarah A. Phinney...EXR: Relative Ino D. Williams, friend W. D. Watts...4 Nov. 1849...Bk. A, p. 133...WIT: John D. & Willis Brown, James Babb.

GRIFFIN Richard Sr.--"Ellinor McClain my present wife 'cert. prop. provided she release right to balance willed' to my heirs"...Est. div. bwt. chn. & their heirs.... EXR: Charles Griffin, James Caldwell of Newberry...2 Feb. 1800--5 Nov. 1805--Wife renounces claim & signed 8 Feb. 1805...Bk. C-1, p. 185-6...WIT: John Cook, George Ball, Jemima Ball.

GRIFFIN William Sr.--Wife Rachel...Sons: William, James (Cason's ck. boundary bwt. them)...Daus: Jane, Peggy, Caty...EXR: Bros. Richard & Anthony & son James...Bk. A, p. 50...27 June 1791...WIT: Charles & James Griffin, Jane Dogharty.

GRIZZLE, Grisel, Grisels John--Daus: Nancy, Judah Garey, "all rest my chn"...EXR: wife Elizabeth...6 May 1810--6 Aug. 1810...Bk. D-1, p. 18...WIT: William Craig, Wm. Grizzle, Stephen Gary.

**HAIRSTON** Peter--Wife Sarah EXR..Chn: John Speak, William Peter, Elizabeth Calmers, Sarah Frances, Martha Catherine...20 Sept. 1844...Bk. A, p. 137...WIT: John Whitten, John W. Owens, John F. Kern.

HALL William--Sons: Abraham, Henry land; after death wife, personal prop. bwt. Elizabeth Carter, Frankie Carter, Sarah Clardy, Mary Bailey...27 May 1797...Bk. A, p. 200...WIT: T. Moore, Abram Hall, James Clardy.

HALL William--EXR: Wife Alsey, William Franks, Adam Potter...26 Jan. 1821--21 Feb. 1821...Bk. E, p. 145...WIT: Charles Allen, John Pope, John Dollard.

HAMBLETON, Hamilton Robert--At death wife Elizabeth, prop. div. bwt. all chn. & gr. son Marshall Hill..EXR: Robert Hollingsworth, Reubin Hill..WIT: Robt. Hollingsworth Samuel Goodman, John Owens...25 Dec. in 35th yr. Amer. Indep...18 Apr. 1812...Bk. D-1, p. 74r

HAMILTON Andrew--To neph. James Downey a minor & niece Eliza Downey both chn. of Samuel Downey....Rem. bwt. Saml. & Alexander Hamilton, Mary Downey, Martha Dorrah, Elizabeth Scoles....EXR: Saml. Downey...Bk. A, p. 114...WIT: Nancy Pitts, Robt. McDaniel, W. R. Molloy...30 Oct. 1848--8 Oct. 1849.

HAMILTON Jane--Daus: Elizabeth Taylor; Margaret w. of William Mills; Nancy McClintock & son John....Gr. chn: Jane & Elizabeth Taylor, Mary Julia Mills...EXR: Son John McClintock...10 May 1834--16 Apr. 1839...Bk. A, p. 5...WIT: John Dean, J. Hutchinson (Hutcheson), F. Dean.

HAMILTON Jane--Chn: Martha Dorrah, Mary Downy, Elizabth Downs, ? Eliza & s.l. James Coles "should he come to this country," Alexander, Andrew, Samuel the tract bought from Jas. Dorrah & Alex. Culberson...EXR: Sons Saml, Andrew...6 Oct. 1842-- 30 July 1844...Bk. A, p. 41...WIT: H. C. Young, Chas. Smith, J. I. Culberson.

HAMMOND Joseph--Sons: Macky, John, Joseph...Gr. son Jos. Hammond...Daus: Nancy, Elizabeth w. of Jack Grizel...EXR: Jesse Childress, Thomas Goodwin...11 Jan. 1817... Bk. D-1, p. 420...WIT: William Owings Jr., Thomas Childress, Rachel Spelse.

HAMMOND Peter--Wife Ann..Sons: William, Isum, Peter...Daus: Riody Robertson, Sally Garrett, Nancy McChurg, Betsy Barrett...EXR: William, Peter & Isum Hammond... 26 Jan. 1816...Bk. D-1, p. 264...WIT: Isiah Couch, Saml Couch, Reuben Roberson.

HANCOCK William--Mother...Dau. Fanny a min...William son of sister Sally Rhoades... Patsey & other surv. chn. of Clement Hancock...James & other surv. chn. of John Hancock...surv. chn. of James Hancock...EXR: Abner Pyles, William Burnside...WIT: James Hancock, William Young, Betsy Pyles.

HAND Robert R.--Chn. 9...Dau. Polly & hus. Robert Thomason & their chn: Sally, Polly, Nancy...EXR: Son Robt. Hand, later changed to Elizabeth w. of Robt. Hand Sr... 9 Nov. 1827--24 July 1840...Bk. A, p. 8...WIT: Arch & E. Young, Thos. Wright.

HARDING, Hardin, Harden William--Sons: Abraham, William, George, Nicholas, Henry's 2 chn. Isaac & Abram; Abner's wid. & his chn. when of age...Daus: Sally, Elizabeth, Susanna & her min. chn...EXR: Sons Nicholas, George...22 May 1809--5 June 1809... Bk. C-1, p. 345...WIT: Zadoc Wood, Jno. M. Clery, John C. Cole.

HARLAN Aaron--Sons: Samuel eldest, George, Joshua, Aaron, Joseph, Isiah (last 3 youngest)...Daus: Sarah, Jane, Mary, Rebecca a min..."married chn. already have theirs"...Wife Elizabeth...EXR: Son Samuel...24 July 1806--17 Nov. 1806...Bk. C-1, p. 239...WIT: Benet Langston, Wm. Sparks, Joshua Galmer...the wid. died bef. 7 Dec. 1835 & Samuel was living in Fayette Co., Ind., so son Joseph appt. Exr.

HATHORN James--Wife Edny...Daus: Nancy Caroline, Mary Ann...EXR: Joseph Neely of Laurens Dist. & Lewis Mitchell of Abbeville...6 Apr. 1817--18 June 1817...Bk. D-1, p. 393...WIT: J. L. Neely, Sam J. Hopper, James Reddon.

HAZLETT Guzzlet--Bro. Robert...Nephs. William McDaniel, Mathew & Nathan & Adam NcDonnold (McDonnal), David Nelson...EXR: Charties Nickles...1 Dec. 1815r--18 May 1816...WIT: William Reed, James Strain Esq...Bk. D-1, p. 294.

HELLAMS William--Wife Constant...Dau. Rachel Allison & her son John P...gr. son Jonathan son of Jonathan...other gr. chn: Sons & daus. of William, Jonathan, W. P., Nancy, Rachel...Chn. are EXR--2 July 1788...Bk. A, p. 8...WIT: John Childress, Richard Owings, John Hellams.

HENDERSON Anne (wid. of James)--Sons: James, Samuel, William...Daus: Polly Irby, Petsy, Fanny, Sarah (last 3 min)...beq. to Nancy & ?Retter Irby...S.L. Wm. Hancock... EXR: John Hunter, William Dunlap, Samuel Henderson...25 Aug. 1801--19 Oct. 1801... Bk. A, p. 308...WIT: Abner Pyles, Saml Henderson, William Dunlap.

HENDERSON Mildred A.--Bro. Abner G. Gary...Sister Peunesy Frances Martin to "take my dau. Frances & raise her"...B.L. John A. Martin of Fairfield...Step. chn: William T., Robert Y., Sarah C., (all Hendersons) get legacy from their gr. father John Boyce dec'd..25 June 1845...Bk. A, p. 78...WIT: Wm. Young, Thos. Wier, Jno. Kern.

HENDERSON Samuel--Chn: Nancy, Justiniana, John, Sally...EXR: Wife Susanna, friend James Young...4 Mch. 1817--15 Apr. 1817...Bk. D-1, p. 378...WIT: James & Anne Young, Alexander Glenn.

HENDRICK Margaret--Sons: Mujah, William...Daus: Fanny Turner, Rachel Hendrick, Mary Burgess, Elizabeth Wright, Martha Willard...EXR: Friend Lewis Graves...2 Jan. 1797...Bk. A, p. 158...WIT: John Middleton, Jacob Clemens, Elizabeth Simms.

HEWIT Charles--Wife Susannah...Sons: John, William, Ashley...Daus; Catherine, Ruth, Susannah Null...EXR: Son John...22 Feb. 1816--4 Mch. 1816...Bk. D-1, p. 263...WIT: William Dunlap, Samuel Bardsdale, George Lick.

HILL Elender, Eleanor--Sons: William, Stephen, Isaac & dau. Anne; David with wife Mary & dau. Mary Turner; Benjamin with wife Susie & chn. Jacob William & Elizabeth Emmeline...Daus: Mary Burns, Catherine Flynn...EXR: Son Benjamin...30 Aug. 1828-- 2 Nov. 1829...Bk. F, p. 235...WIT: John L. Kennedy, Alfred A. Kern, John F. Kern Jr.

HILL Silas--Wife Rebecca...Three bros: Thomas, James, John..."sons & daus."...29 June 1845--18 Dec. 1845...Bk. A, p. 55...WIT: Saml. R. Todd, Jno. D. Wright, Jno. Klink.

HILL Thomas--Fol. Hills named: William, Sarah, F., Robert, James...EXR: Wife Polly, friend Robert Malone, William B. Smith...30 Nov. 1820--14 Dec. 1820...Bk. E, p. 106... WIT: Marshal Pollard, Daniel Jones, Josiah Cason.

HINTON Robert--Wife Elizabeth "& her chn"...Sons: John, Robert, Thomas a min... gr. son Robert Anderson...Daus. Hannah Moore, Elander Hinton...EXR: Wife, son John.. 20 Oct. 1797...Bk. A, p. 173...WIT: Thad. & Wm. Owen, Samuel Anderson.

HITT Elizabeth S.--Sons: Jesse, William, Henry, Benjamin, Martin..."my clothes to son's wives"...EXR: Son William...18 June 1844...Bk. A, p. 141...WIT: J. W. Johnson, John R. Spearman, H. N. Carter.

HITT Henry--Wife Elizabeth Stevens Hitt...Sons: Jesse, Henry, Benjamin, Martin... Dau: Elizabeth Hollingsworth & chn. viz: Mary, Elizabeth, Susan, John R...EXR: Son Jesse, Lewis Ball...3 Mch. 1828-- 27 Sept. 1830...Bk. F, p. 282...WIT: Martha & Willie Ball, Peter H. Boyd.

HOLCOMB Casea (? Cassey)--Sister Phoeby Holcomb EXR..Bro. John & chn: Cassandra, Alfred, Kevel, ? Martral...1 Apr. 1835--10 July 1843...WIT: Peter Simpson, Nathl. Thackston, E. Lyon, Thos. Wright, Stephen & Lucy Griffith...Bk. A, p. 33.

HOLCOMB Richard--Wife Sarah lands on mid. fk. Durbin's ck...EXR: Friend Jacob Robards...22 June 1794...Bk. A, p. 102...WIT: Elisha Holcomb, Reubin Higgins, Joseph Lonins.

HOLDER Jesse--Sons: Solomon eldest, Jeremiah, Willie, Jesse, John...Daus: Delia, Rebeka, Martha, Sarah, Mary, Elizabeth youngest...F.L. Solomon Langston & wife Mary EXR...16 July 1798...Bk. A, p. 200...WIT: Roger Brown, Henry & Sarah Langston.

HOLLAND Jane--Prop. div. 5 pts...Son Thomas, three daus. names..."chn. & gr. chn"... EXR: Son Thos., S.L. John Leek..23 Aug. 1830--9 Nov. 1830...Bk. F, p. 287...WIT: John B. Kennedy, Thomas Wier, John Little.

HOLLAND Regin, Rezin--Sons: John, Thomas, Jeremiah min...Daus: Sarah, Elizabeth, Rachel, Marah, "unborn chn"...EXR: Wife Mary, Joseph Adair...30 July 1802...Bk. C-1, p. 11...WIT: William Saxon, Thomas Holland.

HOLT Sarah--Sons: Larkin, Alfred, Alsey all sur-named Coleman...Daus: Elizabeth Robertson, Gilley Braden, Charlotte Nelson, Deborah Bailey,.EXR: Son Larkin Coleman.. 17 Oct. 1843--2 Dec. 1843...Bk. A, p. 31...WIT: Alsey & A. D. Fuller, Jones Miller.

HOOD Robert--Wife Jane...Dau. Jenny Cunningham...gr. father Kelly Cunningham... EXR: Wife, son Thomas, friend John Cochran..20 Aug. 1796..A, p. 201...WIT: Thomas Richardson, Thos. Harris, John Cochran.

HOPKINS Solomon--Sons: Francis, John, Jeremiah, James...EXR: Wife, son Francis... 19 July 1814--19 Apr. 1815...Bk. D-1, p. 198...WIT: James & Wm. McDonald, Jno. Smith.

HOPPER William--Wife Lettuce...Sons: Joseph, Samuel dec'd & his chn...Dau. Polly Brown...EXR: Saml. G. Williams, James S. Rodgers...19 Nov. 1830--17 Jan. 1831... Bk. F, p. 320...WIT: John S. Osborne, Samuel Irby, H. S. Beadel.

HORTON Enos, Enas--Bro. Rolphly..Neph. John Horton...Niece Mary Ann Horton...EXR: Wife Reobee...8 Sept. 1820--2 Oct. 1820...Bk. E, p. 90...WIT: Robt. Long, Richard Bonds, James Bell.

HOULDITCH William--Chn: 7-James, ?Lily, Zachariah, George, William, Lucy, Polly (last 5 min.)...EXR: Friends James & William Bailey...6 Aug. 1805--19 Oct. 1805... Bk. C-1, p. 74...WIT: Jas. Bailey, James H. Dendy, Jas. Young.

HUGHES Aaron--Wife Margery...Sons: William, Elijah...22 May 1806...Bk. C-1, p. 23.. WIT: Richard & Jesse Childers.

HUNTER Andrew--Land to bro. Robert...Andrew Hunter a horse...cows to sisters Elizabeth & Jane...a verbal will in form of conversation bwt. James Parks & Andrew Hunter & heard by Martha Miller & Margaret Parks...24 Aug. 1795...Bk. A, p. 141.

HUNTER John--Sons: William, John, Samuel, James & his son John B. a min...Daus: Nancy, Mary or Margaret McClintock, lands of Duncan ck (sons lands on Warrior)... EXR: Son Saml..6 June 1818--5 Mch. 1819..Bk. C-1, p. 36...WIT: Alexander Kirkpatrick, Samuel Mills; also Bk. E, p. 19 which names a dau. Peggy & gr. son Wm. Hunter.

HUNTER Langhlin--Wife Esther....Daus: Mary, Esther McDowall, Hetty Simpson, Margaret, Abigail...EXR: Thomas McDowall or McDonald, Jiles Cason...24 Feb. 1798-- 12 Jan. 1803...Bk. C-1, p. 20...WIT: James Young, Wm. Golighly, John Lyon.

HUNTER Matthew--Mother Elizabeth....Bro. James...Neph. Matthew Henry...Chn. of dec'd sister Mrs. L. Henry, viz: Robert, Elizabeth, Sarah, James, Matthew, Ibly, Nancy, Jane...EXR: Capt. John Hunter, William F. Downs...13 Nov. 1813...Bk. D-1, p. 139... WIT: R. Briswell, I. Dunlap, - Richardon.

HUNTER Matthew Senr---Wife Elizabeth...Sons: Matthew, Andrew...Daus: Margaret, Nancy, Betty Jean, Sarah..EXR: James McMahon Esq..Charters Nichels...12 July 1815-- 8 Sept. 1815...WIT: Alexander Austin, Hugh & Samuel Leamon. Bk. D.1.

HUNTER Robert--Wife Isabella...EXR: Matthew Hunter, Andrew Parks, James Parks Jr...26 Jan. 1820--5 Mch. 1821...Bk. E, p. 148...WIT: Charlotte, Thos. Jr., & Wm. Fulton Sr.

HUNTER Thomas--"My chn."...EXR: Wife Maryann, son John...24 Feb. 1824--29 Oct. 1824...Bk. E, p. 426...WIT: William Nelson, Charles W. King, F. Richardson.

HUNTER William--Wife Mary with John, Matthew & William Dunlap EXR...Chn. to get education...21 Mch. 1802...Bk. A, p. 322...WIT: George Miller, Thomas Cason, Andrew Middleton.

HUTCHESON, Hutchinson William Sr--"Each of chn.",.EXR: Son James...28 May 1804-- 10 Jan. 1805...Bk. C-1, p. 141...WIT: Wm. Hutcherson, James Fowler.

HOLLIDAY William--Sons: William, Robert, Matthew...Daus: Margaret, Nancy Rush or Rusel, Polly w. of James Mulaham..."all my chn"...EXR: Wife Jenny, son Robert... 12 Jan. 1822--14 Nov. 1826...Bk. F, p. 53...WIT: Philip West, M. Hood, R. Wait.

IRBY William--Sons: William, Joseph, James H., Samuel...Daus: Nancy w. of John Dice; Frances Cheek; Elizabeth Benham; Henrietta Cook; Sarah Clink...gr. son Irby Dunklin...EXR: James Irby...17 Sept. 1828--20 Oct. 1828...Bk. F, p. 179...WIT: Thomas Jones, William Davis, P. Farrow.

JOHNSON Abraham--Wife Anny...4 single chn: Andy F., Abraham, Mary, Jesse...Others: Sarah Munro, William, Andrew, John...EXR: William Neel Langston...19 July 1829-- 7 Sept. 1829...Bk. F, p. 234...WIT: Andrew Cable, John Hewitt, Wm. Haran.

JOHNSON George--Wife Martha...4 sm. chn: George Washington, Willard Simpson, Sara Ann, John Wesley...other chn: William, Abram, Margaret w. of John Miller Sr... EXR: Bro. Anderson Johnson...21 Feb. 1847...Bk. A, p. 93...WIT: Elihu Watson, Larken S. Monroe, Jesse ?Enterkin.

JOHNSON Jabez, Jubez W.--Chn: William, Jubez, Ann...EXR: Ann W. Johnson...6 July 1842--29 June 1843...Bk. A, p. 33...WIT: Wm. Donnan, Archilles Dendy, Jno. Godfrey.

JOHNSON John--Of Mudlick settlement...Daus: Janet, Agnes, Mary, Margaret...EXR:

Son Douglas, Charles Wilson, - McClintock...25 Nov. 1793...Bk. A, p. 84...WIT: William Fulton, James Wilson, John Wilson.

JOHNSON John--Wife Nancy...Chn: Ezekiel, Aaron, Lofton, Frederick, Isaac, Mary, Elizabeth, Katherine, Martha, Jennette...EXR: Son Isaac...3 Feb. 1844--15 Nov. 1844... Bk. A, p. 52...WIT: James Blackburn, George H. Brown, Susannah King.

JOHNSON Matthew--Son Thomas, dec'd...Daus: Elizabeth Barnett, Fanny Smith, Mary Grant...gr. dau. ?Ethaling Johnson...EXR: William & James sons...14 Nov. 1820 Prv... Bk. E, p. 98...WIT: Robert & Sally B. McNees.

JOHNSTON Abner--Sons: Jabus (Jabuz), Jeremiah, Joseph, Benjamin, George W...Daus: Turnely Neighbors, Mahala, Elizabeth...EXR: Wife Rebecca, friend-Beeks...20 Oct. 1826--4 June 1827...Bk. F, p. 112...WIT: Richard Cannon, Thos. Butler, Jas. Neal.

JOHNSTON Thomas--"youngest chn"...EXR: Wife Ann...23 Mch. 1813--4 Oct. 1813... Bk. D-1, p. 130...WIT: B. Nabers, James H. Lawry, William Burton.

JOHNSTON William--Wife Sally...fol. recv. legacies: Sally Monroe, Larkin Shepherd, Abraham Johnston, Elizabeth ?Guttery, John Munro min...4 Apr. 1798...Bk. A, p. 181... WIT: James & Isabel Gray.

JONES Abner--Wife Esther L...Sons: R. A. & J. M. "land on Durbin ck," & John H. Jones...Daus: Alethia w. of A. W. Harris; Mary Caroline Cooly; Sarah D. Westmoreland; Eliza...EXR: Sons Oliver H. P. & William R. Jones...12 Nov. 1842--13 Nov. 1853... Bk. A, p. 166...WIT: John Jones, Richard H. Vaughan, C. P. Sullivan.

JONES Elizabeth, wid. of Edward...Sons: Gabriel, James, Joseph...Daus; Frances Ward, Mary Burnside, Nancy Burnside (these get money)...fol. 7 get the est: Edward, John, Thomas, Elizabeth, Sarah, Mary or Margaret, Lucy...EXR: Sons Edw. & John...6 Apr. 1809--27 May 1809...Bk. C-1, p. 344...WIT: John Cook, Elijah & Nancy George.

JONES James--Wife Lucy...Sons: Benjamin, Miles, Whitemire, Jesse, Joseph..Daus: Angelia Philips, Jane Duncan, Sarah Bennett...EXR: Son Joseph...23 Oct. 1804--6 Dec. 1804...Bk. C-1, p. 127...WIT: George Whitmore, Joel Whitten, Elizabeth Wason.

JONES John--Niece Joyce w. of Robert Ward...Nephs. Jones & Moses Foster...EXR: Wife Joyce, friends Robt. Ward, Jones Foster...7 Sept. 1804--7 Mch. 1811...Bk. D-1, p. 38...WIT: Thomas Hill, Donel Shell, Samuel B. Shepard, Charles McGeher.

JONES Joseph--Sons: Joseph, John...gr. son Leander Duncan, min...legacy to Nancy & John Watson...EXR: Joseph Jones, John Watson...21 July 1826--7 Sept. 1826...Bk. F. p. 43...WIT: Benjamin Duckett Sr., William Duckett, George Smith.

JONES Joseph--Wife Margaret...."my chn"...Son Samuel...EXR: George Ball, James Neely...3 Nov. 1831--10 Nov. 1831...Bk. F, p. 367...WIT: John Ball, Nathaniel Nickle, Cornelius Puckett, T. B. Leeke.

KIRK, Keirk James--Son John & gr. chn: James, Sarah...S.L. William Brison & his 5 chn. viz: Robert, Sarah, John, James, June...Cousin James Keirk of N. C...EXR: John Kirk, John Hunter...30 July 1799--3 Mch. 1800...Bk. A, p. 231...WIT: John Puckett, Agnes Creswell, Daniel Chawleton (Charlton?).

KELLETT Joseph (Revo. S.)--Wife third pt. while wid. or until youngest ch. of age... Dau. Mary...Son John land along Indian Line...William land over Reedy riv...Div. bwt 4 youngest land where Hugh McHaffy lives, viz: Martha, Ann, James, Martin...EXR: Wife & son William...9 Oct. 1785...Rec. Bk. A, p. 4...WIT: Martin Mahaffy, Corn. McKent.

KELLETT William--Wife Aorna? land Greenville Co...Mother Gennet Kellet lands in Laurens...Sisters: Jennet, Margaret...Div. rest est. bwt. all my bros. & sisters...EXR: Mother...13 Aug. 1795...Bk. A, p. 140...WIT: Edw. Scarborough, Hannah & Jane Kellett.

KERN Elizabeth--Dec'd hus. John F. Kern...Sons: John F., Alfred A., dec'd son P. Daniel & his son Benjamin Daniel & gr. dau. Elizabeth Susan Kern...Daus: Louise

157

Lucy, Eugenia Caroline, Mary Ann Perry, Elizabeth Amelia ?Dason (Deason)...EXR: Sons John, Alfred...23 Mch. 1833--3 Mch. 1834...Bk. F, p. 530...WIT: John Whitmore, Thomas R. Ferguson, Benjamin Hill.

KEVIL Thomas--Wife Agga...Sister Mary Glazebrook...Bro. Benjamin Kevil...EXR: Friends John Westmoreland, Jack Teague...18 Jan. 1813--12 Apr. 1814...Bk. D-1, p. 149...WIT: Joseph Compton, John Edwards, Jinny Edwards.

KINARD Martin--Wife...Sons: H. H., M. T., J. P...Daus: Catherine, Elizabeth Sumner, Martha Garee (Gary), Sarah Dalyrymple, dec'd dau. Huldah M. Henson & chn.–requests that est be settled at Newberry...EXR: Son H. H. Kinard...14 June 1849--30 Aug. 1854.... Bk. A...Codicil 16 Oct. 1852 names gr. son Henry Oliver Henson..WIT: Jacob Eichelberger T. R. Pratt, Jacob Kibler.

KINMON, Kenmon James--Daus: Nancy Cook, Rachel Willison or Williamson...EXR: wife Elizabeth, son Thomas...28 Mch. 1815--2 Feb. 1818...Bk. D-1, p. 432...WIT: Benjamin & Nancy Arnold, George Grace.

KIRKPATRICK Alexander--"As chn. come of age"...EXR: Wife Susan, bro. Thomas, F.L. William Ligon...27 Dec. 1832--4 Feb. 1833...Bk. F, p. 469...WIT: R. Cunningham, R. Hooker, E. Kirkpatrick.

KNIGHT Ephraim--Sons: William, Ephraim, Joel...Daus: Polly, Lucinda...EXR: Son William...27 June 1826--14 Oct. 1826...Bk. F, p. 48...WIT: James & Levi Hill, Joseph Pollard.

LANGSTON Solomon-Wife Sarah..Sons: Henry, Solomon, Bennett..Daus: Amey Christopher, Leodicea Springfild (w. of Thos.), Sarah Miller, Selah Stily, Patty Jones...EXR: Sons: Henry, Solomon...25 Feb. 1810-15 Aug. 1825...Bk. E, p. 513...WIT: John Hitch, John Styles, Basil Wheat (Note: Leodicea, Revo. Patriot).

LEAKE Jeremiah--Wife Jane...Sons: William J., Jeremiah...Daus: Rachel B., Lucinda, Jane Emeline, Isabella, Margaret L. Bonds & dau. Jane E...EXR: Son Jeremiah...4 July 1851--4 Mch. 1853...Bk. A, p. 189...WIT: H. C. Young, B. R. Campbell, Wm. Mills Jr.

LEEK, Leake William Sr.--EXR: Wife Providence & sons Samuel & William...7 Jan. 1807--1 Apr. 1816...Bk. D-1, p. 277...WIT: James Holley, William Carter, Newman Gary.

LEEK George--Wife Margaret..Chn: Samuel, Johnny, William, James, Margaret, Malinda, Jinna, Alzira, Anne a min...EXR: Friends Jeremiah Leek, Samuel & Abner Young, also recv'd bequests..23 Oct. 1819--7 Feb. 1820...Bk. E, p. 61...WIT: Thomas Fulton, Mathew Hunter, Theris Odell.

LEEMAN Samuel--Sons: James, Hugh...Daus: Elizabeth, Mary Bryson, Jane Thomson, Sarah Austin...EXR: Sons Hugh & John, friend James McMahon...8 May 1819--13 Nov. 1821...Bk. E, p. 185...WIT: James & John Hollingsworth, James McMahon Jr.

LEONARD John--Mother Mary...Sister Nancy Pearson...Nancy wid. of G. Leonard... B.L. Ephraim Andrews...EXR: Friend John K. Griffin, neph. Allen Andrews...25 May 1810--26 Apr. 1823..Bk. E, p. 282...WIT: Charles Griffin, Mary Cole, Leonard Andrews.

LEWIS Ellinor--Bros. George, John & Samuel Dalrymple...Samuel's chn. viz: Ellinor & Rosanna; George's dau. Ellinor a min; niece Ellinor Davis; neph Thomas Davis & son John...Sister Rachel Smith & dau. Ellinor...EXR: Bros. John & George...11 Sept. 1787...Bk. A, p. 22...WIT: John Teague, David Mason, John Hill.

LIGON Susannah--Daus: Polly Holman, Susannah Grier..."div. bwt. all chn. or heirs"... EXR: Sons William, Joseph...28 Aug. 1827--15 Feb. 1828...Bk. F, p. 149...WIT: Anthony Golding, Reubin Hill, Eliza Ligon.

LIGON William--Wife Elizabeth...Chn: Thomas, Susan Milan, Patsy Carter, William, Daniel, Joseph T., Robert B., John W., George A. (last 4 youngest), chn. of James dec'd; chn. of Elizabeth Henderson dec'd...EXR: Son Daniel, Henry O'Neal, John Milan... 20 June 1847...Bk. A, p. 130...WIT: James E. Lockart, Aaron Wells, Thomas Nelson, Silas Walker.

LINDLEY Thomas--Sons: James, William 5 youngest, viz: Thomas, Aqula (Acquilla), John, Jonathan, Henry....Daus: Elizabeth, Hannah, Sarah, Mary Abercromie, Nancy Bolt.. EXR: Wife Elizabeth, sons James & William...18 Oct. 1808--Pvd. 6 Jan. 1810...Bk. D-1, p. 5...WIT: Charles Smith, Colvil & John Abercromie.

LITTLE Charles--Sons: Robert Henderson, James ?Clendier, Charles, David...Daus: Catty (Katy) w. of James Kirk & their dau. Sarah; Jean Taylor & dau. Margaret Wier; Ann Mary Bonds & chn. viz: Henry & Caroline of Ga..."minor chn"...EXR: Wife Ann, sons Robert, Charles..19 Sept. 1831--5 Dec. 1831..Bk. F, p. 373...WIT: Robert Creswell, Andrew Kennedy, Jeremiah Leek.

LITTLE David--Wife Charity..."chn"...Step-dau. Mary Farmer...EXR: Wife & Chas. Little...12 Oct. 1812--17 Nov. 1812...Bk. D-1, p. 94...WIT: Robert D. & C. Little, Robert Fleming.

LITTLE David--Wife Sarah..."Son George F. be equal with wife's other chn. had by John"...EXR: J. F. Dorrah...23 July 1850--13 Mch. 1852...Bk. A, p. 151...WIT: W. D. Byrd, E. C. Simpson, J. L. Williams.

LITTLE James---Wife Agnes....Chn: Robert, Mary, Isabel, James, William, David, Thomas....Cousins: Charles & David Little....EXR: Friend James Nickles, Col. John Simpson..29 May 1808--6 June 1808...Bk. C-1, p. 313...WIT: John Munro, James Simpson, David D. Grier.

LOGAN David--Son David...Daus: Polly, Hannah, Cate...EXR. & guard. dur. minority of chn: Angus Campbell, James Caldwell, Pat. Cunningham...Bk. A, p. 14...WIT: Reuben Pyles, Jacon (?Jason) & Mary Gibson.

LONG Elizabeth--"all my chn. consisting of 2 families,--the Mattox & the Long" viz: John & William Maddox(Mattox); Sally Gwin & her son John; Polly Simpson; Elizabeth Davis; Nancy Long; Reubin & Daniel Long & latter's 2 sons, Perry & Micajah..."Nancy lived with me & nursed me"...EXR: Thomas Garrett...9 Nov. 1831--16 Jan. 1832...Bk. F, p. 392...WIT: Ambrose & Hollingsworth & Bennett Garrett.

LONG Robert--Son Daniel...Daus: Susanna, Jane w. of Col. David Cole; Nancy Wier; Rebecca Cargil w. of Dr. John W. Cargil...EXR: John Kern, Dr. Thos. Wier...8 Mch. 1830...Bk. E...WIT: Robt. Owens, William W. Kennedy, Pascal M. Meadows.

LOWE William--Sons: James, Allen, Pleasant...gr. son William Lowe...Daus: Martha C. Crymes; Elizabeth w. of John Young & gr. son. James..EXR: Sons James & Pleasant... 20 Jan. 1844--23 July 1844...Bk. A, p. 20...WIT: James C. Bailey, H. C. Young, Henry Fuller.

McCAIN James--Son John...Dau. Mary...5 Aug. 1786...Rec. Bk. A, p. 3...WIT: John & Henry Hollingsworth.

McCARLEY Thomas--Wife Martha...gr. son Thos. Augustus McCarley...EXR: Son Alexander...13 Dec. 1839--23 Mch. 1840...Bk. A, p. 7...WIT: William & Alexander Power, & C. Williams

McCELLAR Bridget--Dau. Janie Dendy...EXR: son John...1816...Bk. D-1, p. 392... WIT: John Davis, Jno. H. Davis, B. H. Allen.

McCLINTOCK John--Sons: James, John...Daus: Peggy Hunter, Mary Mills, Martha, Betty Fleming, Nancy...EXR: Wife...12 Aug. 1796--1 Aug. 1799...Bk. C-1, p. 66...WIT: Margaret, John and James McClintock.

McCLURE William--Chn: William, John, James already had their pt..."other chn. equal"...EXR: Wife Ruth, son William...13 May 1806--7 Jan. 1822...Bk. E, p. 195... WIT: William Craig, William & John Brigg.

McCLURKEN James--Sons: Samuel, John, James...EXR: Wife Catherine...6 Jan. 1828-- 22 Jan. 1831..Bk. F, p. 323...WIT: Florence & Geo. Washington, Mancil Owings, Sam Cunningham, Sr.

McCONEHY (McConely) Samuel--Daus: Ruth, Amy Scott, Martha Bebe, Peggy Wilson...
EXR: Sons Joseph, James...29 Aug. 1818--2 Nov. 1818...Bk. E, p. 7...WIT: James Bonds,
James Murphy, Peter William Gautier.

McCRADY William--Son James..chn. of son John, viz: Jane, Mary Ann, Caroline....
EXR: Wife Mary, Son Robt. Carter McGrady...3 May 1826--19 June 1826...Bk. F, p.
30...WIT: William & Alsey Fuller, George Nickles.

McCRARY George--Chn: Elizabeth, Lucinda Furgeson, Frances Sheldon, Sara Owens
& Her chn. Robert & Sara, Sophy Smith dec'd & chn.: son Chastine, Edwin home place..
EXR: Edwin McCrary...1845...Bk. A, p. 71...WIT: Edmond Adair, Robert I. & James H.
Adair.

McCRARY Thomas--Sons: Matthew, Charles, Moses, Christopher, Andrew...Daus:
Elizabeth Young, Jean w. of Jno. Greer, Mary Catherine...EXR: Wife Letty, Thos.
Brandor, Geo. Young...9 Jan. 1790...Bk. A, p. 71...WIT: Thos. McCrary, Geo. Bush,
David Bailey.

McCURLEY John--Daus: Nancy Davis, Peggy Shirley, "as 5 single daus. come of age
or marry"...EXR: wife Polly, son George...6 Mch. 1825--11 Feb. 1826...Bk. F, p. 4...
WIT: Martin Graves, Nathan Long, Lemarcus Deale.

McDANIEL Archibald--Wife Mary...Wade McDaniel...Sons: Thomas, Matthew, Joel...
Dau. Elizabeth Moor...EXR: Elizabeth Brook, Jno. Burton, Jas. Boyd...5 Oct. 1825-
2 Jan. 1826 ...Bk. F, p. 2...WIT: Turner Richardson, Joel Weathers, Polly Strain, Jas.
Boyd.

McDOWALL Benjamin--Wife's dau. Patsey Jinnings in Ga. & Anton Jennings, carpenter
tools...30 Aug. 1790...Bk. A, p. 25...EXR: Wife Elizabeth...WIT: Reuben Pyles, John
Tyner, Pat. Riley.

McDOWELL James--Son James EXR...Dau. Jinny Blakely & her son Jas...27 Apr.,
1808--7 Nov. 1814...Bk. D-1, p. 170...WIT: Robt. Creswell, Wm. & Polly Atkins.

McDOWELL James--Wife Jane...Chn: Permelia Hollingsworth, Elizabeth Cannady,
Telitha Bryson, Jane Taylor, Isabella Martin...to wid. Jane McDowell & chn...EXR:
Friend C. P. Sullivan, son James, Jr...20 Feb. 1850--6 Jan. 1855...Bk. A , p. 203.
WIT: Edw. & T. W. Anderson, B. R. Campbell.

McGIN Dannel (Daniel)--Wife Catherine...Dannel Son of Wm. James...Rebecca & Mary,
daus. of Jas Caldwell...EXR: Jas. & Wm. Caldwell...30 Apr. 1806...Bk. C-1...WIT: Jno.
Griffin, Jas. Simpson, Jas. Hamilton.

McGOWN (McGowan) John--Wife Jane..."all my gr. chn."...These named: John McWilliam's
6 chn. viz: Wm, John, Saml, Patrick, Martha, Mary...Dau. Elizabeth Reed's chn:
Jonathan, David, Elizabeth, Martha, Jane...EXR: Son William, Jonathan Reed...27 Apr.
1829--18 July 1830...Bk. F. p. 276...WIT: Jas. & Alex. Austin, Jno. C. Campbell.

McKELVEY John--Chn: James, George, Peggy w. of Jno. Dalrymple, Saml, Hugh, Jabez,
Thos, Rachel Alexander, Nelly, Polly, Isaac, ?Anna..."minor chn. share equal with
those written"...EXR: Wife Mary...29 Sept. 1824--5 Feb. 1827...Bk. F, p. 93...WIT: Jas.
Leak, Jr., Jabez McKelvy, Wm. Fulton.

McKITTRICK George--Wife...Sons: Saml, James, John...Daus: Isabel, Jane, Sarah,
Elizabeth...EXR: son Saml...19 Oct. 1844--12 Nov. 1844...Bk. A, p. 44...WIT: Jas. F.
& Wm. Blakely, Wm. C. Leek.

McKNIGHT Andrew, Sr.--Wife Abigaile EXR:...Daus: Abigail, Jennet...Sons: Andrew,
Archibald "land w. side Rabun ck"...8 Feb. 1787...Bk. A, p. 15...WIT: Martin Huey,
Ino Alexander, David Morton.

McMURTY William (Murtry)--Sons: Wm., Nathan, Campbell, Min...Daus: Jenny Bryson,
Susan Hall, Elizabeth McClussey...Wife Mary...EXR; Friends David Grue, McSeres
Easte...23 Feb. 1808--7 Mch. 1808...Bk. C-1, p. 298.

McNEERS (McNees) Robert--Sons: Saml, Richard, James dec'd...Daus: Susannah w. of

Jno. Milner, Margaret Babb dec'd, Agnes w. of Joshua Teague, Sabra White...EXR: Jos. Babb, Jno. S. James...30 Mch. 1833--23 Jan. 1840...Bk. A, p. 1...WIT: David Dorrah, Jno. Phillips, Elijah Saunders.

McNEES (McNeese) Sally--(dau. of Chas. Allen, who md. 1st Cpt. Lewis Saxon).. "grave of hus. marked"...Daus: Clarissa Downs, Susan Thurston, Polly w. of Ira Arnold & chn. Ruthy, Tabitha w. of Benj. F. Cleveland & chn. Robt. L...gr. dau. Sally Arnold... to Elizabeth w. of Lewis Arnold of Ala...Sons(Saxons): Hugh, Joshua, Lydall, Allen, & his ch. Isabel Weatherall...Other sons: David, Charles...Trustees for daus. Clarissa & Polly were: W. R. Farley & Saml Barksdale...EXR: Sons Hugh, Joshua...25 Nov . 1847 ...WIT: Wm. Leek, Jas. McNinch, Geo. Saxon...Bk. A, p. 175.

McTEER Frances--Daus: Elizabeth, Frances, Margaret ?Olton, Mary Vance & chn. Saml & Wm...EXR: Bro. James Griffin, friend Jas. Simpson...10 Sept. 1803--7 Nov. 1803...Bk. C-1, p. 77...WIT: Alex. Simpson, Wm. Spears, Milling Olton or Alton.

McTEER William--Sons: Nathl, William...Daus: Margaret, Elizabeth, Frances, Jeane, Mary...Chn. & wife to "go to Nathl Vance," all prop. sold...EXR: Nathl Vance, Chas. Griffin...20 Mch. 1800--June 1800...Bk. A, p. 238...WIT: Jno. Simpson, Jas. Wallace, James ?Leffam.

McWILLIAMS Alexander--Chn: David, John, Andrew, Robert, Jane, Mary, Esther & hus. Wm. Crawford...EXR: Saml Leeman, Jno. Wiseman...30 Mch. 1813--7 Apr. 1813...Bk. D-1, p. 117...WIT: Jno. Wiseman, Andrw Hunter, Wm. Crawford.

McWILLIAMS Samuel--Wife Martha...Daus: Martha, Mary...Son Alexander land on w. Cane ck...EXR: son Alex...7 Feb. 1845--10 Mch. 1845...Bk. A, p. 48...WIT: Saml & Mary McWilliams, Jas. Ball, Wm. McGowan.

MADDEN George-- Wife Nancy....Chn: Nancy N., Lacklin L., Fanny, Sarah, Rebecca, Polly, Anny, ?Lewey, Elizabeth Wilbon...EXR: Wife, son Lacklin...3 Oct. 1842--28 Aug. 1844...Bk. A, p. 46...WIT: Wm. & Wait Graves, Thos. Dison.

MADDEN John--Wife Susanna...Chn: Charles, Abraham, William, John, David, George ?Martha..."rest prop. bwt. all my chn."...EXR: Wife, son George...20 Aug. 1795...Bk. A, p. 142...WIT: Richard Pugh, Ann Madden.

MADDEN William--Wife Sarah...Chn: Moses, ?Malso, Eliza Graden, Polly M., Sophia, Hulda...EXR: Sons Moses, Malso...13 Oct. 1849...Bk. A, p. 103...WIT: J. S. Coleman, Hampton Findley, B. F. Madden.

MAHAFFEY Hugh--Daus: Cynthia, Clarinda, "all my chn"...EXR: Friends Wm. & Hosea Mahaffey...31 Dec. 1846...Bk. A, p. 89...WIT: Lewis, Sanford & Cynthia Mahaffey.

MAHAFFEY Martin--EXR: Wife Mary, son Martin...Bk. A, p. 69...WIT: John McMahan, Elisha Hunt.

MAHAFFEY Nancy--Sons: Wm., Lewis, Hosea...Daus: Polly Babb, Sally Cunningham, Cynthia Nesbit, Unice...EXR: Son Hosea...7 July 1832--7 Feb. 1833...Bk. F, p. 466... WIT: James Y. Coker, Wm. T. Downs, E. H. Garrett .

MANLEY (Manly) John--Sons: William, James, John...Daus: Christiana, Jane...EXR: Wife Jane, son Jas...3 Apr. 1808--5 Sept. 1808...Bk. C-1, p. 370...WIT:   J. D. Wright, Jas, McDaniel, B. Smith.

MANLEY William--Sons: Joseph, Washington home place..Chn: Ephraim, Vincent, Nancy, Jeremiah...gr. dau. Dedamia Evans...EXR: wife Elizabeth...11 Sept. 1788--1 Jan. 1801... Bk. A, p. 265...WIT: Joel Burgen, Thos. Burton, John Cochran.

MARTIN David--Wife Nancy...Dau. Levinia Frances Martin...EXR: son Addison P. Martin...30 June 1846--21 Aug. 1846...Bk. A, p. 54...WIT: A. L. Wilson, Wm. Rook, Jr., W. H. Dillard.

MARTIN Edward--Wife Mary...Trustees: Jno. Armstrong, Jas. Davis...Chn: Robt. Jefferson, Margaret Caroline...EXR: David Martin, John Armstrong, James Davis...18

Jan. 1845...Bk. A, p. 66...WIT: Edw. Martin, Turner Milan, W. A. Waldrop.

MARTIN Mary--"Fam. burying ground at father's place"...Friend Robt. Vance Trustee for my step-dau. Margaret Caroline Martin...Est. div. 3 pts. one pt to ea. fol: sister Cynthia Whitworth; William D. Watts in trust for sister? Artemasia Austin & her hus. Saml; Dr. Wm. Philips for sister Elizabeth G. & hus. Robt. Austin...EXR: Friend Dr. Anthony F. Golding...26 Aug. 1846--26 Oct. 1846...Bk. A, p. 56...WIT: T. G. & Rhoda Williams, Eliza Goodman.

MARTIN Reuben--Sons: Reuben, Joseph, Benjamin, Saml, Stephen, John...Wife Joanna... EXR: Sons Henry, Reuben...25 July 1808--5 Oct. 1812...Bk. D-1, p. 88...WIT: Stephen & Sally Garrett, Robertson Moore, Wm. Craig.

MASON David--Wife Isabel...Chn: Mary, John, James, Doritha Ellinor, Samuel, Hannah & chn. of last 3...Needley Davis...Mary Ann Gray...Abner & Saml Young..."ea. of my son-in-laws"...EXR: Sons John James...8 May 1820--20 Oct. 1829...Bk. F, p. 236...WIT: Joshua Teague, Nesby Davis, Elijah Teague.

MATHEWS John--Daus: Olley, Polly, Sally Garrett...EXR: wife Hetty, Jesse Garrett, Jr.. 27 Jan. 1826--1 May 18 26...WIT: Jno. Bolt, Tho. Parker, Andrw. Garrett...Bk. F, p. 22

MAYERS(Mayar) John--Put stone to grave of mother in Columbia...Cous: Rachel & Wm. Brown, Edw. Flannagan...EXR: Edw. Flannagan, Moses Leake, Thos. Craig, esq... 14 May 1829--9 July 1829...Bk. F, p. 230...WIT: Matt. E. & Nancy Cunningham, Sarah Carlisle, Dorcas Leake.

MAYHON Joseph L.--Wife Rachel...son Joseph...EXR: Friend Jas. Powell, son Joseph... 28 Feb. 1819--24 Apr. 1819...Bk. E, p. 25...WIT: Jno. Walker, Jno. Shaw, Isaac Reed

MEADOWS James--Wife Susannah...Sons: Reubin, Jason, ?Ichru...EXR: Wife...28 Sept. 1803--13 Sept. 1804...Bk. C-1, p. 128...WIT: A. Elmore, Reuben Jordan, Polly Saxon.

MEADOWS Mary--Daus: Susan, Polly, Elizabeth..."my husband's & son William's wearing apparel div. bwt. all my sons, viz: Wash, John, Henry, James, Warner, Morris"...EXR: Son Warner...13 Oct. 1827--3 Nov. 1827...Bk. F, p. 137...WIT: Henry & Elizabeth Neel, Thomas Young.

MEADOWS Reuben--Chn. Susannah Prather, Paschal, Polly Pearson, Martha, Reuben, James...EXR: Wife Hannah, son Paschall...9 July 1829--15 Sept. 1829...Bk. F, p. 238. WIT: Isham Milan, Robert Adair, H. S. Neel.

MEADOWS Susannah--Son Reubin & his dau. Anne; sons Jason & John...Dau. Ann w. of James Saxon, Esq...EXR: Son Reubin...18 July 1823--7 Aug. 1826...Bk. F, p. 38...WIT: James Bryson, Wash Meadows, Wm. Fulton.

MEDLEY Edward--Mother Sarah...Bro. James Medly's son Edward Newton Medley a min....Joel Walker's son Thomas Milton Walker a min...EXR: William Coleman...6 Dec. 1821--7 Jan. 1822...Bk. E, p. 194...WIT: John H. Coleman, Alsey Fuller, Jno. Hendley.

MEEK Jno--Chn: William, Betty, Nancy, Jenny, Samuel, John, James  "share equally as they marry"...EXR: Wife Ellinor, Charles C. Neall, William Rowe...13 Dec.1802-- 6 Apr. 1803...Bk. C-1, p. 44...WIT: John Cook, Drury Sims, Benjamin Cason.

MEREDITH Henry--Son Samuel...Dau. Nancy Arnold...Mentioned: Fleming? Mosely, Thomas Waters, Broadwin & Permelia Waters, Sally w. of Benj. Martin, Jane w. of Wm. Bowen, Nelson Meredith, James Meredith's two chn. viz: Amealy, Henry...EXR: Son Samuel...15 Dec. 1842--3 Feb. 1843...Bk. A, p. 34...WIT: William Robertson, John H. Templeton, I. F. Dean.

MIDDLETON Answorth-Sons: Andrew, Thomas, John, James, Hainsworth...Daus: Margaret Hunter, Ann Williams, Judith Sarah, Jane...EXR: John Middleton, Matthew Hunter.... 1 Mch. 1798...Bk. A, p. 119...WIT: William Saxon, Thomas Roberts, James Cobb.

MIDDLETON Jane--dec'd hus...Sons: Andrew, Ainsworth "died in west, no heirs"...

Dau. Jane...EXR: Jane Middleton...8 Jan. 1823--4 June 1827...Bk. F, p. 113...WIT: Coleman & Gideon Carlisle, R. C. Creswell.

MILAN John--Chn: Bartlet, Isam, Wm. A., Henry, John, Milton, Leander I., Betsy Braddock, Ferrie Milan, & fol. Brysons: Patsy, Polly, Jimmy, Nancy...EXR: Feral or Ferrie & Leander Milan...13 Jan. 1857--21 Apr. 1857...Bk. A, p. 272...WIT: William Bailey, Joseph Vance, Robert Bryson.

MILLER Hanse--Youngest son Joseph home place aft. death mother, or if childless, to his sister Betsy, latter also gray mare giving her sister Ellinor 1st colt...Sons: John, Jacob, Jesse, George, James & s.l. James Huddleston...EXR: Wife Susanna & friend John Brown...14 Apr. 1788...rec. Bk. A, p. 7...WIT: Joseph & James Adair, Thomas Ewing.

MILLER John--Wife Margaret...Chn: Nancy Garret, Rachel Addington, Mary Harris, Matthew, Mark, Charles, Wash...EXR: William Hendricks...8 July 1846...Bk. A, p. 75. . . WIT: C. P. Sullivan, Wm. Hance, R. E. Todd.

MILLER Martin--Wife Martha..."all chn. equal with those who have recv'd..." EXR: sons Franklin, Albert...Mgr. of est: Jones Fuller...William Fuller to be schooled...6 Oct. 1827--7 Apr. 1828...Bk. F, p. 159...WIT: Solomon Fuller, Robert & William Bryson.

MILLER Sarah--Bro. Thomas Cason's chn. viz: William, John, Samuel & Elizabeth Buckwalter; Bro. William Cason & dau. Nancy; step-daus: Rebecca Cason & Mary Smith; Sally dau. of Sally Brooks; William Miller; cousin Jeremiah Cason...EXR: Step-sons: John Miller, Joshua Smith...19 Sept. 1828--3 Nov. 1828...Bk. F, p. 173...WIT: Fred Foster, Henry W. Garlington, Alfred Nance.

MILLWEE William--Dau. Margaret...Sons William & James div. home place....Wife Sarah to leave her est to "the child use her best"...Gr.son: Wm. Hudgins schooled... EXR: Wife & son William...26 Jan. 1784...Bk. A, p. 7...WIT: George Ross, James Henderson, William Irby.

MILNER Richard--"all my chn"...EXR: Joshua & James Milner...9 June 1812--3 Aug. 1812...Bk. D-1, p. 79...WIT: Drury Coker, Salathel Shaklee.

MIMS, Mimms John--Wife Martha & only child Charles Ellison Mims. If son leave no issue, one third to neph. Josiah Coggins, same to Sally dau. of Richard & Frances Sims, same to John Strobel Jr...EXR: & Trustees: John F. Carns of Laurens, Josiah Coggons of Newberry, John Strobel Jr. of Colleton Dist...2 Oct. 1831--20 June 1833... Bk. F, p. 466...WIT: Dave, Jesse & Rachel Felder.

MITCHELL Judith--Sons: Thomas, Charles, John, James all "Cobbs"...Daus: Suky Wilson, Susannah Owins...31 Mch. 1826--14 Oc. 1826...Bk. F, p. 46...WIT: James & Temple Cooper, Richard Gaines.

MITCHELL William--Wife Nancy...Chn: Permelia Pyles, Sinthey, Thomas, Isaac, Lewis (sons mins)...EXR: Isaac Mitchell, Wm. Dunlap, Wm. Burnside...15 Oct. 1808...WIT: John ?Casgillva, James Cook, Wm. Dendy...Bk. C-1.

MONRO(Munro) John--Wife Sarah...Daus: Jenny eldest, Sally, Betsy Nancy...Sons: Robert, Alex, Andrew, John (Shepard), Larkin youngest...EXR: Col. Jno. & James Simpson, David Green...WIT: Thomas Fakes, Thos. Witson(?Wilson), Geo. Miller...Prv. 4 June 1821... Bk. E, p. 163.

MONROE Jane--Three chn. now living viz: Margaret, Danl A., John H...EXR: Bro. Larkin S. Monroe & son Danl A. Monroe...22 May 1847...Bk. A, p. 86...WIT: Elihu Watson, Wm. East, James Joye.

MONROE Larkin S.--Wife Rebecca...4 chn...EXR: Friends Anderson Johnson, Elihue Watson...25 May 1849--30 June 1849...Bk. A, p. 107...WIT: William East, R. W. Vance,

James M. Oxner.

MONTGOMERY James--Wife Margaret...Rebecca w. of James Adair; Isabella w. of George Ross...names land in Greenville Co. & in Laurens on Harold Br. of Enoree orig. granted Wm. Lacey...EXR: s.l. Jas. Adair, wife...17 Aug. 1791...Bk. A, p. 52... WIT: John & Isabel Crag(Craig).

MOORE James--Chn: Jesse, James, Jinny min...Wife Valley & her chn...EXR: Cornelius Tinsley...22 Dec. 1805--25 Jan. 1806...Bk. C-1, p. 200...WIT: Jas. Holley, Joel Dendy.

MORRISON(Morison) Alexander--Cous. Alan McDougall...Neph. Alex. Turner...EXR: Benjamin Boyd, Maj. John Simpson...25 Mch. 1799--4 Apr. 1816...Bk. D-1, p. 289... WIT: Arch. Smith, William Boyd, John Luke.

MOSELEY George--(Revo. S.)...Wife Polly(Moore the 2nd w...1st was her sister Lucy)... Chn: George, Robertson, Fleming, Nancy, Tully, Sophia, Thomas, John, Eliza Austin, Elizabeth Moore, Polly Young, Frances Belcher...EXR: Robertson & Fleming Moseley... 10 Nov. 1823...Bk. E...WIT: John Walls, Wm. Ross, James Hunter, Saml Mills.

MOTES Jesse--Wife Sarah...Sons: Jesse Milford, ?Machlin mins..."all that rec'v nothing My lifetime on equal footing with those who have"...EXR: Sons Dendy & Hogan, Alsey Fuller...1 Aug. 1827--25 Aug. 1827...Bk. F, p. 124...WIT: Robt. Campbell, Joseph Willcut, Solomon Fuller.

MOTES Jonathan--Wife Susan...Daus: Dicy Ann Reynolds w. of Benj; Betsy w. of Chesley Motes; Minerva w. of John Pinson...EXR: S.l. Benj. Reynolds...30 Dec. 1845... Bk. A, p. 57...WIT: G. Thomas, Reubin Griffin, H. Finley Sr.

MUNFORD Hugh--Sons: James, Johnston...Daus: Nancy Finney, Margaret Scott, Hannah Bell, Anny...EXR: George Whitmore...30 Oct. 1802...Bk. C-1, p. 238...WIT: Thomas Gibson, William Law, William Dillard.

MUSGROVE Edward--Of Enoree, Laurens Co...Sons: Edward Banks Musgrove, William the home place & mill...Daus: Rebecca Cannon, Mary Berry...Wife Ann plant. lifetime "for self & her 7 chn. viz: William, Margaret, Ann, Hannah, Rachel, Liney, Leah"... EXR: Wife...25 Aug. 1790...Bk. A, p. 28...WIT: George Gordon, Alex. Morrison, John George.

NEELY George--Of Liberty Spgs. & Laurens Co...Dau. Agnes...EXR: Wife Anne, son James...1 July 1793...Bk. A, p. 82...WIT: Joseph Hollingsworth, Henry Hitt, John McCosh.

NEELY James--Wife Mary...Sons: Saml, James, George...Daus: Nancy or Mancy, Betsy... s.l. Joseph Jones...EXR: George & James Neely...19 July 1824--1 Aug. 1832...Bk. F, p. 421...WIT: William Tinsley, William Pollard, Jabez Johnson.

NEELY Joseph--Dau. Rebecca min...EXR: Wife Nancy, son Young...19 Oct. 1824--9 Feb. 1830...Bk. F, p. 255...WIT: Robt. Campbell, Jos. Willcut, D. Anderson.

NEELY Mancy--Wife Elizabeth...Two bros. George, James...Sister Elizabeth Neely... Saml Neely...EXR: Bro. George Neely...30 Sept. 1846...Bk. A, p. 101..WIT: B. T. Watts, I. M. Hill, W. T. Nealy.

NESBITT Samuel--Wife Mary...Chn: Nancy, James, William, Nathan, Demsey, Polly, Samuel, Thomas, Elizabeth...EXR: SON Wm...4 Aug. 1824--4 Nov. 1824...Bk. E, p. 425.. WIT: Drury Boyce, John Nash, Michael Dickson.

NEWPORT Jane--EXR: Dau. Rachel Feagin...4 Oct. 1805--5 Sept. 1814...Bk. D-1, p. 167...WIT: Archeble Young, Danl Wright.

NICKLES Nathaniel--Sons: Nathl, Scott, Robert, James, John (oldest...Daus: Elizabeth, Isabel...s.l. James McDowall...Bro. Wm. Nickles...EXR: Son James, Charles Nickles...

22 Mch. 1804--28 July 1804...Bk. C-1, p. 114...WIT: John Johnson, M. Campbell, James Hollingsworth.

NICKLE Chartis(? Charles)--Sons: John, Robert, James, George, William, Turner, Thomas(last 4 mins)...Daus: Margaret, Polly, Catherine, Ginna, Betsy, Naomi, Sally (last 4 mins.)...EXR: James McMahan, Joseph Hollingsworth...12 Sept. 1819--19 Aug. 1826...Bk. F, p. 40...WIT: James, Joseph, William Hollingsworth.

NICKLES Dr. John--Wife Jane...Daus: Catherine N. Holmes, Mary S. Anderson, Isabella Jane Wright...EXR: Dr. John W. Simpson...25 Feb. 1848--23 Oct. 1850...Bk. A, p. 123... WIT: Willis Benham, J. H. Lockhardt, William F. Martin.

NORRIS Thomas--Dau. Matilda Sadler..."all rest chn. by 1st wife"...Min. chn: Christopher, Felise, Imma, Lewis, Azel...EXR: Wife Sarah...12 Mch. 1833--2 May 1833... Bk. F, p. 488...WIT: Saml Cunningham, J. A. Cheek, Alfred Blackwell.

NUGENT William--Daus: Jane, Martha Elizabeth...gr.dau. Emily F. Owens...EXR: Wm. Blakely Jr...15 Sept. 1836--9 Mch. 1844...Bk. A, p. 28...WIT: Nancy & Nathl Day, Willis Hill.

O'Dell John--Wife Becky...Sons: Thomas, William, John...Daus: Elender, Margaret, Martha..bound-boy Levi Rogers..EXR: Thomas Henderson...20 Jan. 1830--1 Mch. 1830... Bk. F, p. 259...WIT: Stephen Hill, James Duncan, John J. Johnson.

ODELL Rachel--Daus: Margaret w. of Edw. Scribner; Mary w. of Thos. Scribner ; Elizabeth, Rachel...Sons: Thomas, Saml, Levi..."my int. in est. of Baruch Odell...tract of land in state of Ill. Shelby Co. to 5 youngest chn"...EXR: Friend John Odell...16 Feb . 1844--12 Mch. 1844...Bk. A, p. 52...WIT: Josephus C. Babb, Richard M. Owens, John Lusk.

ONEAL Anna Jane--(Hus. John Dec'd)...EXR: Son John Cook...21 Dec. 1808--21 Mch. 1818...Bk. D-1, p. 451...WIT: R. W. Owen, Miller Ligon, William Houlditch.

ONEAL John--Wife Anna Jean...Sons: Barney, William...Daus: ? Market(Margaret?), Jane...land lying on Muclick ck...EXR: Sons Barney, Wm...5 Jan. 1803--25 June 1805... Bk. C-1, p. 160...WIT: Charles Wilson, Samuel Weir.

ONEALL (O'neil) Hugh--Sons: Hugh land on Little Riv; Charles mill & house; Thomas land on Rabun ck...Daus: Patience, Ruth, Ann, Rachel, Elizabeth wife of Thos. McDaniel...4 youngest schooled...EXR: Mearm Babb, William Pearson, Elisha Ford... 3 Oct. 1797...Bk. A, p. 268...WIT: John Hunter, Thos. Wardsworth, P. McDaniel.

OSBORNE Daniel--Sons: Danl, William, Langston, ? Ress...Daus: Amanda w. of Wm. Martin; Polly w. of Jno. Martin; Thoeba Atkins; Elizabeth; ? Eaitha w. of Duke Pinson & gr. son John...EXR: Son Langston...1 Nov. 1822--25 Apr. 1823...Bk. F, p. 6...WIT: John Dunlap, Saml Farar Jr., Addison Pyles...(A dau. or gr. dau. Milly had md. bwt dates of will to Thos. ? Cose).

OSBORNE John--Wife Delphia...Sons: Robertson, Claburn, John & his w. Jane & chn; James & his chn; Nancy Barns...EXR: Thos. F. Jones...8 Mch. 1845...Bk. A, p. 80... WIT: Collier, Beverly & Alfred Barksdale.

OSBORNE William--Sons: John, Edward, Jesse W., ? Etsal...Daus: Polly, Pricilla, Ruthy...EXR: Wife Sally, son John, s.l. Jesse Osborne...24 Feb. 1817--21 Mch. 1817... Bk. D-1, p. 369...WIT: Mitchell Cook, Saml Goggans, John Drake.

OVERLY Meshack--Wife Mary...Sons: Nimrod, Nicholas, Benjamin...Daus: Mary Wells, Elizabeth Green, Anne Edwards, Joana Ross & her chn: Elihu & Mason...EXR: Son Nimrod, s.l. Ross Wells...14 Jan. 1801--2 Aug. 1816...Bk. D-1, p. 323...WIT: Joana Johnson, William Bucks Jr., Benj. Overly.

OWENS Daniel--Mother Mary...Bros: Thomas, Robert...Sisters: Jennet, Elizabeth, Anne, Martha Cabaness..."land I bought of Alex. McQuary"...EXR: Bro. Thomas...29 Mch. 1811--4 June 1821...Bk. D-1, p. 44...WIT: John & Elizabeth Owens, Mary Long.

OWENS John--Wife Mary,..Sons: Daniel, John Jr., Thomas, Robert...Daus: Mary Greer, Martha, Anne, Jean & Elizabeth mins...EXR: Daniel Owens, Jno. Finney...4 Sept. 1806--17 Nov. 1806...Bk. C-1, p. 241...WIT: Robt Long, Manasah & Jno. Finney.

OWENS John--Wife Elizabeth..."chn"...EXR: James Watts, Nathl Day...1 Jan. 1817--3 May 1817...WIT: Robt. Campbell, Wm. C. Ball, Rebec. Childs...Bk. D-1, p. 380.

OWINGS Pressley--Wife Margaret...Son Lanson to live with his M...EXR: Sons Abner, Lanson...10 Mch. 1836--3 Mch. 1845...Bk. A, p. 53...WIT: Robertson Moore, Stephen Garrett, Jonathan Jones.

OWINGS Rachel--Bros. William, Richard, Archibald, John(all Owings)...Sister Nancy Childs...Bk. A, p. 4...WIT: B. K. & James & H. E. Owings.

OWINGS Richard(Revo S.)--Wife Sarah...Sons: Richard, William, Archibald, John (also Jonathan but not named)...Daus: Rachel, Nancy Ann, Sarah, Polly Thomason, Elizabeth Studdard,..EXR: Sons Ricard, William...13 Aug. 1828--17 Mch. 1834..,Bk. D-1, p. 266... WIT: R. K. Owings, Turner Goldsmith, Lavinia Owings, (also Bk. F, p. 541).

OWINGS Thomas--Sons: John, William, David, James...Daus: Jane, Margaret, Rebecca... EXR: Wife Sarah, Son John...23 July 1800--23 Oct. 1800...Bk. A, p. 251...WIT: Rodger Brown, John & Minansah Finney.

PAGE John--Sons: William, John, James...s.l.William Carter...Daus: Betty, Frances , Jenny, Hannah...EXR: Wife Anna, son John...28 July 1803--7 Mch. 1804...Bk. C-1, p. 99...WIT: William Fulton, Betty Page.

PARK Agnes--Daus: Molly Stewart; Elizabeth Blakely; chn. of dec'd dau. Isabella Fowler; Nancy Simpson oldest dau. of my son Andrw Park; Nancy who md. Mr. Pearson; dau. of my dau. Sally Hutchinson...?Celema Brewer who lives with me... EXR: Relative Dr. Jno. Simpson...8 Jan. 1842--25 Mch. 1844...Bk. A, p. 51...WIT: J. D. Wright, B. A. James, C. A. ?Lewers.

PARK Andrew--Sons: William, James, Andrw. min...Daus: Isabella & Marcey Fowler, Nancy, Sarah, Betsy...gr.son Andrw Fowler min...Neph. Andrw. Parks...EXR: Wife Agnes, son James...2 Feb. 1809...Bk. C-1, p. 360...WIT: Robert Hutcheson, James Hunter, James Parks.

PARK James--Br. Wm...Sons: Andrw, John, William, Robert Hunter, Matthew Brown, Thomas Porter...Dau. Elizabeth...EXR: Wife Rachel, James & Andrw Park...11 Nov. 1825--25 Nov. 1825...Bk. E, p. 527...WIT; James Park, Andrew Kennedy, William Fulton, Andrew Spears.

PARKS Charles--Bro. Samuel...Sister Lucinda Parks & her chn, viz: Henry, Sarah, Blueford...EXR: Bro. John Parks, James Boyd...26 Apr. 1833--3 Feb. 1834...Bk. F, p. 524...WIT: James & Elizabeth Boyd, John Coates.

PASLAY(Pasley,Paisly) Robert--"Chn"...Dau. Martha Mitchell...EXR: Wife Elizabeth... 6 July 1818--1 Apr. 1819...Bk. D-1, p. 447...WIT: Asa Chandler, Absolom & William Bailey.

PATTERSON Joseph--Wife Rebecca...Sons: Robert, Joseph...1 May 1820--2 Feb. 1824... Bk. E, p. 358...WIT: Elizabeth & Saml Workman, William Ross.

PEARSON Joel O--Sons: William, Ephias...Daus: Mandy, Mahala w. of M. S. Scruggs; Nancy w. of Osborn Coal; Elizabeth w. of Joel Edwards...EXR: Wife Elizabeth, son Ephias...17 Jan. 1830--17 May 1830...Bk. F, p. 270...WIT: Joseph Brown, Isaac &

Nancy Cooper.

PERRITT Alfred--Wife Mary...Sons: Bryant, Thornberry A...Daus: Nancy Caroline, Sarah A. Ashmore, Abigail C. Ellison, Lucinda F. McDonald...EXR: Wife Mary, son Thornbury...28 Apr. 1845--3 July 1845...Bk. A, p. 47...WIT: Abram Machem, G. B. Riley, Thomas J. Sullivan(Wife Mary was dau. of Saml Bolling).

PETERSON James--Son Benjamin to get all not willed to gr.daus: Patsey, Ann, Susannah Peterson...EXR: Wife Ann...23 June 1799--2 June 1800...Bk. A, p. 237...WIT: John Watts, Wm. Roberson.

PINSON Aaron--Minister...Wife Elizabeth...Sons: Moses, Isaac, John...Daus: Jemiah Kennery, Mary Cole dec'd & chn. as they come of age...EXR: Sons John & Moses... 21 Feb. 1794...Bk. A, p. 159...WIT: John Henry, Aaron Pinson Jr.

PINSON John--Sons: John, Howard, Thomas, Aaron...s.l: Wm. Strain, Richard Duty, Cornelius Pucket, Thomas Weathers...Wife Betsy...EXR: Sons Howard, Thomas...26 June 1811--11 July 1811...Bk. D-1, p. 46...WIT: Robert Carter Sr. & Jr. Richard Puckett.

PINSON M. D.--Wife Elizabeth...Chn. Wash, Mary, Louise, Elizabeth, Joseph, Virginia, Martha, Alpheus...EXR: Geo. W. Sullivan...15 Oct. 1850...Bk. A, p. 136...WIT: Wm. A. Stone, H. D. Pinson, Ruth C. Madden.

PINSON Marmaduke Sr.--Wife Molly...Sons: Bicajah(eldest), Isaac, Marmaduke (youngest)...Daus: Edee, Sally Rucky, Hulsagh, Polly Strain, Ruth(Edee or Edith, 1st w. of Arch. McDaniel had a son Pinson; Hulda md. Jas Cunningham; Sally md. Wm. Madden; Abijah md. Sara Arnold; Marmaduke Jr. md Elizabeth Sullivan)...EXR: Son Bijah, Wm. Madden...26 Apr. 1820--6 Oct. 1820...Bk. E, p. 100...WIT: Isaac Dial, James Boyd, S. Cunningham.

PITTS Milton--Wife Mary...EXR: f.l. William Lovell...13 Nov. 1844--25 May 1845.... Bk. A, p. 50...WIT: W. E. Lindsey, Noah Johnson, Chaplin Lindsey.

POLLARD William--Wife Elizabeth...Daus: Matilda, Elizabeth...EXR: Sons Marshal, Alfred, William...15 June 1817--6 July 1817...Bk. D-1, p. 396...WIT: John Robeson, James Mitchell, Braxton Watts.

POLLOCK James--Wife Ann...Sons: William J; John & his chn. including James; Samuel & his chn...Daus: Gennet Henley, Isabel, Elizabeth Gray & her son James; Sarah Darymple & her son James...gr. dau. Ann Scott...Rec. 26 June 1793...Bk. A, p. 101.

POOL Elizabeth--Chn: William, Rebecca Patterson, Nancy Compton, Mary Coleman... gr. dau. Mary E. Moseley's part in trust by son Berry P. Pool...EXR: son Berry,.. 24 Sept. 1850--23 Oct. 1850...Bk. A, p. 121...WIT: W. S. Smith, Saml Mills, A. S. Hutchinson.

POTTER Thomas G.--Chn: Weyman H., Francis A., Thomas G., Allen T., George W., Moses, Mary H. Kennedy of Ga. & chn; Elizabeth H. Potter...EXR: Son Weyman...3 Feb 1842--16 Feb. 1842...Bk. A, p. 193...WIT: Wm. Young, Thomas Wier, John H. Kern.

POWELL Samuel--Chn: Thomas, Samuel, Elizabeth Bailey...gr.chn. Oliver Powell... EXR: Thomas & Saml Powell & s.l. Zachariah Bailey...June 1820--4 Oct. 1824...Bk. E, p. 418...WIT: James & Silas Bailey, Benj. James.

POWELL Thomas--Wife Lucinda...Sons: Thomas, Samuel, William, Robert...Daus: Margaret Delia, Marietta w. of David Goodman, Elizabeth, Nancy Bailey dec'd...EXR: Sons Thos & Saml, friend R. F. Simpson...Pvd. 3 Mch 1834...Bk. F, p. 539...WIT: Hugh Buster, John T. Woody or Weedy, Thomas P. Williamson.

167

POWELL William--(married more than once)...Chn: Wm. Wesley, Nancy, Elizabeth Gaines, Rhody, Peachy, Polly, Belinda, Milly, Virginia, ?Avoney...EXR: Bro. James Powell, s.l. Philip Waits...19 Nov. 1816--28 Dec. 1816...Bk. D-1, p. 343...WIT: David Brademan, Wm. Braden, Martin Norman.

PRATER(Prather) Ann--EXR: Son Israel, John Allen...12 Jan. 1834--4 Mch. 1834...Bk. F, p. 546...WIT: Saml Young, Moses Baty, John Roberson, Margery McMiller.

PRATHER Josiah--Wife Ann--Sons: Israel, Thomas, Jesse, Amos...Daus: Polly, Sabitha J., Deliliah, Rachel Ensley...EXR: Joseph Duncan, Thomas & Jesse Prater...6 Apr. 1822--18 Nov. 1823...Bk. E, p. 329...WIT: John & Josiah Atcheson.

PRATHER William--Wife Mary...EXR: Dau. Dorcas...3 Nov. 1788...Bk. A, p. 12...WIT: A. Gray, John Lindsey, John Wallace.

PUCKETT James--Dau.. Susannah w. of John Pinson & her son Joel; Jean w. of John Beasley & her chn. viz: Nancy, Chainey; Patsey w. M. Walker...son James min...Others: Richard, Dabney, Neeley, Jueen or Queen...10 Feb. 1796--20 Feb. 1800...WIT: Wm. Ball, Martha Avery, Meshack Avery...also 20 Sept. 1797--3 Mch. 1800...EXR: Wife Mary, son Wm...Bk. A, p. 229...WIT: Jno. Hunter, Wm. Dandy, Saml Leek.

PUGH John--Sister Elizabeth Gilbert...neph. Jesse Pugh...EXR: Wife Nancy, Wm. Gilbert... 2 Dec. 1815--21 Feb. 1816...Bk. D-1, p. 189...WIT: Thomas Roberts, John Hezzery, James Garrett.

PUGH Richard--Gr.dau. Nancy Cochran...4 step-chn: John, Wm, Saml & Margaret McClanahan...EXR: Wife Mary, Jno. McClanahan...10 June 1796--Bk. A, p. 148...WIT: William Boyd, Saml Mattles, John Cochran.

PYLES Abner--Sons: Newton, Milton, Adison "who recv'd prop. bef. he left here," T. Jefferson youngest...only surv. dau: Susannah H. Tribble & her chn...also named: Richard & Maryann Shackleford gr.parents of "my oldest dau. Matilda Teague dec'd & Matilda's chn. Elizabeth & Eliza"...EXR: sons Newton & Jeff...12 Apr. 1844...Bk. A, p. 87...WIT: W. T. Campbell, William Blakely, W. A. Waldrop.

PYLES Hewlett--Wife Nancy, pregnant...Chn: Estha, Diadama...EXR: Father John Pyles , bro. Nathl Pyles...10 May 1834--6 Sept 1842...WIT: Joseph Sullivan, Chas. H. & Wm. Simmons(orig. not in files Prob. Judge)...Bk. A.

RAGADALE Edmond--Wife Sarah...Sons: Peter, William, Edward C., John's two sons Robert & Thomas...Daus: Marinda, Ann, Jane...EXR: Edw. C. Garrett...9 Nov. 1848-- 6 Mch. ?1856...WIT: William Bolt, Sarah Saxon, Thos. J. Sullivan.

REAFS(Reass, Rees) Nancy--Daus: Betsy Pugh, Polly Yorke & her son Jonathan Allison, min...EXR: James Allison, William Pugh...3 Feb. 1808...Bk. C-1, p. 332... WIT: Nancy Wright, Danl Wright.

REED David--Chn: Jonathan, Elizabeth, David, Matthew...EXR: wife Elizabeth & bro. William Reed...11 Sept. 1815--29 Oct. 1815...Bk. D-1, p. 229...WIT: John W. Williams, John & James Nickles.

REED Mary--Sister Elizabeth Strain(Strange)...gr.chn: Mary, Caroline...EXR: William Reed, bro...28 Mch. 1831--16 Apr. 1831...Bk. F, p. 345...WIT: Katherine Whiteford, Letty King.

REEDER(Reader) Simon--Sons: William, Thomas...Daus: Sarah, Patsy, Charlotte...9 Nov. 1818--18 Nov. 1823...Bk. E, p. 328...WIT: Robert Long, Robert & Thos. Owens... Wife ment.

RICHEY(Ritchey) John--Wife Margaret...Dau. Jane Harris....s.l. Joseph Graves...Samuel Richey...EXR: son William & friend Martin Shaw...3 July 1819--8 Nov. 1819...Bk. E,

p. 41...WIT: David Caldwell Jr., Arch Holte, Owen Fuller.

RIDDLE John--Wife Mary...Sons: Harris, Newton, Melmouth, Berry, Fealden...Daus : Catherine Garner, Elizabeth w. of Elihu Garrett; Mary w. of John Cannery; Matilda C...19 Aug. 1850--6 July 1855...Bk. A, p. 209...EXR: Berry Riddle, Wm. Power...WIT: Reubin, Jeremiah, Fountain & Benjamin Martin.

ROBERSON John--Sons: Reubin, Toliver, John with w. Marah, also Menoah, William Barnett appear to be sons...Daus: Fanny, Peggy, Polly, Melley...23 Feb. 1802--19 Nov. 1803...Bk. A, p. 321.

ROBERTS Jacob--Sons: John, Isaac, Jacob, Thomas...Daus: Elizabeth Meadows, ?Allemon Brown, Sarah Gilbert, Morah Roberts, Claresy, Copey Gilbert dec'd & her chn. viz. Miledy & Lucinda...EXR: Wife Mary, Isaac Roberts, John Meadows...3 Jan. 1804--15 Apr. 1806...Bk. C-1, p. 217...WIT: David & Jno. Wright, Ezekiel Griffin.

ROBERTS James--Sons: James, George...Daus: Susannah, Mary Ann, Patty B., Sally Fuller...EXR: Richard Shackleford, William Bailey...23 Jan. 1801--30 Jan. 1801...Bk. A, p. 272...WIT: A. Rodgers Jr., Zachariah Motes, Peter Roberts.

ROBERTS James--Wife Sarah...Bro. Edward...EXR: Jacob Niswonger, "if he fails then James Crocker"...26 Jan 1816...Bk. D-1, p. 326...WIT: Jacob Niswonger, Wm. McFerson, James Crocker.

ROBERTSON Manoah--Wife Loucreacy...2 min. daus...EXR: William Owings...18 Nov. 1844--9 Dec. 1844...Bk. F, p. 55...WIT: John Garrett, Mary Owings, E. Hilton.

ROBIRSON William--Sons: John, Thomas, Robert, ?Isor...EXR: Friends Fred Burts, Wm. Green...1 Mch. 1812--21 Mch. 1812...Bk. D-1, p. 69...WIT: John & Joseph Cook, David Caldwell.

RODGERS Andrew--Sons: Abner, Andrew & his dau. Peggy Young; chn of my son William; chn of son John...Dau. Anna Frier...EXR: Son Abner...7 Dec. 1820--3 Sept. 1821...Bk. F, p. 175...WIT: James & Matthew Henry, John Leek.

RODGERS John--Wife Sally...Chn: James L., Lavinia Brownlee, Tabitha w. of Berry Martin, Jane...EXR: Son James, s.l. Thomas Brownlee, friend Charles Allen...20 July 1827--7 Apr. 1828...Bk. F, p. 160...WIT: Wm. Pitts Jr., Mary Reynolds, Henry S. Beadel.

RODGERS Sarah--Son James...Dau. Tabitha...gr.dau. ?Menima Martin...EXR: Friend R. T. Simpson...1 June 1832--20 Aug. 1832...Bk. F, p. 424...WIT: Saml Downs, C. W. & Jonathan Allen.

ROOK William--Wife Elizabeth...Sons: Saml, Thomas I., William...Dau. Catherine w. of Benj. Lyles...1 Feb. 1848--5 Nov. 1850...Bk. A, p. 129...WIT: P. C. Caldwell, Chas. C. Wells, John Suber.

ROSS Catherine--Chn: John, Jane, Sara, Francis, Elizabeth, James youngest...EXR: Son Francis, s.l. William Cowan...11 Oct. 1826--14 Nov. 1826...Bk. F, p. 52...WIT: Samuel Fleming, James & Alex Mills Sr.

ROWLAND Christopher--"personal prop. bewt. all chn"...EXR: Wife Mary, son Robert. 29 Mch. 1796...Bk. A, p. 153...WIT: Silver Walker Sr., Matthew LeFoy, Mary Rowland

ROWLAND Henry B.--"my chn. equal"...EXR: Wife Lettice, John Whitmore...24 Apr. 1828--12 Feb. 1831...Bk. F, p. 325...WIT: James Blackburn, Aaron & John Johnston.

RUNNOLD Joseph--Chn: Polly, Betsy, Anna, Lunorda, William, ?Pearly...EXR: Wife Elizabeth, John Cook...25 Jan. 1815--16 Feb. 1816...Bk. D-1, p. 332...WIT: Reubin

Goldin, Anthony Goldin, Joseph Jones.

RUSHING Aquila--Wife Mildred...Daus: Sarah, ?Higrah...EXR: Wm. Rushing, Joseph Owen...6 Jan. 1805--11 July 1805...Bk. C-1, p. 167...WIT: A. N. Owen, W. Hollingsworth.

RUTLEDGE William--Bro. John Knight...Uncle Joseph Rutledge..Sisters: Polly, Nancy... EXR: Joseph Rutledge, Cornelius Cook Sr....Pvd. 5 Jan. 1823...Bk. E, p. 222...WIT: Larkin Gaines, Betsy Gaines, Robt. T. Duff.

SADLER John--Mother Mary...Son Pleasant..."my chn"...EXR: Wife Mary, Pleasant Sadler, Lewis Ball...15 Sept. 1812--9 Dec. 1819...Bk. E, p. 43...WIT: Henry, Hitt, George Ball, Peter Ball.

SATTERWHITE Mary--Daus: Martha Hill, Sarah Whitlow...gr.dau. Mary Hill,..EXR: Sons John & James Mitchell...2 Mch 1820--27 Nov. 1824...Bk. E, p. 437...WIT: Elihu Creswell, Benj. Hatter.

SAXON Charles Sr.--Daus: Sally w. of John Rodgers; Polly wid. of George Anderson; Sally Allen McNees; son Lewis Saxon's wid...EXR: gr.son Charles Saxon Jr...named also, Tilly Anderson, Bailey Rodgers (prb. gr. ch)...WIT: Jonathan Downs, Ezekiel & Rebecca Mathews...2 June 1816--7 Oct. 1816...Bk. D-1, p. 336.

SAXON Hugh--Sister Susan W. Thurston...to Capt. Saml Barksdale in trust for sister Mary Arnold & chn. & niece Ruth Arnold...Neph. Hugh son of Saml Saxon dec'd...to Hugh Saxon Allison son of cous. Jane...to Mrs. Omey Stone...to Hugh S. son of Wm. R. Farley...prop. of est. of Polly Harris & John L. Harris...aunt Cynthia Williams dec'd & her chn: Monima Brooks, Matilda Little, Nancy Parks...Uncle Lyddall Allen & chn: Frances Allen, Lucy Arnold(others were: Jonathan, Isaac, Cynthia N, Chas W., Mary D., Sarah)...Clarissa Downs dec'd...names mother as living...niece Mary w. of Henry Sullivan...EXR: Bro. Joshua, friend Willis Wallace...11 Nov. 1851...Bk. A, p. 142... WIT: Geo. W. Connors, N. Barksdale, Jeremiah Glenn.

SEURLOCK(Scurlock) Ann--Daus: Frankey, Dolly...2 gr.sons, Reubin & Joshua Scurlock... EXR: Friend Lewis Banton...18 Sept. 1796...Bk. A, p. 165...WIT: Sarah Arrowood, Chester Ware, Claborn Goodman.

SEILLION Hugh--Daus: Jane, Amey, Patsy...EXR: Wife Jane...July 1806...Orig. not in J. P. Of. but recd. Bk. D-1, p. 325...WIT: Basil & Keziah Prater, Z. D. Keron.

SHEA Patrick P.--EXR: Wife Elizabeth, Robt. Campbell...8 Oct. 1815--7 Aug. 1817... Bk. D-1, p. 407...WIT: Jno. Roberson, Martin Shaw, David Madden.

SHEARS Jude--Son Saml...EXR: Dau. Lethere...22 June 1830--15 Oct. 1830...Bk. F, p. 285...WIT: Ursula Brooks, Thos. Harris, Meliona Crocker.

SIMMONS Charles--Chn: Sarah, John, Mary McCas, with fol. minors: Charles, William, Elizabeth, Jean...EXR: Wife Elizabeth & son John...7 July 1791...Bk. A, p. 47...WIT: Joshua Downs, John Rodgers, James Floyd.

SIMMONS Elizabeth--(dec'd hus. Charles)...Sons: William, John, Charles...Daus: Sally Madden, Elizabeth Smith, Jane Franks...EXR: John Garlington...27 Mch. 1822--7 Oct. 1833...Bk. E, p. 338...WIT: John Dunlap, Henry C. Young, R. F. Simpson.

SIMPSON Alexander--Sons: John, James...Daus: Mary Hutcheson, Margaret Glenn, Agnes Dunlap, Elizabeth, Sarah...EXR: Sons James & John, Saml Austin...13 Apr. 1811--5 Sept. 1814...Bk. D-1, p. 165...WIT: John Blake, Ann Haron, John Sheer(Shear).

SIMPSON John--Wife Sarah...Sons: William W., John, Richard F...Daus: Jane & hus. John Nickles; Mary & hus. Capt. Anthony Griffin; Kitti & hus. Major R. Griffin; Nancy & hus. Major Thos. Wright...sister Agnes...Bros: Alexander, James...EXR: Sons W. W. & J. W. Simpson...13 Feb. 1815--2 Oct. 1815...Bk. D-1, p. 218...WIT: Ezekiel

North, Rover Gray, John Felts.

SIMPSON John--Wife Harriet...Chn: "equal pts.".. EXR: Henry R. Shell...17 Aug. 1846...
Bk. A, p. 106...WIT: James & Joseph Hipp, Isaac Lovelace.

SIMMS Charles--Chn: George R., James D., Judith, Lucy Ann, Pelina C...EXR: Wife
Sarah, Clough Shelton, Bernard Glenn...25 Apr. 1813--1 Nov. 1813...Bk. D-1, p. 131....
WIT: John McCoy, Benj. Saunders, Danl Long.

SIMMS Francis--"my chn. & their heirs" viz: Starling; William; Chn of Elizabeth
Gidding viz: Wm. C., Jno. L., Elizabeth I.; Haney Fowler; Priscilla Cheek; Polly
Walker...EXR: Son William, s.l. Willis D. Cheek...4 June 1845...Bk. A, p. 128...also
named a gr.dau. Elizabeth ? Geons...WIT: Wm. Jones, R. S. Woodruff, Danl Lanford.

SIMS William--Wife prop. dur. wid.hood or until youngest ch. of age...Chn: Nathan,
Ann, Reubin, Simpson, Rhoda, John, Messor Babb Sims(confused)...EXR: Wife Rebecca,
Fred K. Burts...20 June 1805--10 Sept. 1805...Bk. C-1, p. 173...WIT: John Sims Jr.,
Lewis Graves, M. Burts.

SMITH Drury--Sons: George, James, John & "rest of chn. viz: Elliott, William, Sarah,
Elizabeth Cheek, Mary Ford"...EXR: Wife Sarah, John Smith...12 Aug. 1797...Bk. A,
p. 182...WIT: Danl Ford, Henry Vaughan.

SMITH John--EXR: Wife Susannah...20 Nov. 1807--15 June 1816...Bk. D-1, p. 312...
WIT: Nelson Sanders, John Smith, R. M. Owen.

SMITH Lucy--Daus: Sarah McNeese, Mary Harris...Son Charles Allen money due me
in Virginia, said Chas. to pay: to Sally Atkins, dau. of Lydall Allen for Schooling;
to Frances & Cynthia Allen, daus. of Lydall...to gr.son Joel Allen...to Milly wid. of
Lydall Allen...to gr.dau. Sara Crisp & her dau. Lucy...to gr.daus. Lucy Bacon Allen,
& Harriet Saxon...EXR: Son Charles...9 Feb. 1826...Bk. F, p. 250...WIT: Colvill
Abercromie Jr., Mary Marshal, E. S. Roland(apparently Lucy Smith was the former
Lucy Bacon who md. as 1st hus. Chas. Allen Sr.)

SMITH Robert--EXR: Son William...29 June 1817--16 Feb. 1818...Bk. D-1, p. 434-435..
WIT: John W. & James. Smith, Saml Kennedy.

SMITH William R.--"All my chn. & their Heirs"...chn of dec'd son Marshall...EXR:
Sons Ezekiel & Archibald Smith...24 Sept. 1850--7 Apr. 1857...Bk. A, p. 271...J. H.
Irby, C. C. Higgins, W. B. Henderson.

SOUTH William--Wife Cathy(Catherine Daniel)..Sons: Daniel, William, John, Gabriel,
James, Zedekiah dec'd & left wid. Ruth & chn...Daus: Nancy(w. of Wm. Hall) & her
chn. Wm. Fr. & Patsy Robertson; Rachel(w. of Jesse E. Clardy); Hannah(w. of Jno.
Norwood); Sarah(w. of Reuben Hall)...EXR: Son Gabriel, s.l. Jesse E. Clardy...2 Sept.
1842--5 Aug. 1844...Bk. A, p. 38...WIT: Philip Waite Sr., John C. Hall, R. L. Waite.

SPEIRS(Spears) William--Wife Elizabeth...Son Andrew & his sister..."all my chn"...
EXR: Son William...10 Jan. 1845...Bk. A, p. 100...WIT: J. P. Hutcherson, M. B. Sheldon,
John Stewart.

STARNES Ann--Sons: Aaron W., Ebenezer, John...Daus: Molly Murphy, Ann Jones,
Rachel Hughes, Rebecca Sims...28 Nov. 1800--1 Oct. 1802...Bk. C-1, p. 4...WIT: Rachel
& David Anderson.

STARNES Ebenezer--Sons: Aaron, Ebenezer, John...Daus: Mary, Ann, Rachel, Rebekah...
EXR: Wife Ann, son Aaron...4 Nov. 1789--Bk. A, p. 24...WIT: Saml Wharton, John
Field, Roger Murphy Jr.

STARNES Mary Ann--Chn: Moses, chn. of dec'd son John; chn. of dec'd dau. Ann
Sherby; Susan w. of Berryman Sherby; Rebecca w. of Lewis Graves; Elizabeth w. of

Aaron Hill; Sarah w. of Isaac Edings...EXR: Martin Shaw, friend...20 May 1843...
Codicil 28 Jan. 1851...Bk. A, p. 256...WIT: Joel Laidson, Asa Fogy, James McPherson...
Codicil names Mary w. of Wm. Cobb, apparently a dau; gr.son Joel son of Ann Sherby
dec'd & Mary Berry sister of Joel.

STEVENS John--Sons: John, James, David, Solomon...Daus: Janey, Elizabeth, Mary...
EXR: Wife Mary...8 Aug. 1793...Bk. A, p. 81...WIT: Zachariah Bailey, Elizha, Wiles..

STEWART Francis--Chn: William, Robert, John Allen, Mary...Mother of these chn:
Sarah Lipp Stewart...EXR: Friends Wm. Blakely son of Wm. Blakely, James L. Young...
6 May 1845...Bk. A, p. 63...WIT: Alex & Hugh McKeby, John Dalrymple.

STIMSON(? Simpson) Enos--Adopted dau. Mary Simpson all prop...EXR: Friend & Neighbor Saml Wharton...7 July 1798--8 Dec. 1800...Bk. A, p. 262...WIT: Thos. & John
Davenport, Benj. Watson.

STONE John--Sons: Rolley, Lewis, William, Reubin, Elin(?Elam...Dau. Nancy...EXR:
Wife Mildredge (Mildred), son Rolley...25 Jan. 1797--17 Mch. 1800...Bk. A, p. 253...
WIT: Danl & H. Wright.

STONE John--Chn: John, George, Janey, Polly Kennedy(youngest daus: Polly, Fanny)...
EXR: Rev. Zachariah Arnold, Dr. F. Conn...30 Aug. 1826--6 July 1827...Bk. F. p.
117...(John Stone renounced all claim to house at Mineral Spring, purpose of spring
bathing)WIT: Geog. & John Comer, Gable Trenton.

STRAON(Strain, Strange) David--Sisters: Susanna, Jane...EXR: Susanna Strain...20 Oct.
1831--8 Nov. 1831...Bk. F, p. 363...WIT: David Strain, Andrw. Rogers, Wm. Green,
Nathl Nickle.

STRAIN James--Sons: David, John, William...Dau. Susannah...Dau. & s.l. Ferguson...
EXR: Wife Jane, son David...9 Oct. 1812--14 June 1813...Bk. D-1, p. 104...WIT: James
Nichols, Jonah Johnson, R. Campbell.

STWART(Stewart) John--Oldest son Francis...y.dau. Nelly...s.l. David Stodard...EXR:
Charles Little...3 Jan. 1806--4 July 1806...Bk. C-1, p. 225...WIT: James Brown, Joseph
Vance.

SULA William--Son Geo. Moore Sula...wife Sarah...5 Aug. 1840--11 Sept. 1840...Bk.
A, p. 7...WIT: John Wm. Simpson, M. Garlington, Richard Denron.

SULLIVAN Joseph--Wife Temperance...Bro. Thos. Jefferson Sullivan prop. in trust
for wife permitting her reside on land, get toll of mills & labor of slaves...Chn:
Milton A., Wm. Dunklin, Chas. Pleasant, John H., Kezziah McCullough, Mary Ann
Eppes, Malinda C., Temperance(latter gets land including "the Hickory Tavern")...
Bro. Geo. Wash Sullivan trustee for son Milton, minor who gets land bounded by
Andrw. McKnight, Jno. Bolt, Willis Cheek, Pleasant Shaw, Jno. Mears, Christ'pr Posey...
all chn. to be educ...EXR: Bro. T. Jefferson Sullivan...WIT: E. B. Gambrell, W. H. &
Thos. Manly...27 May 1846--12 Nov. 1849...Bk. A, p. 109.

SUTHERLAND Joshua--Son Samuel & "rest of family"...EXR: Wife Eleanor, Wm. Leak,
Andrew Rodgers...28 Apr. 1801...Bk. A, p. 298...WIT: Elijah Edwards, Martha Leak,
Andrew. Rodgers.

SWAN Timothy--Son Alexander...Daus: Rebecca, Isabella...EXR: Wife Sarah, friend
Wm. F. Downs...21 July 1816--7 Oct. 1816...Bk. D-1, p. 338...WIT: James Hutchinson,
John Simmons, David Sloan...Mother named.

SWINDLER(Swindle) Michael--Sons: John, Daniel, George...Daus: Deliah, Susy Saxon...
EXR: Bro. George, Aaron Cloar...3 July 1809--8 July 1815...Bk. D-1, p. 210...WIT:
Philip Wait, Wm. Washington, Jones Box.

TANNEY John--EXR: Wife Elizabeth...Nieces: Peany Raney, Susannah Taney...4 Sept. 1798..Bk. A, p. 202...WIT: Thos. Honor, Ambrose Johnson, John Gamble.

TAYLOR Alexander--Wife Margaret...Daus: Jane, Margaret, Hannah, Catherine Ransom, Mary...gr.son Alex McCarley...EXR: Sons Robert, John, James...25 Dec. 1821--22 Feb.. 1822...Bk. E, p. 203...WIT: Wm. Cowan, Charles & William Taylor.

TAYLOR James--Mother Martha...Bros: Samuel, chn of bro. John ,dec'd...also ment: Mary w. of Hugh Workman, Jane Goodwin, Robert Taylor, Elizabeth w. of Wm. Speers... 19 Oct. 1843--13 Nov. 1843...Bk. A, p. 30...WIT: J. C. Wright, J. H. Irby.

TAYLOR John--Wife Barbara...Sons: Alexander, William...Daus: Barbara, Mary & step-dau. Rebecca...EXR: Alex Taylor, Wm. Cowan...22 Feb. 1818--5 Mch. 1818...Bk. E, p. 18...WIT: James Hutcherson, William Young, Hugh Crooks.

TAYLOR John--Wife..."all my chn."...6 Apr. 1833--2 June 1833...Bk. F, p. 489...WIT: Nathl Day, Samuel Templeton, Saml Taylor Jr.

TAYLOR Margaret--Sons: James, Robert...Daus: Jane Chambers, Catherine Roberson, Margaret, Hannah..."to Alex. McCorley"...EXR: John & James Taylor...21 Nov. 1829--

5 July 1830...Bk. F, p. 273...WIT: Robt. Caldwell, Saml Pearson, Sterling Tucker.

TAYLOR Martha--Chn; Robert, John, Samuel, James, Elizabeth Speers, Jane Goodwin, Mary Workman...EXR: Saml Taylor Sr...14 Feb. 1831--12 Oct. 1843...Bk. A, p. 29... WIT: John & Henry Taylor, Nathaniel Day.

TAYLOR Robert--EXR: William W. Sloan...Fol. appear to be chn: Margaret w. of Julius Martin; William Taylor's son William I; John, James, Jane...3 Apr. 1843--26 Sept. ?1851...Bk. A, p. 139...WIT:--Taylor, John & James Goodwin.

TAYLOR Robert--Sisters: Kitty Goodman, Rebecca w. of Humphrey Willis & their chn: Sally Goodman...Bro. Bluford...EXR: Duke Goodman...25 Oct. 1851...Bk. A, p. 147... WIT: James Parks, J. J. Atwood, W. D. Watts.

TAYLOR Samuel--Sons: Andrw, Kennedy, John, David, William dec'd...Daus: Martha, Margaret, Katherine w. of Robert Taylor, Mary Ann.w. of Joseph McCullum, Nancy w. of Wm. Taylor, Jane...EXR: Wife Jane, son David...3 Jan. 1842--3 Nov. 1843...Bk. A, p. 15...WIT: Andrew Kennedy, Thomas & Feril Milan, relative Robt. Gilliland.

TEAGUE Elijah--Sons: Robert, heirs of son Joshua...Daus: Elizabeth Hipps, Sarah McAdams, Mary Wilson, Catherine McAdams, Rebecca Teague...EXR: Son Abner, s.l. Joseph Hipps...2 Oct. 1824--18 Apr. 1826...Bk. F, p. 20...WIT: Elijah Teague, Charles Mchesky, John Miller.

TEAGUE Joshua--Lands from Wm. Caldwell & John Lewis, one line being Indian creek... Sons: Israel, Elisha, Isral, Willaim, Abner, James...Daus: Isabel Mason, Sophia Lyon, Susan ?Mafer, Mary Adam...s.l. Wm. Gray...EXR: Sons Elijah, Israel...12 May 1804-- 2 May 1808...Bk. C-1, p. 308...WIT: Nathan Jones, Thomas Dalrymple Jr. & Sr.

TEMPLETON David--Sons: David, James, Robert, William, John...Robt. Hanna & gr.son David Hanna...EXR: Dr. George Ross, Creek William Craig...19 Apr. 1817--2 June 1817...Bk. D-1, p. 390...WIT: William Craig, James Templeton, Hezekiah Rice.

THOMAS Isaac--Sons: Evan, John, ?Jeremiah, William yg., Edward, Isaac, Abel the 3 ods sons...yg. daus: Sarah, Phoebe; ods. daus: Mary Weisner, Elizabeth Cox...EXR: Wife Mary, son John...4 June 1802...Bk. C-1, p. 164...WIT: Jacob & Mary Weisner.

THOMASON Nancy--"my 5 chn", named are James D., Cathy P., both min., Polly & Step-dau. Nancy Thomason...s.l. Wm. Thomason EXR...27 May 1837...Bk. A, p. 211... WIT: M. P. Evins, William Studdard, Gideon Thomason.

THOMPSON Henry--Chn: Rebecca Richey, John, Polly, Nancy, Jenny, James...EXR: Wife Catherine, son John...17 Feb. 1825--4 Dec. 1833...Bk. F, p. 503...WIT: Martin Shaw, Menoah Forgy, Joseph Irby.

THREAT(Threet, Thweatt) Sarah...Hus. Reuben...Son Tom..."5 young chn"...EXR: John & Robert Dunlap...5 Apr. 1819--6 Sept. 1819...Bk. E, p. 38...WIT: John H. Davis, Robert Bell, William Brown,

TINSLEY Abraham--Son William...Daus: Sarah, Mary..."pay Joseph Cason from money collected from Chas. Huet"...EXR: Bro. James, wife Nancy, f.l. Henry Johnson...5 Jan. 1804--5 Feb. 1810...Bk. D-1, p. 8...WIT: Frances Stewart, George Dalrymple, Elijah Teague.

TINSLEY Cornelius--Daus: Patsy Weeks, Betsy Tribble...gr.son Corn. Tinsley...EXR: s.l. Jeremiah Tribble...3 Dec. 1817--8 Dec. 1817...Bk. D-1, p. 423...WIT: Saml Vance, John Dendy, J. Underwood.

TINSLEY Zachariah--"raise & educ. chn"...EXR: Wife Betsy, John Dendy...25 Mch. 1830--18 Nov. 1830...Bk. F, p. 286...WIT: Abner Pyles, Joel Dendy, Saml Vance.

TODD Andrew--"Wife"...Daus: Letitia, Margaret...EXR: Saml B. Lewers & s.l. Enoch Agnew...6 Aug. 1835--4 Dec. 1843...Bk. A, p. 23...WIT: Joseph Cooper, James Dorrah, Charles Smith.

TODD John--Wife Nancy...Sons: James, Charles, Robert, John...Dau. Mary...s.l. Robt Bryson...22 Jan. 1821--4 May 1821...Bk. E, p. 162...WIT: Wm. McClonahan, Jas. Todd, John Hobbs.

TODD Patrick--Wife Jane, at death div. est. 7 pts...Sons: Ar `ar, William, `ndrew, Dr. Patrick, James & his chn., John & 2 chn. viz: Martha Winn, Pat Todd 2   lf-bro. of Martha..Daus: Jane McCall; chn. of dec'd dau. Ellen `4. McFall...EXR: John D. Williams, son Dr. Patrick...15 June 1852--11 Dec. 1852...Bk. A, p. 151...WIT: Wesly Smith, Francis Hill, John H. Goodman.

TODD Samuel--Bros. John, Andrew...sister Jane Hamilton...nephs. Saml & John Hamilton & Saml Todd...nieces Martha Hamilton, Eliza`.eth & Jane Todd...1818-1830...Bk. E.... EXR: Samuel B. Luers(Lewers).

TODD S.T.H--Bros: Robert E., William W., James R.--"all my bros. & sisters including chn. of dec'd sister Mary W. Higgins"...mother a legacy...EXR: Robert E. Todd... 6 Aug. 1843--30 Dec. 1844...Bk. A, p. 45...WIT: C. P. Sullivan, E. W. Simpson, Robt. Thompson.

TOMPSON(Thompson) William--Wife Nancy...Sons: William, Abraham & son Wm... Daus: Molly, Elizabeth Lemon, --Williamson...EXR: Anthony F. Yelding..11 Nov. 1826-- 22 Dec. 1827...Bk. F, p. 137...WIT: Sally M. Hall, Cynthia Armstrong, Martha Cheppbell (Chapel).

TOMPSON(Thompson) William--Chn: Sarah Ann, Isabella, Elizabeth, Nancy, Jane, Mary..."young chn. equal to those md."...EXR: Wife Jane, John W. Perry(Penny)...23 Sept. 1836--18 June 1840...Bk A, p. 2--also Bk. F, p. 2...WIT: John, Allen & Wm. Coleman.

TUCKER Lavinia--Bros: David & Ezekiel Higgins...Chn. of sister Lavinia Rofs...sister Haney & hus. James B. Higgins dec'd & chn...William son of sister Nancy Fowler... Elizabeth w. of James French...neph. Benj. B. Higgins..."balance bwt. bros. & sisters"... EXR: James B. & Benj. B. Higgins, b.l. & neph...17 Dec. 1842--Codicil 24 Dec. 1845 (She was apparently wid of Genl Wm. House Tucker & bwt. 75-80 yrs. old. Statements from Joseph Prior who talked with her 14 Mch. 1837, Wm. Fowler in 1850 & Wm. Powers in 1855)...Bk. A, p. 230

TURK Mary--Bros. & sisters: Hannah Pitts & chn. & bro. Henry Pitts...Jean & James Bolen & chn...Ordery & Jonathan Motes & Chn., one being Joseph...bro. Benj. Collier's chn...neph. Jos. Motes chn. Mary, John...EXR: Sister Ordery's son Joseph Motes, friend John Simpson...16 July 1799...Bk. A, p. 217...WIT: Wm. Rason, Zachariah Motes, Archibald Sayers.

TURK Rachel--Bros: Archibald & Matthew McDaniel & sister Margaret McDaniel; neph. Matthew O'Daniel, min...16 July 1797...Bk. A, p. 171...WIT: Matthew Johnson, Arch McDaniel.

UNDERWOOD James--Sons: Robert, James, Mathew, William, John & Isaac dec'd... Wife...Daus: Jane, Mary & step-dau. Nancy Copeland...EXR: s.l. John Blakely, son John...29 June 1822--18 Nov. 1823...Bk. E, p. 333...WIT: Robt. Caswell, John H. Davis, Watson Deen.

VANCE Mary(She was Mary Dunbar McTier & hus. Nathl Sr.)...Chn: Saml, John, James W., Joseph H., Nathl, Allen, David, William dec'd, Frances Greer, Mary(Williams)... EXR: Son Joseph...-1840--16 Nov. 1841...Bk. A, p. 9...WIT: John & J.W. Watts, Elihu Attom.

VAUGHAN Claiborn--Son John, "all my chn."...EXR: Wife Mary...11 June 1816--5 July 1819...Bk. E, p. 31...WIT: Coleman, Elizabeth B., & Joanna Lewis Carlisle.

VAUGHAN Walter P.--EXR: Bro. Drury Vaughan & his dau. Elizabeth, Charles Eggerton...18 July 1827--5 Nov. 1828...Bk. F, p. 184...WIT: Charles Eggerton, Arch. Todd, S. B. Cook.

WALKER Elizabeth M.--m.l. Mrs. Susannah Walker...sister Eliza Garey...Bro. John L. Young...niece Theodora dau. of G. W. Young...EXR: Bros. John & James Young... 18 Jan. 1842--11 Aug. 1842...Bk. A, p. 35...WIT: Wm. Young, W. W. Templeton, Jno. H. Dendy.

WALKER Keturah--Chn: Allen, Bones, Hogan, Azariah, Elizabeth Shaw, Debly Ann Wilcott, Emily Shaw, Emaline Madden, chn. of Patsy Milan dec'd viz: Wm, John. Debly Ann, Jane, Elizabeth,...EXR: Son Hogan...9 Mch. 1843--5 May 1845...Bk. A, p. 50...WIT: John H. Coleman, Wm. Nelson, Azariah Walker.

WALKER Moses--Wife Elizabeth...Chn. mins...Bro. Jathrow..."Elizabeth & John Walker agree to abide by abv. writing"...1 June 1791...Bk. A, p. 36...WIT: Thos. East, Jas. Bell.

WATKINS Charles--EXR: wife Eli§abeth, James Abercromie...30 July 1810...Bk. D-1, p. 427...WIT: Charles Watkins, Mary, Nancy & John Cochran.

WATTS James--Son James.."my chn"...named are: Elihue C. Watts, Priscilla Griffin, Narcissa Goodman, Betsy Chapman...EXR: Elihue, William & John Watts...2 Oct. 1839-- 7 June 1842...Bk. A, p. 27...WIT: W. B. Meriwether, Hazel & Elizabeth H. Smith, Marcus Dendy, Martha Walker.

WATTS John--Wife Peggy...Sons: Richard, John Pollard, Braxton, Beaufort...Daus: Elena K., Louisa, Narcissa, Cornelia, Elmira, Peggy, Matilda Vaughan...EXR: Sons Beaufort, Braxton, Richard, Nathanl Day...14 Sept. 1812--26 Oct. 1812...Bk. D-1, p. 90...WIT: James Vaughan, Similion Deale, Mrs--Pollard.

WATTS Nancy C--2 y.daus: Sarah P. & Margaret E. "all my chn"...EXR: son James W. Watts...8 Mch. 1845--10 Mch. 1845...Bk. A, p. 49...WIT: J. E. Gray, John D. Williams, H. M. Phinny.

WELLS Aaron--Est. to mother Rebecca & sister Elizabeth Wells...Bro. Elisha...EXR: Bro. Moses Wells...pvd. 30 May 1806...Bk. C-1, p. 233.

WELLS Elisha--wife Elizabeth, EXR...1 Nov. 1813--27 Feb. 1820...Bk. E, p. 65...WIT: John Cook, Drury Sims Jr., John Hitt.

WESSON(?Wasson) John--Wife Elizabeth...Chn: Hicks, Sarah, Polly, Marhta...EXR: Father Henry Wesson, Jesse Jones...1 July 1805...Bk. C-1, p. 165...WIT: Absolom Harwell, Benj. Wesson.

White James--"chn"...EXR: Wife Elizabeth...19 July 1807--5 June 1817...Bk. D-1, p. 368...WIT: William Chiles, Rhoda & James Young.

WHITEHEAD William--Chn: William, John, Nancy, Benjamin, Thomas, Donel, Stephen, Sarah Strain, Jane Alberson, Linsa Adkins, ?Milla...EXR: Wife Margaret, Charters Nickels...22 Mch. 1805--8 Oct. 1805...Bk. C-1, p. 178...WIT: J. N. Johnson, Jas. Strain.

WHITMORE Joseph--Dau. Sarah Duncan...gr.son George Whitmore, min..."prop. div. bwt. all chn. & heirs of those dec'd"...EXR: Son George...27 May 1803--20 Nov. 1803... Bk. C-1, p. 131...WIT: Whitmore & Dred Jones, Reubin Flanagan.

WHITTEN John Sr.--Chn: Sidney, John Jr., Sally Henly, Ann Jacks, Fanny Ray, Susan Kennedy...EXR: Son Sidney, Claxton Ray...3 July 1828--2 Jan. 1832...Bk. F, p. 381... WIT: John F. Kern Jr., Alfred Kern.

WHITWORTH Cinthea(Cynthia)--Dau. Frances Elizabeth gets all...Trustees & EXR: Daniel Rudd of Newberry friend & relation, Henry Burton...14 May 1846...Bk. A, p. 98...WIT: Anthony F. Golding, John H. Goodman, A. G. Cook.

WILKS Whitehead--Wife Eliza...3 pts. one to dau. Eliza & her hus. Samuel Henderson... to chn. of dec'd son Cornelius...to son Joseph...to son Thomas all claim I have to my father's est...EXR: J. H. Irby, Dr. John Davis...8 Nov. 1847...Bk. A, p. 123...WIT: Saml Fleming, R. E. Todd, William J. Blakely.

WILLARD John--Wife Patty...Daus: Polly, Elizabeth, Sarah...EXR: Son Meager...29 June 1816--2 Nov. 1816...Bk. D-1, p. 342...WIT: J. L. Neely, Walter Burges, Elizabeth Davenport.

WILLIAMS David--Sons: Samuel M., Henry R., Joseph H., Leonard, Robert, Ephraim, William A., Dr. James(sons all had col. educ.)...Daus: Elizabeth A. Miller; Frances Clary; Mary Metts...EXR: Sons Henry & Leonard...26 Mch. 1853--11 Oct. 1853... Bk. A, p. 163...WIT: W. J. Whitmire, R. C. Cannon, A. C. Garlington.

WILLIAMS James A.--Wife Mary...Sons: Daniel, John & 4 youngest, viz-James Alwood, Franklin, Washington, Elihu...Daus: Sarah Cooper, Elizabeth Ann Cooper...EXR: s.l. Charles & Reubin Cooper...6 Jan. 1816--20 Jan. 1816...Bk. D-1, p. 252...WIT: William Hudgens, R. H. Owins, W. Tinsley.

WILLIAMS Mary--Sons: Elihue Duke, Franklin, Washington W...Daus: Elizabeth w. of Reubin Cooper & her dau. Mary Amanda...EXR: Sons Elihu, Wash...12 Aug. 1826--15 Apr. 1828...Bk. F, p. 162...WIT: Anthony Golding, Saml Goodman, John W. Williams.

WILLIAMSON Agnes--Dec'd hus. James...Sons: Dr. Wm. Williamson, James McCollums... Dau. Jane w. of Hamon Miller...Trustees: Albert & Franklin Miller...9 Jan. 1845... Bk. A, p. 76...WIT: John Nickles, Willis Benham, James Davis.

WILLIAMSON Elisha--"If wife Elmina should not have a living child by me"...Dau. Essie Brown & her chn. John & Clarissa Lovelace...gr.chn: Elisha Williamson, Elizabeth L. Arnold...EXR: wife...7 Aug. 1851--23 May 1853...Bk. A, p. 156...WIT: R. L. Stephens, John K. ?Suson, Charles Murphy.

WILLIAMSON Jane--Dau. Mary Campbell...EXR: Son Sanders Williamson, Ira Gambrell... 29 Apr. 1840--8 Oct. 1842...Bk. A, p. 24...WIT: Benj. Arnold, Joel Stone, Stephen Stone.

WITSON(?Wilson) Benjamin--Sons: David S., John, Benjamin, James...Daus: Elizabeth

?Gray, Mary Burns, Isabella McConnel, Jane & hus. Abraham Gray, Larey w. of William Boyd, Martha, Margaret, Ann Scott a min...EXR: Wife Elizabeth, James & David S. Wilson...23 Apr. 1815--3 June 1815...Bk. D-1, p. 207...WIT: Wm. Neal, Enos

WILSON Charles--Dau. Mary...Sons: James, Charles, "six other chn"...EXR: Son Thomas, friend Elijah Watson...4 June 1820--13 June 1820...Bk. E, p. 82...WIT: Charles & James Crawford, Charles Wilson Jr.

WILSON John--Mother personal prop...land to William, James, Jeane Grant, William Ware or Mare...EXR: William Ware...11 Dec. 1800...Bk. A, p. 266...WIT: Edmond & M. Wood.

WILSON John--Wife Jean..."all my chn" mins...EXR: Turner Richardson, Robert Allison Sr...11 Aug. 1823--3 Apr. 1826...Bk. F, p. 14...WIT: James Todd, J. A. Lynch, C. Stone.

WOLF George--Son George...Dau. Nancy...EXR: Wife Nancy, Capt. Saml Henderson... 7 Jan. 1806--30 Jan. 1816...Bk. D-1, p. 258...WIT: Wm. Dunlap, Wm. Montgomery, John Swelevan(Sullivan).

WOLF John F.--Daus: Isabella Saxon, Elizabeth Milner...EXR: Wife Mary, son George, Samuel Davis...prop. left in trust of Hugh Saxon, George Wolf...3 Feb. 1820--5 Mch. 1820...Bk. E, p. 150...WIT: Saml Davis, Patillo Farrow, J. A. Mathews.

WOLFF Mary--Son George F. Wolf & his 5 chn. viz-John S., Melton Y., Charles S., James R., Mary...gr.sons: Lewis, Elizabeth & John Saxon...EXR: John F. W. Saxon... 26 Feb. 1842--4 Jan. 1845...Bk. A, p. 46...WIT: Christopher Burns, H. & R. C. Saxon.

WOOD Joseph--Son Zadock...EXR: Wife Elizabeth...13 Mch. 1817--3 Nov. 1817...Bk. D-1, p. 419...WIT: James H. Harden, Coleman Carlisle, James Bobbs.

WRIGHT Samuel--Sons: Eldest William G., minors James & Samuel...Daus: Elizabeth, Frances, Polly, Nancy, minors...Wife Patience, educ. chn. & at her death, div. bwt. all...EXR: Bro. William Wright...23 Sept. 1808--6 Jan. 1809.

YOUNG Abner--4 chn: Dorothy, Isabel, James, Emma Florella or Hosalla(confused)... EXR: Wife Rebecca...Dau. Lucinda dec'd...20 Mch. 1833--2 Sept. 1833...Bk. F, p. 497... WIT: John Mason, John & William Hunter. (The dau. Dorothy md. T. E. Herbert; Isabella md. Dr. Geo. Young)

YOUNG George Sr.--Chn: George, Elizabeth, Mary, Lettie Rowland, Jane Whitmore, Thomas' two chn: George & Thomas...EXR: A. McCreary, Bro. Christopher Young, son George...1 Feb. 1826--4 Nov. 1839...Bk. F, p. 497...WIT: Thos. Young Jr., Christ Young Jr., John Boyce.

YOUNG James--Sons: James & Robert youngest chn. & "should they move to western country, sell my lands...rest of chn. have had theirs"...25 May 1796...EXR: Wife, sons James & Robert, George Anderson...WIT: Andrw. Middleton, Abner Young...Bk. A.

YOUNG James Sr.--Sons: John, James...Daus: Betsy Carter, Polly Medley, Betty, Lucy, Sally...EXR: Zachariah Bailey, William Burnside...21 Nov. 1807--7 Dec. 1807...Bk. C-1, p. 283...WIT: James Holley, Thomas & Mary Powell.

YOUNG James--Wife Mary Ann..."my chn"...EXR: Sons Gallatin & Wm. Augustin, friend Turner Richardson Esq...25 June 1824--16 Oct. 1824...Bk. E, p. 429...WIT: William Moore, Hugh Saxon.

YOUNG Joseph--Chn: Robert, Joseph, John, Elizabeth Roland...EXR: James son of Wm.

## NINETY-SIX.

Fort Ninety-Six.

Ninety-six stands near the scene of the first bloodshed in South Carolina during the Revolutionary War. Here the British built a star-shaped redoubt in 1780, which was besieged by General Greene in 1781. Later in the same year the fort fell to the Americans, and Ninety-Six was moved to the railroad a short distance from the original site. Greenwood State Park is near by.

Courthouse, Newberry

OLD COURTHOUSE (1826), CAMDEN; Designed by Robert Mills

first American architect, one of South Carolina's most gifted sons.

Winnsboro Courthouse, begun in 1820-

178

# MISCELLANEOUS REFERENCE DATA

Most of the original claims for Revolutionary Service are filed at the State Historical Commission in Columbia, S. C. These were paid by "INDENTS" or script money and the majority were settled by the state with public lands or forfeited estates. Mr. A. S. Salley, as Secretary to the Historical Commission, has edited and printed for the Commission, nine volumes of STUB ENTRIES TO INDENTS, Three, of ACCOUNTS AUDITED (thru letter B) which are filed in approximately some 10,000 envelopes, two volumes of NAVY RECORDS, and other books. The Commission also has custody of the records that were filed in the Secretary of State, Comptroller General, Treasurer's and Surveyor General's offices. Mortgages, marriage settlements and miscellaneous books are indexed. There is a file of loose manuscripts, also photostatic copies from the War Department, Washington, of some companies of the Revolutionary War.

At the State Library in Columbia is available, what is known as the MORTALITY SCHEDULES-census records of 1860, 1870, 1880--which give such data as: names of persons dying the preceding year, date of death, residence, age; Caroliniana Library: Copies of the wills of the counties of the state formed before 1853, except these: Beaufort, Colleton, Chesterfield, Georgetown, Lexington, Lancaster, Orangeburg. The earliest records were filed in Charleston, but after the Revolution, in the various districts, until about 1785 when the separate counties were functioning. The Charleston Library Society, founded 1748, has an extensive collection of South Caroliniana. In each county, estates settled in Court of Equity, furnish much genealogical material and original manuscripts, while these Court-houses offer records that can be found nowhere else.

Among books furnishing proof for Revolutionary service for South Carolinians, we name: Gibbes Documentary History of S.C; Memoirs of American Revolution As Relating To State of S.C. by John Drayton; McCrady, History of S.C. in the Revolution 1780-1783; Mills Statistics & Handbook; Force's American Archives; Saffell's Revolutionary Record; South Carolina Histories by Ramsay, Chapman, Simms, White, Landrum, Wallace, Yates-Snowden; Historical Register of Continental Army by Heitman; History of The Old Cheraws by Greeg; O'Nealls Annals of Newberry; Historic Camden by Kirkland & Kennedy; History of Edgefield by Chapman; History of Spartanburg by Landrum etc; D.A.R. Lineage books and Magazine; S. C. Histl. & Geneal. Magazine; Transactions of Huguenot Soc. of S. C., and other books named within these pages.

AN AMERICAN RIFLEMAN.

Goose Creek, Episcopal Church in Berkeley County,
oldest church building standing in South Carolina. (1711-19), NEAR CHARLESTON

The Oldest American College Library Building,
University of South Carolina

WOODROW WILSON SHRINE

First Presbyterian Columbia for a time had as it's Stated Supply Pastor, Dr. Joseph Wilson, the father of Woodrow Wilson, and a few blocks is the former Wilson home designed by the mother of the President and built by his father; it is now a shrine, purchased by voluntary subscriptions and is in charge of the American Legion. The home contains many of the original pieces and relics of the former home. The parents and sister of Woodrow Wilson are buried in the First Presbyterian Church yard.

Ruins of Millwood ante-bellum home of General Wade Hampton

Calhoun Mansion. Members of this family were massacred by Indians in 1760. A descendant, John C. Calhoun, the great statesman, member of Congress, Secretary of War, Secretary of State, Vice-President of the United States.

From the massacre of the Anthony Hampton family, five sons were left. One son, Wade served in the Revolution. His son, Colonel Wade II, with Andrew Jackson. His son, General Wade III was governor of South Carolina 1876-1878.

# THE GREAT SEAL OF THE STATE

From Drayton's Memoirs of the American Revolution (chapter 18,

" So soon as the government under the Constitution of March, 1776, were organized, the necessity of having a public seal became evident; and, on motion in the General Assembly, it was resolved, That his Excellency, the President and Commander-in-Chief, by and with the advice and consent of the Privy Council, may, and he is hereby, authorized to design and cause to be made a Great Seal of South Carolina, and until such a one can be made, to fix upon a temporary seal.*

" In pursuance of this resolution, William Henry Drayton, and some of the Privy Council, were charged with designing the Great Seal, and causing it to be made; and in the mean time, a temporary public seal was adopted by the President and Privy Council, for purposes of State. The first use of this temporary seal (which appears to have been the Seal-at-Arms of the President) was for commissioning the civil officers of the government, and for a pardon issued by President Rutledge, dated 1st May, 1776, in favor of a person who had been convicted of manslaughter before Chief Justice William Henry Drayton, and his Associate Justices, at a court commenced at Charles Town on the 23d April, 1776.† In these commissions, it was called his (the president's) seal, but in pardons and other instruments, it was afterwards called ' the Temporary Seal of the said Colony,' or ' the Temporary Public Seal'; and, it was used from that time throughout the year 1776, until about the 22d May, 1777; as on that day, President Rutledge issued a pardon under ' the Seal of the said State,' omitting the word temporary; whence there is reason for believing the Great Seal was then made; and from that time the temporary seal does not appear to have been used. ‡

---

[* See Journals of the General Assembly of South Carolina for 1776, in the office of the clerk of the House of Representatives, at Columbia.]

[† See Book of Miscellanies and Bills of Sale in the secretary's office, Charleston, S. S., pages 1, 2.]

[‡ The author remembers seeing the mould or *dye* of the Great Seal, brought by the artist who was engraving it, to his father, William Henry Drayton, at his residence in Charles Town, for his inspection; but he cannot fix what particular time it was. From some circumstances which occurred, he believes it was not in the winter.]

"The device for the armorial achievement and reverse of the Great Seal of the State of South Carolina, is as follows:

"ARMS.—A Palmetto tree growing on the sea-shore, erect; at its base, a torn-up Oak tree, its branches lopped off, prostrate; *both proper*. Just below the branches of the Palmetto, two shields, pendent; one of them, on the dexter side, is inscribed March 26th, the other, on the sinister side, July 4th.

"Twelve spears, *proper*, are bound crosswise to the stem of the Palmetto, their poitns raised; the band uniting them together bearing the inscription QVIS SEPARABIT. Under the prostrate Oak is inscribed *Meliorem Lapsa Locavit ;* below which appears in large figures 1776. At the summit of the Exergue are the words SOUTH CAROLINA; and at the bottom of the same, ANIMIS OPIBUSQUE PARATI.

"REVERSE. A woman walking on the sea-shore, over swords and daggers; she holds in her dexter hand a laurel branch—and in her sinister, the folds of her robe; she looks towards the sun, just rising above the sea; *all proper*. On the upper part is the sky, *azure*. At the summit of the Exergue are the words DUM SPIRO SPERO; and within the field below the figure is inscribed the word SPES. The Seal is in the form of a circle, four inches in diameter, and four-tenths of an inch thick.

" It was not designed until after the fort at Sullivan's Island had defeated the British fleet, as all its devices will prove. The fort was constructed of the stems of the Palmetto trees, (*Corypha Palmetto*,) which grow abundantly on our sea-islands—which grew on Sullivan's Island at the time the fort was made, when the battle was fought, and which grow there at this day.

"The ARMS were designed by William Henry Drayton, and the original executed by him with a pen, bearing a great similitude to what is represented on the Seal, is in the possession of his son. It, however, contains more devices, but this is easily reconciled, by supposing all he had designed was not deemed by the President and Privy Council necessary for the Great Seal. The explanation of this side of the Seal is the following: The Palmetto tree on the sea-shore represents the fort on Sullivan's Island; the shields, bearing March 26th and July 4th, allude to the Constitution of South Carolina, which was ratified on the first of those days; and to the Declaration of Independence, which was made by the Continental Congress on the last of them. The twelve Spears represent the twelve States which first acceded to the Union. The dead Oak tree alludes to the British fleet as being constructed of oak timbers—and it is prostrate under the Palmetto tree, because the fort, constructed of that tree, defeated the British fleet; hence the inscription, *Meliorem Lapsa Locavit*, is appropriately placed underneath it; under which 1776 is in large figures, alluding to the year the Constitution for South Carolina was passed; to the battle fought at Sullivan's Island; to the Declaration of Independence, and to the year when the Seal was ordered to be made.

16

"The REVERSE of the arms is said to have been designed by Arthur Middleton, often mentioned in these memoirs, and who was the father of Henry Middleton, at present ambassador from the United States of America to the Court of Russia. The Woman walking along the sea-shore strewn with swords and daggers, represents Hope overcoming dangers, which the sun, just rising, was about to disclose in the occurrences of the 28th of June, 1776; while the laurel she holds signifies the honors which Colonel Moultrie, his officers and men gained on that auspicious day. The Sun rising in great brilliancy above the sea, indicates that the 28th of June was a fine day; it also bespeaks good fortune."

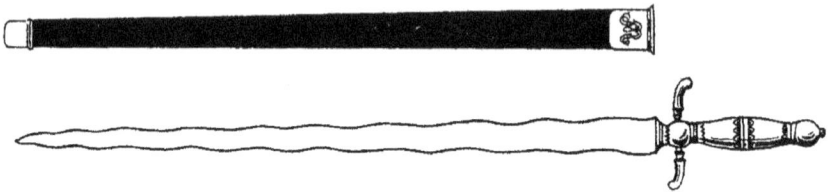

# THE SWORD OF STATE

This sword hangs from the front of the Senate Rostrum during daily session of the Senate and is carried by the Sergeant-at-Arms on all State occasions. It was made in Charles Town (Charleston) and bought May 5, 1704, for £26 11s 3d ($129.00).

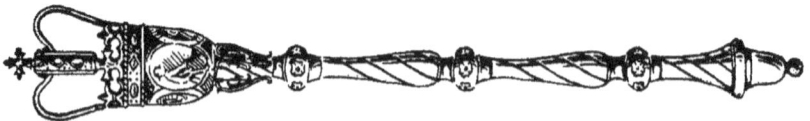

# MACE

The mace is the emblem of authority of the House of Representatives. Whenever the House officially attends in the Senate Chamber, and upon state occasions, the mace is always borne at the head of the procession. It was made in London in 1756 and is solid silver with gold burnishing. It is possibly the only mace in use in the United States which antedates the Revolution. It was used by the Commons House of Assembly until the Revolution.

Mottoes

"Animis Opibusque Parati"
(Prepared with minds and resources);

"Dum Spiro, Spero"
(While I breathe, I hope.)

# Chief Agricultural Products and Commercial Industries

Farming: cotton, tobacco and truck produce

Farming

Textile manufacturing

Lumbering

Hydro-electric power production

Fishing and marketing sea foods

Canning foodstuffs

Fertilizer manufacturing

Mining: gold, tin, k a o l i n, granite and quarrying

Poultry and pigeon raising

Hog raising

Fruit growing and marketing

Shrubbery and flower nurseries

Operation of tourist hostelries

Paper manufactur

# The Palmetto State

## MAP OF SOUTH CAROLINA

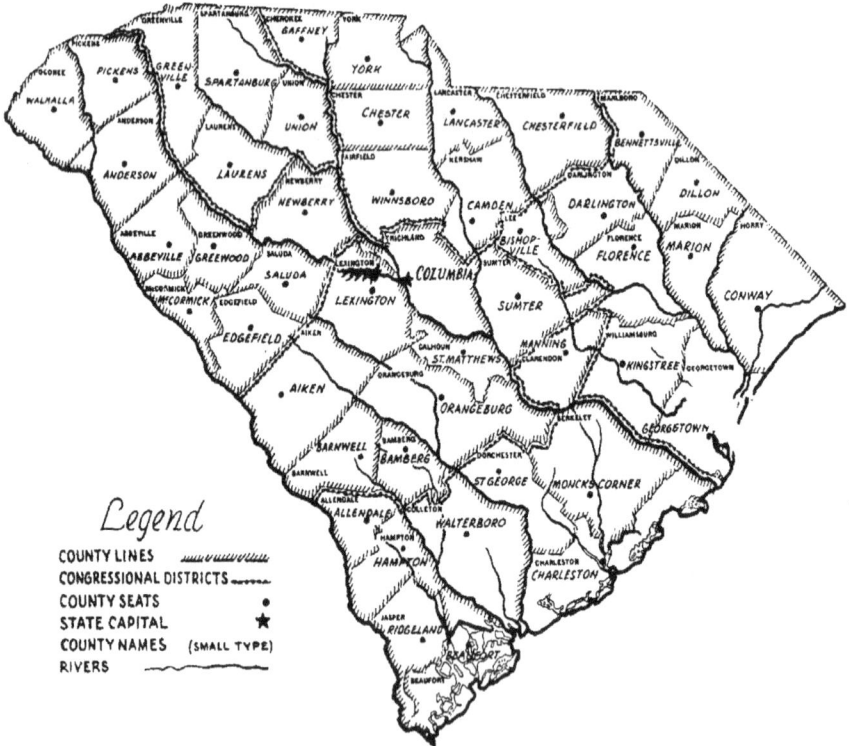

GREENVILLE SPARTANBURG CHEROKEE YORK
GAFFNEY
PICKENS
OCONEE GREEN YORK
PICKENS VILLE SPARTANBURG UNION
LANCASTER CHESTERFIELD MARLBORO
WALHALLA CHESTER
ANDERSON CHESTER LANCASTER CHESTERFIELD BENNETTSVILLE
LAURENS UNION FAIRFIELD
ANDERSON LAURENS DARLINGTON DILLON
NEWBERRY KERSHAW
NEWBERRY WINNSBORO CAMDEN DARLINGTON DILLON
ABBEVILLE GREENWOOD RICHLAND MARION HORRY
ABBEVILLE GREENWOOD SALUDA BISHOP-VILLE FLORENCE MARION
MCCORMICK EDGEFIELD LEXINGTON COLUMBIA SUMTER FLORENCE
MCCORMICK EDGEFIELD SALUDA LEXINGTON SUMTER CONWAY
EDGEFIELD AIKEN CALHOUN MANNING WILLIAMSBURG
ST.MATTHEWS CLARENDON KINGSTREE GEORGETOWN
AIKEN ORANGEBURG
ORANGEBURG BERKELEY GEORGETOWN
BAMBERG DORCHESTER MONCKS CORNER
BARNWELL BAMBERG
BARNWELL ST.GEORGE MONCKS CORNER
ALLENDALE COLLETON
ALLENDALE WALTERBORO
HAMPTON CHARLESTON
HAMPTON CHARLESTON
JASPER RIDGELAND
BEAUFORT
BEAUFORT

### Legend

COUNTY LINES
CONGRESSIONAL DISTRICTS
COUNTY SEATS •
STATE CAPITAL ★
COUNTY NAMES (SMALL TYPE)
RIVERS

186

# THE SULLIVAN FAMILY
# IN IRELAND AND AMERICA

Archeology leads us to believe that the Gaelic Race conquered Ireland about the 4th century B.C. They came from some country east of Gaul by way of the North sea, which later became known as SCYTHIA. The ancient progenitor of the Sullivans about 1,000 B.C. was Milesius, king of the Gaels. His son, Heber, was ancestor of Aengus. There follows Owen Mor, King of Munster who married Beara, daughter of the King of Spain. His son, Oilioll Olum, was 237th monarch of Munster and died A.D. 234. Finghin was the 14th Christian King and grt-gr-father of King Aengus. There were seven generations before SUILDHUBHAIN who lived about A.D. 950 when surnames were first adopted. There were 101 generations from the beginning to SUILDHUBHAIN (O'SUILEABHANS, pron. Sooeeliavan, Sullivan).

The Sullivans were living along the river Suir in eastern Ireland when the overwhelming hordes of the Anglo-Norman invasion (about 1169) compelled them to migrate to the southwest (counties of Cork, Kerry, Limerick). The southern branch of Sullivans in America, descend from Sir Owen O'Sullivan, who sat in Parliament 1585 (reign of Queen Elizabeth). It is not to be assumed that everyone who bears the name SULLIVAN today, descends from this line. One must establish that his ancestor left Ireland during the Cromwellian period or the great upheaval of 1641-1654, when "all the nobility . . . were banished and their lands confiscated . . . any still there by 1 May 1654 would be put to death." Many fled to Spain and other countries. Reaching America was John Thomas Sullivan to Virginia 1655 (our line). Florence Sullivan was Master of a ship bringing first settlers to Charleston, S.C., and he was also Surveyor-General of the Province, and Sullivan's Island named for him. The ancestor of General John Sullivan of the American Revolution settled in Maine.

## SULLIVAN FAMILY DESCENDED FROM

CHARLEMAGNE 742/814, EMPEROR OF THE KNOWN WORLD, married
    HILDERGARD 757/782 (can trace to Geoffrey Plantagenet 1113/1151) m.
    Matilda of England 1103/1167, grdau. of

WILLIAM THE CONQUEROR, whose grdau. Eleanor, married Alphonse, 9th King of
    Castile who died 1214)

CHARLEMAGNE, married Princess Hildergarde of Swabia . . . had-

LOUIS LE DeBONNAIRE, King of France born 778, d. 840, reigned 814/40, m.
    Judith, dau of Guelph, Count of Andech & Bavaria. They had—Giselda & Louis,
    King of Bavaria. (Latter had - CAROLMAN who had Arnould, who had
    HEDWIDGE.)

PRINCESS GISELA (Giselle) m. 867 Eberhard, Count of Burgundy, son of Henrock,
    Duke of Friuli. (Wurts, Magna Charta) had -

PRINCESS ADELHEID, Countess of Burgundy who m. Ludolph, Duke of Saxony (Burke
    Vol. I, Ped I) Had -

OTTO, DUKE OF Saxony d. 912, m. Princess Hedwige dau. of Arnolph, Emperor
    887/99 & wife, Otta of Bavaria. (Arnolph was son of CAROLMAN, son of
    Louis I, King of Bavaria, son of Louis Le Debonnaire) Otto had -

HENRY THE FOWLER, Emperor 919/36 (born 876, d. 936) m. 2n Matilda of
    Ringelheim, dau of the Saxon count, Thiederick. (For mother of Henry, see -
    Burke Royal Fam. Vol. 1 Ped. L; also Royal Fam. by Lavoisne). Henry &
    Matilda had -

HEDWIDGE d. 956, m. Hugh Capet, Duke of France (p 184 Wurtz Magna Charta, Vol. I & II) They had -

HUGH CAPET, KING OF FRANCE 938/996, m. Adele or Adelaide, who according to Burke, was dau..of Otto I. Had -

ROBERT THE PIOUS 971/1031, m. 2n - Constantia. She was called "Constance of Provence," & was dau of Berenger Count of Provence. Had -

HENRY I, King of France, b. 1005, d. 1060, reigned 1031/60, married Anne of Russia, grdau. of the 1st CZAR Vladimir (3rd wife & dau of Jaroslaud). Had -

PHILIP I, King of France 1052/1108, reigned 1060/1108, m. 1071 as 1st wife, Bertha, dau of Florient Count of Holland. Had -

LOUIS VI, King of France 1081/1137, m. Alice or Adelaide of Savoy in 1115, dau of Hubert II, Count of Piedmont. Had -

LOUIS VII (1119/1180), m. 3rd Adelaide or Adela, dau. of Theobold II, Count of Champagne. He went on 2nd Crusade. They had -

PRINCESS AGNES OF FRANCE, married Adelem de Burg, Steward to King Henry II of England, Governor of City of Wexford, Ire. He was son of Wm. de Burgh, Earl of Cornwell (oldest Duchy of England) son of Robert, son of Harlowen de Burgh who married Arlotta, mother of William the Conqueror. (De Burgh, one most powerful families of Ireland, governors under the Kings of England. They trace through Geoffrey, Duke of Lorraine, who led the Crusades 1097, refused to wear a crown in Jerusalem. After him, the family have the cross on their armorial bearings.) Princess Agnes had -

WILLIAM FITZ-ANDELEM de Burgh, Lord Gov. of Ireland 1177, died 1204, m. 1st Lady Isabel of England (widow of Llewlyn, Prince of Wales). Had -

RICHARD MOR de Burgh the Great, Lord of Connaught & Trym; Lord-Lieut. of Ireland 1227. He died 1243, m. Lady Hodierna de Gernon (grdau of King Odo O'Connor & dau. of Robt. de Gernon by Una O'Connor). Had -

WALTER de BURGH, Baron of Connaught, Earl of Ulster & Constable of Ireland, who d. 1271. He m. Maude de Lacie, d. 1303 (dau. of Hugh de Lacie, Earl of Ulster & Constable of Ire. Sir Hugh came to Ireland 1171, was Lord Palatine & a descendant of Charlemagne.) Had -

RICHARD de BURGH 1259/1326, was 2n Earl of Ulster, Lord Justice of Ireland in 1296, died 1326, married Lady Margaret de Burgh, (dau. of John de Burgh, Baron of Lanville.) Had -

LADY JOAN de Burgh who m. 1st - 1312 Thomas Fitzgerald, 2n Earl of Kildare, d. 1359 (her father was Richard, known as "the Red Earl"). (McMurrough King of Leinster, in a power Struggle with other Irish Princes, asked some English nobles to come over & help him. Among these were the Fitzgeralds. These newcomers merged with the Celtic mass, - intermarried, adopted Irish language & customs. Maurice Fitzgerald was Justice of Ireland 1229. His descendant, 5 generations removed, was crowned King of Ireland 1315 at Dundale.) Had -

MAURICE FITZGERALD, 4th Earl of Kildare, d. 1390, m. Lady Elizabeth Burghersh (dau. of Sir Batholomew, Burghersh, Knt; 3rd Baron of Verdon, Lord Justice of Ireland, by 1st wife, Lady Maude Mortimer, dau. of Sir Edmund Mortimer, Baron of Wigmore) Had -

GERALD FITZGERALD, 5th Earl of Kildare, Lord Justice of Ireland in 1405, died 1410 who m. Lady Margery Rocheford (dau. of Sir John de Rocheford, Knt;

Lord of Thistledown by his wife Lady Margery Bereford dau. of Lord of Kill, Leixlip & Casthewarren). Had -

JOHN-CAM FITZGERALD, 6th Earl of Kildare, d. 1427. (He built the castles of Maynooth & Kilkea. The former was the famed stronghold of the Geraldines. The Earls of Kildare ruled in "the Pale" and intermarried with the Irish for some 300 years, until it was said they "were more Irish than the Irish," and her most loyal supporters). He had by wife Margaret de la Herne

THOMAS FITZGERALD, 7th Earl of Kildare, Lord Duputy of the Kingdom in 1454 & 1463 & d. 1478. He m. Lady Joan Butler who d. 1486. (Dau of James Butler, 7th Earl of Desmond & of royal descent from Edward I of Eng.) The Earls of Desmond's great territories extended over Limerick, Kerry, Cork & Waterford, and included some 575,000 acres. This land was confiscated in Elizabeth's reign & parcelled out to English settlers.) Had -

GERALD FITZGERALD, 8th Earl of Kildare, Lord Duputy of Ire. & in effect, actual RULER. He married Lady Allison (dau. of Sir Rowland Eustace of Harristown by Lady Maude, dau. of Jenico d'Artois, widow of John Dondall of Newton). In 1534 the Kildares declared war on England, and later 6 of them were hung.) Gerald had -

LADY ELEANOR FITZGERALD (sister of Gerald oge, 9th Earl of Kildare). She married 1st Donnell Mac Fineere Mac Carthy-Reagh, Prince of Carberry in Ireland. His mother was dau. of Donnell, 9th Lord of Bearehaven who d. 1520. Had -

LADY JULIA MacCARTHY, married DERMOD O'SULLIVAN, the Powdered, 11th Lord of Beare & Bantry, of Dunboy Castle, who d. 1549. (Donnell Mor, 8th Lord in descent from the first who assumed the name O'SULLIVAN, & lineal descendant of Eogan Mor, was the 25th in descent from Olioll Olum, the 237th Monarch of Munster, Ire. thru his son, Owen. This Donnell Mor's grt-gr-son, Aura-ny-Lacken, Lord of Desmond, was the 1st Lord of Beare & Bantry in Munster, & direct ancestor of Dermod the 11th Lord, who m. Julia MacCarthy.) Issue: Owen, Donel, Philip, Dernod, Joan

SIR OWEN O'SULLIVAN (or Eoghan) sat in Parliament 1585, died 1594, m. Helena Barry (dau. of James, Lord Barry, Fitz Richard Barry Roe by wife Ellen, dau. of Cormac na hory MacCarthy Reagh) Issue: Owen, John, Donel, Julia

OWEN O'SULLIVAN, flourishing 1612 (Carew's Pacata Hiberna p. 293. He had a regrant of DUNBOY Anno 9 James I.) Died 31 Aug. 1616. Married Helena dau. of Pierce Butler of Gregolt. She d. after 1616. Issue: Owen Donel, Dermod, Philip, Connor, Helena, Julia

OWEN-DONEL, b. after 1599, joined Rebellion of 1641, was attainted & fled the country. His family scattered among relatives & friends, and some came to America. He married Jo-Ann Elizabeth dau. of Thos. Brown & grdau. of John Brown. Issue: John (or called John Thomas for two maternal ancestors); Derman to American 1656 & left will; Elizabeth, Anne

JOHN O' SULLIVAN b. 1637, came to America 24 Oct. 1655 (Patent Book 3, p. 392, Land Office, Richmond, Va.) He came as minor with relative Elizabeth Sullivan. He appears in "a list of Lower Norfolk People in 1673 as 36 yrs. old (Clerk's Office, Norfolk, Va.; Wm. & Mary Quart. Vol. 26). He married 1st - Mary dau. of Owen Hayes of Lynhaven Parish (see his will). He m. 2n Sara dau. of Thos. Gore. In the early Virginia records the name is variously spelled: Usehullevan, Usuliman, O'Swellivant, O'Sullivan, Sullivan. The will of John Sullivan is recorded in Princess Anne County, Va.: Lynhaven Parish, dated 12 May 1698, prv. 7 Sept. 1698, Bk. 1, p. 194; see also State Library, Richmond, Va. Lands owned by him are mentioned in the will of Matthew Brinson 12 June 1681 (Jour. Irish - Amer. Soc. 25/103. Abstract of will of Owen Hayes, 25, 99). Issue: Owen, Morris, Mary, Amie & John with wife Hester who died bef. Father & had son John, m. Catherine Bright.

OWEN O'SULLIVAN I, b. Lynhaven Parish, Prin. Anne Co., Va. abt. 1673/4, was granted 240 acres 7 Nov. 1700 at Dam Neck, near Owen Hayes at Fish Pond (Prin. Anne Co., Va., Bk. 4, fol. 126) also granted 862 acres in Lunenburg County 10 Sept. 1755 (Pat. Bk. 32,631) granted 225 A 15 July 1760 (Bell's Free State); granted 160 Acres 10 Sept. 1755. The tithable List of Wm. Caldwell, taken 1749 for Lunenburg shows Owen Sullivan (Wm. & Mary Quart. 11, 57). Owen's will dated 12 Oct. 1768, prv. 6 Feb. 1769 in Charlotte County (this county cut off from Lunenburg 1764). Family records state he married several times, once in 1693 to Elizabeth, born 1678/9 dau. of Lt. Col. Thos. Claiborne (1647/1685) who m. Sara Fenn. Owen Sullivan's last wife appears to have been Mary Ruth Pleasants b. 1671/4, dau. of John I (1644/98) who m. abt. 1666 the widow Jane Larcome Tucker. The names - Owen, Claiborne, John, Pleasant, Elizabeth, etc. come down thru generations to present. Issue: 13 - Owen II, Charles, William, John, Pleasant, Mary (Mullins), Temperance (Farmer), Esther (Hart), Madeline, Margaret, Frances, Patience, Elizabeth.

OWEN SULLIVAN II, b. in Lunenburg, Va. 1699, d. 1790, m. May 1721 Mary Margaret Hewlett (Hulit, Hughlett, etc.) b. 4 March 1707 (dau. of Wm. Hewlett & Mary Fearne who was dau. of John Fearne & Mary Lee). Owen II is named in father's will. By deed 1 Oct. 1781 Owen Sullivan conveys to Chas. Crenshaw 151 acres "including the late dwelling house of the late Owen Sullivan deceased, devised to said Owen Sullivan by Will of Owen Sullivan deceased" (Charlotte Co., Va. D BK 3, p. 571). There are records of other sales from Owen Sullivan to James Mullins, Stephen Farmer, etc. A History of Sullivan family was compiled 1882 and published by Wm. D. Sullivan 1913. In it he states that the above Owen and wife Margaret Hewlett had 5 children to move from Virginia to South Carolina. They were: 1-James, m. 1st Meta Bolling; 2n Sara Harrison Choice; 2-Owen III, grant in S.C. 1773, m. Sally O'Dell Nelson; 3-Margaret, m. Col. Samuel Wharton; 4-Pleasant, m. Milly Kelly; 5-Charles, next in line

CHARLES SULLIVAN, b. Charlotte Co., Va. 2 Apr. 1728 died in Greenville County, S.C. 3 Nov. 1808, buried Lebanon Meth. Church, grave marked as Revolutionary soldier. He married 15 June 1749 the widow, Mary Charlton (Johnson) She b. 1 June 1722, d. 20 Dec. 1837. Issue 5 viz: 1-Moses, m. Milly Chandler; 2-Sara, m. Joseph Dunklin; 3-Claiborne, m. Mary Harvey; 4-Stephen m. Martha Powell; 5-Hewlett

HEWLETT SULLIVAN b. in Va. 28 Dec. 1763, d. Greenville County, S.C. 11 July 1830 Revolutionary solider. (Organized Company of Scouts) Married 19 Dec. 1787 Mary dau. of Joseph Dunklin (Revo. Patriot) She rendered Revo. Service also. He was large land and slave owner, Senator, buried at Lebanon Church yard. Issue 12: 1-Judge Dunklin Sullivan, m. Mary Mayberry dau. of Rev. soldier, moved to Ala.; 2-Dr. John C. Sullivan, m. Anne Hendricks Arnold; 3-Geo. W. Sullivan, m. Jane Washington Brooks; 4-Joseph P. Sullivan, m. Temperance Hamilton Arnold; 5-Elizabeth, m. Rev. Marmaduke Pinson; 6-Frances, m. Squire Calhoun; 7-Jane m. Samuel L. Moore; 8-Mary, m. James M. Latimer; 9-Thos. Jefferson, m. Sara Cureton; 10-Chas. P., 1st-Sara Smith; 2nd-Zelene Boyd; 11-Hewlett, Bach.; 12-James M. married 1st-Sara Mimms; 2nd-Lizzie Vaughan.

THOMAS JEFFERSON SULLIVAN I, b. 28 Dec. 1807, d. 13 Jan. 1866, m. on 12 Sept. 1833 Sara Moon Cureton. He was extr. of his father's estate. Issue: 1-Henrietta (Parkins); 2-Frances (Goodgion); 3-Adelaide (Huff); 4-Sara (Mahaffey); 5-Claudia (Huff); 6-John S., m. 1st-Clinkscales; 2nd-Allen; 7-Charles, m. Arrah Watts; 8-Thos. J. II

THOMAS JEFFERSON II, b. 24 Dec. 1852, d. 5 Nov. 1923, m. 11 Nov. 1884 Felicia Arnold Sullivan b. 9/1/1865, d. 5/26/1927. Issue: Joseph Giroud and Capt. Claudius (WWI) unmarried; Rev. Humbert Sullivan, Capt. WWII, m. Grace Pitts; Dr. Charlton Sullivan, m. Evelyn Peele; Malinda C., m. Arthur Holley. Sara next in line.

SARA LUCILE SULLIVAN, m. 6 March 1907 Erasmus Powe Ervin (descendant of Col. John Ervin of Revolution) Children 2-Elizabeth Felicia, m. Albert Stephens of Laurens; Houston Sullivan Ervin, m. Sara Louise Graham.

This New index, that was completed for this reprint, does not cover the section on Laurens County, SC Wills. For the researcher looking for persons within tghis section, we sugest a book that is in print by Southern Historical Press and compiled by Colleen Elliott: Laurens County SC Wills, 1784-1840. This book can be purchased at: southernhistoricalpress.com

# Index *to* South Carolinians *in the* Revolution

Samuel 95
**BLAIKLEY,**
**BLAKLEY,** Thomas 42
Wm. 17, 42, 96
**BLAIR,** James 96
Jno. 120
**BLAKE,** Edward 85, 86
John 57, 85, 86
Wm. 115
**BLAKNEY,** John 121
**BLALOCK,** Jeremiah 52
**BLAMEYER,** Wm. 57
**BLAND,** Robert 96, 108
**BLANDING,** Wm. 108
**BLASSINGAME,** Jno. 96
Julian 108
**BLEAKEY,** John 67
**BLEDSOE,** Bartlett 96, 118
Berryman 118
**BLOUNT,** Chas. 108
**BLUNDEL,** Nathan 85
**BLYTHE,** Samuel 96
**BOBBITT,** Wm. 34
**BOBO,** Sampson 121
**BOCQUET,** Peter 115
**BODDIE,** Nathan 96
**BOEVIE,** Rhonda 96
**BOGGAN,** Patrick 96
**BOGGS,** Aaron 96
**BOLES,** Samuel 119
**BOLLING,** Samuel 96, 125
Wm. 96, 125
**BOLT,** Abram 42
Robert 125
**BOLTON,** Agnes 90
Matt 96
Robert 96
**BONDS,** Morris 80
**BONE,** Jno. 81
Wm. 81
**BONEY,** Jacob 80
**BONHAM,** Absolone 98
**BONNEAU,** Ann 90
Anthony 114
**BONNER,** Jas. 121
Will 83
**BONNIOT,** John 85, 86
**BOOBE,** Sarah 90
**BOONE,** Thos. 115
Wm. 115
**BOOTH,** Jno. 44, 96
Henry 108
Mary 94
May 90
**BOOZER,** Henry 108
**BOQUET,** Peter 86

**BORDEAU,** Daniel 85
Natl. 86
**BORDIN,** Rich. 84
Wm. 84
**BOSTIC,** John 120
**BOSTWICK,** Littleberry 96
**BOSWELL,** Jesse 29
**BOTHWELL,** John 115
**BOTSFORD,**
Rev. Edmund 96
**BOUCHELLON,** Joseph 96
**BOUEQUETT,** Peter 86
**BOUNETHEAU,** Mary 90
Peter 67, 85, 96, 115
**BOURDEAUX,** Daniel 86
Nathl. 86
**BOURK,** Jno. 81
Robert 81
**BOWDERS,** John 84
**BOWELL,** Thomas 83
**BOWEN,** Benj. 30
Robert 96
**BOWER,** Catherine 90
**BOWERS,** David 96
Sylvana 90
**BOWIE,** John 57, 108
**BOWMAN,** James 81
Sarah 90
**BOX,** Margaret 90
Mary 90
**BOYCE,** Alex 57
Jno. 96
Wm. 84
**BOYD,** Ed 84
Elizabeth 90
David 96
Jas. 125
Jno. 96
Martha 90
Samuel 125
Thos. 119
Wm. 34, 125
**BOYER,** Jno. 82
**BOYKIN,** Burrell 96, 114
Francis 57, 83, 120
Sam 67
**BOYLS,** Martha 90
**BOYS,** Nathan 96
**BOZEMAN,** Ralph 120
**BRADLEY,** Francis 46
Jas. 87
**BRADWELL,** Nathaniel 57
**BRACEY,** Sackfield 96
**BRACKET,** Samuel 96
**BRADFORD,** Jno. 96
**BRADLEY,** E Uzabeth 89

Margaret 90
**BRANDON,** Mrs. Agnew 90
Christopher 51
Matt 84
Thomas 67, 115
**BRANFORD,** Wm. 119
**BRANN,** Wm. 119
**BRASWELL,** Henry 44
**BRATCHER,** Samuel 28
**BRATTON,** Martha 89, 94,
120
Wm. 67, 96
**BRAZEL (L),** Hannah 90
Richard 84
**BREED,** Priscilla 90
**BREESE,** Timothy ..119
**BREMAR,** Francis 57, 86, 118
**BRENT,** Jas. 96
Jno. 120
**BREWSTER,** Hugh 81
Jno. 81
Wm. 30, 96
**BREWTON,** Mary 89
Miles 114
**BRIAN,** Jas 96
Matt 83
**BRICE,** Margaret 90
**BRICKEN,** Jas 85, 86
**BRIDGEMAN,** Erasmus 108
**BRIDGES,** Mary 90
**BRIGES,** Jno 82
**BRISBANE,** Adam 120
**BRITT,** Richard 20
**BRITTON,** Daniel 67
Henry 67
**BROCK,** Reuben 30, 96
Uriah 119
**BROCKINGTON,** John 40
**BROCKMAN,** Jno 96
**BROOKS,** Zach. S. 37
**BROOKSHIRE,** Jno 39
**BROOM,** Jno 37
Thos 81
**BROTHERS,** Jno 121
**BROTHERTON,** Wm 81
**BROUGHTON,** Alex 115
Ann 90
Thos 119
**BROWN,** Grizell 90
Sarah 90
**BROWNE,** Alex 80, 81
Archibald 14, 67, 96
Bartlet 96, 120
Benj. 57
Bernard 96
Chas 57, 96

# Index *to* South Carolinians *in the* Revolution

Mary 89, 111
**DUNLAP**, George 98
Jos 85, 87
Margaret 91
Wm 11, 42
**DUNN**, Andrew 82
Jeremiah 98
**DUPRIEST**, John 83
**DUPUY**, Jno 98
**DURANT**, Henry 98
**DURHAM**, Charnel 38, 69, 86
**DURKINS**, John 98
**DURN**, Elizabeth 91
**DUSENBURG**, Charles 98
**DUTARQUE**, Louis 57
**DWIGHT**, Nath 114
**DYSERT**, Corn 84
**EARLE**, Bayliss 98
Jno 98
Samuel 57, 98
**EARNWOOD**, Wm 80
**EASTERLING**, Wm 98
**EBERLY**, John 85
**EDDINS**, Benj 98, 119
**EDENFIELD**, David 120
**EDERINGTON**, Francis 69
**EDMASTON**, John 84
**EDMONDS**, David 57, 58
Jas 85, 86
**EDSON**, Jas 118
Jno 118
**EDWARDS**, Abel 114
Elizabeth 91
Henry 120
Jno 69, 85
Margaret 91
Mary 91
Rebecca 91
Rich 98
Sarah 91
Thos 98
Warren 85
Wm 120
**EGAN**, John 85
**EIKESTER**, Mary 91
**ELAM**, Wm 98
**ELBERT**, Sam 120
**ELDRIDGE**, Christopher 98
**ELDSWORTH**, Susannah 89
**ELIOTT**, Chas 82
Jno 83
Thomas 69, 85
**ELKINS**, Ann 91
Jno 83
Johnson 20

**ELLERBE**, Robert 111
Thos 69, 111, 114
Wm 98
**ELLINGTON**, Amerinthta 91
**ELLIOT**, Barnard 57
Benj 69, 79, 114
Elizabeth Knox 119
Jos 57, 85
Sam 69
Thos. 57, 69, 86
Wm 80, 84, 85
**ELLIOTT**, Ann 89, 94
Jane 89
Mary 91
Sabina 91, 94
Sarah 91
Susanna 89, 94
**ELLIS**, Elizabeth 91
John 23
Mary 91
**ELLISON**, Elizabeth 91
Robert 98
**ELLSWORTH**, Chas 98
**EMBRY**, Joseph 119
**EMERSON**, Henry 49
Jno 98
**ENGLAND**, Wm 119
**ENLOW**, Deason 25
**ENSIGN**, Jno 98
**ENTELWEIN**, Martha 91
**EPES**, Peter 98
**EPTING**, Adam 98
**EPPERSON**, David 108
**ERVIN**, Elizabeth E 89, 111
Elizabeth J 89, 111
Hugh 111
Jan W 89, 111
John 69, 98, 111
Samuel 111
**ERWIN**, James 69
Wm. 98
**ESKRIDGE**, Burdett 118
**ESOM**, John 57
**ESPEY**, Samuel 98
**ESTILL**, Wm 98
**EUBANK**, John 69
**EVANCE**, Jas 82
Jno 84
Thos 57, 98
**EVANS**, Batte 17, 98
Chas 69
Elizabeth 91
Enoch 69
Ezek'l 98
Geo 57, 69
Jno 85, 121

Perry 28
Roland 98
Nathan 98
Philip 39
Wm 98
**EVELEIGH**, Gei 57
Michael 57
Nich 57
Thos 85, 86
**EVERETT**, Thos 98
**EVINS**, Alex 121
**EWELL**, Jas 98
**EZELL**, Hartwell 120
John 84
**FAIN**, William 98
**FAMBROUGH**, Thos 108
**FARLEY**, David 120
**FARMER**, John 39
Shadrack 39
**FARR**, Jno 58
Robert 24
Thos 69, 115
William 98
**FARRABE**, Caleb 108
**FARRAR**, Field 58, 79
Thos 58, 120
**FARROW**, Rosan W. 98
Rosannah Waters 89, 120
Thos 50, 69
**FARQUHAR**, Robert 98
**FARSON**, Jno 82
**FATHERN**, Benj 81
**FAUST**, Burrell 98
**FAYSSOUX**, Peter 58, 79, 85, 98
**FEARN**, Jno 98
**FEASTER**, Andrew 98
**FELDER**, Henry 98, 121
Jno H. 98
Sarah 91
**FELLOWS**, Nath 119
**FENNER**, Rich 121
Robert 121
**FENWICKE**, Thomas 69
**FERGUSON**, Elizabeth 91
Mary 91
Moses 80
Samuel 79, 98
Thos 86, 114, 115
**FERIS**, James 87
**FIELD**, James 58
**FEW**, Wm. 98
**FILES**, Abner 119
Jeremiah 119
**FINDLEY**, Jas 98
Jno 31, 121

Jesse 14
Jno 84, 120
Jos 99
Owen 117
Ralph 121
Rich 99
**GRIFFIS**, Thos 82
**GRIFFITH**, Jos 70
**GRIGSBY**, E 108
**GRIMBALL**, Sarah 91
Thos 70, 85, 86
**GRIMES**, Wm 82
**GRIMKE**, Fred 115
Jno F. 58
John P 115
**GRISHAM**, Moses 34
**GRIST**, Benj 47
**GROSS**, Francis 86
**GROTT**, Francis 85
**GRUBER**, Philip 41
**GUERRARD**, Benj 85, 86
**GUERRAUD**, Elizabeth 89
**GUERRY**, Samuel 58
Stephen 58
**GUEST**, Wm 47
**GUILLAUD**, Jas 86
**GULES**, Wm 83
**GUMEAS**, Elias 99
**GUIN**, Jno N. 99
**GUNNUNGUST**, Fred 108
**GUNTER**, Henry 20
Jno 26
**GUNNELL**, Henry 108
**GUPBELL**, Elizabeth 91
**GUTHERY**, Jas 51
**GUYTON**, Aaron 30
**GWIN**, Jno 129
**HADDON**, Jennett 92
Mary 91
**HADDICK**, Sarah 92
**HADDOCK**, Sarah 92
**HAGER**, Cymon 83
**HAIGLER**, Jacob 46
**HAILE**, Benj 121
Jos 21
**HAILEY**, Wm 99
**HAINS**, David 83
**HALBERT**, Wm 99, 108
**HALCOMB**, Jno 3
**HALE**, Wm 120
**HALEY**, Jno 79
Mary 91
**HALKS**, Jas 26
**HALL**, Geo Ab 70, 85, 86
Jesse 47, 99
Jno 58, 117

Mary 91
Mary Ann 91
Samuel 83
Sol 32
Susan 91
Susanna T 91
Thos 58, 85, 86, 121
Wm 85, 86, 115, 99, 121
**HALTIWANGER**, Jno 99
**HALLAM**, Jno 121
**HAMILTON**, Andrew 48, 70,
99
Ann K. 99
David 38, 47, 85, 86, 99
Jas F 81, 111
Jno 58, 99, 111
Jos 70
Thos 99, 119
Paul 121
Rachel 91
Wm 82, 111, 121, 100
**HAMBRIGHT**, Fred 99
**HAMMOND**, Abner 100
Chas 100
Geo 70
Job 121
Jno 70
LeRoy 70, 115, 100
Samuel 37, 70, 100
**HAMPTON**, Edward 70
Jno 58
Henry 59, 70, 81
Thos 100
Rich 58
Wade 58, 80
**HANBY**, Mrs. Jeremiah 92
Susannah 92
**HANCOCK**, Clement 86, 87
**HAND**, Jno 81
**HANNA**, Robert 53, 119, 121
Thos 50
**HANSON**, Walter 100
**HARBISON**, Geo 120
Jas 35
**HARNETT**, Thos 99
**HARRIS**, Tucker 108
**HARCHFIELD**, Henry 100
**HARDAWAY**, Joel 58
**HARDEE**, Wm 20
**HARDEN (IN,ING)**,
Elizabeth 92
Geo 119
Henry 100
Lewis 14
Wm 70, 120
**HARDGROVE**, Jno 84

**HARDWICK**, Wm 114, 120
**HARDY**, Christopher 87
Jno 100
Tho 100
**HARDYMAN**, Jos 70
Thos 70
**HARGETT**, Jno 81
**HARGRAVE**, Robert 70
Samuel 70
**HARIOT**, Robrert 114
**HARLESTON**, Ann 92
Isaac 58
Jno 70
**HARLOW**, Benj 70
**HARNSBERGER**, Conrad
100
**HARRELL**, Jeremiah 121
Lewis 100
Zack 121
**HARRINGTON**, Drury 51,
119
Henry 100
Wm H 70, 114
**HARRIS**, Aaron 11 7
Arthur 100
Drury 81, 84
Edward 81
Goodman 12
Griffin 84
Hugh 100
Jas 81
Jno 30, 80, 81, 82, 100,
129
Mason 84
Matt 100
Robert 100
Sherwood 100
Thos 85, 86
Tucker 79
Wm 82
**HARRISS**, Micajah 70
**HARRISON**, Benj 100
Constan 84
Jas 100
Reuben 121
Richard 100
**HARRY**, Charles 119
**HART**, Ann 91
Arthur 114
Derrill 70
Jas 84
Jacob 82
Jno 58
Jos 84
Martha 120
Oliver 58, 79, 86

Wm 83
McCRADY, Edward 85, 86
McCRAVY, Thos 103
McCREE, Wm 84, 103
McCREERY, Robert 73
Thos 103
McCREIGHT, Tobt 38
McCRERY, Archibald 26
McCULLOUGH, Geo 73
McCUNE, John 15
McCURBY, Archibald 82
McCURDY, Jno 81, 103
McCUTCHEON, Jno 119
McDANIEL, Archibald 73
Ed 121
Wm 84
McDAVID, Jas 103
Jno M. 130
McDEARMON, Thos 121
McDILL, Jno 35
Thos H 121
McDONALD, Adam 59
Archiabld 117
Chas 86
Donald 45
Jas 51, 59
Jno 49, 119
Pat 83
Rachel 92
McDOUGAL, Alex 121
McDOW, Thos 41
McDOWELL, Chas 103
Jas 83, 103
Jno 117
Margaret 89, 103
Thos 82, 84
McELVEEN, Mary 92
Wm 49
McELWEE, Wm 103
McENTIRE, Robert 83
McFADDEN, Isaac 82
Rob 103
McFALLS, Jno 83
McFARLIN, Geo 32
McFERRING, Archibald 120
McGACHY, Jno 81
McGAUGHEY, Samuel 119
McGARROUGH, Jos 103
McGAW, Wm 120
McGAY, Wm B. 120
McGEE, Jesse 130
Mich 103
McGIBENAY, Hugh 83
McGILIVRAY, Robert 115
McGILL, Hannah 92
Jno 111

Sam 111, 103
McGINNIS,Chas 59
McGIANE, Jno 83
McGOCH, Jno 84
McGOWAN, Wm 121, 130
McGREW, Wm 84, 103
McGREGOR, Jno 103
McGUINES, Andrew 83
McGUIRE, Elij 119
Merry 59
McGWIGIN, Dan 82
McHAFFEY, Oliver 21
McILVEEN, Mary 92
McInSMITH, Catherine 92
McINTOSH, Alex 59, 73
Wm 30, 49, 121
McIVER, Chas 118
Evander 103
McJUNKIN, Jane 94, 120
Jos 9, 73, 103
Sam 103, 115
McKASKELL, Kenneth 40
McKAY, Mrs. Cabton 92
McKELVEEN, Mary 92
McKENZEY(IE), Alex 81
Will 83, 103
Wm 83
McKEOWN, Alex 108
McKINDRICK, Catherine 92
McKINNEY, Jas 6
Jno 121
McLAHANY, Wm 87
McLEAN, Jane 86, 89
McLEON, Eph 103
McMASTER, Hugh 103
Jas 103
McMORRIS, Wm 103
McMAHON, Archibald 47
Jno 42
Peter 30
McMANESS, Thos 73
McMICHEA, David 83
McMILLAN, Daniel 35
Jas 33
McMILLIAN, Daniel 120
McMULLEN(AN), Alex 117
Jas 120
Jno 81, 109
Rowley 121
McMURRY, Jno 41
Wm 108
McNEELY, David 84
McNEESE, Jno 114
McNEILL, Dan 60, 79
Hector 103
McPHERSON, Sarah 92

McQUEEN, Alex 59
Jno 73
McRAE(W), Duncan 73
Fran 103
McWATERS, Jno 84
McWHARTER, Elizabeth 92
McWHERTER, Aaron 81
Alex 81
Geo 81
Jas 52
Jesse 81
Jno 103, 119
MACHEN, Henry 102
MACK, Jno 102
MAAFIELD,Jno 81
MACAULY, Jno 72
MACKEY, Jas 102
Thos 41, 108
MAGDALEN, Mary 92
MAGEE, Elisha 73
MAGNER, Henry 12
MAGRUER, Elijah 82
MAHAFFEY, Martin 114
MAHAM, Hezekiah 59
MAID, Ann 92
MAIN, Rachel 89
MAJORS, Benj 119
Jno 119
MAKENTIER, Jno 82
MALLARD, Susan 92
MALLETTE, Gideon 120
MALONE, Corn 119
MALOY, Wm 118
MALTBY, Elizabeth 89
MAN, Elizabeth 92
MANGUM, John 119
MANN, Susannah 92
MANNING, Lawrence 102
MANSON, Fred 102
MARBURY, Thos 102
MARION, Benj 72
Esther 94
Fran 59, 115, 117
Gabrel 102, 121
Jos 121, 102
Catherine 92
Patrick 130
MARKHAM, Jas 87
MARLEY, Jno 115
MARLOW, Jno 117
MARR, Andrw 115
MARQUES, Isaac 102
MARSH, Rob 29
Wm 102
MARSHALL, Jas 102
Mary 92

# Index *to* South Carolinians *in the* Revolution

Stephen 119
**NONES**, Benj 86
**NOOT**, Angelen 89
**NORRIS**, Jno 103
Patrick 119
Wm 103
**NORTH**, Edward 75, 85, 86
**NORTON**, Ichd 103
**NORWOOD**, Geo 103
Jno 74
Thos 32
**NUCKOLLS**, Jno 103
**NUNN**, Joseph 118
**OAKES**, Daniel 103
**O'BANNON**, Abigail 92
**ODAM**, Aaron 28
**ODEN**, Alex 119
**ODILL**, Thos 103
**ODINGSELL**, Chas 115
**ODOM**, Dan 3
Levi 44
Sion 44
**ODORN**, Margaret 92
**OFF**, Isaac 82
**OGIER**, Geo 60
Lewis 103
**OGLETREE**, Wm 103
**OLDHAM**, Geo 30
**O'HEAK**, Jas 109
**OLIPHANT**, Catherine 92
David 60, 79,
87, 114, 115
Rob 83
Wm 60
**OLIVER**, Alex 103
Jas 117, 120
Pete 46
Tilson 47
**OLT**, Abram 74
**O'NEALL**, Samuel 121
Wm 121
**ORR**, G. 109
James 103
**OSBORN**, Ephrm 103
Jno 50
Robert 83
**OSHEALS**, Jno 50
**OSMUN**, Geo 81
**OSTEEN**, Sol 120
**OSWALD**, Margaret 92
Wm 74
**OTTERSEN**, Samuel 74
**OTTERSON**, Mrs. Samuel
89, 94
**OTIS**, Eph 103
**OTT**, Abram 103

**OUSBY**, Thos 60
**OUTLAW**, Alex 119
**OUTSON**, Jonthn 84
**OUTZ**, Peter 103
**OVERALL**, Nathaniel 103
**OVERLY**, Henry 119
**OVERSTREET**, Sarah 94
**OWEN**, Elizabeth 89
Fredrick 31
Jno 86, 119
**OWENS**, Jas 103
Jno 84
Thos 26
Wm 41
**OWINGS**, Richard 42, 130
**PACE**, Newsome 103
**PAGAN**, Jennett 92
**PAGE**, Jno 103
**PAGETT**, Joel 118
**PAGGETT**, Sarah 93
**PAINE**, Dav 104
Thos 118
**PALMER**, Daniel 52
Job 35, 86
Josh 52
Jno 103, 121
Jonathon 104
**PARCIVAL**, Benj 104
**PARHAM**, Drury 50, 104
**PARKER**, Dan 81
Dav 104
Jos 85, 86
Jno 74
Moses 104
Wm 86
**PARKINSON**, Jno 104
**PARKS**, Abrm 114
Jas 119
Sam 104
**PARR**, Arthur 121
**PARROTT**, Thos 48, 74
Jno 104
**PARSONS**, Dav 117
Jas 82, 114, 115
Susan 92
Wm 109, 131
**PARTRIDGE**, Wm 60
**PATRICK**, Cain 104
Henry 131
**PATTON**, Jane 92
Sarah 93
**PASLEY**, Robt 74
**PATE**, Jno 104
Matt 104
**PATTERSON**, Alex 32
Josh 104

Wm Jos 104
**PATTON**, Jacb 111, 114
Jno 121
Matt 52, 104, 111
**PAUL**, Jacob 118
Jno 119
**PAULLING**, Wm 104
**PAWLEY**, Benj 114
Geo 114
Wm 114
**PAWLING**, Wm 84
**PAYNE**, Josh 104
Jno 104
**PAYTON**, Jno 104
**PEARCE**, Josh 104
Jno 26
**PEARSON**, Jno 74
Moses 74, 104
Tabitha 93
**PEARMAN**, Wm 104
**PECH**, Bela 104
**PEERS**, Valentine 74, 104,
114
**PEEPLES**, Henry 104
Jno 81
**PEGUES**, Claud's 74, 104,
114
Wm 114
**PELLAM**, Wm 81
**PELOT**, Frances 92
Mary 92
**PENDARVIS**, Sarah 93
**PENDERGRASS**, Darby 115
**PENDLETON**, Henry 115
Jno 83
Philip 131
**PENNEY**, Ann 92
**PENNINGTON**, Kinchin 84
**PENRICE**, Edmund 117
**PERKINS**, Dav 74
Geo 119
Thos 45
**PERONNEAU**, Henry 60
Jas 60
Jno 60
**PERSE**, Silas 104
**PERRIN**, Theus 114
**PERRITT**, Needham 28
**PERRY**, Benj 79, 104
**PETERS**, Chris 85, 86
Jno 104
**PETERSON**, Jno 47
**PETTIGREW**, Alex 104
Jas 119
**PETRIE**, Alex 60
Peter 121

# Index *to* South Carolinians *in the* Revolution

# Index *to* **South Carolinians** *in the* **Revolution**

Jno 87
Jos 87
**SINGLETON**, Ann 93
Edmond 24
Jno 75, 105
Matt 75, 105
Rich 60, 82
Ripley 86, 105
Thos 85, 86
**SINGLEY**, Rachel 93
**SINQUEFIELD**, Francis 75
**SISON**, Wm 118
**SISSOIN**, Fredick 118
**SIZEMORE**, Ephraim 50
**SKIRVING**, Chas 62
Elizabeth 93
Jas 75, 105
Sarah 93
**SKOTTOWE**, Samuel 86
**SLAPPY**, Henry 120
Isabella 93
Sam 120
**SLOAN**, Alex 121
Dav 105
Jas 84
Jno 38, 75, 81
Rob 83
Geo F. 43
**SMITH**, Aaron 62, 75, 121, 105
Anna M 93
Annanias 105
Austin 32
Benj 75
Buckner 47
Catherine 93
Chas 81, 105, 120
Mrs. Christopher 93
Dan 62, 79
Dav 81
Eleazr 87, 114
Elizabeth 93
Henry 84
Isac 29
Janet 93
Jas 52, 76
Jno.18, 23, 81, 83, 105
Jno C 62
Jos 119
Josh 85, 86, 105
Jonthn 105
Mary 93
Merriwether 105
Nathan 82
Phil 84, 85
Press 62

Ralph 81
Roger M 105
Rob 62, 79, 86
Sam 52, 62, 75, 82
Simeon 17
Steph 105
Smallwood 118
Susan 93
Thos 5, 75, 82, 83, 105
Wm 28, 50, 82, 83
Zopher 82
**SNELLGROVE**, Sarah 93
**SNELLING**, Wm 86
**SNIDER**, Mary 93
**SNIPES**, Wm C 75, 82
**SNODDY**, Andw 80
Fergus 81
Jno 121
**SNOW**, Hannah 93
Wm 75
**SNOWDEN**, Aaron 120
Ester 120
Jas 119
**SNYDER**, Paul 86
**SOUTHERN**, Gipson 19
**SPANN**, Chas 49
Jas 49, 105, 120
**SPARKS**, Daniel 75, 114, 120, 105
**SPEARS**, Obediah 49
**SPEER**, Wm 135
**SPENCER**, Benj 84
Calv 105
Tho 105
**SPIVEY**, Geo 75
Moses 17
**SPRING**, Dorothy 93
**SPRINGS**, Rich 109
**SPIGNER**, Frederick 105
Margaret 89
**SPOFFORD**, Jos 105
**SPOOTWOOD**, Alex 109
**SPRAGUE**, Jos 105
**SPURLOCK**, Elizabeth 93
**STACKHOUSE**, Wm 105
**STANLEY**, Sam 105
**SPRINGER**, Sylvester 62, 79, 117
**St. GEORGE**, Geo 27
**St. JOHN**, Andion 75
**St. JULIEN**, Susan 93
**STAFFORD**, Arth 86
Thos 117
**STANDARD**, Wm 75
**STANDRIDGE**, Jas 47
**STANYARNE**, Ann 93

Elizabeth 93
**STARKE**, Jno 75
**STARR**, Daniel 105
**STARMES**, Daniel 86
Jno 83
**STEEDMAN**, Edward 35
Jno 105
**STEEL (E)**, Elizbeth 89, 105
Fran 105
Jas 84
Jos 105
Jno 82, 117
Sam 119
Wm 87
**STEEN**, Jas 105
**STERNS**, Joshiah 105
**STEPHENSON**, Hugh 119
Jno 86, 120
**STERLING**, Silas C 120
**STEVENS**, Dan 36, 76, 86
Jervis H 76
Jno 105, 120
Wm S 62, 79
**SIMEON**, 106
**STEWART**, Chas A 76
Dan 80
Jas 15
Jno 36, 81
Wm 120
**STILES**, Benj 106
Edward 86
**STILL**, Murphy 121
**STILLWELL**, Jno 106
**STINSON**, Dav 81
Jas 86
**STOBO**, Jacob 87
**STOCK**, Jon 106
**STOKES**, Jeremiah 106
**STOLL**, Phoebe 93
Rebecca 93
**STOCKMAN**, Christopher 45
**STONE**, Benj 76, 120
Chas 86
Jacob 38, 106
Jas 121
Jno 106
Jonthan 106
Reuben 119
Ruth 93
Wm 86, 119
**STONER**, Peter 83
**SOUTHERLAND**, Jas 47
**STOREY**, Anthy 120
Henry 119
**STRAIN**, David 120
**STRANGE**, Amos 43

# Index *to* South Carolinians *in the* Revolution

# Index *to* South Carolinians *in the* Revolution

www.ingramcontent.com/pod-product-compliance
Lightning Source LLC
Chambersburg PA
CBHW031121020426
42333CB00012B/174